"Gil Evans began casting his spell on jazz in a day when arrangers were invisible men, and (largely by choice) he remained an elusive figure even after his landmark collaborations with Miles Davis. Stephanie Stein Crease masterfully illuminates Evans's music, and brings the man himself out of hiding."

—**Francis Davis**, author of *Like Young* and *The History of the Blues*

"At long last, a book on one of jazz's most pivotal (and enigmatic) figures! Stein Crease gets as close to Gil Evans as one could hope for, and writes with grace and sensitivity about the unique and often difficult life of a jazz arranger. A great contribution, and a pleasure to read."

—**John F. Szwed**, author of *Jazz 101* and
Space Is the Place: The Lives and Times of Sun Ra

"That Gil Evans was one of the great figures in American music, a composer and orchestrator of breathtaking originality, is increasingly acknowledged. He was also a pleasing puzzle, one of those rare beings who never quite crossed what Conrad called the shadow-line (separating youthful optimism from adult dread), never sacrificed pleasure or principle, never sullied his gift, never succumbed to bitterness—a genuinely free spirit. In *Out of the Cool*, her aptly titled biography, Stephanie Stein Crease has performed an exceptional service, bringing order to the facts and shining a light on an eminent and exemplary life."

—**Gary Giddins**, author of *Bing Crosby: A Pocketful of Dreams*
and *Visions of Jazz: The First Century*

"Without question one of the most important jazz biographies in recent years. Stephanie Stein Crease explores this enigmatic man's life with insight and compassion. Until now Evans's story was known only in sweeping brushstrokes, but Crease produces a well-rounded portrait so full of inner detail that it makes you return to his recorded works with even greater admiration."

—**Stuart Nicholson**, author of *Ella Fitzgerald* and *Billie Holiday*

"Elegantly written and scrupulously researched, *Gil Evans: Out of the Cool* is a stunning contribution to the literature of jazz. Stephanie Stein Crease has uncovered a wealth of new information that will delight anyone with an interest in modern jazz. She has also found the keys to unlocking the memories—often for the first time—of many who were present at the creation of some of the greatest jazz records ever made. And it's a joy to read! I couldn't put it down."

—**Krin Gabbard**, author of *Jammin' at the Margins: Jazz and the
American Cinema*, and the editor of *Jazz Among the Discourses*

"A meticulously drawn portrait of one of the great contributors to what is probably the least well understood (and undervalued) aspect of jazz— arranging. Stein Crease's biography reveals Evans to be one of the original American bohemians on the scene from the thirties to the eighties, perennially short of cash, but always faithful to his jazz muse."

—**Linda Dahl**, author of *Morning Glory: A Biography of Mary Lou Williams*

GIL EVANS

GIL EVANS
out of the cool
his life and music

Stephanie Stein Crease

a cappella

Library of Congress Cataloging-in-Publication Data
Is available from the Library of Congress

"Blues in C" by Ron Overton reprinted from *Hotel Me: Poems for Gil Evans and Others*, ©1994 by Ron Overton, by permission of Hanging Loose Press, Brooklyn, New York.

Use of material from the Teo Macero Collection, Special Collections, New York Public Library for the Performing Arts, by permission of the Library and Sony Music/Columbia Records.

Cancion del fuego fatuo (from El Amor Brujo)
By Manuel De Falla
©1996 by Chester Music Ltd.
International Copyright Secured. All Rights Reserved.
Reprinted by Permission from G. Schirmer, Inc.

Every effort has been made to obtain permission for the use of all photographs reproduced for this book. In some cases (those in which no photographer is credited) the photographers remain unknown.

Jacket and interior design: Lindgren/Fuller Design

Jacket photo: © Carol Friedman

© 2002 by Stephanie Stein Crease
All rights reserved
First edition

Published by A Cappella Books
an imprint of Chicago Review Press, Incorporated
814 North Franklin Street, Chicago, Illinois 60610

ISBN 1-55652-425-0

Printed in the United States of America

5 4 3 2 1

To R.P.C.

Sounds of surprise
a page turns—click
ideas fly
ears tilt, mind turns
love soars
to you.

CONTENTS

Introduction and Acknowledgments / xi

1. Stockton / 1

2. Prince of Swing / 19

3. Hollywood / 46

4. Claude Thornhill—His Band
and His Sound / 71

5. Wartime / 98

6. 52nd Street Annex / 124

7. Moon Dreams / 146

8. Jambangle / 180

9. Out of the Cool / 219

10. Svengali / 258

11. Sweet Basil / 298

12. Epilogue (Parabola) / 325

Notes / 331
Bibliography / 343
Selected Discography / 349
Index / 375

INTRODUCTION AND ACKNOWLEDGMENTS

His mother told him he fell from a star. In truth, there was something ethereal about Gil Evans. He crossed numerous boundaries—musical and personal—that handicapped many of his contemporaries. His sense of freedom and adventure led him to become a relentlessly innovative arranger and composer. Like a handful of other American artists—Duke Ellington and Aaron Copland, Martha Graham and Alvin Ailey, Louise Nevelson and Jackson Pollack—Gil Evans did not merely contribute new forms to his medium but created his own inimitable world. His was a world of sound.

The arc of Evans's life (1912–1988) and career paralleled and often foreshadowed the quickly changing world of American jazz through the century. A self-taught musician who first learned about arranging by copying instrumental parts from 78rpm records note by note, Evans went on to lead his own high school dance band at the end of the 1920s. Within a few years, Gil Evans and His Orchestra became popular with the college crowd in southern California, and he and some of his musicians went on to work in Hollywood. By 1941 Evans was an assistant arranger for Claude Thornhill's Orchestra, whose sound, style, and instrumentation veered off from most of the big bands working at that time and were integral to Evans's artistic development. In the late 1940s, Evans became a key figure in New York City. His basement apartment, a few short blocks from the buzz of 52nd Street, was an important meeting ground for young progressive black and white musicians of that time, including Dizzy Gillespie, John Lewis, Johnny Carisi, Gerry Mulligan, George

Russell, and Miles Davis. The Miles Davis Nonet and the "Birth of the Cool" scores of the 1950s were the outcome of the nonstop musical discussions at Evans's place; so were Evans's and Davis's later trailblazing collaborations *Miles Ahead, Porgy and Bess,* and *Sketches of Spain,* which indelibly changed the course of modern jazz arranging, instrumentation, and conceptualization and brought out new facets in Davis's playing. In the late 1950s and through the 1960s, Evans enhanced the distinctive voices of other leading jazz musicians—such as Steve Lacy, Cannonball Adderley, Paul Chambers, Elvin Jones, Johnny Coles, Budd Johnson, Jimmy Cleveland, Kenny Burrell, Wayne Shorter, and Phil Woods—with his arrangements. By decade's end, Evans started experimenting with electronic instruments, synthesizers, percussion, electric guitars and basses, and freed-up rhythms. His scores became more flexible, and he relied more heavily on his musicians as improvisers, collectively and individually. He had an innovative way of willing his musicians to go "beyond notation," as one colleague put it. In the 1970s and 1980s he attracted a new generation of performers and collaborators. The band he maintained for the rest of his life was a hotbed of strong musical personalities: virtuosic avant-gardists alongside the best studio musicians, classically trained and Brazilian percussionists, and bebop- and Jimi Hendrix–inspired guitarists.

Yet histories and documentaries often marginalize or even overlook Evans's work, mentioning him in passing as the one who arranged Miles Davis's masterpieces. There are several reasons for this neglect. One is that Evans was an arranger, and jazz history focuses largely on star performers and soloists. Gil often worked behind the scenes, invisible to all but those who were familiar with the nature of that work. Another reason has to do with Evans himself. He was often reserved and had no interest in business or self-promotion. While others would have leapt at the chance to hitch a ride on Davis's stardom, Evans downplayed his role. Still another reason is that, while jazz has always involved fusion—it has always been a music of borrowings—few musicians fused elements as daringly as Gil Evans did. Since jazz criticism has frequently been invested in erecting and defending boundaries, Evans's music (like that of Miles Davis) was often challenged and excoriated as "not jazz."

The story of Evans's life does not have the high drama often associated with jazz musicians such as Charlie Parker or Charles Mingus. He did not torment colleagues or lovers, and he never knifed anyone onstage nor spent time in a drug rehabilitation center. Gil Evans lived to get his senior citizen's half-fare pass in New York City, and he considered it a badge of honor. When he was celebrated as a Founding Artist at the Kennedy Center in Washington, D.C., it was not posthumous.

Evans's story, however, is full of pathos. There were lows: his artistic plans were dashed right and left, he was ripped off by record companies and promoters, and he was ignored by critics or audiences who wanted to hear *Porgy and Bess* but not his current developments. Unlike composers and songwriters, arrangers do not receive royalties, and Gil received only a flat fee for his recorded arrangements. For much of his life in New York City he lived hand-to-mouth, putting a strain on his family. He turned down offers that didn't interest him, some of which could have been lucrative.

Yet his resolute choices also brought priceless highs: a close family life; enduring friendships with intensely creative people like Davis and Lacy; devoted musicians who were willing to work even when there was no money; and the ability to produce a body of artistic work of unparalleled force, whose freshness only increased as he got older.

Writing the biography of a jazz musician is a difficult balancing act: one must discuss the person's life, the history of jazz, and the cultural context of the music without overplaying or unduly reducing any of these components. The story of any one musician has to be woven into an account of the ever-evolving story of jazz itself. Yet jazz is a musical phenomenon that also has to be understood in musical terms. On one occasion I was at a jazz library while researching this book and going over some scores. A jazz scholar came over and voiced surprise that I could read music, especially something as complicated as an orchestral score. Such knowledge is essential if one hopes to understand certain processes involved in the making of jazz, especially when it is expressed in written music.

Delving into a life and art as rich and complex as that of Gil Evans has been a process of its own. I would not have been able to attempt or complete this book without a great deal of encouragement and assistance. I would like to extend my deepest gratitude to Anita Evans and Anita's and Gil's sons, Noah and Miles. Over a period of several years, they were always generous with their time and insights and allowed me to go through a considerable number of Gil's original scores, notebooks, and tapes. This material will form the basis of the Gil Evans Archive (which has yet to find a permanent location). Anita Evans has also been unstintingly patient—as soon as she helped me resolve one batch of questions about Gil's activities, habits, tastes, and experiences spanning several decades, a new list had already formed.

I was very fortunate to have been introduced to Steve LaVere, a photo and music archivist and music historian from California. Steve found and interviewed many people about Gil Evans's youth and early career, including friends, band members, and a former officer and colleagues from the Army. In the process he unearthed a trove of material, including scrapbooks, letters, telegrams, newspaper ads, recording contracts, and radio logs. This was a welcome assignment for Steve and an adjunct to the documentation of the career of the late Charles LaVere, Steve's father, who was a gifted pianist, multi-instrumentalist, singer, songwriter, and active studio musician in Southern California from the mid-1930s until his death in 1983. Steve LaVere was meanwhile involved with his own long-term project, the documentation of the life and music of the Mississippi Delta blues musician Robert Johnson; it was through his efforts that the copyright status of Johnson's music and photographs is now protected and secure.

My agent, Susan Ramer, remained confident and encouraging through the long course of this project. My editor, Yuval Taylor, was enthusiastic, incisive, and patient despite lapsed deadlines.

I would like to thank those who read the manuscript in its entirety or portions thereof: George Avakian, Robert P. Crease, Krin Gabbard, Michael Jarrett, Peter Keepnews, Emily King, Jeff Sultanof, and John Szwed.

Many other people, some of whom are now deceased, contributed in ways both large and small to this book. They include George

Adams, George Boujie, John Carisi, Rudy Cangie, Mark Cantor, Maybeth Carpenter, Herb Crawford, Jack Crowley, Laurent Cugny, Linda Dahl, John DeSoto, Robin Dewhurst, Bunny Edwards, Carmene Calhoun Ennis, Sue Evans, Carol Friedman, Gary Giddins, Ira Gitler, Ellen Goldstein, Gil Goldstein, Maxine Gordon, Ann and Greenlaw Grupe, Ray Hagan, Skitch Henderson, Jon Hendricks, Roc Hillman, Noris and Imogene Hurley, Howard Johnson, David Joyner, Mrs. Jessie Judd, Masabumi Kikuchi, Bill Kirchner, Stan Klevan, Lee Konitz, Steve Lacy, Tom Malone, Abby Mattas, Jimmy Maxwell, Pat McGuirk, Kati Meister, Helen Merrill, Louis Mitchell, Gerry Mulligan, Kenneth Noland, Kenny Olson, George Paulsen, Fred Peters, Andy Phillips, Brian Priestley, Bruse Ross, Jimmy Rowles, George Russell, Maria Schneider, Ichiru Shimuzu, John Snyder, Noel Silverman, Lew Soloff, Dave Taylor, Elizabeth Tilton, Evan Vail, Ben Wallace, and the family of Ryland Weston.

I would also like to thank George Boziwick, director of the Music Division, New York Library for the Performing Arts; Dan Morgenstern and the staff of the Institute of Jazz Studies; and Robert O'Meally and the Jazz Study Group at Columbia University.

Last, I would like to thank my husband, Robert P. Crease— philosopher, dancer, writer, historian, poet, lover, the embodiment of a renaissance man—whose support, generosity, brilliance, and love have been all-encompassing. This project would not have come to pass without his constant caring and his insight, good will, and great sense of humor, every step of the way.

1   stockton

On a golden day in early October 1987 in New York City, Gil Evans was walking with a friend through some of the densely wooded paths in the middle of Central Park. His step was brisk, his blue eyes clear. His wizened, aging features relaxed with the beauty of the morning. The last few months had been unusually hectic for Evans, now seventy-five years old. Over the summer his band had been to The Hague, the south of France, Italy, and, most recently, Brazil for four days. He was finally settled back at home, half a block away, in a tiny fifth-floor walk-up apartment on West 75th Street that doubled as a studio.

He walked deeper into the woods and started rummaging around in the pockets of his well-worn jeans and flannel shirt. Leaning against a big, old oak tree, he pulled out a small, gnarled hardwood pipe, which he filled with marijuana from a leather pouch. He wordlessly offered the pipe to his companion and slowly took a couple of puffs. He then pulled out a small bird whistle he had ordered from a Sierra Club catalog. The whistle's lifelike trill—not too harsh or metallic—attracted scores of birds, who flocked around the huge oak within minutes. Evans named ten or so varieties of birds whose calls he could pick out, then paused to savor the mixture of their voices. His fascination with sound was as keen as it had been when he was a child. Suddenly, he stretched out his thin, now reedy arms in greeting, marveling at his newly assembled orchestra.

ıΙ Iıı I

Gilmore Ian Ernest Green was born on May 13, 1912, to Margaret Julia McConnachy, who was in her late forties at the time of his birth. She was an adventurous and imaginative Scotch-Irish woman, qualities she passed along to her son. Little is known about Gil's biological father or his relationship with Margaret. She told Gil as a child that his father was a doctor who died before Gil was born, in a hospital in Toronto that had burned down. She also told him that he was her gift, that she'd found him on a beach where he had fallen from a star. Gil later said that until he was about eleven, he didn't suspect anything different.

Gil's mother's adventures and travels have made her life and his childhood difficult to document. Those of Gil's friends who knew Margaret remember her as a thoroughly charming woman with a British accent, but Gil himself was unclear about his parents' background. In 1936, in what is probably Gil's first press interview—for the local paper in Santa Ana, California, where he played with his ten-piece dance band—Gil said that both his parents were born in Australia. Many years later, he said his mother was Scotch-Irish and that dire poverty had driven her from the British Isles. She took a route common to other poor, respectable young women in the late 1800s and responded to ads for housekeepers abroad. She moved to South Africa, Australia, and then Canada. Maybeth Carpenter, a vocalist with Evans's band in 1938, who Gil's mother befriended, said that Margaret told her she had married five times. She said that Gil's father, Green, a Canadian doctor, was her fourth husband, and he had died before Gil was born. She separated from her fifth and last husband, John A. Evans, another Canadian, when Evans was a teenager and the family was living in Stockton, California. There is no documentation of any of Margaret's marriages or the deaths or separations from her first four husbands. But, like other women who hired themselves out in similar positions, she may have had more than business relationships with some of her various employers.

John Evans, a miner, became Gil's stepfather when Gil was a young child. The family migrated to wherever the older Evans could get work—in Saskatchewan, British Columbia, Washington, Idaho, Montana, and Oregon—before eventually settling in California. Gil remembered the bitter winters of Saskatchewan, going to a different school every year, and occasionally riding a horse to school. Years later, he described with awe the way his petite mother—she was less than five feet tall—served up Paul Bunyan–sized breakfasts at logging and mining camps. His first obtainable school records, from Stockton High School, show that he attended the ninth and tenth grades at Berkeley High School, and that he spent the first six weeks of his junior year in Burbank before entering Stockton High in October 1928. His grades in Berkeley were excellent, all As and Bs, but during his last two semesters at Stockton, they slipped; though he graduated on June 19, 1930, he flunked both English and algebra and received a D in elementary music.[1]

One can only speculate about that D. During his senior year, Gil was preoccupied with music; transcribing songs and arrangements from records, playing with his band, and related activities kept him very busy. As a young child, he was totally fascinated by sound, any kind of sound. He could recognize visitors by the sound of their cars or even their footsteps. He became interested in jazz in Berkeley when a friend's father had set up a piano, phonograph, and drum set in the basement; he started teaching Gil basic chords and how to pick out tunes on the piano. (Years later, Gil realized that he was taught the names of certain chords and inversions incorrectly.) Gil considered his friend's father "advanced" for encouraging the kids to play and listen to jazz. He heard his first jazz records in that basement—Duke Ellington, Louis Armstrong, Fletcher Henderson—and the father took Gil and his own sons to hear Ellington at the Orpheum Theater in 1927. Gil fell in love with what he heard.[2]

Gil began spending a lot of time at the local record store, where he could sit and try out records before he bought them. He was also spellbound by the remote radio broadcasts that started proliferating from the mid-1920s on, playing the music of the day—hot, danceable jazz. "When I was coming up, radio was really the big thing. There would be remote broadcasts from all over the place. Armstrong came on all the time, and so did Duke, and the Casa Loma band. Don Redman had a wonderful band of his own that used to broadcast live a lot. I caught all those broadcasts as much as I could and it was a wonderful education, really."[3]

When the Evans family moved to Stockton in the autumn of 1928, the city had a population of about 20,000, and downtown Stockton looked almost like the pioneer town it had been half a century earlier.

The main street was lined with storefronts with two-story facades and wooden sidewalks; some men still toted guns. The town was largely supported by agriculture. There was a large Asian community: Chinese immigrants who came in the mid-1800s to build the railroad and Filipinos who supplied cheap farm labor. Stockton also had its upper crust. The Holt family, who hired Gil's mother as their children's governess in 1930, were the originators and first manufacturers of Caterpillar tractors. They remained one of Stockton's foremost families for decades. The Grupe family, whose son Greenlaw became one of Gil's close high school friends, developed a thriving real estate dynasty, which the family has kept a close grip on since the early 1900s.[4]

Gilmore Evans, John A. Evans, and June M. Evans were listed together in the Stockton directory of 1929, with an address on North Center Street. Within a year, all three had separate addresses. John Evans became a brakeman with the Western Pacific Railroad. Margaret and Gil both moved into the Holt household, where she was hired as a governess, which put Gil at a disadvantage socially. He frequently ended up staying with friends, and when he was seventeen, he rented a room in a boarding house near the center of town. After 1931, John Evans no longer appeared in the city directory.[5]

When Gil first entered Stockton High, he was a tall, attractive sixteen-year-old whose natural poise and independent style were very apparent to his peers. Quiet yet affable, within weeks he gravitated toward other students who either played instruments or were excited about music. For the most part, his new friends came from fairly well-off families who, later on, weathered the Depression gracefully. He especially gravitated to the homes of friends whose families owned pianos. One of them was Ben Wallace, an outgoing, generous teenager, whose father's steady business—a funeral parlor—allowed the family to live in a large, well-equipped home. Ben's mother used to delight at listening to Gil play the piano for hours after school; Ben listened from the next room, marveling at the beauty of Gil's explorations.

Ben was sometimes asked to play drums for the casual gigs Gil and his friends began to get around town. Wallace himself admitted that his playing was not that good; he got invited because he usually could borrow his family's car and had some cash.

Gil was also happy to spend time at Ben's house because Ben had an extensive collection of 78rpms featuring Louis Armstrong's small recording groups: his Hot Five and Hot Seven played some of the most innovative improvisational jazz of the era. Gil was enthralled by these recordings and borrowed freely from Ben's collection, a couple of records at a time. Many years later, when Gil achieved a certain degree of fame, he used a stock response with journalists asking about his early influences: "Everything I ever learned about jazz came from Louis Armstrong. As far as how to handle a song and how to love music, I learned from him. I bought every Armstrong record between 1925 and 1932, that was his most creative period, you know." Ben Wallace showed the good-natured generosity of his youth when he spoke about Gil some sixty years later. "When Gil left Stockton in 1931 to go to college," Wallace said with a laugh, "he took all my Armstrong records with him. I didn't have a single one left."[6]

Gil also frequently stayed with Leroy Judd, who was a much better drummer than Ben Wallace and became a member of Gil's first working band in 1929, playing for high school dances and parties. Gil was very fond of Leroy's mother, who was musical herself. He spent a great deal of time at the Judds, at the piano or hunkered over their phonograph copying music from records. Gil's five-piece band often used the Judd's basement to rehearse, and a couple of years later, so did his ten-piece band.

Gil and his friends were a close-knit group. Since fraternities were not allowed at their high school, they decided to form a club, which they called the "Goober Club." They took in enough members to rent an old house with a large water tank that they sound-proofed and made into a card room. The club's instigator and money man was Greenlaw Grupe, who was already following in his family's business-savvy footsteps and was the club's secretary-treasurer. As a music lover, budding entrepreneur, and patron of the in-crowd, Grupe became the manager of Gil's newly formed combo; he did everything from seeking out gigs to financing incidentals to running interference when trouble came up.

Gil's little band played the most popular dance numbers of the day, such as "China Boy" and "Limehouse Blues." Everyone was dancing, and in the late 1920s, up-tempo arranged dance music, played by ten- or twelve-piece bands and spiced up by exciting jazz soloists, was the rock and roll of its time, just as swing music—played by even bigger dance bands—would be a few years later. Gil's very first arrangement was based on the then-current hit by Red Nichols and His Five Pennies, "Ida, Sweet as Apple Cider." Gil's arrangements of the hits of the day, the results of his painstaking record copying, made his band a big attraction at parties. Members of the Goober Club usually came along for the ride.

Bruse Ross, the club's vice president, who later ran a small business in Stockton, recalled:

> He [Gil] was smart. He was a real student, but he'd get every-thing without even trying—Latin, mathematics, anything, the whole bit. He was of a different breed, I'll tell you. Things came easy to him. He had no musical education at all—he picked it up all by ear. I can remember him playing a piece over and over, play that much on a record and take it off, play it over again with his ear cocked down there. But jeez, when he used to play piano [illustrates with foot stomps], the whole building could hear him clobber down, boy.[7]

ı' lı ı

While most of Gil's friends led fairly sheltered lives, Gil lived inde-pendently and ate many of his meals in restaurants. He didn't seem to have to account to anyone, though he remained very close with his mother, a cheerful, seasoned wanderer who made do in all kinds of circumstances. Gil, who inherited her creative resource-fulness, managed to have a part-time job of some kind and one car or another from the time he was sixteen. And these cars, though used, were classy. Gil was paid under the table by cafe owner Gus Terzakies to haul students over to his cafe at lunchtime in his Pierce Arrow, an elegant old roadster that was finally wearing out, part by part. This scheme lasted about a year until the car had its final breakdown. Gil also scared up other part-time jobs while in high school—delivering gas canisters and playing solo piano at tea time at the elegant Hotel Stockton. The Pierce Arrow and its successors—a LaSalle, a Ford, and later a Cadillac—were paid for by loans, mostly from Greenlaw Grupe. But no matter how well used these vehicles were, they reflected Gil's adventurousness and independence.

Gil's personality already manifested certain contradictory elements that would last throughout his life. His growing prowess as a bandleader and pianist gave him cachet with his high school crowd, but he was neither exhibitionistic nor egotistical about his talent. His musical activities made him a ringleader, but he was actually a loner who didn't follow the crowd. He could be a prankster, but he was also gentlemanly and soft-spoken, and he completely charmed his friends' mothers. He had an almost innate sense for quality items, like the Pierce Arrow, but didn't desire luxurious things for their own sake, and he was usually broke. For all the unreturned loans or records, his friends thought of him neither as a con artist nor as particularly deprived.

None of his friends really knew much about Gil's early life or his family's circumstances. In those days, people didn't reveal intimate details about themselves and their families the way they do today. Ben Wallace said he sometimes felt sorry for Gil, but couldn't exactly describe why. Others thought Gil was the most interesting and unusual person they knew, and they never got any indication that he was lacking in any way, emotionally or otherwise. If anything, they romanticized his autonomy.

Music was already ruling Gil's life. He made his way through high school and was regarded as extremely bright, even excelling at a couple of courses. Most of his waking hours were devoted to music in one way or another, and particularly to his band. Performing for school parties and functions was the ideal social leavening agent, and having a band was an adventure that everyone could partake in. It was also an experience that took on a life of its own and had its own necessities—a place to transcribe records, rehearsal space, transportation, and money for gas, food, tuxedos, and publicity. Gil's direct, unassuming manner helped him get what he needed for his fledgling combo—plus enthusiastic support from his friends. He learned to become a smooth operator without ever seeming like one—an unoppressive mooch. As his future friend and colleague Jimmy Maxwell once said, "He was one of these very captivating people that would come over and eat you out of house and home, and somehow you'd end up thanking him."

ı' Iı I

When Gil graduated from Stockton High in June 1930, his year-book photo was accompanied only by his name. The rest of his class-mates had captions running on for a paragraph or two, listing their accomplishments, goals, and dreams, but Gil never got around to submitting his blurb. Gil was uncomfortable about documenting his accomplishments, musical or otherwise. This self-effacing attitude—a strange mixture of modesty and lack of confidence—and his readiness to get on with the next project followed him to adulthood.

As a young man graduating from high school, Gil's accomplish-ments, and even some realized dreams, were beginning to mount up. His little band was playing in and around Stockton three or four nights a week, and he was working on new material in every spare minute. He wasn't alone, either. By this time, when dance bands were sprouting up all over the country, several young musicians performed around the Stockton and Modesto area as collaborators and competitors. Most of Gil's musicians, and his audience, were fellow students. Gil graduated from high school in June 1930 and entered the College of the Pacific in Stockton in September. In January 1931 he transferred to Modesto Junior College, a bigger school eighty miles from Stockton that attracted students from all over the state and provided new opportunities for Gil's band.

Ned Briggs, a bass player who graduated from high school with Gil, had a small band that also worked fairly steadily. He often used Gil on piano, and both he and Gil organized various combos for specific engagements around the countryside. The gamut ran from playing for cowboys in the Mother Lode country to fraternity and sorority dances at the colleges to family picnics at Loma Lake. During the summers of 1930 and 1931, Gil and his five-piece group played their first long-term engagement—three weeks—at Harbin's Hot Springs, a resort up the Russian River in Mendocino County. A photograph from this time has a caption that points to the owner's daughter, Helen Booth, as Gil's girl. Most of his friends thought of

Gil as having no romantic interests. But Ben Wallace remembers the gossip when the band returned from this job: that Gil was really taken with this girl, but didn't want to let his band members know of his interest.

Gil and Ned Briggs were friendly rivals for a couple of years because there was never quite enough work to go around. Ned's group usually consisted of trumpet (played by his brother Clark), sax, drums, piano, and himself on bass. The Briggs band's music tended to imitate the style of a smooth, schmaltzy San Francisco hotel band. In 1932 Briggs's combo got a fantastic break that Gil couldn't possibly compete with—through a family connection, Briggs and his group were hired as the entertainment aboard the S.S. *President Cleveland* steamship, which traveled through the Far East for four months.

Gil, who left Modesto Junior College after a year and moved back to Stockton, turned Briggs's absence to his own advantage. He cornered most of the work, for one thing, and his own band, which now numbered seven pieces, and his skills really started to gel while Briggs was gone. Even at this time Gil's arrangements showed some finesse. His tastes ran toward the jazz-oriented dance music of the day, played to a true 4/4 swing beat, rather than the sweet, smooth style that was prevalent in that era. Shortly after Briggs returned, the two young bandleaders officially joined forces and became the Briggs–Evans Band. They rehearsed at the Briggs's and the Judds' homes in Stockton, and Gil wrote virtually all the band's arrangements.

Abby Mattas, a fellow schoolmate from Stockton High who joined the band in the early summer of 1932, remembered that Gil organized the rehearsals like any diligent bandleader. The band met around nine A.M., three or four times a week, and rehearsed until noon when they'd break for lunch. They'd return and rehearse for a couple more hours in the afternoon. Gil wanted them to rehearse after dances too, but that idea didn't go over very well. After a while, with Gil setting the rehearsal schedule, composing the arrangements, and essentially establishing the band's style, the direction in which the group was moving was obvious. The band was now billed as Gil Evans and His Orchestra, and Gil was clearly the leader.

Pat McGuirk, who eventually had a successful career in radio and television, became a close friend of Gil's at this time. A music lover and trumpet player himself, McGuirk eagerly followed the band's formation and development. He thought Gil was an absolute genius for being able to copy arrangements from records, as did the rest of Gil's crowd. "Almost everything Gil was doing in those days was larger than life. He just lit up everything. You never quite knew what Gil was going to do or say next. He was always exciting, always interesting; he kept you alert. His ideas were things that other people didn't think about and his approach to things was uncommon. But there was always the music, always the music."[8]

The band now had nine members: Ralph Liscom on trumpet; Clark Briggs on trumpet and valve trombone; Noris Hurley on trombone; Abby Mattas, who played clarinet, tenor sax, and guitar; Ryland Weston on alto sax; Herb Stowe on tenor and baritone sax; Ned Briggs on bass (and utility trombone); Leroy Judd on drums and violin; and Gil on piano. Abby Mattas was the youngest member until Gil hired seventeen-year-old Jimmy Maxwell, a talented young trumpet player who still had one more year to go in high school in Tracy, a small town twenty miles south of Stockton.

Gil had been wanting to expand his brass section to two trumpets and two trombones, and Ryland Weston, also from Tracy, recommended his friend Jimmy to Gil. "So I went up to Stockton and tried out and fortunately for me I got the job, which changed my whole life, or led the direction that my life went," Jimmy Maxwell said in 1989, when he'd finally retired from a rewarding career as one of New York's top studio musicians.

ı¹ ıı ı

The Casa Loma band, all but unknown today, was the most influential white jazz-oriented band of the early 1930s, when the broad sweep of the Swing Era was still a couple of years away. The band, based in Detroit, had a dashing, dapper appearance (impeccable tails and white tie was the look), and their enthusiasm was infectious. It adopted many of the musical elements of the best black dance bands led by Duke Ellington, Fletcher Henderson, and Bennie Moten, whose popular Kansas City–based band later gave rise to the Count Basie Orchestra. Moten's swinging, riff-based, call-and-response arrangements were a huge influence on Gene Gifford, Casa Loma's chief arranger and guitarist. Gifford emulated Moten's arrangements but wrote with his own colleagues in mind and polished the southwestern style to a sheen. Gifford's scores "required a very high level of expertise...and this the Casa Loma band possessed in abundance."[9]

Casa Loma developed its own precise, snappy style and projected an energetic unified swing sound. The band played catchy instrumental arrangements of tunes such as Wingy Manone's "San Sue Strut" and "Casa Loma Stomp"; interspersed in the up-tempo numbers were romantic ballads—such as "Smoke Rings," the band's theme song—that were ideal for close dancing.

Casa Loma's frequent radio broadcasts helped create a large, mostly white, collegiate audience for the band, particularly in eastern cities where swing already had a foothold in ballrooms and nightspots, but the band also had a following in small towns around the country. "In 1930 the average small-town white boy who loved jazz heard only the Casa Loma band...on phonograph records, in ballrooms and on the air," wrote jazz and jazz dance historian Marshall Stearns.[10] Gunther Schuller, in his comprehensive book *The Swing Era*, called Casa Loma "the band that set the stage for the Swing Era, the first white band consistently to feature jazz instrumentals and pursue a deliberate jazz policy."[11]

The Casa Loma band was the obvious musical model for Gil's struggling combo. Casa Loma's polished musicianship and stylish verve also had a big influence on Benny Goodman, then a very well paid New York studio musician, when he was getting ready to start his own big band in 1934. Within a year, Goodman's orchestra outshone almost every one else's. By 1936 the Casa Loma band was displaced by the King of Swing and other white swing dance bands that followed Goodman's lead. [12]

Before Goodman's star ascended, Gil and his musicians emulated the Casa Loma band, musically and otherwise. According to Maxwell, "We even had snazzy uniforms. Ned Briggs, who read *Esquire* faithfully, the bible of the natty dresser, also worked in a fancy clothing store. So he got us these uniforms and we had these photographs made where everybody stands sideways with their hands in their pockets and the instruments are stacked up in a tasteful pile." But while the Casa Loma band's financial success easily allowed for their elegant attire, Gil's band (which also modeled itself financially on the Casa Loma Band, a "cooperative") spent six months paying for theirs.[13]

The band played Casa Loma's arrangements and solos note for note thanks to Gil's faithful transcriptions. Gil approximated Casa Loma's sound by encouraging his musicians to double on a variety of instruments: Abby Mattas was equally at home on tenor and clarinet and occasionally played some guitar; Clark Briggs doubled on cornet and valve trombone. As the band became more established over the next two years, Gil urged his reed players to play—and buy—flutes, oboes, and English horns. His use of woodwinds in a dance band context was almost unheard of at the time. Twenty years later, Gil's scoring for these instruments in a jazz setting was still considered unique and helped comprise his signature sound and texture.

Even in 1932, Gil veered from the sectional writing (brass versus saxes) that was almost standard among dance bands at that time. He ferreted out every orchestral combination he could from his musicians. As Jimmy Maxwell said, "Gil had a knack for writing for ten pieces so that it would sound like a twelve- or fifteen-piece band. The trombone would play the fourth sax part or one of the sax players would fill out the brass section so that we got all kinds of colors with the use of mutes. And as you know, Gil was very skillful early on at making colors, making beautiful sounds."[14]

Gil's musicians especially prided themselves that theirs was the only band around that played absolutely no stock arrangements, which were simplified orchestrations of popular songs. In the lingo of the day, all of Gil's arrangements were "specials," either a completely original score or an arrangement copied from a record with all its intricacies. Following the jazz ensemble style of that time, Gil left space in his arrangements for short solos and encouraged his players to improvise. Most of them chose to memorize solos they'd heard on records or that Gil would copy for them. All in all, the band was starting to have a degree of finesse and to swing.

Many years later, Gil was not shy about the fact that he was a musical autodidact, but always added how much he learned from "everyone he ever listened to." Copying arrangements from records, note for note, was the best way he knew to learn the arranger's art; it was his apprenticeship. It is an exacting skill, especially when applied to determining all the notes a group of instruments are playing. Musical transcription requires a fairly developed ear in the first place, and it is an invaluable aid in further increasing the ear's discernment. The rest of Gil's musicians were not without talent, either. Abby Mattas could play almost any challenging solo on the clarinet that Gil handed to him. And Jimmy Maxwell would return from a dance job at two or three in the morning and then sit around playing Louis Armstrong solos—which he'd transcribed and memorized—for another three hours.

ı' Iı ı

By the winter of 1933, Gil's band was working almost every night. They played sorority and fraternity dances, proms, and weekly dinner dances for the local elite at the Hotel Stockton. They made their first broadcasts at the local radio station KWG, located in the basement of the Medico-Dental Building in Stockton, a space they also used for rehearsals. Every Saturday night that summer, the band (and all their instruments) would pile into Gil's LaSalle to go play at a ballroom overlooking Loma Lake, where they packed the place. Gil often stopped at a bootlegger on the way out of town, another example of his worldly savvy—though in this case his purpose may have been more to show his "cool" than anything else. He might have one drink at the beginning of the night, and maybe one more later, but that was it. None of his friends ever remembered seeing him drunk or his music being affected in any way.

Gil and company considered it a real coup when, that same year, they were hired by the Dreamland Ballroom in Stockton to play three nights a week. The Dreamland was the spot where the town's working people came to have a good time; it was not the band's usual college crowd. In fact, some of the Goober Club members gave Gil some flak for playing there because they thought it was too working class. For the band it was a steady job, and some of these performances were broadcast locally.

Johnny De Soto, who became the band's drummer in 1932 and eventually became a studio musician in Los Angeles, said that Gil's band played all the fraternity and sorority dances for the College of the Pacific:

> We had that pretty well locked up. Well, we had a good band, that was number one, and there wasn't anybody that could have competed with us, because Gil copied note for note all those Casa Loma arrangements. I used to play with Ned Briggs, too, but he didn't have the kind of talent that Gilmore did. He was more interested in having a hotel-type band, that schmaltzy kind of thing. I went from Ned's band to Gil's band, and then Ned went to Gil's band.
>
> We played mainly for all the young people from school who had grown up together, so everybody knew each other. The band was friends with the customers and the customers were friends with the band. It was just a hometown thing, and that's as far as we thought we would ever go. Most of us had no intention of being professional musicians or anything like that, or even leaving town.[15]

During this time, Jimmy Maxwell often spent the night with Gil in his boardinghouse room after dances or rehearsals when it was too late to hitchhike back to Tracy. The close friendship they developed lasted until Gil's death in 1988. Maxwell, born in 1917, is a large man with a keen intelligence and sense of humor. His career began with Gil, but his reputation as a first-rate, world-class trumpet player became firmly established with Benny Goodman's band from 1939 to 1943. He vividly recalled how much Gil influenced him in their youth:

> I always thought it was kind of elegant that he lived all by himself and ate at restaurants, and all those exciting things. He'd go to a whorehouse once a week or so, which I thought was very classy.
>
> We talked an awful lot when I spent the night. Mostly we'd talk about "when we were famous." But Gil was also quite a thinker. He read books like *The Seven Pillars of Wisdom* and his

favorite, *Generation of Vipers*, which I think was the first book to criticize modern American civilization. I was still a very devout Catholic at that time and he used to torment me with remarks about the Church. He'd sort of grin and get this glint in his eye and tell me all kinds of obscene stories, and gave me the occasion for sin whether I listened to him or not.[16]

According to Maxwell, Gil was still following the Casa Loma band's lead in terms of musical conception, sound, and style until Benny Goodman's band started really taking off between 1934 and 1935. Trying to broaden the scope of things, Maxwell produced a couple of arrangements that he'd copied from recordings by Duke Ellington and Jimmie Lunceford, which Gil used a few times but didn't incorporate into the band's book.

The steady rehearsals and growing work experience were beginning to pay off for Gil Evans and His Orchestra. Their reputation as a great band for dancing had spread as far as the Bay Area. In the fall of 1933 the band started getting invitations to play for fraternity parties and pep rallies at the University of California at Berkeley.

They considered their first gig at Berkeley—playing for a rally—the most prestigious job they'd had thus far. Gil had recently acquired a Cadillac, a used touring car, to replace the La Salle that ferried the band around the Stockton area for two years. Though the car was roomy, the band members still had to take turns sitting on one anothers' laps on the back seat. For this occasion, they rented a trailer to carry the instruments so they wouldn't arrive at Berkeley—a good seven-hour drive from Stockton in those days—looking completely crumpled.

About halfway there, Maxwell, who was sitting in the front seat next to Gil, realized they had lost the trailer. Gil glanced out the rearview mirror. Sure enough, the trailer was nowhere in sight. Gil quickly pulled the car over to the shoulder of the road, and they all piled out.

They walked about a quarter of a mile back up the road and found the curve where the trailer had come unhitched. It was overturned, with a tangle of instruments, cases, and music spilling out over the embankment. Their dreams for this important day faded as the wind swept sheets of music farther into the ravine. Maxwell counted himself lucky—as a matter of course, he never let his trumpet out of his hands. But Ned Briggs's bass, which had been on top, was almost fractured in two within its fabric case. Abby Mattas's sax had a peculiar new curve to it, as did one of the trombones.

While some of the musicians were very upset and almost in tears, Gil stood in the middle of the road and burst into laughter. His laughter was enigmatic, double-sided. One facet was Gil's natural response to the turn the day had taken, an expression of his genuine lightness of spirit—like the sheets of music freely wafting about in the wind. The other side was hard to figure, hard to reach. His laughter distanced him from his peers, as if this day weren't so momentous after all. "He thought it was the funniest thing he'd ever seen," Jimmy Maxwell recalled. "This was one of those things about Gil that was charming as long as you didn't have to live with it. Otherwise it was pretty hard to take."

When everyone calmed down they decided to push on to Berkeley. They had allowed themselves plenty of time to get there, so they could still make it to the rally. Most of the instruments were still playable, and Ned Briggs hoped he could borrow a bass from a friend. They managed to set the trailer to rights, repacked the instruments, and resumed their trip (without their fastidiously copied music). Remarkably, the day was not a total disaster. They actually played through the entire gig from memory. For once, the musicians were thankful that Gil was so insistent about putting in a lot of rehearsal time.

In the summer of 1934, the band had a still more important gig. Gil Evans and His Orchestra was hired to be the house band for the entire summer at Globin's Cabins and Chalet, a family resort at Lake Tahoe. They were hired by Kupie Martin, an oversized, overweight singer/comedian who was going to front the band and also perform impersonations. Martin had recently defected from a band led by Dick Jurgens, a more established bandleader who had been covering the Tahoe resort circuit for a few years.

Globin's Cabins and Chalet was built out over Lake Tahoe and attracted people from the Bay Area and Sacramento. It consisted of a sprawling rustic hotel with several cabins nearby, about a half-mile from the more dressed-up Chalet, where an old boathouse served as a ballroom for dancing.

Away from the Stockton area, Gil and his musicians felt like real working professionals. This was their highest paying steady job to date: each musician received fifteen dollars per week plus room and board. They took their meals in the hotel itself (which they dubbed "El Tahoe") and slept in the attic of the boathouse.

Though the band was thrilled to be in this vacation dreamland, the accommodations were not completely idyllic. They had to put their mattresses up in the rafters because of the rats, for one thing. And five nights a week (they took Sunday and Monday nights off) they had to carry their instruments the hilly half-mile from the boathouse up to the hotel to play for dinner and then haul everything back again to play for dancing. They also had their regular share of youthful mishaps. Gil, who loved sunbathing, once got so sunburned he couldn't make it to work. And on one night off, Gil and five of his band members rented a boat with an outboard motor. While they were fiddling with it after it stalled in the middle of the lake, the motor was accidentally overturned, and it sank immediately. Again, Gil burst out laughing despite the fact that six people would have to paddle the boat miles back to shore. "He was delighted," Jimmy Maxwell said. "Nothing ever seemed to bother him. I guess it didn't need to. We were so upset it made up for anything that might trouble him."

Meanwhile, Gil and the band continued to develop musically. Both Abby Mattas and Jimmy Maxwell recalled that, by this time, Gil's arrangements sounded more and more original. He'd been listening to a wide range of classical and twentieth-century music. He was particularly influenced by the music of impressionist composers such as Ravel and Debussy and the Spanish composer Manuel de Falla. Tinges of their orchestral palettes started showing up in Gil's work.

The vacationing college kids came flocking to hear Gil's band, not so much for the impressionistic colorings, but because the band played great dance music. Dick Jurgens's band, which was working a few miles away at another resort, finally had some competition. Jurgens's band played all stock arrangements and had the smooth romantic sound that was once Ned Briggs's ideal. Jurgens's

commercial streak had its appeal—that fall he and his band were
booked for their most prestigious engagement to date, at the St.
Francis Hotel in San Francisco. But the word was out. Jurgens's
musicians started coming to hear Gil's band rehearse, and on their
nights off they came to hear all of Gil's "specials."

Between the rats, the rafters, and endless requests for the summer's hit songs, Gil and his band transformed themselves into a
much more professional group, even if their playing wasn't quite
on a par with Casa Loma's. Their camaraderie and high spirits
shone through their music, often compensating for their technical
lapses and rough edges. "That summer was our big break," said
Maxwell. "We thought we were famous. It was our big start in the
big time."

2 prince of swing

The "big time" proved elusive. That fall, the group found getting new gigs was still one step forward, two steps back—all the way back to Stockton. "We got a job in a nightclub in Sacramento and we moved there and we were all set to go," Jimmy Maxwell recalled. "The day we were supposed to open, we were rehearsing with a hula dancer or something like that and a guy from the union came in. We all belonged to the Stockton local, and he wouldn't let us play. So we were stuck in this hotel for a week and we didn't have the money to get out and we didn't eat. The club fed us for a couple of days. We managed to get back to Stockton and got our job at the Dreamland Ballroom back."[1]

In September 1934 the band fell back into the jobs they had had the previous year. In addition to playing at the Dreamland five nights a week, they did broadcasts from Stockton's KWG, resumed playing for sorority and fraternity dances for the colleges in Stockton and Modesto, and occasionally performed for events at the University of California in Berkeley. Once in a while the band played for dances at upscale hotels in San Francisco. Gil, now twenty-two, knew that a career in music was exactly what he wanted. He'd completed another semester at Modesto Junior College the previous spring and did not re-enroll once the band was back in the area; neither did Johnny De Soto or Ryland Weston, who had been fellow students. Though their career goals were not as whole-heartedly musical as Gil's, for the moment they and the rest of the band were content to follow Gil's lead. They were making more money than their friends, and even in Stockton the musician's life had an aura of excitement. Jimmy Maxwell, eighteen years old at the time and the best musician in Gil's young band, was the only band member attending college that fall. He entered Modesto Junior College as a freshman and hitchhiked the twenty-five miles back to campus after the band's gigs at the Dreamland, often returning at five in the morning since "in those days there weren't that many cars on the road."[2]

Travel to jobs out of town often seemed jinxed. The secondhand cars and dubious trailer hitches belonging to Gil or one of the others were fine for cruising around the flat farmland surrounding Stockton but didn't hold up on long arduous trips, let alone the hills of San Francisco. On the way to a job at the prestigious Fairmount Hotel at the top of San Francisco's Nob Hill, Ralph Liscom's Essex— laden down with musicians and towing the trailer full of instruments—wasn't able to make the steep grade leading to the hotel. "We all had to get out and push the trailer up the hill," said Abby Mattas. "Then we were so grubby looking the Fairmount's doorman didn't want to let us in."

By the early spring of 1935 Gil was ready to take some risks, and so were some of the others. Greenlaw Grupe, the former treasurer of the Goober Club and the band's self-appointed manager, discovered a vacant ballroom in the coastal resort town of Capitola, near Santa Cruz, about sixty-five miles from Stockton. Grupe convinced Gil that it would be a great idea to lease the ballroom and book the band into it for the summer. Grupe, who'd been lending money to Gil for years and had financed Gil's latest car and the insurance for it, and Hart Weaver, another former officer of the Goober Club, were willing to invest in the band—with some strings attached. They thought the ballroom had potential as a business. Gil's interest was in furthering the band; he wanted to jumpstart the band out of Stockton into a setting where he and the boys could work steadily, be their own bosses, and get more exposure.

Capitola served as a resort for people from Stockton, Modesto, Sacramento, and Fresno—inland valley towns that got really hot in the summer. The town's summer population of about a thousand had decreased significantly from a decade earlier, but it was beginning to recover from the Depression. The 1935 Santa Cruz County

Business Directory prefaced its Capitola listings with this description: "Capitola-By-The-Sea, an attractive beach resort located 5 miles SE of Santa Cruz on the northern shores of Monterey Bay. Has an extensive power plant, a large casino and a wide sandy beach...possesses all the attractions of a modern, up-to-date recreation resort. Fresh and salt water bathing, dancing, canoeing, fishing, golfing, riding stables."

The Capitola Ballroom was a medium-sized dance hall that could accommodate six hundred people. It was right on the scenic esplanade, across the street from the boardwalk and a wide swath of white beach. Down the block was the Venetian Court, the very first condominium development in California, constructed in segments during the 1920s. There were reasons why the ballroom could be rented at a cost affordable to Grupe et al. It was vacant, dilapidated, and badly in need of paint and repairs. It contrasted starkly with the Cocoanut Grove in Santa Cruz, *the* nightspot in the area, an expansive nightclub/ballroom that was attached to the town's casino. The Grove could accommodate about two thousand people and had just that year been refurbished with the bright-colored trappings of a tropical garden, providing big-city glitz and glamour to the region.

For the most part the entertainment offerings at the Cocoanut Grove were geared for the area's white, well-heeled resort clientele. The Grove occasionally splurged on a nationally prominent band such as Ben Bernie's (the "Ole Maestro"), the band that made a hit out of "Sweet Georgia Brown" when it introduced the song in 1925. Ten years later, Bernie's band was more distinctive than the "sweet" bands that proliferated at that time; its playing could border on swing, and it had a couple of able jazz improvisers in its ranks.[3] Black entertainment was featured at the Grove only one night that entire summer and billed as if it were an exotic show from a foreign country. A large ad in the June 5, 1935, edition of the *Santa Cruz Sentinel* read, "Harlem Comes to Santa Cruz— Lionel Hampton, 'World's Fastest Drummer' and His 16-piece All-Colored Cotton Club Orchestra." The floorshow featured Willa May Lane, "America's Most Beautiful Colored Entertainer," and Villa and Lovett, "Red Hot Harlem Dance Demons." The truth was that Hampton had been working in California since 1928. He'd been the drummer for the Les Hite Orchestra between 1930 and 1934, years in which the Hite band was one of the most successful of the handful of black dance bands then based in California.[4] In the summer of 1935, Hampton was leading his own dance band so he could feature himself prominently on the vibraphone—now his preferred instrument—rather than drums.

Most frequently, the Grove featured California bands like the Scott Held Orchestra and Griff Williams and his Hotel Mark Hopkins Orchestra. "Sweet" bands such as these had the tame hotel style and sound that people were accustomed to and wanted. The "sweet" bands reigned through much of the 1930s, not just in California but all across the country. To contemporary ears, the music of the "sweet" bands sounds hopelessly predictable, and the bands seem barely distinguishable from one another. The sentimental sounds that flooded the airwaves in those years served as an antidote to the Depression; the music was eminently danceable and as soothing as comfort food. As Louis Erenberg pointed out in *Swingin' the Dream*, "Popular music registered the deflation of expectations. As hotter jazz groups disbanded and live entertainment shrank drastically, sweet (melodic) bands took over the commercial radio airwaves, content to comply with radio's insistence on inoffensiveness and the audience's desire for soothing sounds. Such bands also controlled the best remaining 'location jobs' in hotels and cafes." [5]

By the summer of 1935, a change was in the air—both economical and musical. Recordings by swing bands were topping the charts. "Let's Swing It" by Ray Noble and "Rhythm Is Our Business" by Jimmie Lunceford jostled against sweet and sentimental ballads by Bing Crosby and Guy Lombardo for number one hits that July and August. This tug—the "sweet" versus the youth-led exuberance of swing—was played out in many areas of the country, Capitola included. Gil's band, though ragged around the edges technically, was in the latter camp. Gil and his musicians didn't think of the entertainment offered at the Grove as competition; they felt, rightly, that they had the swing sound all to themselves. But they'd overestimated the extent to which a new sound alone would give them an audience—they hadn't thoroughly reckoned with the drawing power or the assets of the well-established Grove.

Greenlaw Grupe and Hart Weaver optimistically set everything in motion. They put up all the money for the rental of the Capitola ballroom, a house for the band, a cook, and general expenses. They also paid for some repair and maintenance costs and for a set of microphones. The two young businessmen also ran back and forth between Capitola and Stockton that summer, trying to keep the ballroom afloat while also running a gas station back in Stockton that they were partners in. However, the details of the Capitola financial arrangement were not entirely out in the open. Unbeknownst to Gil's musicians until months later, Gil, Grupe, and Weaver made an agreement that Gil and the band would share the income, if any—and the losses, if any—from the ballroom with Grupe and Weaver. This agreement was uncharacteristically secretive for Gil with respect to the band, which was left under the impression that it was a cooperative, with Gil as musical director. "Everything that came in went into a pot," said Rudy Cangie, a tenor saxophonist who joined the band that summer. "Room and board came out of that. There was never anything left over. We ate well! We had our own cook. We had a fun time, but no money, no money."[6]

No one, including Grupe, shied away from all the dirty work involved in cleaning the place to get the ballroom ready to open. "The first thing we had to do was to scrape the dance floor," Johnny De Soto recalled. "We were working on that dance floor on our hands and knees for about a week." Gil and his musicians also served as their own promoters. They cruised through town with a billboard strapped to the top of Gil's car, while one of them hung out the window, barking praises of the band through a megaphone.

The band's cook was another frugal move on Grupe's part; it was more economical to have a cook than to have the whole band eat out three times a day. Anne Grupe, née Dervin, who became engaged to Greenlaw Grupe the following year, remembered the band members getting outraged at Grupe because he was so stingy with them. "They'd say, 'You know what that Greenlaw is having us do now? He won't let us eat butter! We have to eat margarine!' They were just furious at him, really furious."[7] Most of them were from Stockton's elite families and never worried about penny-pinching; except for Gil, none of them had lived on his own. (Eating margarine was a draconian measure—oleo had only recently been widely manufactured in the United States and tasted genuinely awful.)

On opening night at the ballroom, all the former Goober Club members and other fans came down from Stockton with their girl-friends. The atmosphere was as exuberant as the band's college dances at home—band and ballroom fit the college crowd like a glove. At the end of the evening, the Stockton gang celebrated by raising a real ruckus. A parade of honking cars moved slowly through the small town. Rowdy enthusiasts hung out their car windows cheering as if they'd just witnessed a victory by the local football team. Annoyed residents spent the next few days talking about gathering a petition to close the ballroom. These marauding teenagers were a far cry from the older, genteel resort crowd that the Cocoanut Grove attracted.

In June, Grupe and Weaver started running their own small ads in the *Sentinel*: "Follow the Crowds Tonight and every night but Tuesday to Capitola Ballroom. Music by Gil Evans and His Orchestra. Admission 55 cents Sat. Nights; 40 cents week nights." The band garnered enough attention to earn a listing in the paper's weekly entertainment highlights. Gil and the boys began to attract a small but steady audience.

Gil still modeled his band largely on the Casa Loma band, which was still an enormous success. It was featured on the very popular, nationally broadcast "Camel Caravan" radio show, and young col-lege crowds across the country "regarded it as the hottest thing around," wrote Albert McCarthy. Gil continued to encourage his musicians to double on other instruments. Abby Mattas said:

> Gil got everything he possibly could out of our band, even if it meant playing three notes on some other instrument, if that was what he wanted for an arrangement. So we had Ned Briggs playing the trombone, even though he was the bass player. If Gil needed some trombone, Briggs came up front with the horns, played those notes, put the trombone down and went back to the bass. He even had me playing guitar—he knew my father had a guitar and told me to start bringing it. So I had to put my horn down, play what he wrote for guitar, then go back to the horn.[8]

Though the full sweep of the Swing Era still lay ahead, Gil knew that the art of arranging was key to a band's success. It was also a paramount challenge, whether Gil was assigning parts for sections or individual instruments or writing toward the strengths of particular musicians. Well-designed arrangements could also obscure the inconsistent skills of Evans's young musicians; they could enhance everyone's playing—even at this stage. On this subject, Benny Goodman himself wrote, "The art of making an arrangement a band can play with swing...one that really helps a solo player to get off, and gives him the right background to work against—that's something that very few musicians can do. The whole idea is that the ensemble passages where the whole band is playing together or one section has the lead, have to be written in more or less the same style that a soloist would use if he were improvising."[9]

Shortly after opening night in Capitola, Gil started holding auditions for new musicians. He needed to replace Abby Mattas, who played tenor saxophone and clarinet, and he wanted to expand the band. Mattas's mother couldn't envision a life for her son on the road and wanted him to come home to Stockton. ("Those old-time Italian mothers—you just do what they say," said Mattas). For the first time, Gil started seeking musicians from outside the original nine-piece Stockton gang. Rudy Cangie, a saxophone player, went along for the ride, while his friend Nick tried out for the singer's spot at one of the auditions. "They didn't think Nick would work out," said Cangie. "I had all my horns in the car, so they tried me out too, and Gil said, 'When do you want to start?' They were really looking for a jazz man, but they didn't get one."

"Jazz man" was the trade term for an improviser, a soloist—specifically, a hot soloist. When dance bands, black and white, started proliferating in the late 1920s, a hot soloist was the draw, the celebrity, the crowd pleaser whose improvisations would add drama and excitement to a performance. The "jazz man" had the responsibility of improvising in addition to playing his scored part in the ensemble.[10] Most of Gil's musicians were strictly section players whom Gil pushed as far as he could—to be good ensemble players, to swing together, and also to occasionally play written-out solos that he'd painstakingly copied from records. The only jazz man in the bunch at that time was Jimmy Maxwell, who had developed his improvisational skills to date by copying and playing Louis Armstrong's solos.

By mid-June the band had added three new members: Cangie, who played tenor sax and clarinet and could sing; alto saxophonist Dick Nelson, a schoolteacher who joined for the summer; and Sheldon Taix, a trumpet player who occasionally doubled on guitar. The band now numbered twelve. Gil at twenty-two was the oldest of the group, while the average age of the others was nineteen. Photographs from the band's scrapbook, maintained by Ryland Weston, show them as a bunch of all-American guys, a happy-go-lucky group of young men romping with their girlfriends on the beach and living it up. Though Gil was hardly an autocratic bandleader, his seriousness about music and his sense of discipline went far beyond that of his musicians.

"I was nineteen at the time, and music was a glamorous business," said Rudy Cangie, who later became a California sideman and studio musician and worked for big-name bandleaders such as Ozzie Nelson, Alvino Rey, and Liberace. "You sit up half the night, shoot the bull, never practice—just have fun. That was not Gil's idea. Gil said, 'Hey, we're going to have a band, and if you want to play, I want to hear some practicing.' We didn't argue with him because we knew he was right. We also knew we weren't as good as he wanted us to be. We got the gist—we either start practicing, or else out! And he laid down the law, for which, to this day I am thankful. Otherwise I would have been just another ten-year musician with some mediocre dance band, and that would have been the end of it."[11]

ı' ı, ı

During the summer of 1935, swing music and swing dance were becoming a mass cultural phenomenon in the United States. The great black dance bands, Fletcher Henderson's, Bennie Moten's, Duke Ellington's, Cab Calloway's, and, later, Jimmie Lunceford's, had been swinging along for years; the musical groundwork was well in place. The powerful sounds of these big bands, whose arrangements could heighten the rhythmic drive of swing, was irresistible to jazz-oriented white musicians such as Benny Goodman. Over the course of the next two years, a combination of forces—a partial recovery from the Depression, a revitalization of the record business, a rising entertainment industry, and the more widespread radio medium—ignited a cultural brushfire across the country. That swing music and dance were inseparable gave the movement even more impetus. Dance halls and ballrooms were now acceptable places to go for growing numbers of young people—from a spectrum of class backgrounds and, in some cities, of different races—who exalted in the freedom of the lindy hop.

Dance fever spread to the homogeneously white Capitola audience, too. "Dancing Crowds at Beach Break All Time Record!" ran the *Sentinel*'s headline for July 26, 1935. The throngs of dancers showing up at the Cocoanut Grove hadn't been as consistently large since before the Depression. According to the *Sentinel*, about fifteen hundred people flocked to the Grove on Saturday nights that summer, and the weeknight average was around six hundred. Gil's band didn't fare nearly as well. The crowd it attracted to the Capitola Ballroom was younger than the one at the Grove. It was composed mainly of college kids who found their way to the ballroom through word of mouth. In July, Grupe and Weaver targeted their ads: "Youthful-Peppy Music by Gil Evans & His Orchestra." Gil and company also tried to draw a larger audience by having novelty nights, such as a Country Store Night, and holding amateur nights for "any kind of act" on Fridays. These novelty nights were smaller echoes of such events at prominent big-city ballrooms. "At the Palomar in Los Angeles, Monday was a 'candid camera' night ... Wednesday featured a Mardi Gras Carnival atmosphere ... Harlem's Savoy featured ... Thursday Kitchen Mechanics' Nights, bathing beauty contests, and Saturday night car giveaways." [12]

Gil's most loyal fans came for the music. "Swing was just coming in, and we were popular because of the Casa Loma and Goodman influence," said Cangie. "On weekends we did great. The college kids really liked us; they'd all come in from San Jose State." Despite the disparity between the size of Gil's audience and the far larger Saturday night crowd at the Grove, Gil's following was in the vanguard at the moment. Gil's jazz-oriented East Coast swing style set his band apart.

Gil kept an ear tuned to the East Coast bands and, according to Maxwell, started paying greater attention to the music of Duke Ellington and Jimmie Lunceford. By midsummer, Gil wanted to add even more instruments without incurring the expense of hiring any extra musicians.

"'OK, guys, I need more instruments,'" Cangie recalled him saying. "'Oboe, English horn, and flute. Who wants to do it?' Wes took the flute, and that left the English horn and oboe to me, which turned out to be the life-saver for my musical career. I was hired so many times later in life because of that."[13]

While Cangie and the other woodwind players doubled on other wind and reed instruments, Jimmy Maxwell and the other trumpet players were recruited to double on valve trombone. Gil quickly abandoned the use of that instrument because, remembered Maxwell, "Valve trombones don't automatically sound in tune and the result wasn't too good." Gil continued to arrange every tune, leaving his special mark on it, even though he was extremely slow, much to the frustration of the other band members. Gil was a deliberate writer who could brood over a couple of measures for hours, if not on and off for days. If anyone asked where Gil was, a standard reply was that he was "up there staring at a lead sheet," Cangie recalled. "Personally, the band was a brotherhood. Musically, the band was Gil's, totally. Everybody respected Gil and did as he said, even when it came to [forcing us into] learning new instruments. When Gil delivered a new arrangement it was a cause for celebration."[14]

Personally, Gil was always friendly and caring to his musicians, but he also tended to be a bit reserved, maybe because he was older than the others. More significant was his total preoccupation with music. Anne Grupe, who was also from Stockton, was one of the very few people who remembered a more private side of Gil during that summer in Capitola. Anne was the younger sister of Bernyce, whose relationship with Gil had run hot and cold since high school. Even then, Gil's devotion to music and his desire to be a professional scared Bernyce off. "I spent every summer in Capitola with my grandparents," said Anne. "That's how I happened to be around that summer in such close contact with Gil Evans. They—Bea and Gil—were really very much in love. She didn't see him at all that summer because she was staying with a friend in Carmel, but I saw him every day at the beach—my grandparents' house was right at the beach.

"I was only sixteen then, I wasn't really dating yet, and Gil was actually kind of boring. When you're sixteen, you're not really that interested in a man's problems. He would sit there on the steps of my grandparents' house by the hour and tell me how much he loved my sister."[15]

Gil often seemed removed from the lively social life that his band members enjoyed that summer (the band's scrapbook shows several photos of the others arm-in-arm with girls at the beach). Gil had very specific visions about his future, as is evident in a letter to Grupe a few months later, in which Gil expressed his feelings about Bea:

> She's stopped writing to me so I guess she's either found someone else or decided I don't love her. The terrible part is, I do, but I could never marry her while I'm climbing up in this business. She says she thinks she'd like it, but I know she'd never be happy if she were away from Stockton where all her friends are. All I'll be doing for the next few years is playing every night, rehearsing after the job, arranging, recording, etc., during the day. When would I have the time for a home life? So that's why I never write to Bea. I want her to forget all about it, although I never will.

Gil's vision was uncannily correct. He would indeed spend nearly all his free time arranging, rehearsing, and playing—even at Capitola, as the leader of what was still a band of kids. For him, music would remain all-consuming for the rest of his life—Gil did not marry until he was thirty-eight years old and had his first child, with his second wife, at the age of fifty-two.

Gil seemed positively ancient to Anne, who was then just starting to date. (A year hence, like many of her teenage peers, she would be radically transformed into a married woman.) "I did have one date with Jimmy Maxwell, but Marvin Gennetti [another friend of the band] said, 'You can't go out with him!' He warned me away from Jimmy because he smoked marijuana! I'd never heard of marijuana in my entire life, but Jimmy was just darling. The next year he came into our bedroom blowing the trumpet when Greenlaw and I were on our honeymoon."[16]

As the summer progressed, the locals accepted Gil's band and hired it to play for town picnics, dances, and beauty contests—all worth front-page coverage in the *Santa Cruz Sentinel*—and Capitola became more and more of a hot spot to go dancing. On August 6, Bob Millar and his twelve-piece orchestra, with vocalists Bert Douglas and Maybeth Carr, came to play at the Grove. Millar's band was a prominent hotel band and Hollywood studio outfit, and Millar was considered an "Eddie Duchin of the West." The band drew immediate raves from the *Sentinel*; they played to a record-breaking crowd of almost two thousand people on their first Saturday night there and were asked to stay on for another week. Gil and his musicians heard Millar's and other bands on their breaks and were checked out in turn by the touring musicians. The contact would prove especially worthwhile.

Winding down at the end of August was disappointing. There were some profitable Saturday nights, and word had spread about Gil's band, but their venture never really caught on. By the end of the summer, Grupe and Weaver, the band's backers, were not able to recoup any of their initial twelve-hundred-dollar investment, and the group had incurred an additional nine hundred dollars' worth of debt. The band members still didn't know about the deal making them liable for the losses; knowing they had no money, Grupe and Weaver saw no reason to mention it.

The band's last gig at the ballroom was the last Saturday night in August, and there was not much of a crowd. Because they made no money that night, in a final, spiteful farewell, some of the band members stood in a row at the edge of the bandstand and peed on the dance floor—the same one that they'd so carefully scraped at the beginning of the summer. "The Big Rain" was what sax player Dick Nelson called it in a letter to Gil some months later.

ı' ıı ı

Shortly before closing night, Gil and his musicians got what turned out to be a huge break. Bob Millar recommended Gil and his band to his booking agency, the Music Corporation of America (MCA). Even at this time—before the music industry machinery went into high gear—MCA, whose main office was in Radio City in New York, was the largest and most powerful booking agency for white bands in the country, with integral ties to radio networks, sponsors, prominent hotels and ballrooms, and record companies. An MCA contract meant, for the likes of its top sweet bands such as the chart-topping Vincent Lopez Orchestra (and very soon, its top swing bands, such as Goodman's), prime seasonal bookings at the Hotel Pennsylvania in New York, national tours, radio access, and record contracts, for which MCA extracted its 10 percent cut. For smaller fish such as Bob Millar, it meant the Cocoanut Grove in Capitola and the better hotels in San Francisco at the same 10 percent and a pedigree comparable to the "Good Housekeeping Seal of Approval."

On August 26, 1935, Gil received a letter from MCA agent Norman Doyle, who was following up Millar's recommendation. Doyle wanted to set up an audition with an MCA rep in San Francisco. "In as much as the expense for one of our representatives coming up to Capitola would be $21.05 for railroad fare and Pullman as well as additional expense for meals, I thought it would be advisable to take the band into San Francisco for an audition for Earl Bailey, who is in charge of all of our northwest territory...." If that arrangement didn't work, Doyle agreed to come to Capitola from Los Angeles before Gil's closing night—which was all of five nights away.

It did not take long for Doyle to prove his worth as an agent. A day later, he secured an audition for a potential booking. On August 27, Gil received a telegram from Doyle confirming a paid (union scale) "live" audition at a matinee dance for Labor Day, Monday, September 2, at the prestigious Rendezvous Ballroom in Balboa Beach. The Rendezvous needed a replacement for Dick Jurgens, Gil's old rival from Lake Tahoe, who was off to a posh hotel engagement in San Francisco. The dance was to start at three P.M., but Doyle asked the band to arrive at the ballroom at ten in the morning so he could meet Gil and hear the band himself. This was a fabulous opportunity for the band. The Rendezvous was a well-established, glamorous ballroom on the pristine Newport Beach peninsula. It was famous among dancers as the home of the Balboa, a fast-paced dance done to swing music but without the upper body gyrations of the lindy hop. (Most of the action took place in the feet, which would shuffle furiously while the torsos of the dancers remained almost still.) Gil and his crew were ecstatic—this was just the kind of opportunity they'd been hoping for.

The drive to Balboa included, predictably, another trailer incident. "We left Capitola and drove to Balboa overnight to make the afternoon audition at the Rendezvous," said Rudy Cangie. "This time, we had a seventeen-foot house trailer, which would start waggling like mad all over the highway when anybody lay down in it, which of course Gil wanted to do because he was so tired. In Santa Barbara, the hitch broke causing a three- or four-hour delay, which put us in Balboa an hour before show time. Everyone was dead tired, but we made the matinee—and we were accepted! In fact, we had just gone down for the showing, thinking we'd be there for the day and go back home, but the management said, 'No, no, you stay here! We can use you!'"[17]

That one audition earned them both a gig and a contract with MCA. "Gil Evans and His Youngsters" were hired for that Wednesday and Thursday and through the next weekend. As things turned out, the band performed at the Rendezvous Ballroom on and off for the next seventeen months. They played there weekends that fall and winter and were the house band from Easter week through Labor Day for the 1936 and 1937 seasons. Starting in mid-September 1935, the band was also hired to play a couple of nights per week at the Valencia Ballroom in Santa Ana, California, ten miles away from Balboa. The boys were jubilant. They had an agent, a contract with MCA, a new job in another beautiful beach town, and they were actually going to get weekly paychecks! It finally seemed like they had left Stockton for good.

For the first few months Gil and the boys lived at the YMCA in Santa Ana, another idyllic California coast town that seemed immune from hardship. The Rendezvous Ballroom was right on the beach. Again, photographs from various scrapbooks show Gil and everyone else looking like they were having a great time. Professionally, they were certainly on their way up. An ad for the Rendezvous in the *Balboa Times* for January 4, 1936, read:

Last Opportunity to Hear and See
LES HITE and MAE DIGGS,
California's Outstanding Colored Orchestra at the
    RENDEZVOUS, BALBOA
SPECIAL SUNDAY
Both LES HITE and Orchestra and your Favorite
    Gil EVANS and Orchestra
DON'T MISS THIS

It was unusual for a black band and a white band to be paired together at that time in California, and in this instance Hite's band was far more prominent than Gil's.

Gil and his musicians often spent their leisure time together, too. Photos in the band's scrapbook dated October 8–9, 1935, show Rudy, Gil, and several of the band members on a jaunt in Ensenada, Mexico. "It was a good job in the summertime," said Jimmy Maxwell. "We made good pay, maybe forty or fifty dollars a week. In the wintertime we made twelve dollars a week, but in those days you could live on that. Pay two dollars for a lesson, one dollar for a pint of whiskey, and the rest for room, board, and cigarettes. So it was a happy life, an exciting life, because we were sure that the great day would come when Benny Goodman would hire all of us!"[18]

Spirits were dampened only by the revelation of the agreement among Gil, Greenlaw, and Weaver. Now that the band was starting to receive weekly paychecks, Grupe and Weaver finally informed Gil's musicians of the losses incurred at Capitola and that they owed Grupe and Weaver money. According to Grupe, the Capitola venture was twenty-one hundred dollars in the hole. Grupe and Weaver wanted their initial investment back. Weaver was owed a thousand dollars and Grupe two hundred dollars; the band was also to pay off the additional nine hundred dollars' worth of debt.

"They [Grupe and Weaver] lowered the boom on us when we got down to Newport," said Johnny De Soto. "They came to see us and said, 'You know we went in the hole in Capitola and you've got to pay it back.' And we said, 'Pay it back?' We didn't make any deal with anybody—we were a bunch of absentminded kids, just thinking about music. But we said OK. We were making thirteen dollars a week at Balboa, playing weekends going into the winter season, and we paid Greenlaw three dollars a week, each one of us. We went through with it, and we got along OK—we were batching it, three or four in a room, and things were cheap. But that was one of those things that happened that none of us really liked very well, but we lived with it. I think Greenlaw still hollers about it. 'Oh, I lost a lot of money!' I think Greenlaw still has the first dollar he ever made."[19]

ı'ıı ı

"Good evening, everyone! Once again it's Swing Time at the Pasadena Civic Auditorium, and tonight playing for the Pasadena Community Dance we bring you the swing tunes of Gil Evans and His Orchestra. Here's an original number to start our half hour of dancing music by Gil Evans, and it bears the thoughtful title of 'Thinking About You.' "

The radio announcer slipped his introduction neatly in and out of the band's slow and sultry theme music, which faded under the announcer's smooth voice, the signature of a suave radio professional in March 1936, when the broadcast was made. "Thinking About You," he repeated. "Let's have it, Gil!" The band picked up the tempo and launched into the tune, an Evans original, with an easygoing swing beat made for dancing.

"Thinking About You" is an instrumental number with a fairly catchy melody and a typical AABA pop song form. The tune and arrangement are reminiscent of some of Goodman's lesser-known recordings from 1935, such as "I'm Livin' in a Great Big Way" arranged by Fletcher Henderson, or "Hooray for Love." The first chorus is played with closely harmonized saxophones with accents from the trumpets. The chorus that follows is more unusual; a paired clarinet and trumpet play lead on a melodic variation, with a muted brass background, giving way to clarinets soaring over trombones. The band swings as hard as it can on the ensemble chorus, and a charming *soli* passage reveals Gil's penchant for writing ensemble lines with an improviser's phrasing and flair, even at this stage in his career, with his unevenly skilled band. Gil's endless rehearsals paid off—a tape of this broadcast shows that the band could swing and that on romantic ballads Rudy

Cangie could croon with the best. There's no question that the band still sounded ragged around the edges and lacked the punch and power of the truly professional bands. At the Pasadena Civic and other local dances, however, Gil Evans and His Orchestra were a living presence—to their fans, they were as great as the big-league dance bands on the radio.

Gil's band was still in a precarious financial situation. Gil received a letter from an annoyed Grupe that summarized all that he and Weaver were owed and alluded to money that Grupe had loaned Gil personally, which had left him very strapped. Gil wrote a ten-page handwritten apology in reply in March 1936. "I don't blame you for thinking I'd pooped out on you," he began, expressing his appreciation to Grupe for not being angrier. He itemized what he thought the band owed Grupe, which came to $273.78. "Christ! What a lot of dough. No wonder you're short on cash." Gil mentioned some additional new expenses of his own—for car repairs, dental work, and a new suit for his band appearances. As soon as the band received their first check from the Rendezvous on April 12 (seventy-five dollars per man for Easter vacation; thirty dollars per man per week from April 12 to June 21; then fifty dollars per man for the summer), Gil promised to send him fifty dollars per week. "I'm really sorry that I've drained all your dough...but I can honestly say I haven't wasted a penny," wrote Gil. "I stay home all week arranging music, and some nights when the crowds are small I stay home and arrange to try to keep up with the new tunes because we've got to have them all from now on. In case you don't know it, you dumb shit, if it weren't for you we wouldn't have any band or job with the Music Corporation and I wouldn't have any car. In other words we'd still be on the stage of the beautiful Dreamland Ballroom."

The letter also reveals that Gil's Rendezvous gig, which was now confirmed through the summer, had been threatened. The trouble had been stirred up by Pops Tudor, a powerful local entrepreneur who had run the Rendezvous for eighteen years until it was taken over by a Mr. Burlingame. Tudor, who, Gil wrote, had "been at the ballroom so long that he can't stand to see a band there that he hasn't organized or been able to dictate to," had decided that the band needed a leader out front. Tudor had one in mind: Ray West, a local middle-aged musician whose claim to fame was that he had played at the Cocoanut Grove a decade ago. "He's the biggest bull-shitter I've ever met," Gil wrote to Grupe. "The kids in the band said nothing doing. They'd rather lose the job than have an outsider in front of the band. So now Pops is sorer than hell at us and he goes around telling everyone how lousy we are." That was not all. Tudor had also been surreptitiously organizing a band, led by Vido Musso, then California's best man on tenor sax, to replace Gil's band in time for the Rendezvous's summer season. Burlingame stood up to Tudor and insisted that Gil's band stay, but when Burlingame told Gil his band could keep the job, he added a few strings. He said that the band needed another pianist, a couple of singers, and a leader out front—Gil himself. Gil professed horror at this last condition. "Can you imagine me leading a band? Neither can I, but I have to do it. Boy, I'll be a scared and embarrassed bastard!"

After successfully navigating these obstacles in what Gil called "their climb through the business," the band members settled into a routine. They moved into the Jaroso Apartments in Balboa, which Anne Grupe described as "a horrible dump," where three and four of them bunked together. Gil dutifully tried out several piano play-ers, including the young Stan Kenton. Kenton, born in Kansas but raised in Los Angeles, had worked at the Rendezvous on and off since 1933 with a swing-oriented jazz band led by Everett Hoag-land. He subbed as a pianist for several other bands as well. Although Kenton filled in for Gil several times that spring and summer, Gil preferred Buddy Cole, then nineteen, whom he hired on the spot after hearing the young pianist in a little club. Cole's first night with Gil's band was the first night of Easter vacation. Burlingame himself hired another youngster who'd been popular at previous engagements at the Rendezvous to sing novelty num-bers; to Gil's relief, the singer got on very well with Gil and his boys. Meanwhile, Gil auditioned female singers "by the dozens." A female singer had to not only sound good but look good as well, and Gil couldn't find anyone with the right balance of assets. "They've either got a good voice and no looks or a lousy voice and good appearance," he wrote Grupe.

At the Rendezvous, the band began to attract a steady and enthusiastic college following, and they were frequently hired for dances and events in the area. That June, Gil and his band were the featured performers for a dedication of Newport Harbor, organized by none other than Pops Tudor himself, who had been won over. The band played at the Pasadena Civic Auditorium at several community dances, which were held every Friday and Saturday night and often broadcast. Starting in June 1936, the band began to broadcast regularly from the Rendezvous, which gave them an audience far beyond the local area, and Gil began receiving fan letters from other states. But their most avid fans came from the local college crowd. In spring 1936, the band was featured at the Fiesta Ball, the biggest event of the year for Santa Ana Junior College. "Evans has planned a program calculated to satisfy the many high school and college students who will gather," wrote the local college newspaper. Other local newspapers referred to Gil as the "Prince of Swing."

On Gil's twenty-third birthday, May 13, 1936, he was interviewed for the first time, for a feature article in *El Serape*, the student paper of Santa Ana Junior College. The article, written by Vic Roland, was typically sophomoric, ranging from the idiotic ("The number 13 jinx and all its accompanying superstition has evidently been neglected by our interviewee.... He was born, May 13,...He will be 26 years old [twice thirteen].") to the prosaic (while Gil's original ambition was to become a doctor, "fate, discovering his strongest talent, had different plans for him"). Gil and his band were said to play swing music because it was "more fun for the band to play that type than any other." According to the article, "Gil's foremost ambition at present is to be America's best bandleader." The article declares, "Hundreds of collegians have adopted the motto, 'If life is a song let's swing to it with Gil Evans!'" The article concluded with an accurate prophecy: "We take off our hat to a band and its leader which we predict will become prominent."

That spring, Gil's band also received its first pan. A review by a Chuck Cochard in the *Daily Trojan*, the student paper from the University of Southern California, declared that "Gil Evans' Orchestra is lousy." That judgment, however, did not go over well, and an irate respondent replied, " They are not only an up-and-coming outfit, but they are already here, and boy are we glad of it. It may interest Mr. Cochard that Benny Goodman, upon hearing this worst combo took such an interest in them as to give them his own personal arrangements of two of his finest numbers, 'King Porter Stomp' and 'Dixieland Band.'" There is no evidence that Goodman and Evans met at this time. In all likelihood, Evans's band played Gil's transcriptions of these arrangements (by Fletcher Henderson and Deane Kincaide, respectively).

As Gil was making a hit with the local college crowd, he and his musicians were also becoming more visible in professional circles. They all became members of the AF of M Local 687 in Santa Ana. In April 1936, the band's personnel were listed in that month's *Tempo*, the journal of Local 47. The National Band Directory of April 13, 1936, reported that the band had opened at Balboa that Easter week for the season with eleven musicians: Gil Evans, piano and arranger; Ryland Weston, Reuel Lynch, Herb Stowe, Rudy Cangie, saxes; Ralph Liscom, Jimmy Maxwell, Sheldon Taix, trumpets; Noris Hurley, Pete Carpenter (formerly with Bob Millar), trombones; Johnny De Soto, drums, and Clarence Ewing, bass. The list omitted Buddy Cole, possibly because he was a recent hire.

Gil's name was getting around, well beyond the network of local professional musicians. Officials of Lucky Strike, the cigarette company that sponsored the *Let's Dance* program, asked Gil as part of a survey for a list of the fifteen songs most frequently requested from the dance floor. The list Gil sent back in reply reveals that Goodman had firmly replaced the Casa Loma band as his model: hits by Goodman and his orchestra, including "Goody Goody," "Stompin' at the Savoy," "King Porter Stomp," "Christopher Columbus," and "Let's Face the Music and Dance," make up almost half the list; the remaining numbers included "Robins and Roses," "Will I Ever Know," "Tormented," "The Day I Let You Get Away," and "All Alone at a Table for Two." Gil also began receiving letters from song pluggers working for various publishers and was sent lists and requests to play certain songs. Several of Gil's horn players were featured in instrument advertisements. Jimmy Maxwell and Ryland Weston appeared in local trade publications endorsing Selmer trumpets and saxophones; their names were suffixed "with the Gil Evans Orchestra."

Despite this increasing visibility, only Gil of all the band members really understood that the band did not have the kind of crack professional sound or musical finesse of the top-ranking bands. "They were all high school boys," said Cangie. "They really hadn't had all that much experience. Gil was hoping to shape them into a good jazz band. Some of the guys took to it, but it never seemed like it satisfied Gil, but he struggled with it and drove the guys to practice and to become better musicians, and a few of them did. But as far as being a proficient band—we lacked the real professionalism that Gil was in competition with and I'm sure Gil felt that!"[20]

In the summer of 1936, Gil finally found a female singer that he and the band liked—seventeen-year-old Elizabeth Tilton. Liz was the younger sister of vocalist Martha Tilton, who would join Goodman in the summer of 1937. Gil asked Martha first, but after she turned him down she mentioned that her sister, a high school girl on summer vacation, might be interested. Liz Tilton did not have quite the voice of her sister, but she had the classic cute-girl-next-door look and was a crowd pleaser. After a week of stern coaching and coaxing from Martha and her mother, Liz went to Balboa to try out, using "Is It True What They Say About Dixie?" for her audition number. She got the job, and she started the following Friday night. Since Gil was slow at coming up with new arrangements for her and she had a limited repertoire, Liz sang her audition number four or five times a night for a couple of weeks.

An article written by Elizabeth's mother, Frances Tilton, offers an interesting window on the low repute that swing music had in social circles. The article was entitled "My Daughters Sing Swing" and subtitled "A modern mother who defends her daughters' singing with dance bands and defies you to prove she's wrong."

I have always considered myself a pretty typical American mother. But, since Mart and Liz started traveling with swing bands, I have become aware that some people, finding out that I am the mother of two swinging daughters, look at me as if they thought I might be out of my mind, permitting my girls to be exposed to what I am sure these people feel are the dangers of swing music in general—and swing musicians in particular. And as for allowing Mart and Liz to travel—the only girl with twelve or thirteen men—allowing them to stay up all hours of the night in public places where liquor is sold, allowing them to

ride unchaperoned in buses or trains with drummers and trumpet players and saxophonists—well, I guess there's many
another mother who thinks I am sending my daughters straight
down the path to perdition.[21]

Frances Tilton wrote that she "would never have consented to let
either of the girls sing with any of these pick-up, fly-by-night bands
that work in questionable neighborhoods or cheap cabarets," and
when her daughters first started singing, she went along on tour.
She soon realized that her daughters were "a lot safer with all those
boys" than with a single escort, and added, "I don't consider my girls
are in any more moral danger singing in a night club than they
would be typing in an office." They "probably make more money"
than stenographers. They also wrote home to Mom regularly.

Another new asset that summer was woodwind player Jack
Crowley. Crowley was the band's first eastern import. He had
worked in Kansas City for a couple of years in the early 1930s when
it was a musician's paradise. He often went to the Reno Club to hear
Count Basie's band, then to the East Side Musicians' Club where
musicians typically jammed all night. In 1935 he'd hitchhiked to California with another musician friend and had been working with a
small Dixieland band in Los Angeles when he heard that Gil was
looking for a clarinet player. Crowley, who felt like a worldly outsider
compared to Gil's clean-cut college kids, initially got a cool response
when he auditioned on clarinet at a dance at the Rendezvous. Maxwell really liked his playing, but Gil was ambivalent and asked him
to audition again. This time Crowley played a Johnny Hodges–style
alto saxophone solo on an Ellington tune. He was hired.

The hottest and most well-known musician Gil hired that summer
was twenty-three-year-old Vido Musso—the same Musso whom
Pops Tudor had wanted to recruit a few months earlier to front a
band at the Rendezvous. Born in Sicily, Musso grew up in Detroit,
then moved to Los Angeles in 1930, where he played clarinet with
Stan Kenton and acquired a strong local reputation on tenor. Musso
was a bona fide improvising jazz musician, and his hefty, muscular
sound and style were modeled, like so many other saxophonists of
that era, after Coleman Hawkins. However, Musso could not read
music at all and didn't seem to have much in the way of band-leading

ability. That spring Musso tried leading his own group at the Hermosa Hut, in Los Angeles. He "knocked 'em silly for a few weeks," reported *Tempo*, "but it was soon apparent that he wasn't adapted to the maestro role." The band broke up, and Musso joined Gil and was a star attraction with the pros who came to hear the band.

Early that summer, the Rendezvous dances were broadcast nightly on KFWB. A small press clipping with Gil's picture captioned "New Maestro" says the band has "quickly become a favorite of many a dance enthusiast." Crowley recalled, "On 'Plenty of Money and You,' which was played fast with four baritones, the band would stop playing in the middle of the bar and let the sound of the dancers become dominant."

The summer of 1936 was a high point for the band. They had a steady gig at a prominent location, avid local fans, an audience that was growing—at least through the Western states—thanks to weekly radio broadcasts, and several top-notch musicians. Sunday matinees at the Rendezvous were usually reserved for "name" bands. Gil's musicians got to mingle with the sidemen from Jimmy Dorsey's band or from the other bands that came through. They were on the periphery of the big time.

The biggest single thrill for the band in its gig at the Rendezvous took place in August 1936, when Benny Goodman himself—the idol of virtually all of Gil's musicians, and of Gil himself in terms of musical direction—came to hear them with tenor saxophone player Art Rollini in tow. In the short year since Goodman's legendary appearance at the Palomar, Goodman had become a hero to legions of admirers. The Goodman orchestra traveled to Los Angeles by Pullman, in which Goodman had a private car, instead of caravanning across the country in cars and buses. The band played at the Palomar through July and August 1936 at three times the fee of the previous year, and for three weeks of that engagement they were also involved in filming *The Big Broadcast of 1937*.[22]

Goodman never went merely to hear someone else's band—he was perpetually scouting for new talent. In particular, he was looking for a good tenor sax player because he had fired Dick Clark, who'd been with him since January 1935. Goodman may have heard about Vido Musso; he might even have heard Musso on the radio with Gil's band broadcasting from the Rendezvous. In his own autobiography, Art Rollini claims the credit for hearing Musso first: "Time went on and Dick Clark was leaving. Ena and I had gone to hear Gil Evans' band near the beach. Stan Kenton was playing piano and Vido Musso was on tenor. Vido impressed me. I told Benny and he said, 'Send him down.' "[23] (It is likely that Rollini, one of the star tenor players of that time, had heard Kenton, who subbed with Gil's band—but at this point Gil's main piano player was Buddy Cole.)

"We were thrilled to death about Goodman showing up," remembered Cangie. Gil and his musicians were also a little bit nervous. "We had an arrangement of 'Dallas Blues.' When we were first rehearsing the chart, Gil told me, 'For Christ's sake, Rudy, learn the chorus [the solo]!' He gave me the record, and I copied Art Rollini's chorus. The night they came to see us, Gil pulled out 'Dallas Blues,' so I got to stand up and play Art's chorus, note for note. Later, Gil was so embarrassed, and said to me, 'Did you have to play it note for note?' But that was the only way I knew it!"[24]

It was a giddy few days. Goodman asked Musso to come and audition, which meant performing during the third set at the Palomar. By coincidence, Abby Mattas, one of Gil's first saxophonists, had hitchhiked down from Stockton to visit. He and the entire band went to the Palomar to "cheer Musso on," Mattas remembered. "Vido gets up there—now Vido can't read music, but he's a musician and when he hears something he locks it in his head and he can play it. They [Goodman's band] played 'Honeysuckle Rose'— I'll never forget this—and Musso got up and took a chorus, and then took about ten choruses, and the band was going crazy! Krupa was back there. So Benny says, 'You're hired!' Then later that night, Gil told Goodman, 'Well, Musso can't read music,' and Benny said, 'We'll teach him!' "[25]

Goodman asked Musso to attend a rehearsal the next day and to show up early to go over the tenor book with Rollini: "We turned to the first number in the book, 'Minnie the Moocher's Wedding Day.' Vido struggles. He couldn't read. We went over it and over it, but with the highly syncopated charts he was lost.... Vido sweated that night out [his first performance with Goodman's band] and made his famous remark: "It's not the notes that bother me, it's them damn *restes*!"[26]

After Vido's audition and the set were over, Gil, Abby, Vido, and the rest of Gil's boys, along with Goodman and John Hammond, all went to the Paradise Club to hear Lionel Hampton, who was playing vibraphone with a small group. Gil had already come to hear Hampton several times. "They [the jazz writers] got that Hampton deal all wrong, about who discovered Hampton," said Mattas. "Gil had heard Hampton, and that's how Goodman found out about Lionel Hampton. We were all sitting at a table, John Hammond was there, and the announcer says, 'We've got a special guest here!' So they put the spotlight on Benny, and Benny got up to play with the band, with Lionel on the vibraphones.

"Meanwhile—Jesus, I meet Benny Goodman, Gil introduced me to Benny! That was one of the greatest things that ever happened to me!"[27]

John Hammond, already a powerful figure in the jazz world, singled out Gil's band in an article in *Tempo* that fall that discussed the music scene on the West Coast. Hammond opined that the "music situation in L.A. was little less than appalling. No local bands with even the simplest ingredients of swing." In a second article, Hammond admitted his statement was a bit broad but did not retract it. However, he expressed

favorable comment on the band Gil Evans has at Balboa; in fact he was more impressed than the local musical fraternity by the Evans band, which may mean that Evans has been denied due credit, or that he may have been the victim of that well-known slowness of all communities to appreciate "home-town" talent. Evans has undertaken the worthy but difficult ambition of creating a band fashioned definitely after Good-man's, and thus he has thrown himself open to the charge of being an imitator.... Evans, thanks to the efforts of Hammond, is in line to make some recordings. These records will give a better opportunity for a true evaluation of the band, as weak spots always show up on wax.

The article further comments that the best musicians in town were under contract at the movie studios, with restrictions on them, leaving a void of really first-rate players in the world of dance bands and radio orchestras. Further, the writer continues, not one local radio station has a knowledgeable swing DJ—according to Hammond—

> and other DJs protest that swing programs would not be commercially viable. But it does not seem too much to expect that at least one LA station might attempt something along this line for one or two periods a week considering the amount of time a week devoted to wholly uninteresting dance records.... Everything considered, Los Angeles would have a pretty fair musical rating except in comparison with the cities that are as yet the real centers of musical activity in the U.S., New York and Chicago.[28]

The fact that Musso was picked up by Goodman created a buzz and started other rumors connected with Gil's band. Another clip from *Tempo* and a fan letter both asked the same question: "Is it true that four members of Gil Evans' orchestra have joined Benny Goodman's band?" As it turned out, Musso was the only one, though Goodman hired Jimmy Maxwell later on. "We had Vido Musso in the band," said Maxwell, "and Goodman heard him and hired him, and he thoughtlessly did not hire me at that time, and I didn't forgive him for that for a long time." Other personnel changes in Gil's band occurred in mid-September, when the band shifted back to the Valencia Ballroom during the week and played at Balboa only on weekends. Reuel Lynch repossessed the lead tenor chair after Musso left; Ned Briggs reclaimed the bassist's spot from Clarence Ewing, who'd played most of the summer; and Buddy Cole was now officially on board, featured on piano and on an electric vibraphone played from a keyboard, which he'd invented. Jimmy Maxwell made it into the "bigger" time after all—he was hired by Jimmy Dorsey, as was trombonist Pete Carpenter. Three other musicians, Bob Petkere, Bill Watt, and Jackie Pierce, vocalist, were briefly in and out of the band that summer—none of whom were hired by Goodman.

There was no denying Gil's status as a big fish in a small pond. Just like his band's big-time counterparts, he and his musicians received fan letters, often with requests for photos. "I have listened

to your orchestra for quite some time and find it very entertaining.
Your arrangements are swell and your vocalists really deliver the
goods."

After the hubbub with Goodman, the band lapsed into the familiar rhythm of their gigs at the Valencia and the Rendezvous during
the fall, with occasional dances and broadcasts. But things were
looking up. Doyle had booked them on a tour of the Northwest
scheduled to start in January 1937.

Typically, Gil and the boys were enthusiastic. They thought the
booking proved MCA's confidence in them and were convinced this
tour would land them in the big time once and for all. To them,
going on a tour of the Pacific Northwest—though very much off
the loop—was as significant as going to Chicago or Detroit.

3 hollywood

In late January 1937, Gil took the train to Seattle. The rest of the band went by car, and it took them almost three days. That winter was one of the worst on record for the West Coast, and on this trip the inevitable car mishap involved failure of the heating and defrost systems. "It was so cold and dreary," said alto player Jack Crowley, "that one of the guys had to keep hanging out the window and scrape the windshield to keep it clear of ice and snow."

Seattle was covered with snow. The band's first engagement was at the Trianon Ballroom; by all accounts, Gil's band was one of the first real swing-dance bands to play there. Like many ballrooms outside big cities such as New York or Chicago, the Trianon usually served up a mixture of regional bands, touring bands of widely varied expertise, and occasional appearances by the top-tier big bands. Even so, it required a lot of effort for ballrooms such as the Trianon, which took up an entire block, to maintain enough clientele to support the bands it brought in. As did more famous ballrooms such as the Savoy or Roseland in New York, the Trianon offered regular dance lessons, held weekly dance contests, and had its own dance group, the "Trianon Steppers." The Trianon also had a weekly newsletter, the *Trianon Saturday Night*. Though its covers were hand-drawn and its contents poorly typed, the newsletter championed life at the ballroom and the bands that played there.

When your friends ask where you are going, just say, "I'm going to swing it at the Trianon, to the music of the finest swing band in the West." Gil Evans and his band open Saturday, coming direct from a sensational 17-months engagement at the Rendezvous Ballroom at Balboa Beach. Competition with all the other Los Angeles bands, and the many big-name bands, have built the Gil Evans organization into one that does not have to take its hat off to any other swing band, with the exception of the master of Swing, Benny Goodman.[1]

Opening night, a Saturday, was jammed despite continuing harsh weather. The personnel were the same as a few months earlier at Valencia, with thirteen musicians in all: Gil as the leader and arranger, four reeds, two trumpets, two trombones, Buddy Cole on the piano and organ, Ned Briggs on the bass, John De Soto on drums, and Elizabeth Tilton on vocals.

Several friends of the band sent celebratory telegrams for Gil's opening, including trombonist Pete Carpenter, who had played with the band for a couple of months the previous winter, and his vocalist wife, Maybeth. Pete, who within a few years would become an A-list Los Angeles studio player and arranger, had just quit Jimmy Dorsey's band after a brief couple of months. According to Maybeth, "he hadn't had enough experience to be with the Dorsey band, he really hadn't. And that was the only job where he ever got a hard dose, in all the years that we were married, and he was kind of devastated."[2] A couple of days later, the couple sent Gil a second wire asking if Gil would hire both of them.

After the Friday night performance, the band's sixth night in Seattle, Gil went back to his hotel and wrote the Carpenters a lengthy reply.

Everything is going fine up here. Up until now they've always had sweet bands (that is, no sour ones), so we're still a little worried; but the crowds are pretty good although they sometimes put their hands over their ears. As long as they keep them away from their noses, I guess we'll get by.... What a madhouse this last week has been. Of course we all landed here broke and the main problem has been trying to establish credit in the various eating establishments—no easy task I assure you. We all stayed at various hotels the first night and because of lack of funds we've been forced to remain thru this week. Naturally I got stuck at the most expensive one—a mere $29.46. So tomorrow I'll have to find a place where I can cuff until next payday. What a life![3]

Gil also wrote that, just two nights after their arrival, the band was broadcast via remote wire from the ballroom, and the Columbia network would continue to transmit Gil's band for a half-hour spot twice a week in Seattle and to all of its western stations. Broadcasts were the ultimate exposure for any band, but this otherwise enviable situation created some unexpected headaches right away. "We've been having quite a lot of trouble getting permission to play some of our tunes over the network, the catch being that I didn't know the names of the publishers," Gil wrote. He spent a week and a fair amount of cash sending telegrams to New York for the information. He wrote that now that everything was in order and the programs "ought" to be better. "Please listen when you get a chance and let me know what's wrong so we can try to remedy it before the following week."

The second half of Gil's letter addressed a number of delicate issues:

Now, Peter, here's the straight dope on our situation with no exaggerations or mincing words: I can think of no happier day for all of us, no greater cause for celebration than the day you rejoin our band and we proudly present Maybeth as our featured vocalist.... At no time since you left has anyone felt that you were gone for good nor has a week ever gone by that someone hasn't expressed the wish that you'd hurry up and get back. However, I haven't told anyone yet that you've left Dorsey, because they'd immediately want to know if and when you were coming back.... You undoubtably have been expecting this next question so I won't disappoint you. When you rejoin the band will it be permanent, provided that musically and financially the band continues to improve? It's unnecessary for me to explain to you how detrimental it is for an organized band to lose any of its members; consequently, Pete, I'd want your word that you'd never leave simply for the sake of a temporary increase in your income.... Your salary while we're here would be $35.00 a week and Maybeth's would be $30.00 a week. I sincerely hope you'll both be with us soon and in the meantime I'll be trying to think up a delicate way to give Bobby [Blair] and Tillie their notice. Say hello to Maxwell and tell him to write.[4]

The next morning, Gil's band had an uncommon surprise. Duke Ellington's band was scheduled to play the Saturday matinee engagement at the Trianon, but the day before, a blizzard in California had delayed Southern Pacific trains for eighteen to thirty-six hours. Thus, on January 30, 1937, Gil's band wound up substituting for Duke Ellington's and managed to keep the crowd happy despite the absence of the legendary headliner. According to the *Trianon Saturday Night*:

Well over a thousand Ellington fans were turned away at the scheduled matinee. Many had traveled a long way to hear this famous attraction.... We even went so far as to have two United Airline transport planes ready to meet the train in Portland at 7:30. This train, already twelve hours late, did not arrive until midnite which was too late for us. We greatly appreciate the patronage of the large crowd that did come in Saturday, knowing that Duke would not appear. Gil Evans and his boys put on a fine program and everyone had a good time, dancing to his fine swing music.[5]

The same issue noted the huge popularity of Gil's band and stated, "Present indications are that Gil Evans and his band are going to be at the Trianon for a long time."

By this time the Carpenters had received Gil's offer and were overjoyed. On Tuesday, February 2, Gil received a telegram: "We accept your offer and terms with pleasure. Shall we join you there or will you be back here soon. Rent due on apartment. Shall we pay month two weeks or week. Answer collect. What about uniforms for us." Gil advised them to join him in Seattle, in a little over two weeks' time, so he could give proper notice to trombonist Bobby Blair and Elizabeth Tilton (who would return to finish high school in California). When the Carpenters set out by car in mid-February—

"nobody could afford to pay for the train then," recalled Maybeth—
Maybeth's father was hospitalized with a serious case of pneumonia.
The couple's reunion with the band in Seattle was marred by the
news that Maybeth's father had died while they were en route.

Maybeth and Pete were feted at the ballroom, though, and the
Trianon decided to hold the band over for several more weeks.
"Gil had the difficult task of introducing swing music to Seattle
dancers and he did a fine job of it," declared the *Trianon Saturday
Night*. "Seattle dancers are much more swing-minded now." The
local radio announcers were billing Gil's band as one of the "chief
exponents of America's modern syncopation."

Logs of Gil's live broadcasts on KOL indicate that the band's
repertoire at this time drew heavily from Benny Goodman's book.
The log from February 17, 1937, seems fairly typical and includes a
generous mix of romantic ballads and swing tunes such as "I've
Got My Love to Keep Me Warm," "Avalon," "I've Got You Under My
Skin," "Blue Moon," and "Moonglow." Fan letters rolled in from as
far away as California and the Midwest.

Radio was the central link to a band's success during the Swing
Era. The radio medium initially popularized Benny Goodman's
sound coast to coast, and it was on the radio that John Hammond,
sitting in his car in Chicago tuned in to the Reno Club in Kansas
City, first heard the Count Basie band. As commercial forces
during the Swing Era consolidated in favor of bands such as Goodman's, radio reinforced the power relationships between bands,
booking agents, and the most prominent venues. David Stowe noted
in *Swing Changes*, a study of the era, "By controlling access to key
locations, such as New York's Hotel Pennsylvania, which served to
launch Goodman, Tommy Dorsey, Shaw, and Miller, booking agen-
cies essentially controlled a band's commercial horizon." [6] In the
case of lesser-known bands such as Gil's, radio broadcasts helped
introduce their music to the public and also to other musicians;
this was especially valuable when these bands had no recordings.

Networking took place in other regards as well. Vido Musso
telegrammed Gil asking about a spot for clarinetist/saxophonist
Bill Depew, who wanted to leave Goodman's band. Goodman's
sidemen were then making an average of two hundred dollars per
week to Gil's thirty, but Goodman's intimidating personal style with

his musicians had been the subject of many items in the trade magazines.[7] One example was Goodman's seemingly capricious firing of tenor player Dick Clark, whom Musso had been hired to replace the previous summer. According to Art Rollini, Goodman let Clark go because Clark was prematurely balding and Goodman wanted a young, good-looking crew.[8]

Gil's last night at the Trianon was Thursday, March 4, 1937. The next and last stop on the band's tour was a week-long engagement at the year-old Uptown Ballroom in Portland, Oregon, where, again, Gil's authentic swing music was very well received.

Gil and the band were scheduled to return to the Rendezvous in Balboa on March 24 for the traditional spring break engagement and for another idyllic summer. Maybeth Carpenter recalled:

> I had to set the alarm to wake up by noon if I wanted to get a good tan. We played a tea dance Sunday afternoon, and that night we didn't work as late. Our third meal of the day was after work, late at night. Gil was a great one for never having cash—he wouldn't cheat, he'd just forget. He was unconcerned about money—as long as he could do what he wanted. Saving and having a lot of money never interested Gil.... [But] we had two salaries, so we did better than anybody, and we did save a little money. And the band looked marvelous. We had uniforms, and Ned Briggs was like a wardrobe mistress. Each night before we left the bandstand, he told everybody what to wear the next night (boutonniere, what color shirt, etc.) And Wes was old eagle-eye—we'd get fined if we wore the wrong thing. We were not allowed to wear our uniform or shoes off the bandstand at all. If anybody was caught off stage wearing something they got fined. It was deducted from your salary. We all paid for our own uniforms. And that band always looked great—immaculate. Girls flocked around the band.[9]

Whether being back at Balboa was idyllic or not, it had become routine—the same crowd, the same dancers, the same tensions between dancers who liked the up-tempo numbers and those who were after the sweet numbers. A week after the band returned, Jack Parrent wrote in his music column for the *Daily Trojan*,

"Trojans who hopped (danced isn't the word for it) to Gil Evans's band at Balboa have come back with several interesting comments. The major objection was that he played too many 'romp' numbers in comparison with the slower, sweeter tunes. Though the innumerable high school and jaycee lads and lassies would rather do the 'Balboa' than eat, the majority of the home guard still enjoy a more than occasional non-race dance."

It was also a return to the same old routine with Gil. Ever the perfectionist, he still wanted to rehearse as much as possible. "Pete and I were very much in love," said Maybeth, "and here was that darn Gil, calling a rehearsal on our one night off a week. It used to make us angry. But he didn't care, he'd just fluff it off and say, 'The band needs it.' He was pretty good at fluffing off what he didn't want to hear or be bothered with."[10] More annoyingly, Gil continued to fluff it off with the band's MCA agent Norman Doyle. Jimmy Maxwell, who moved to Los Angeles and started playing with other bands that summer, recalled:

Through MCA we had a contract with Victor Records but Gil wouldn't record because he said we weren't good enough. That was the source of much anguish and quarreling in the band. We'd visit Norman Doyle every Monday on our day off and say, "When are you going to get us a really good job?" A hotel job was what we thought was a good job, it paid $60 a week. And Norman would say, "Well, Gil, do you think your boys are ready?" We'd say, "Sure!" But Gil would say, "Well, Norman, maybe a few more months, the band needs a little polishing up." I'd take Gil aside, and say, "Come on Gil!" But Gil was not that way. He didn't think we were ready and he told people that. Then Norman would say, "He's the leader, he should know." Norman didn't know a damn thing about music—he was a businessman. He was just waiting for Gil to say, "Yeah, we're ready. Let's go!" I didn't know a damn thing about life either, but I knew one thing—if you keep telling a guy you're not good enough he's going to believe you.[11]

In some ways, Gil had a point. The band did not have the spit and polish of Goodman's or Lunceford's or the other top bands whose music Gil followed. But judging from air checks, Gil could have taken the band to the next step—beyond the Rendezvous Ballroom or the Pasadena Civic Auditorium.[12] Gil's skills as an arranger might have been more apparent with a more experienced group of musicians. An item in the *Pasadena Star-News* that October mentions that Gil turned down an offer to work for Goodman:

> A young swingster who received the distinction of being invited by the "King of Swing," Benny Goodman, to give up his own orchestra and join the Goodman aggregation as an arranger should go far, and Gil Evans, who plays at the Pasadena Community Dance tonight and tomorrow, claims this distinction. But still he clings to his own musicians, wishing to make a name for himself in his own way. At the Trianon ballroom, Seattle, and the Uptown Ballroom, Portland, he was a great success, and those who know his music from his long Balboa Rendezvous engagement can understand why.[13]

Gil was intensely loyal to his musicians, but by failing to press Doyle to do more—and even putting him off—Gil had allowed opportunities to slip away. As 1937 drew to a close, no promising jobs were in the offing—only their off-season gigs back at the Valencia Ballroom in Santa Ana, one-nighters at the Rendezvous, and local dances. Because Gil continued to insist that his band wasn't ready, MCA relegated the band to the bottom of its list.

In early 1938, an opportunity finally presented itself—but one that, for several band members and for Gil himself, caused a lot of conflict. Skinnay Ennis, who had been a featured star in Hal Kemp's orchestra, was going out on his own as a leader and was shopping around for a ready-made band to front.

Ennis, one of the first of the early big band crooners, had been working with Kemp ever since Kemp first formed his band in the mid-1920s, while the two were fraternity brothers at the University of North Carolina. Ennis was the drummer at first, then was coaxed into singing. Over the course of a dozen years the band acquired a reputation, toured Europe, and began landing decent gigs upon their return; a stay at New York's Hotel Pennsylvania in 1934 clinched the band's popularity. In the late 1920s, Kemp's was actually a "hot" band and included "hot" trumpet soloists such as Jack Purvis and a young Bunny Berigan. But over the course of the next few years it turned "sweet." The Kemp band's style was crafted by its arranger, John Scott Trotter, who made the most out of the corps musicians' technical limitations. Trotter created a signature sound with linear, sustained unison parts for the clarinets and muted trumpets, playing in a clipped, almost preswing fashion. With Ennis as its star singer, by the mid-1930s the band became "a wonderfully smooth, sophisticated-sounding outfit that twice was voted Best Sweet Band by *Metronome*'s readers."[14]

Ennis was no Bing Crosby. Still, his wispy, intimate delivery—a result, Ennis himself admitted, of the fact that he was not really a singer—was "haunting and sexy," wrote George Simon.[15] Ennis was featured in several of the Kemp band's successful recordings for Brunswick during the mid-1930s, including its theme song, "Got a Date with an Angel." In the fall of 1937 he also made a minor splash in the Paramount film *College Swing*, which featured George Burns and Gracie Allen, Martha Raye, Betty Grable, and a hot new comedian named Bob Hope. Ennis's increasing visibility inspired him to strike out on his own as a soloist and bandleader. With Kemp's blessing and the able assistance of Kemp's own manager, Alex Holden, Ennis left Kemp's band in late November 1937. No one doubted that Ennis would succeed.

Ennis aimed to keep the recognizable sound of the Kemp band but with himself as leader and unequivocal star. He also wanted to skip the growing pains of starting a band from scratch. Holden began contacting agents and big band leaders; Gil's band soon emerged as an obvious and excellent choice. Ennis had probably heard the band at the Rendezvous, where Kemp's was one of the bands that came through on Sunday afternoons. Maybeth Carpenter recalled an episode in late fall of 1937: "We were playing a job—a one-nighter in a high school in a little town like Glendale. Lo and behold, we're playing along and somebody said, 'Look who just walked in—Skinnay Ennis!' Someone else said, 'What's he doing here?' And Gil, raising his eyebrows, said, 'I'm afraid I have a pretty good idea.' Gil knew that MCA must have sent him over to hear the band."[16] Shortly thereafter MCA informed Gil that Skinnay wanted to take over the band.

Gil's musicians knew that their predicament was at least partly Gil's fault. "There were no bookings," Rudy Cangie explained. "MCA had said, 'We can't book you guys!' The Victor contract was never consummated because he [Gil] felt we weren't ready to record."[17] Meanwhile, Ennis had already lined up a very prominent gig for himself and an orchestra at the Victor Hugo, a glamorous, first-class Beverly Hills restaurant that catered to the stars. Gil put the decision to have the band be taken over by Ennis to a vote. His musicians really had few options.

The majority chose to go with Ennis. Both Jack Crowley and Rudy Cangie were engaged to be married and wanted more financial stability. "It was a good job so we went for it," said Cangie. Though Gil tried to keep his feelings out of it, he was not entirely successful. "Gil cried," Maybeth recalled. "Not in front of us, but we found out later he had. MCA sold Gil down the river."

The newly reminted band, billed as Skinnay Ennis and His Orchestra, opened at the Victor Hugo on April 14, 1938. Personnel are listed in *Tempo* as Ryland Weston, Jack Crowley, Rudy Cangie, Herb Stowe, saxes; Ralph Liscom, Ross Matjasic, trumpets; Pete Carpenter, Noris Hurley, Carl Loeffler, trombones; Gil Evans, piano; Johnny De Soto, drums; Ned Briggs, bass; and Sonny Dawson, guitar. For the moment, at least, Gil's Balboa band was largely intact and still included eight members of the original Stockton gang; but three of Gil's top musicians—Maxwell, Cole, and Maybeth Carpenter—were not in Ennis's band.

Despite the conflict, it was a good move—the band was steadily employed again, and most of them stayed together. Gil and some of the band members shared a house in Hollywood half a block below Sunset Boulevard. "A place called Victor's Steak House was right on the corner," recalled Johnny De Soto. "The house was a twenties-style old wood house with a porch. Six or seven of us were there—Briggs, myself, Dawson, Ryland, I think Stowe, and Gil. Gil had this dog there. Leave it to Gil. He couldn't have a nice little ordinary dog—he had to have a big Great Dane."[18]

There was one hitch: Gil and his musicians faced a formidable union problem that would break them up over the course of the next year. They were still members of Santa Ana Local 687 rather than Los Angeles Local 47, which technically made them a traveling band. Union regulations designed to encourage the hiring of local talent imposed a 10 percent "tax" on leaders who hired nonlocal musicians. But for nonlocal musicians to turn local and get a local union card required a huge sacrifice—not working at all for the first three months, and playing only casual engagements for another three. Still, several of Gil's musicians—including Cangie, Crowley, De Soto, and Stowe—eventually made the switch and were in fact rehired by Ennis after the required time had elapsed. Others played as long as they could as traveling musicians before getting bumped for the L.A. regulars. This process, set in motion by the Ennis take-over, took a toll on the band over the next two seasons, giving rise to rifts and resentments and causing personnel changes.

The breakup of Gil's band began the minute Skinnay took it over. A press clipping from *Tempo* magazine reviews the band's debut at the Victor Hugo, April 14, 1938. The article vivifies Gil's dilemma—musically and commercially:

> Skinnay Ennis, erstwhile singer and drummer with Hal Kemp, who recently took a fling at the movies, makes his debut as bandleader fronting Gil Evans's band, which drew plenty of favorable comment during engagements at Balboa Beach and other West Coast spots, and not so long ago was considered the coming swing-style unit on the Coast. MCA's recent failure to find a spot for the band under Evan's leadership is puzzling. Possibly because of recent lay-offs, but more likely because of the deadening influence of the gilded dullness of the Victor Hugo, the band wasn't performing as solidly here as it did in the freer environment of the Rendezvous Ballroom in Balboa. The fact that the boys didn't feel at home yet in new somewhat Kempish arrangements is another reason for spotty perform-ance, but consensus is that the band, which is comprised of capable young musicians can be built into a good outfit. A standout man is Jack Crowley, one of the few white alto men of the Johnny Hodges school.
>
> Ennis officiates only with the baton and on vocals. Gil Evans, still with the band on piano, probably retains business interest in the band.[19]

The Ennis Orchestra came off more favorably in the Third Hollywood Swing Concert, held at the Palomar on July 31, 1937, and sponsored by Local 47: "in view of the fact that this band used to play at
Balboa before Ennis took it over, the boys know how to play hot and
did some of the best on the whole program." The review also states
that "the concert wasn't well represented as to 'swing' "—too many
girl trios and show bands. The name big bands that appeared were
Floyd Ray's, a prominent L.A.-based black band that received the
biggest hand (and had stolen the show the previous year); Casa
Loma, which got "the second biggest hand, strictly on musical
merit"; and Tommy Dorsey's band, which got the third biggest hand
and closed the program. (Tommy Dorsey's band would achieve
widespread fame a few months later with its double-sided hit record
"Marie" and "Song of India.") The program also included a band
led by Vido Musso, which "must have been thrown together judging by the sounds it emitted." The entire event looked as though
"there were too many people running around directing and order-
ing," with bands being pushed on and off the stage hastily.[20]

ı' Iı I

When the Ennis Orchestra closed the spring-summer season at the
Victor Hugo in early September 1938, Jimmy Maxwell was back
on board. Maxwell, who'd moved to Hollywood before the Ennis
takeover, had been working with Maxine Sullivan near the Hugo
when Gil et al. started playing there. Sullivan's engagement in a
"showy ornate little Hollywood nite club" was quite a prestigious
job for the sextet assembled for her appearance, led by L.A. bassist
Darryl Harper. The group played the Claude Thornhill arrangements Sullivan had brought with her from New York (where she
had been appearing at the Onyx on 52nd Street), with a violin taking over a saxophone part. "The band is better than you'd ever
guess. If Reuel Lynch [clarinet], Jimmy Maxwell and Johnny Black
[piano] weren't 'hometown' boys, local musicians would be going
overboard about them." [21]

Maxwell, who'd worked with various groups since leaving
Evans's band the previous summer, recalled reuniting with Gil and
the boys via the Ennis organization.

When she [Maxine] was due to close, Ralph Hallenbach [a trumpet player and arranger with Skinnay] came over and auditioned me, so to speak. And there was a great to-do about whether I would like to come work for Skinnay's band, and of course, I needed the work. So I went back with the band—and Gil was still there. He and whoever in the band wasn't married and the dog all shared this house. They used to pick me up on Sunset Boulevard. I'd walk down to the foot of the hill and wait for them to pick me up, which they often forgot to do. I also used to go over to the house every afternoon to practice because I couldn't practice where I lived.

Truthfully, to this day I regret Gil's band breaking up. We had a huge library, a couple of hundred arrangements. And he gave it all to Skinnay for nothing. Always in the back of my mind, I really thought the band would get back together—until the day Gil died.[22]

That fall, the Ennis Orchestra was carving a niche for itself in the upper echelon of the Los Angeles music scene. The Casa Loma band was at the Palomar, while Vido Musso, who had left Goodman for the first (but not last) time, was again trying his hand at leading a band, this time at Villa Venice. *Tempo* reported that Musso "surprised us all by pulling a band out of a hat that is as promising an outfit as anyone has put together around here in a long time." Its members included Reuel Lynch, Evans's former sax player, and the "rhythm section has a solid man in Stan Kenton, an asset in any man's band."[23]

Ennis, still on the way up, then landed a spectacular job backing up one of the brightest new stars in the entertainment world— Bob Hope.

Hope was a hit maker in all the major entertainment venues: Broadway, radio, and movies. After coming up in vaudeville and small theaters through the previous decade, he made a big splash on Broadway in the 1936 *Ziegfeld Follies*, sharing the spotlight with Fanny Brice. Hollywood soon beckoned, but meanwhile the comedian was featured frequently on radio. In May 1937, he signed a twenty-six-week radio contract for the *Woodbury Soap Show*, broadcast from NBC in New York. In the summer of 1938, after he had traveled to Hollywood to film *The Big Broadcast of 1938*, Hope continued the show via transcontinental hookup. By fall 1938, Hope was signed by Pepsodent for his own show on NBC.

Hope met Ennis in the late fall of 1937 while both worked on the Paramount film *College Swing*. It was Hope's second film and Skinnay's first. Hope took an instant liking to Ennis at the time and hired him and his band to accompany his new variety-format radio show.

The *Pepsodent Show*, like other regular radio shows of the day, ran once a week for a season: thirty-nine weeks starting in September, then off the air for thirteen weeks in the summer, and back on again in the fall. The cast would rehearse for two hours early Sunday evening, take a break, then preview the show in front of an audience to work out the kinks. A three-hour rehearsal took place on Tuesday, followed by a two-hour break, and then the show was broadcast with a live audience, airing for a half-hour, 7–7:30 P.M. and 6–6:30 P.M. in the spring.

The show first previewed before a live audience on September 18, only a few days after the Ennis Orchestra closed at the Victor Hugo. The show's regulars eventually included three other comedians: Jerry Colonna and Brenda and Cobina (Brenda Frazier and Cobina Wright, Jr.). Jerry Colonna, with his trademark huge mustache, was a trombone player with Ozzie Nelson before he became a big radio star as a comic. The regular cast also included the vocal group Six Hits and a Miss (one of the most innovative vocal groups of the time), Skinnay Ennis and His Orchestra, and well-known announcer Bill Goodwin. In the Hope show's second season, 1939–1940, Judy Garland was a frequent guest. The format was standardized from the beginning and included an opening theme ("Thanks for the Memory"), a Hope monologue, an Ennis number, a guest spot, Six Hits and a Miss, another Hope routine, the closing theme, and the credits and sign-off. When the Ennis band started making records, about a month after the debut of the Hope show, the band played the songs it had recorded. Almost immediately the Hope show became a Tuesday night habit among many Americans, bringing Hope a bigger radio audience than he had ever had before.

Meanwhile, Ennis's career was proceeding nicely on several fronts. That fall, he recorded his first two 78rpms for Victor as a leader, "Garden of the Moon" and "The Girlfriend of the Whirling Dervish." Both songs were written by Johnny Mercer, Al Dubin, and Harry Warren for the film *Garden of the Moon*. The recordings feature Ennis as vocalist accompanied by Evans's musicians plus newcomers Dawson, Schlegel, and Fred Whiting, with Gil himself on piano. These sides are Evans's very first commercial recordings as arranger and pianist. The piano parts can barely be heard on these recordings, but as examples of Gil's arrangements these 78rpms are fascinating artifacts.

"The Girlfriend of the Whirling Dervish" is the more interesting of the two. A novelty number, Gil milked it for drama and humor. Tom-toms and low clarinets punctuate Skinnay's ironic delivery ("They tell me a whirling dervish is a Bombay gait, who through simply whirling and uncurling, makes those Hindu jitterbugs blow their oriental tops about jitterbug"). The ensemble bursts forth through the nonsensical verses with flair, trumpets and trombones growling. The instrumental solo spots are terrific: a hip-for-the-time alto saxophone solo (probably by Jack Crowley) accompanied only by tom-toms (by drummer Johnny De Soto), and a dazzling trumpet solo by Jimmy Maxwell on the out-chorus. The sax tom-tom duo passage had already been popularized by the Goodman Orchestra's recording of "Sing, Sing, Sing" (released earlier that year). The requisite Middle Eastern effect is provided by warbling clarinet obbligatos. The band—still largely the Evans band—plays with far more precision than had been revealed by their air checks from eighteen months earlier. The B-side, "Garden of the Moon," is a winsome little two-step, treated in a much more Kemp-ish style. It is a standard lightweight romp; a muted Maxwell restates the melody after Ennis's breathy delivery. A couple of double-time passages challenge the band and sounds quite modern in their linearity.

These sides hardly point toward Gil's future artistic leanings. In all likelihood the songs themselves were probably chosen for some song-plugging deal. But there are some passages in each recording where one finds Gil's arrangements stretching the limits of standard pop fare. All in all, these sides reiterate how varied the pop mainstream was during the Swing Era, when the hits of the day did not *all* swing.

In mid-September, the Ennis band closed at the Victor Hugo for a two-month hiatus, but they immediately began a weekly engagement at the prestigious Hotel Mark Hopkins in San Francisco. According to *Tempo*, Skinnay's opening there was one of the most successful at the Mark Hopkins in years, and the band was "packing 'em in." Ennis flew back and forth to L.A. every week for the radio show until the band resumed playing at the Hugo in November. A front-page article in the *San Francisco News* on October 7, 1938, explains how Ennis managed to have jobs—and bands—in San Francisco and Los Angeles at the same time:

> There are two Ennis bands. One is his honest-to-goodness band at the Mark Hopkins with which he hopes to go places as a bandleader. The other is strictly a radio-hour band carrying his name for radio purposes only. Two bands and he's only been in the business eight months!... He doesn't think his kind of singing will stay popular forever, without something else behind it.... That's why he's molding his band to a particular and different style—the style he believes will replace swing tomorrow.[24]

The article goes on to say that Ennis's radio band was largely composed of musicians in John Scott Trotter's band, a roving troop of ex-Kemp musicians, who all played with several radio bands simultaneously. In other words, they were the "radio men" who had most of the commercial work in Los Angeles sewn up. Furthermore, since Gil's musicians were still on transfer from the Santa Ana local, Ennis would have had to pay the union the 10 percent extra as a traveling band, so it was to his economic advantage to use local musicians for the radio show. But Skinnay was dedicated to his dance band, though he stuck to the conservative California "hotel" band style, sidestepping what he considered a fad—swing: " 'I wouldn't think my future was worth 3 cents if I had a swing band,' he says. By his sulphurous language when he talks about sensationalism in swing, he makes it unanimous as far as the five band leaders at San Francisco's big hotels are concerned."[25]

Ennis's exposure as an all-around entertainer was enhanced considerably by the Hope show. Hope made sure that Ennis received a few key lines for laughs—mostly playing straight man to Hope—

on every broadcast, which anted up Ennis's booking status as a bandleader. When the Ennis band reopened at the Victor Hugo in January 1939, it was a Hollywood favorite and a bigger draw than ever.

Where did that leave Gil? Apparently, not very happy—although, characteristically, one would never have known it from his demeanor. Gil's responsibilities as the Ennis band's arranger were demanding and time-consuming. Though some of Gil's "sweeter" arrangements were perfectly appropriate for the Ennis Orchestra, a batch of new arrangements had to be tailored for Skinnay's sound and personality and for the hotel and restaurant crowds. They were not the effervescent swing charts Gil had been working on for years. Gil's responsibilities also included rehearsing the Hope show band and the Ennis dance band. Musically, the thrill had gone for Gil and for many of his musicians. As Cangie recalled,

> Ennis was a nice guy but we didn't respect him musically, not after Gil. When Skinnay took the band over it became a very unhappy band.... Gil didn't want to play piano anymore, so there were different piano players. They hired Skitch Henderson and Charles LaVere. I'm sure Charlie came one of those nights just to bail Gil out. Skitch played with us for many weeks, but he didn't go to San Francisco. Gil played piano in San Francisco with Skinnay when Skinnay didn't have anybody else. We were all thinking of ways to jump.[26]

The pianist Charles LaVere had just recently settled in Los Angeles and was working with Frank Trumbauer after touring with Paul Whiteman's orchestra for a year (the following year he became Bing Crosby's regular accompanist).[27] Skitch Henderson, who went on to become the music director at NBC in New York during the 1950s and founded the New York Pops in the 1980s, was then a hungry young actor and musician under contract to MGM. MGM didn't come up with any film roles for him so the studio hired him as a rehearsal pianist. Within a few months, Gil stopped playing piano for Ennis almost entirely. LaVere primarily played at the Hugo and in San Francisco, and Henderson played for the Hope show. Henderson recalled:

What everybody forgets is that nobody had any money. I got paid $3.00 a week for being rehearsal pianist, a slave job. I rehearsed with the stars—Judy Garland, Deanna Durbin, people who came on the lot and had music to do. After the composer would come and play their vehicle, whoever it might be—Kern or Berlin, Youmans, all the biggies—then I was the next person in line. I would get the right key for them and write a sketch. When Skinnay got the Victor Hugo booking, he asked me if I would come there and work with the band. That was my beginning of a very close association with Gil. He and Ralph Hallenbach were the arrangers.[28]

Henderson remembers this as an eye-opening period in his musical career. For one thing, he was impressed by the stark contrast between the arranging styles of Gil Evans and Ralph Hallenbach.

It was so incredible to have two men with such violently opposed poles as far as how to write for a band. For Ralph it had to be perfect, you didn't do anything without checking a book. Gil was the creative arranger and [only] about a third of what he wrote ever ended up in the book. The rest of it was on the floor, because it was a little beyond the pale, certainly of Skinnay. The band at the Hugo was a Mickey Mouse band really. It was Hal Kemp—the triple-tongued trumpets and all of that. It was a strange amalgamation of Gil trying to make it a musical band and Skinnay wanting what we called in those days a "hotel" band. Gil wrote really off the wall for those years, considering the musicianship we had—the class of player. I don't want to insult anybody, but I realized as I got older how he strained the limits of the Ennis band by the kind of charts he brought in. He wrote bass parts that would strike people dumb today.... I remember a song called "Honolulu," an arrangement of Gil's that haunted me all of my life because of his creativity with that horrible song. Skinnay hated it, but whenever I led the band we always played it. [Henderson, sixty years later, began to sing it.][29]

Around the time that Skitch started working with the band, Gil was also handed a new responsibility: Carmine Calhoun. Calhoun, who would marry Ennis in December 1939, was a glamorous but completely inexperienced singer who started working with the band after Maxine Grey, a holdover from the Kemp band, left to get married. Carmine, then eighteen years old, was related to Hal Kemp's wife. Raised in Texas, she was the daughter of a wealthy cattleman and was "reared as a society girl."[30] She had known Skinnay for years and tagged along with him when he settled in California. She managed to convince Skinnay to try her as a singer at least with the dance band, though not on the Hope show. The sometimes unpleasant task of teaching her music was handed to Gil.

> I didn't know much about music [Calhoun recalled], so Skinnay turned me over to Gil. Gil taught me how to sing, and change keys. And Gil wrote fantastic arrangements for me— "Old Devil Moon," I get goose pimples thinking about it. Gil did magnificent vocal arrangements! I don't think that was what he really wanted to do, but he was very good. He wasn't only a good musician, he was kind of a sneak. He put me into the [vocal] trio with Pete Carpenter and Sonny Dawson, and taught me my part in harmony, but he made me believe that was the way the song went. If I thought he was teaching me how to sing harmony, I wouldn't have been able to do it.[31]

Carmine had a crush on Gil and flirted with him openly, even after she and Skinnay were married. Many years later, she described her relationship with Gil as mutually adoring ("we were even going to run off and get married one day"). Gil was a gentleman, however, and did his job, some of which was squiring her around, a situation that as a headstrong young woman she may have misread. Several of the band members thought her extremely manipulative and an instigator of false rumors, which at times caused ill will between Skinnay and others.

Meanwhile Gil was constantly under pressure to come up with arrangements. At no other time in his career was he under such duress to constantly write appropriate material in such a range of styles ("I've always learned from practical work")—or with such a commercial bent. As his later career proved, being a "pen for hire" was just not what Gil wanted to be.

ı' lı ı

Toward the end of October 1938, Gil did get some help with the arrangements for the Hope show. Shortly after the show started airing, the Hope organization wanted to hire a more experienced vocal arranger, one who might also have some name value. An oft-told story is that Gil's own opinion was sought, and he recommended the arranger/pianist Claude Thornhill, a musician who would become a key figure in Gil's artistic development. At this time, Thornhill was considered the best vocal arranger around. He'd had several chart-topping hit records in the previous year, most notably the beautifully swinging "Loch Lomond," which launched the career of vocalist Maxine Sullivan; Benny Goodman then asked Thornhill to arrange this tune for his big band, and it became a big hit for Goodman as well, sung by Martha Tilton. Furthermore, Skinnay and Alex Holden both knew Claude personally; Thornhill had worked as a pianist and arranger for the Kemp band in 1930 and 1931. According to *Tempo*, October 1938, Thornhill was hired by the Hope organization to shape up the Ennis band and write arrangements for the *Pepsodent Show*; he moved to Los Angeles that month.

Thornhill was well regarded in New York jazz and popular music circles as both an arranger and pianist with original ideas. Born in 1909 in Terre Haute, Indiana, Thornhill was considered something of a *wunderkind* on piano, which he started studying as a child. Then, at the age of fourteen, he ran away from home and got a job playing on a riverboat. During periods of reconciliation with his parents, Thornhill studied at the Cincinnati Conservatory and later at the Curtis Institute in Philadelphia. In the late 1920s Artie Shaw, a former band mate and friend, got Thornhill a job with Austin Wylie's dance band in Cleveland, and both musicians moved to New York in the early 1930s. Thornhill quickly became an A-list studio pianist and arranger and worked for Paul Whiteman, Hal Kemp, Freddy Martin, Benny Goodman (in his first big band), and Bing Crosby. He was in the all-star band that Ray Noble performed with at the Rainbow Room and was then hired for André Kostelanetz's radio show. Meanwhile, he also recorded with several prominent jazz musicians, including Billie Holiday.

Thornhill, often described as pixieish, was—even then—a heavy drinker, who also consumed endless cups of coffee and cigarettes. Gil had "a fixed image in my mind from this time, of Claude with his cigarette holder and his eternal cup of coffee. They were his badges. So were his Adler Elevator shoes."[32] In Hollywood, Thornhill quickly established a reputation as an eccentric. Carmine Calhoun recalled:

> He used to come into the Hugo, laugh hysterically, and crawl around on the floor, barking at people. Being drunk in those days was looked on differently—drinking wasn't looked on as a disease of alcoholism. If a celebrity like Claude did crazy things, it was passed off as a joke. All the stars did that. Thornhill and Gil were together a lot during that time. I always thought that Gil was too smart and that he loved the music part of it too much to get too far out.... Gil wouldn't let himself get too out of control because it would harm his ability.[33]

Jimmy Maxwell remembered that Evans and Thornhill became very close right away and that Gil gleaned a lot from Thornhill musically. "Even then," Gil told Nat Hentoff in an interview in 1957, "Claude had a unique way with a dance band. He'd use the trombones, for example, with the woodwinds in a way that gave them a horn sound." [34]

Thornhill arranged almost all the vocal numbers for the show, and Gil wrote the Ennis orchestra's instrumental numbers, some of the vocal features, and the bulk of the Ennis band's dance book, which Thornhill had nothing to do with at all. Claude—often with Gil's assistance—did the arrangements for other featured guest stars such as Frances Langeford and Betty Hutton, and those for Six Hits and a Miss.

However, according to Skitch Henderson, Gil wrote more for the Hope show than his band members realized. For instance, most people thought Judy Garland's arrangements were all written by Roger Eden, who was already in the upper echelon of the music department at MGM when he became Judy Garland's music director. Said Henderson, "Roger Eden would never hear of Gil Evans writing an arrangement for Judy Garland. Never in a hundred years! So I would bring these atrocious, screaming arrangements from Metro and secretly Gil and I would—behind the scenes—kind of adapt them for the Skinnay Ennis orchestra, which was not a virtuoso orchestra by any means."[35]

Meanwhile, Ennis was also trying to keep up as a recording artist, but it is unclear how much influence or direction Gil provided in this realm. Ennis cut his next sides for Victor just a month after his first, on October 25, 1938. The songs were "Deep in a Dream," "Gardenias," and "I'm Forever Blowing Bubbles" (the latter side was never issued). On this occasion the personnel only included one Evans stalwart, saxophonist Reuel Lynch; the rest were big band honchos and studio men, including Manny Klein on trumpet, Artie Bernstein on bass (who would join Benny Goodman in May 1939), Dick Clark on tenor, and Thornhill himself on piano. Most likely, Thornhill was the arranger for these sides. None of Ennis's recordings from this period made it onto the charts. But interestingly enough, the band was getting a reputation. It was mentioned in *Down Beat*'s "Review of the Year" ("These Events Made Music Headlines in '38") with other September items: "Skinnay Ennis' new crew clicked on Pacific Coast."[36]

Evans's role in Ennis's next recording sessions, in March 1939, was more pronounced. Ennis went back into Victor's Hollywood studios accompanied by Evans's personnel—Maxwell, Noris Hurley, Pete Carpenter, Rudie Cangie, Ryland Weston, Johnny De Soto—with Charles LaVere on piano. Gil was the arranger for two of the sides: "Strange Enchantment," the theme from the film *Man About Town*, and "Wishing Will Make It So" from the film *Love Affair*. Claude Thornhill also did a couple of arrangements for the same date: "That Sentimental Sandwich," also from *Man About Town*, and "Hooray for Spinach" from *Naughty but Nice*. "Strange Enchantment" and "That Sentimental Sandwich" both were recorded again April 13, 1939. (The second version of "Strange Enchantment" was reissued on compact disc for the first time in 1998 as part of an unusual big band compilation in which the repertoire goes far beyond the warhorses of the era.)[37]

Like "The Girlfriend of the Whirling Dervish," "Strange Enchant-ment" barely fits into what one might consider the easy listening patterns of the day. It is a light fox trot, but its dreamy introduc-tion with clarinet, celeste, and muted trumpet, a recurring vacilla-tion from major to minor, and a quasi-oriental clarinet-led interlude take the song to a different dimension. Clarinets and muted trum-pet play the first chorus, which opens into a full ensemble state-ment. The "Arabian Nights" interlude sets up Skinnay's typically half-sung, half-whispered vocal chorus, accompanied by celeste and low clarinets. This part of the arrangement is dreamy and ethereal yet tongue-in-cheek—a combination Gil became quite adept at later in his career. The third chorus takes a different tack, with trom-bone out front; suddenly the piece is swinging with brass—a new attitude that carries through the last chorus, which repeats the tex-ture of the first.

Professionally, Gil and company were doing what they'd been dreaming of—playing steadily in a glamorous Hollywood restau-rant, getting paid well, being featured on a hit radio show and—finally!—making records. Working for the Hope show, complete with plenty of celebrities coming and going, provided many opportunities for Evans and his musicians to network and find other work. Rudy Cangie recalled that Gil was unhappy about los-ing his band to Ennis, and the way he showed it was by not play-ing piano. He used subs frequently, and by April 1939 he left the piano chair completely. Otherwise, Gil carried on with his business professionally.

Skitch Henderson remembered this period with great affec-tion. "Those were very happy times for me at the Hugo. Gil shared a house in Beverly Hills, I lived with Jimmy Van Heusen. That was the mafia, we were all very close together. We were all stumbling for a living in those days. The Hope show was thirty-five dollars a week—that was the scale, and then between the contractor and the union dues, I think I got a check for twenty-nine dollars or thirty-one dollars. But it was a very important gig to have."[38]

With Ennis, certainly, Gil had lost control of his musical world. Whatever yearning Gil had had for nurturing a band of his own and arranging and performing jazz and swing music was placed in abeyance. By April 1939, just a year after the "takeover," Ennis had replaced almost all of Gil's original sidemen with Local 47 musicians. The "traveling" status of Gil's musicians was a ready excuse. *Tempo* reported, "Among those who left or are to leave the band: Evans (piano), Liscom (trumpet), Hurley (trombone), Stowe (sax), De Soto (drums). Replacements so far include Harry Johnson (trumpet), formerly with Ozzie Nelson; Charlie LaVere (piano), one-time Whiteman bandsman; Jimmy Murphy (trombone), Fred Peters (sax). New set-up will enable band to take local engagements. Gil Evans remains on staff as arranger."[39] Two months later, *Tempo* reported that "Skinnay Ennis (Victor Hugo) reorganization completed with signing of Saxmen Hilly Harwick and Reuel Lynch. De Soto remains on drums." Other longtime Evans colleagues—Jack Crowley, Jimmy Maxwell, and Pete Carpenter—were still with Ennis, at least for the moment. Later that summer, Jimmy Maxwell was finally hired by Benny Goodman. The next time Maxwell played at the Hugo it was with the Goodman orchestra, when it appeared on the West Coast for the first time in two years (August 10–17, 1939).

The Ennis Orchestra finished their residency at the Victor Hugo on May 22, 1939, and the last Hope show aired on June 20. Ennis had a busy summer season lined up for the dance band, which got to revisit a couple of former Evans haunts, such as the Rendezvous at Balboa and the Cocoanut Grove in Capitola, with a lot more fanfare ("In person—direct from Hollywood! Skinnay Ennis with his Famous Broadcasting Orchestra and Stage Revue"). The band did a West Coast tour, starting in Capitola, and played at theaters, ballrooms, and amusement parks in Seattle; Portland; Vancouver, BC; and Salt Lake City. In Seattle, the band played an extended run at the Palomar Theater. A press clip from Jack Crowley's scrapbook highlights Gil's work there: "The arranger had done a fine job on the music. It's original, it has plenty of color, and there are no rough edges between numbers." By popular demand, the band played a special one-nighter at Seattle's Trianon Ballroom. The *Seattle Post Intelligencer* covered the event in a few paragraphs that were duly reprinted in *Trianon Saturday Night:*

> The first thing you learn about throbbing-voiced Skinnay Ennis, the band leader is that he's not skinny... The second thing you learn is that Skinnay is another alumnus of that remarkable

college generation, circa 1925... which spewed out so many top-flight band leaders, among them Kay Kyser, Jan Garber, Hal Kemp and John Scott Trotter.... The third thing you learn is that Skinnay is an extraordinarily shrewd young man, fully aware that the professional life of a ranking leader is seldom longer than five years, and that the time to save money is now, not in the distant and uncertain future. Give Skinnay five more years and he'll be comfortably fixed for the rest of his life.

Skinnay has a smooth-working 13-piece organization, more sweet than swing.... Curiously there are no stringed instruments in the Ennis band. Those soft effects he gets from muted brass.... "I've tried to get an all-purpose band here," he says. "This aggregation will work commercial radio, theatres, big ballrooms and one-night stands with equal success. String music sounds swell in a hotel dining room, but there's no great future in hotel dining rooms."[40]

Interestingly, the newsletter does not mention Gil Evans's name at all. The authors of the *Trianon Saturday Night* made nothing of the fact that the Ennis band comprised largely the same group of musicians who were greeted so enthusiastically two and a half years earlier, when Gil Evans and his swingsters wowed the Seattle audience with its first exposure to authentically played live swing music.

4 thornhill—his band and his sound

In the fall of 1939 Claude Thornhill, the Hope show's head arranger, decided to strike out on his own and form his own dance band. Thornhill had been unwilling to go on the road with Skinnay Ennis during the summer and may have already started thinking about leaving the Hope show at that time. He returned to New York to scout around for musicians with a sheaf of arrangements in hand, and in February 1940 the new band had its first performances. By the following summer, Gil began to split his time between the two leaders: Ennis, whose dance band still included a few of Gil's original Stockton musicians, and Thornhill, whose fledgling band wound up in southern California. Gil worked for both bands, with varying degrees of commitment, for the next two and a half years.

Gil swerved from one set of circumstances to the other. The Ennis band was relatively successful commercially and, via the Hope show, reached a wide audience, but the dance band's fundamental hotel style was bland. The Thornhill band, by contrast, was moving in the direction of a genuinely new sound and was critically acclaimed from the outset. But its prospects for steady work were often hampered by uncannily bad timing. Its existence was tenuous at times, thanks to Thornhill's lack of business acumen—a lack as far-reaching as Gil's would turn out to be. Disinterest might be a better way to put it.

In the fall of 1939, the Ennis orchestra was busy and sought after. It reclaimed its spot at the Mark Hopkins in San Francisco and at the Hugo in Hollywood. The band was again the accompanying band for the Hope show, which was gearing up for its second year.

Thornhill's decision to leave the Hope show was due to a number of factors, the most important being his growing ambition to have his own band. Carmine Calhoun Ennis recalled, "When we left to go up to San Francisco, Claude didn't want any part of that. He didn't want to just travel around with us as an arranger, he was too important a musician, so Alex Holden helped him get his own band started, too."

Carmine also claimed that Thornhill's work was falling off because of his increasing drinking problem. "Some of the things he brought in were terrible, the most mish-mash horrible mess you ever saw. His arrangements got so crazy it was almost impossible to play them.... The Hope show had to let him go. When he was sober he wrote the most gorgeous things you ever heard."[1]

ı‖ıｌı

As George Simon wrote, "For sheer musical beauty, for gorgeous musical moods, for imagination and wit and taste and originality and consistently fine musicianship, there was never a band that could match Claude Thornhill's."[2]

A vivid example of Thornhill's unusual thinking was recalled by clarinetist George Paulsen, one of Thornhill's first band members: "We were making our first trip across the U.S. heading for California and we stopped at the Grand Canyon in Arizona. Claude asked us to get our instruments out. We lined up facing the canyon— he called off chords and we listened to the echoes. Some interesting sound effects resulted. They should have been recorded—they would have been recorded today! It drew a crowd of interested spectators."[3]

The way Paulsen met Thornhill is typical of how Claude collected the talented young musicians who eventually made up his new band, for which he'd already written forty scores. Paulsen was working with a dance band at Child's Paramount restaurant in Times Square. "Claude had a waitress call me over to the table; he told me his plans and wanted to know if I'd be interested in making a rehearsal at the Nola studio.... The rehearsal I attended was the first one Claude's band had. There were four saxes and two clarinets in the reed section—I was playing clarinet. I was completely thrilled with the sound of the arrangements."[4]

Paulsen's enthusiasm was partly a result of the overgorged commercialism of the big band scene of the day. In 1939, the big business of big bands—a top white band with the right machinery could net as much as $250,000 a year—still inspired the formation of many new bands.[5] Superstar sidemen, notably Gene Krupa and Harry James, formed their own bands. So did Lionel Hampton and Teddy Wilson, who had both come to fame with Benny Goodman (as members of Goodman's trio and quartet).

The musical variety among the big bands was—as it had been all through the 1930s—remarkably broad. The hard driving, riff-based playing of Goodman, Basie, and Lunceford—what we might think of today as the quintessential music of the era—still commanded a vast audience. So did the more eclectic approaches of Tommy Dorsey and Artie Shaw, who made hits out of such unlikely material as "Song of India" and "Frenesi" and became Goodman's de facto archrivals thanks to the entertainment media. Ellington's completely individualistic style kept his orchestra and his music in a class of its own. "Sweet" bands that might sound hopelessly dated and bland today, such as those of Freddy Martin, Guy Lombardo, or Shep Fields, were very successful; their records occupied the top slots on *Your Hit Parade* for weeks at a time.

Clearly, though, there had been a sea change. In 1939, the Glenn Miller Orchestra, after struggling for two years, found resounding success and had a string of million-selling hits, notably "In the Mood" and "Moonlight Serenade." Miller's sound and style perfectly married sweet and swing and appealed to an even wider audience than Goodman's band did. Louis Erenberg wrote:

Once he decided he would never outswing Goodman, Shaw, or Basie or best Tommy Dorsey on trombone, Miller emphasized his strengths—arranging and organizing the talents of others into a more unified, romantic sound. The result was a synthesis: "sweet swing," a clean-cut version of jive suitable for expansion into the nation's heartland via jukeboxes and radio.... Miller took the edge off the hard-charging Goodman style and made it comfortable for the less experienced white dancers. Thus his codification of the major elements of big band performance into a streamlined sweet swing made his musical product appealing to a much wider audience. It was Miller, not Goodman, who set the pattern for white bands after 1939.[6]

Musically, Miller's smoothing agent consisted of, among other things, a clarinet lead playing an octave above the other reeds, which rounded out the band's sound considerably. The arrangements were tight, with carefully planned solos that hardly ever varied; the band was wonderfully consistent, but there was little room for inventiveness on the part of the musicians or the arrangers for that matter—Miller altered everything to fit a certain mold. Further, Miller's perfectionism extended to the band's clean-cut collegiate good looks—he and his band lent big band jazz an unassailably respectable aura. Miller's success allowed a band like Thornhill's, often clarinet-led and certainly smooth sounding, to garner critical attention early on, and to receive optimistic and endless comparisons to Miller as well.

Claude Thornhill's band initially had twelve instrumentalists: four saxophonists (who doubled on clarinet), two clarinetists (who played *only* clarinet), two trumpets, one trombone, and three rhythm, including Thornhill on piano. Thornhill also hired a twenty-three-year-old Princeton graduate named Bill Borden as arranger when the band was first being formed. Many years later, Borden said that at first the band sometimes "sounded like Jimmie Lunceford, sometimes like Bob Crosby." Claude and Borden quickly crafted an alluring quasi-orchestral sound by using (at times) five or six clarinets in unison and mixed voicings between the brass and reeds; they wrote deftly for woodwinds, including occasional use of the flute, and later on French horns were added to the band. With the exception of arrangements by Ellington, Billy Strayhorn, and Eddie Sauter, the use of "mixed" voicings between brass and reeds and unexpected instrumental couplings were still unusual; straight-ahead sectional writing for the brass and saxes was the norm.

A 1941 article in *Down Beat* about Borden ("Man Behind the Band") described the Thornhill–Borden working relationship.

> Borden and Claude together have worked out a style unlike anything any other band is using. It employs a lot of weird clarinet stuff. Thornhill uses six clarinets at times...and as Borden says, "we try to make each section sound good by itself in every score." A flute and five clarinets voiced above the leader's simple one-finger pianistics is another trick which has proved popular. Using two bass clarinets and four regular clarys also makes for a "different sound." ...He [Borden] is quick to point out that Claude suggests ideas and patterns and oversees his work.[7]

Gil would inherit this collaborative rapport.

Thornhill's repertoire, featuring romantic ballads, medium swing tunes, and his ingenious reworkings of classical or traditional themes ("Hungarian Dance Number 5," Borden's "O Sole Mio") reflects the leader's eclecticism and creative imagination. A completely distinctive feature for the time was that Thornhill had his horns playing without vibrato except for specific instances where he wanted it used. "That distant, haunting no-vibrato sound," as Gil described it—first without, then later with French horns—blended with the brass and reeds in various combinations, creating and altering moods in very specific ways. Thornhill also trained his musicians in the use of dynamics; the band could swell from a whisper to a full ensemble forte in a flash. And Thornhill used soloists much in the way Ellington did, in short passages; the soloists—including Thornhill—emerge from the texture of the arrangements in an organic way.

The jazz press responded favorably. In February 1940, a mere six weeks after the Thornhill band was formed and before it had even played any major engagements, *Metronome* featured it in its Showcase column. "Thornhill's New Troupe Good Hotel Prospect— Unique Clarinet Feature Should attract lovers of Pure, Sweet Dance Music," the headline read. The article singled out the band's uniqueness in having "two men whose job is to play only clarinet. Around these two rests the distinctiveness of the orchestra, for they are employed not only to produce a rich woodwind section (probably the richest and most brilliant in any dance orchestra today) but also to add unique tone coloring to the ensemble and to supplement the brilliance of the relatively small brass section."[8]

Despite the acclaim, the Thornhill band got off to a rocky start business-wise. "Its first engagement, a two-week spot, was scheduled for a swank spot in Virginia Beach," George Simon wrote. "The night before the opening the place burned to the ground." The band subbed sporadically for Glenn Miller's band at the Hotel Pennsylvania and for Sammy Kaye's at the Commodore. The first solid engagement was for five weeks at Capitol Park Casino in Hartford, Connecticut, from April 8 through May 15. Shortly thereafter, the band drove across the country to California to play the summer season at—of all places—the Rendezvous ballroom in Balboa.

Gil, who had maintained contact with Thornhill, helped him secure that job.[9] But it too proved somewhat disappointing. Despite the ballroom's radio wire, playing at the Rendezvous proved to be a strictly local affair, as it had for Gil's band: it had no relevance to the far more active big dance band scene in the Midwest or on the East Coast. Nonetheless, it was a plum engagement for a new band, and Claude could afford to hire three more musicians—another trumpet and trombone player and vocalist Jane Essex. Thornhill's young musicians had a golden time at Balboa, as had Gil's own musicians. "After being around New York and the East Coast it was simply heaven to be at Balboa," George Paulsen wrote. "What more could a young man want—living on the ocean shore—lots of beautiful girls—enjoying playing with a good band—fun, excitement—you name it!"[10]

Gil, meanwhile, continued to work for Ennis. The Hope show never replaced Claude; Gil took up the slack through the 1939–1940 season, and he was now the principal arranger for the Hope show and for Skinnay's dance band. Though Gil functioned behind the scenes, he had become indispensable to Skinnay's working units.

In late May 1940, just as Thornhill and his new band were settling in at Balboa, Gil went on the road with the Hope show. They played theater dates through the Midwest on their way to a Pepso-

dent convention in West Virginia, then headed to a splashy opening at Loew's Times Square Theater in New York. In a letter to the
Carpenters postmarked May 24, 1940, Gil conveyed the idiosyn-
crasies of the professional musician's world while on the road.

> An old pit drummer who got his traps out of storage for the
> date, a military trumpet, one sax player who had an old silver
> tenor and could only play in the low register on clarinet. He
> told me confidentially that he was forty-five and that flute was
> his real instrument which he had played the hell out of with
> John Phillip Sousa. Another "sax player" was a water salesman
> and after the program he gave me his card which read: "Ever-
> pure—have a mountain spring in your home."...by the time
> Dolores [Hope] got through changing her arrangement...we
> didn't have much time for the band number. You probably
> noticed how the sound men and technicians messed up other
> parts of the show. As Hope would say: Oh brother, it was mur-
> der, *believe* me.

While in Chicago Gil went to hear Bob Crosby, Bud Freeman,
and Stuff Smith ("all very good and uninteresting") and spent a lot
of money on food and taxis. He left Chicago for New York City
with Jack Douglas, the "mad gag writer" for the Hope show (Douglas was a frequent guest on the Jack Paar TV show in later
years), with whom he shared a train compartment. Hope and company were finishing their theater engagement in Chicago, but
Douglas was in a hurry to get to New York. This was Gil's first trip
there, and New York's buzzing jazz scene, especially on 52nd
Street, grabbed him right away:

> Douglas and I gave New York a quick once-over last night. The
> Edison where we stay is right downtown, half a block from
> Broadway, so we walked to a lot of the spots. Saw Roy Eldridge
> (who is the greatest I've ever heard) and Billie Holiday (who
> is beautiful and the greatest I've ever heard). Went to the Hotel
> Pennsylvania and saw Jimmy Dorsey.... Lennie Hayton was
> there. He's arranging for Jimmy.... Please write soon. I
> arranged a couple of tunes: "Fools Fall in Love" and "Louisiana

Purchase."... I just read this letter over and it's pretty corny
and drab, but it's true.

ıⁱıₗı

When Gil returned to California, Skinnay and the band were about
to embark on a West Coast tour, but Gil did not accompany them.
Among other things, he was the contractor for four sides recorded
by Six Hits and a Miss for Okeh (he most likely acted as the
arranger as well). For the most part, Gil spent time with Thornhill
and his musicians, unhampered by the usual demands of his work
for Ennis. Gil's association with Thornhill established the groundwork for their own future collaboration, a tie that would prove
intrinsic to Gil's musical development.

Gil's presence around Thornhill's band during the summer of
1940 became the subject of one of those multiversion jazz anecdotes that are the bane of scholarship but the stuffing of so much
jazz history. Version number one is from Paulsen's memoirs.

This is a photo taken 6-24-40 on a small boat en route from
Newport–Balboa to Catalina Island. This [snapshot] is Gil
Evans and Jane Essex (Dover). Jane was very seasick when
this was taken (we all were, except Gil) as we hit some very
rough water.... We were going to hear Benny Goodman's band
on their final night.... He broke up the band for some time
after that. When I said "we" above, I meant Claude's whole
band. Several of the fellows refused to return by boat—they
flew back the next day. Those of us who returned by boat were
pleasantly surprised to find the water as smooth and calm as a
mid-western lake.... At any rate *this will verify that Gil was
with us at Balboa*—at least part of the time. We were there from
May 15 until September when we went up to San Francisco to
work at the Mark Hopkins Hotel.... The S.F. World's Fair was
still going.... At the time Artie Shaw was at the Palace Hotel
and Freddy Martin was at the St. Francis. There were many
bands playing in San Francisco and Oakland and at the Fair—
bands like Basie's. When we were at Balboa, Kenton's band
was at Hermosa Beach and Jimmie Lunceford was in the

Watts area. Kenton's men used to come to hear Claude's band all the time.

Gil told version number two himself. While Claude was at the Rendezvous, Gil recalled, he took the band out to Catalina—and in this version, Thornhill rather than Gil is the only one who doesn't get seasick: "Thornhill took the band out to hear Benny Goodman and Eddie Sauter, who had just joined Goodman. He rented an open fishing boat, and the water was very rough. Everybody was, like, whoof. Except for Claude, who sat there smoking his cigarette and drinking his coffee."[11] While Gil was Ennis's chief arranger and the Ennis band was working constantly, Gil spent the summer hanging out with the more interesting Thornhill band instead.

The Rendezvous gig had other benefits for the Thornhill orchestra besides the glorious setting. It acted as an incubator for the band in its first few months, and it provided the kind of stable environment that helped the band gel as an ensemble.

The Thornhill band made its first recordings for the Okeh label in Hollywood. On July 11, 1940, while the band was in the midst of its Balboa engagement, it recorded "Chicken Reel," "Corinna Corinna," "Old Wien," and "Love Tales." The first two sides were never issued. "Love Tales" was re-recorded in September, along with six other new sides; backed with "Old Wien" ("Old Vienna"), it was released the following spring, and the other sides gradually followed. It is the most interesting of these first releases, a fine example of the band's style on ballads, along with "The Doll Dance," a swing treatment of a tune that was popular at the turn of the century. "Love Tales" opens with Claude's spare handling of the melody, rising over very soft unison clarinets, which then joins a lush, full ensemble to play the second chorus. Thornhill's ballad style, especially when featuring the band's first vocalist Dick Harding, was what made all the critics allude to Miller. This recording is punctuated with enough surprises—Claude's witty tremolos, the luminous unison clarinets, the no-vibrato brass sounding like French horns—to make you wonder exactly what you are hearing. By contrast, "The Doll Dance" reveals that the band—and Claude—could boogie and swing with the best. In this case, clarinets and saxes play straight sectional roles, trading riffs with the piano, leading into a short but gutsy tenor solo, then followed by a solo on muted trumpet as an antidote; Claude's tremolos usher the ensemble back in. This early arrangement points toward the original treatment that Claude and Borden would give to classical or traditional themes a few months later with startling results.

The Rendezvous engagement provided Thornhill with a couple of other West Coast opportunities. In fall 1940 the band performed at the Glendale Civic Auditorium and the Ambassador Hotel and started playing at the Hotel Mark Hopkins in San Francisco in late September, succeeding Ennis's own engagement there. Following a pattern that would be repeated time and again, the band met with critical kudos but mainly blank stares from the dancers. A clipping from Jack Crowley's scrapbook in the *San Francisco Examiner* ("Around Town"), touted the Thornhill band's opening: "The biggest news of the month…is the opening of Claude Thornhill's very excellent band." But for all its quiet elegance, the Thornhill band's music seemed out of place, too unfamiliar and unclassifiable to win Nob Hill's affections. "Claude didn't sound at all like Henry King or Joe Reichman," wrote George Simon, "the flashy society-type tinklers who were local favorites, and soon the Thornhill band was invited not to come back."[12]

Meanwhile, the Ennis orchestra enjoyed a busy and successful summer. In July the band filmed its first short for Warner Brothers, which featured "La Plight," "Three Little Words," "Let's Do It," and "The Birth of the Blues." It toured the Northwest, performing at theaters and amusement parks in Portland; Seattle; Vancouver, BC; Reno; Denver; and Salt Lake City. And it garnered the opposite reaction from the general press and the trade magazines that the Thornhill band had—popular appeal but critical ennui. A clipping from Jack Crowley's scrapbook applauded the band and Ennis's easygoing charm: "It's a sweet band with just enough swing showing through here and there to make things lively. But the sweetest part of it is the effortless technique of the 12 musicians. They do the most amazing things quite unobtrusively and you don't realize how startling they are until about two minutes too late to applaud. Not that they don't draw plenty of applause—they do."

The jazz reviewers were not always as generous toward Ennis. George Simon's review of a broadcast from the Wilshire Bowl in Hollywood in *Metronome* accused the leader, among other things, of pandering to song pluggers:

> He's introing all his numbers now, and he prefixes their hearings with words like "this is a nice number that's going to go places," or "here's a brand new number which looks like a hit." And then what he does is play a slew of tunes you've never heard before. Pioneering in small doses is all right. But Skinnay has too much to offer—too much that's most effective when not presented via unknown mediums. Specifically, the "too much" is his own singing, and the mellow mood that his voice, when properly presented, produces...the band is trying to do more. It's using arrangements that try to make it sound like a big band, which it isn't, and which consequently, they don't. The voicing is thin, and Paramount Publix endings, such as the one in "High on a Windy Hill," border on the musically ridiculous.... Of course it's reminiscent of the Kemp group, and good clean reminiscing it is, too. If it would only play ballads the way Kemp's bunch did in the days when it featured Skinnay, this new band could turn into one of the country's most popular bands.[13]

In fall 1940 Gil worked exclusively for Ennis. Simon was obviously not impressed with Gil's attempt to go for a complex orchestral sound or his nonformulaic arrangements, as can be heard on the 1939 Ennis recording "Strange Enchantment." Ennis's musicians couldn't always pull off Gil's intentions, but this did not deter Ennis's admirers. The band returned to the Mark Hopkins in San Francisco for three weeks, from August 25 to September 16, and in November was back at the Hugo, where it continued to be a big draw, ever enhanced by Ennis's connection with Bob Hope. Hope's career was flourishing more than ever. He was considered America's number one comic on stage, screen, and radio and was a huge attraction wherever he appeared. The Hope show, including the Ennis band and Hope's comic sidekicks Jerry Colonna and Brenda and Cobina, was the featured entertainment for the 25th

Annual Pacific Automobile Show, held in San Francisco from October 26 to November 2, 1940. Hope's appearance was hailed as his last (at least for a while), before starting the filming of *The Road to Zanzibar* with Bing Crosby and Dorothy Lamour, the first of the Hope/Crosby "Road" comedies.

ı' Iı I

After Thornhill's unsuccessful stay at the Mark Hopkins, he decided to see if he would have a better reception back east. In late fall 1940, the Thornhill band was taken on by the Shribman brothers, who booked the New England dance band circuit. The Shribmans had most of the circuit sewn up and booked Glen Gray, the Dorseys, Glenn Miller, Goodman, and other top-ranking bands for that "territory." As Paulsen recalled, "We were always preceding or following some band like Miller or Goodman." At this time, Miller's band was enjoying its peak popularity, spurred on by its national broadcasts from the famed Glen Island Casino in Westchester, New York, through spring 1939. The band's radio presence, in conjunction with "Little Brown Jug," a big hit that spring, initiated a chain of recording, performing, and broadcasting that finally gave Miller, an ambitious and disciplined bandleader, the success he so zealously sought.

In a promising stroke, the Glen Island Casino booked the Thornhill band in March 1941. With that prospect, Thornhill started hiring more musicians. Among them were trumpet players Lyle "Rusty" Dedrick and Conrad Gozzo, who had been working with Red Norvo's band at a hotel in Boston six nights a week. This particular Norvo ensemble had, like Thornhill's, a sophisticated sound and approach that had enormous appeal for musicians and critics but did not really attract a large audience. Norvo's book included arrangements by Eddie Sauter, who by this time was writing for Benny Goodman and others. Sauter, like Thornhill, had a predilection for unusual voicings and textures and didn't fall back on any formulas. Thornhill came to hear Red's band frequently in between the Shribman circuit one-nighters. Dedrick remembered when Claude contacted him:

I was back in New York with Red's band, staying at the Century Hotel, and at 2:30 in the morning the phone rings. It was Claude, and he asked me if I would like to join his band. He gave me the build-up—he had a recording contract and soon they were going to open at Glen Island. I said I was too happy working with Red Norvo, Red was like a father to me. So, for the next 24 hours, I searched for Red. If the money was short you could never find him, and that was the case. I was so angry at Red that when Claude called back at 2:30 the following morning, I accepted. Well, by ten A.M. there was a knock on my door. It was Red. He was steaming! He said, "I wouldn't mind if you were going with Tommy or Benny or somebody like that, but *that band!*" He was really upset because Thornhill's band wasn't even on its feet yet.

But we opened at Glen Island, and one night Gozzo nudges me and says "Look, look!" Red was coming in the door. We were like scared little kids. We finished the set and we were about to hide out in the band room downstairs. But Red came right up, grabbed a hold of us and asked us over for a drink. "I was wrong!" he said. "The band is so beautiful."[14]

Several other outstanding players joined the Thornhill band for the Glen Island engagement. The most prominent was the New Orleans–born clarinetist Irving Fazola (born Prestopnik; "Fazola" was a nickname that stuck, based on the musical syllables fa-so-la). According to George Simon, it was Faz's presence in Glenn Miller's first big band (1937) "that indirectly led to the clarinet-with-saxes sound that set the [Miller] band's style."[15] But the clarinetist's reputation also had a dark side. Fazola, an extremely overweight alcoholic whose behavior could get out of control, resigned from Bob Crosby's Bob Cats, in which he was a star soloist, because of a fistfight with a fellow band member. By the time Fazola reached Thornhill's band, he was still a heavy drinker, but there are no enduring tales of violence.

Other musicians hired during the Thornhill band's second year also had some sterling credits. Among them was Danny Polo, whom Thornhill knew from childhood. Polo had been a featured soloist in the best European dance/jazz orchestras for several years; he returned to New York in 1939 and played with Jack Teagarden for two years. Polo and Fazola were briefly together in Thornhill's band and both used the older Albert system clarinets. In the awed words of a Thornhill alumnus, the pair were "two of the most beautiful sounding clarinetists in the world."[16] Thornhill hired drummer Nick Fatool, who'd played with the biggest names in the business—Benny Goodman and Artie Shaw. Other less well-known musicians were hired who soon acquired great reputations in the musicians' community, such as guitarist Barry Galbraith, who played a large part in Gil's later work. There were numerous woodwind players, and George Paulsen said he played each of the woodwind chairs at one time or another. "I was the only flute player Claude ever had while I was with him. Flutes were not commonly used at that time, as they are today. Faz played oboe, but seldom with the band."

The Glen Island gig finally allowed Thornhill to hire Gil as an additional arranger. It was what Gil had wanted from the moment Thornhill left Ennis—"I haunted Claude until he hired me as an arranger in 1941," Gil once remarked.[17] Bill Borden had suggested that Thornhill hire Gil, who he knew "wasn't happy with Skinnay Ennis." In a way, the timing was perfect for Gil. The elements of Thornhill's sound and style—the lack of vibrato, the use of mixed woodwinds, the orchestral ambiance, the integration of soloist and ensemble, the mood—had become natural to Thornhill's musicians. These elements became integral to the music Gil developed a few years later and paved the way for cool jazz.

Gil brought a companion when he moved to the East Coast for his new job—Cyclops, his Great Dane. Having a pet seemed completely impractical for someone who moved and traveled as often as Gil did. But the dog may have fulfilled the time-honored role of a good nondemanding friend. "My first experience with Gil is that he blew into New Rochelle in a convertible with a big Great Dane sitting next to him," recalled Dedrick. "He had driven all the way across the country."

The Glen Island Casino was one of the finest ballrooms in the country at that time, and the club's numerous radio wires made it a big hit with radio audiences nationwide.

Glen Island itself is not a "maker of bands." But Glen Island's many advantages added to the fact that the bands which have played the spot "have what it takes" have spelled success for Larry Clinton, Glen Gray, Tommy Dorsey, Jimmy Dorsey and Ozzie Nelson.... Added to the Casino's advantages is its ideal setting. Constructed several hundred feet above the rippling tides of Long Island Sound, it overlooks glittering waters scattered with anchored cruisers and yachts. Winding paths and overhanging trees surround the Casino proper—with a college charm and beauty.[18]

Thornhill and his band received this much-needed break, and the band stayed at Glen Island for a luxurious two months. George Simon's review of the Thornhill band's debut in *Metronome*, May 1941, was a rave.

Chalk up Claude Thornhill's as the band of 1941 with the highest P.P. rating. "P.P." stands for "Potential Popularity." Which means that of all the new dance bands this year, and so far as this writer is concerned, for all years since the advent of Glenn Miller, Claude Thornhill's stands the greatest chance of turning out to be the nation's No. 1 dance orchestra.

The style, the first really new one to emerge in recent years, and one that often borders on modern, classical music, is a Thornhill creation.... That ensemble is a joy to hear. Claude's arrangements and those of Bill Borden are responsible in part. But so is the expert musicianship of the entire group, with its power-house brass section, its well-blended reeds, and the tasty potent rhythm section.[19]

The review singled out lead trumpet player Gozzo for his brilliant tone and fine control, which in turn helped shape the band's highly controlled dynamics.

When the band returned to Glen Island a few months later, in August 1941, Thornhill added two French horns, then unheard of in a dance band. Gil recalled, "He [Claude] had written an obbligato for them to a Fazola solo to surprise Faz. Fazola got up to play; Claude signaled the French horns at the other end of the room to come up to the bandstand; and that was the first time Fazola knew they were to be added to the band."[20]

From today's vantage point, Thornhill's French horns and clarinets would not, in all likelihood, be anyone's idea of music representative of the Big Band Era. If anything can be gleaned from readers' polls conducted by *Down Beat* and *Metronome* in 1941, when the Thornhill band was indeed making a name for itself, it was hardly representative of the era even then. The top five bands in the sweet category (let alone swing) for the 1941 *Down Beat* readers' poll were the orchestras of Glenn Miller, Tommy Dorsey, Jimmy Dorsey, Duke Ellington, and Benny Goodman. Though Thornhill had a few records that made it onto the charts in 1941—"Snowfall," "Sleepy Serenade," and "Autumn Nocturne"—the band didn't garner enough votes in any band category of either magazine even to be listed. Thornhill didn't have the forceful ambition of Goodman or Miller or the manic bossiness of a Tommy Dorsey or an Artie Shaw. Perhaps forceful personalities really were requisite to make it in the big band business; the stakes were big, the competition brutal, and the media relentless—just like rock music of today.

Thornhill was a taskmaster in getting exactly the right sound he wanted, but in other areas he was more relaxed. In many ways, this was the kind of leader Gil himself would become. George Paulsen wrote:

> There is no doubt that Claude was a truly great musician. He was definitely ahead of his time and too musically advanced for the general public. He was more of a musician than a businessman. He was a fine person and got results with his musicians by treating them properly. I don't recall him being harsh in rehearsals. He was an easygoing kindhearted person. I think of the impish boyish smile or grin or the twinkle in his eyes when I think of him. He had some very serious moments, too. He was a perfectionist and demanded that things be just right...this meant some long hard rehearsals...often we had to record something shortly after we had obtained the new arrangement...then a few weeks later after playing it on the job it would sound 100% better.... But here it was on record sound-

ing worse...much of the best music Claude played never was
recorded.[21]

These disparities and ironies—about commercial success versus
musical success or achievement, and the vagaries of the recording
industry—would trail Gil's career in the same way.

᠌ᴵ ᴵᵢ ᴵ

Even though Gil was finally working for Thornhill, he continued to
do some work for Ennis on and off through 1941. For one thing,
Ennis had a hard time replacing Gil, and for another, Gil probably
needed the extra money; however, this was Gil's last season with
the Hope show. When the Thornhill band went on the road for the
summer, Gil went to Chicago with the Ennis orchestra for an eight-
week stay at the prestigious Palmer House. Typical of the time for
restaurants or nightclubs, the band was part of an elaborate floorshow, which in this case included "fiery South American dancers"
and comedians. The band provided accompanying music for some
of the other acts and also played for dancing. In a news item about
the job, *Tempo* listed Ennis's lineup as a "crack crew," four of whom
were originally members of Gil's band. "The Ennis band (Evans is
still main cog in the combo, being arranger and musical director)
has been one of the outstanding musical aggregations ever produced in this territory and is the out-and-out favorite of every
West Coast cat. But they all figure Evans made a wise choice in
submerging his own personality to go under the Ennis banner.
Rarely do Western leaders make the grade under their own
names."

Just four days after the Ennis Orchestra opened at the Palmer
House, the band suffered a terrible bus accident. Considering how
many big bands were on the road during the Big Band Era, it is
remarkable that band bus accidents weren't more frequent. An
Indiana newspaper reported on July 1, 1941, "Skinnay Ennis'
famed 13-piece band came to grief today at 1:25 A.M. when the entire
ensemble, excepting the leader himself and his vocalist-wife, Carmine, were injured in a crash of their chartered bus after playing
an engagement in the Gary armory." The bus crashed into a trolley

pole, and the entire front end of the bus was crushed. All thirteen of the men were hospitalized after the crash, and seven were kept for serious injuries. "With so many injuries it was considered a miracle that no fatalities resulted," *Down Beat* reported.

Fortunately, Gil, Carmine, and Ennis were not on the bus. According to Carmine, "At the time of the accident, Gil was with us, in Evanston. Gil and Skinnay and I had driven to Gary—we went in Gil's car because we were late, and didn't make the bus. That's why we weren't in the accident. Lucky that no one was killed." The most severe injuries were suffered by George White, bassist, whose leg was broken in three places, and Louis Mitchell, Kenneth Olsen, Ralph Liscom and Jack Crowley, who had to remain in the hospital for a couple of days. The Lew Diamond Orchestra, the regular off-night band at the Palmer House, took over for a few days until most of Ennis's musicians recovered.

In a letter Gil wrote to the Carpenters from the Palmer House in the late summer of 1941, he noted that the Ennis band was almost back to normal, with the exception of George, who, like everyone else involved in the bus accident, was being treated fairly by the insurance company:

> I surely hope for your sake that, besides being dull, this isn't all second-hand news to you, and speaking of rehearsals, we hold them in the same room where the hotel carpenters remodel and repaint the bedroom furniture. Their sawing and hammering, the brass yapping and my yelling at everyone in general about nothing in particular makes a very amusing scene, I've been told, although I haven't as yet appreciated it.
>
> Benny just came on the air, bringing to mind our little chum, Jim [Maxwell]. He's playing lead on a jazzer and I hope he gets through because we had a big Italian dinner tonight with much red wine.... He feels fine and looks fine except that he has a rather deep scar on his cheek from the operation he had on his jaw as a result of that tooth infection. His playing has really improved and he plays lead on most of the tunes now. His mental attitude has also improved and he's fast becoming distressingly normal. In fact, he and Gertrude are to be married in September (in case he hasn't already told you this—it's *very*

confidential and although he'd probably strangle me if he knew I'd told anybody, us girls must have our little secrets!)

Skinnay's band will be at the Palmer House another three weeks—where incidentally he has been a terrific success, breaking Eddie Duchin's record and then on to the Chicago theater for two weeks.... There have been many rumors about the first program [of the Hope Show] being here in Chicago and the next two in New York, etc.... most of them come from Carmine, who is still her same sweet altruistic self. About the only thing Max [one of the writers for the Hope show] (with whom I live) and I have in common is our opinion of that——— * [deleted for political reasons only].

Music and Rhythm ran a lengthy feature article about Ennis in its October 1941 issue, with the pointed title "My Band Doesn't Play Hal Kemp Music." The article was based on an interview with Ennis during the band's Palmer House engagement. "Why should we copy anyone when we've got an original arranger like Gil Evans?" said Ennis, who describes Gil as "a former terrific jazz arranger. It's taken me several years to tone him down to my speed. He does everything for the band now and has for some time done all the stuff on the Hope Show." Ennis mentions that Leonard Joy from Victor Records wanted to re-record some of the band's older material, but that Ennis himself was interested in recording some medleys. "For instance, we've got a *Porgy and Bess* medley arrangement that's really fine. Matter of fact, they're playing it right now." [22]

George Gershwin's *Porgy and Bess* had been completed in August 1935. *Porgy* ran for a money-losing 124 performances in New York that fall, shortly after its Boston premiere. Recordings of several songs featuring Metropolitan opera stars Helen Jepson and Lawrence Tibbett (instead of the original cast members) were made during the show's New York run.[23] The songs, however, did not achieve the hit status of other Gershwin songs until years later. The fact that Evans arranged a medley from this work in 1941, three years after Gershwin's death, when the show was virtually forgotten, is indeed fascinating. The recordings, or possibly the sheet music from *Porgy*, caught Evans's attention.

With this in mind, it is startling to read about the twenty-seven-year-old "former terrific jazz arranger" when Evans's most far-reaching work in jazz lay ahead, including his 1958 arrangement of *Porgy and Bess* for Miles Davis. As Skitch Henderson pointed out, most of Gil's work for the Ennis band wasn't even played. Gil had to rein in his writing for the tasks at hand—vocal accompaniments for the Hope show and dance numbers for the hotel/night-club crowd. Gil did not write for the swing/jazz audience—the Goodman audience that Fletcher Henderson or Eddie Sauter was writing for. Neither was he writing for the jazz sophisticate or dancer that thronged to hear Duke Ellington. Gil undoubtedly found the Thornhill band a more appropriate vehicle than the Ennis band and Thornhill more receptive to unusual ideas.

Meanwhile, Gil's letter to the Carpenters divulges his real passion: Great Danes. He writes enthusiastically about Cyclops, the dog that rode across the country earlier that year, one to which he was particularly attached. After mentioning Carmine, Gil wrote:

> Speaking of bitches (of a much superior type however) reminds me to tell you that I'm going out to a kennel tomorrow to buy a female Dane. I already have a male 13 months old.... He should throw marvelous puppies provided I can find him a female of the same excellent conformation and genetically suited for breeding (please note my newly acquired breeder's talk).... The dog's name is Cyclops, but don't worry he has two eyes.
>
> Before you kiddies stifle any more polite yawns I'd better cut out (Harlem talk). Don't be a heel like me—write me another long letter right away.

Over the next few months, Gil's connection to the Ennis band became even more tenuous. Gil kept on talking of leaving, and one day he made it stick. "Gil and Skinnay had some arguments sometimes," said Carmine. "We were on the road once and I was in the hotel, and Gil came up to the room, and said 'I'm leaving the band.' We all got on a train the next night and he just left. No two weeks notice or anything—we were in St. Louis or someplace. I don't think we saw him again until the Army."[24]

Ennis returned to Los Angeles without Gil at the end of the summer. Gil returned to the East Coast to rejoin Thornhill, who was about to resume playing at Glen Island that fall. According to *Down Beat*, Thornhill had an unusual twelve-month contract with the Casino; he could leave and return any time he chose. Gil left Ennis for what he certainly thought was the last time.

ı¹ lı ı

Charles Garrod, in his Claude Thornhill discography, credits Gil Evans with a dozen arrangements recorded by the Thornhill Orchestra between 1941 and 1942.[25] Among the best known are "Buster's Last Stand," "There's a Small Hotel," and "I Don't Know Why." One of the most striking is Evans's swing treatment of "Arab Dance" (written in 1942 but not recorded until 1946), from Tchaikovsky's *Nutcracker*. This arrangement exemplifies how Gil, even at this stage of his career, was able to masterfully deconstruct and in effect "recompose" the music of others. After a soft intro-duction stated by trombones and French horns, with quiet toms and bass accompaniment, the woodwinds play a rhythmically dis-placed, almost boppish statement of the first theme, expanding into an ensemble burst. Following the clarinet solo, the orchestra enters in a staggered fashion, revealing a brilliantly architected motific development that culminates in a full ensemble statement. The band subsides as Claude enters on piano, then the brass and saxes rally in a blues-oriented shout chorus, with fluid descending lines from the saxes that sound startlingly Ellingtonian.

"Buster's Last Stand" is a much more straight-ahead arrange-ment, a joyous romp worthy of Goodman's or Lunceford's bands. With the Thornhill orchestra, Evans achieved what he had always aspired to with his own band: precise playing, great intonation, and the truly unified propulsive drive that swept up audiences during the Swing Era. The band achieves this swinging unity with Evans's "Arab Dance," and the band's recordings of both of these arrangements defy a common complaint that the Thornhill band could not swing. More significant, the quality of Evans's arrange-ments at this time—the meticulous way all the instruments were handled, the deliberation in phrasing and building toward musical climaxes—shows Evans reaching a new level of mastery of his trade. As Borden said, the Thornhill band was like a lab for Gil, and he used it well.

The Thornhill band recorded frequently for Columbia from October 1941 through the spring of 1942. The band also made four "soundies" in January 1942: "Somebody Nobody Loves," "America, I Love You," "Count Me In," and "Where Has My Little Dog Gone." According to newly documented research by Mark Cantor, the music film historian, the first three were Evans arrangements (though "Count Me In" may have been a collaboration with Claude), and these films are typical of the period. Attention was mainly given to Claude and the vocalists, and while the entire ensemble acquit themselves well and Evans's arrangements are effective, "neither the material selected nor the 'on-screen' coverage does full justice to the band," said Cantor. In June and July 1942, the band recorded another ten sides for Columbia, which included Gil's most popular arrangements from this period: "Be Careful, It's My Heart," "Buster's Last Stand," "There's a Small Hotel," "I Don't Know Why (I Just Do)" and "Moonlight Bay." These were made before the controversial union recording ban brought commercial recording to a complete halt on August 1, 1942.[26]

But the hectic and insular world of the big bands had already begun to unravel for far more ominous reasons. The increasing turmoil of the war in Europe and unfolding events in the Pacific began to affect many aspects of American life, and a limited draft was already in place. The United States managed to stay out of the European conflict for two years, but on December 7, 1941, the Japanese bombed Pearl Harbor, and within a day the United States finally entered the war.

Rusty Dedrick recalled that the Thornhill band was playing a Sunday matinee at Glen Island that pivotal day. His story echoed that of many others, especially musicians:

> I was about to be drafted, they were trying to draft me even before Pearl Harbor. We had a matinee that Sunday afternoon. The waiters came up and said, "The Japs bombed Pearl Harbor!" We all said, "Where's Pearl Harbor?" Nobody knew from

nothing! I just knew immediately—I had been fighting the draft and now I knew it was hopeless. The band left for some date on January 1, 1942, in a bus and Fazola and I saw them off. A little later I was standing at the Forrest Bar with Red Norvo and I was still hanging out, knowing that I had to go.[27]

The Thornhill band was in a state of upheaval that winter, as were many big bands. Gil described the havoc wreaked on the band in a letter to the Carpenters postmarked January 1942; the letter does not fail to mention Cyclops the Great Dane:

We've had quite a little turnover in the band—10 changes. Claude let Nick and Fazola go, chronic moping and griping being the trouble. They're both nice kids in their own funny way though, and I wouldn't be surprised to see them back sometime. Faz got "stoned" a couple of weeks ago and joined the Navy, although I haven't heard yet whether he was accepted. He's a little on the heavy side—close to 300 pounds. His daily gin ration is always well over a quart and a half, but he rarely shows it physically and almost never in his playing which, after working with him, I realize is matchless. We've cut out one reed chair entirely and the rest of the changes were either an improvement or "inductees", mostly the latter....

We gave up the house on Clay Drive since Claude will be on the road playing theaters and one-nighters till May when they return to Glen Island for the summer. Cyclops and I have a nice big room in a private home here in Pelham. The lady is very nice—although insane—and loves dogs, so Cy has the run of the house and the grounds—both of which are enormous.

I spent the last couple of days in Newark, N.J., where the band is playing a theater engagement. Remind me to devote all of my next letter to Claude as master of ceremonies on a stage show. Brother!!!

Love to all, Gil

Despite all the upheaval, between spring 1941 and fall 1942 the Thornhill sound and style crystalized. Several factors were at work. Among the foremost, as Gunther Schuller pointed out, was

"Thornhill's recognition that what the world needed in 1940 was not another riff-tune swing band in the image of Goodman or Miller." Second, between 1939 and 1941, all ASCAP compositions were effectively banned from radio broadcasts. This forced band-leaders to write new material and register their work with the newly formed licensing organization, BMI. Bandleaders and arrangers also hunted up material in the public domain, reviving the "swinging the classics" trend that arose in the mid-1930s as a novelty ("Loch Lomand," the 1937 hit record with Thornhill's arrangement, helped promote this trend).[28]

"Thornhill went about this with a vengeance and—it must be said—with more taste and skill than most," wrote Schuller. At the same time, Thornhill's originals were "extraordinarily effective and beautiful in their own unique way. Indeed some of the opaque orchestra textures and blends, rich harmonizations and dense voicings, were completely novel, never been having heard before in either jazz *or* classical music." [29] The band played the entire summer of 1942 at Glen Island and continued to win accolades from the critics. "Claude's Clever Crew Rates Rave," was the headline of Barry Ulanov's review of the Thornhill band at Glen Island during that time. "There aren't many bandleaders who will even think about experimentation. Claude Thornhill's whole band is built around new ideas. And so Claude deserves acclaim for his rare quality as an experimenter, if nothing else. But there is a lot else. Mr. T. has done a topnotch job in whipping his organization into shape as an all-around performing body that can knock off ballads and jazz and novelties and strange fruits of the strange brain of Thornhill with equal facility."[30]

While Thornhill's fortunes were seemingly on the up, the effects of the war on civilian life in the States were increasingly manifest. Though music was deemed very important for general morale, through the course of 1942 the draft, rationing, and manufacturing curtailments affected the music industry and the world of big bands and musicians in a variety of ways. Musical instrument manufacturing was cut back due to restrictions on the use of pre-cious metals, and there was a ban on jukebox manufacturing. In May 1942, record production was slashed by one-third because of shellac shortages. By August, gas rationing was reduced to two gallons per week and bands had to travel by train or car—no buses. By this time the big bands were scuffling to keep their chairs filled.

Gil expressed frustration with his job, but it was of a personal nature. In a letter to the Carpenters in August 1942, written over the course of several weeks, Gil sounded clearly depressed:

> It's like I was telling you in the car that night on the way to the Casa Mañana—I can't live a happy natural life in the arranging business. I haven't got what it takes to routine myself, and consequently, whenever I go visiting or have a date, that little devil conscience spoils everything by telling me I ought to be home staring at the "88." So five weeks ago I gave Claude my four weeks notice and was supposed to have been through last Wednesday. But the picture date was set ahead almost a month and Claude said it was impossible for him to find anyone since they had to leave immediately to go on one-nighters and will only arrive there in time to start the picture. So I'm stuck for another eight weeks, but at two hundred per—when the picture starts. Nice as it sounds, I would still rather have quit.... the one consolation will be seeing Mother and you kids.
>
> I went up to hear Benny on a one-nighter. Stayed all evening and came back to NYC with Benny and his wife and Jimmy [Maxwell] and Goit [Gertrude, his wife]. By a curious coincidence they start their picture at Universal on the same day as Claude's band. Benny offered me the job doing the picture [*The Powers Girl*[31]]—married life must be making him light-headed. Of one thing I'm sure: it's making him light-hearted. You never saw such a change in a fellow. He acts like an enthusiastic young kid about his band instead of the old warhorse bastard he used to be; laughs when the band messes something up instead of the old "ray;" even smiles at the people and acknowledged their applause.

"One Friday later," Gil expresses the most profound grief—in fact, it was the most profound emotional expression to be found in his letters—to the Carpenters. The cause is not what one would expect:

Tonight I have been crying my eyes and heart—the first time since Claude and Skinnay started the great purge by firing Ned [Briggs, the bassist from Stockton, who went on with Gil to work with Ennis]—and feeling the desperate need of company for my misery, I must write and tell you that he's dead. Sad eyes, glorious head—tiger-like body—colt-like antics—great heart—child-like faith—affectionate and fearless disposition—irreplaceable companion. All are gone. Cy is dead. Ironically his great size was the great tragedy of his life. It was that which killed him. He rarely found another dog that would play with him—the delight of his life. They invariably became terrified and would attack him in what they thought was self-defense. The accident was freakish. He raced up the street from our house with another dog, which, as usual, misinterpreted his intentions and bit at him. His attention momentarily distracted, he did not see a fire hydrant into which he crashed at top speed. His only apparent wound was fearful enough looking, but it certainly didn't look fatal. His front leg was ripped wide open...after an hour of stitching at the hospital it looked pretty good again and the doctor said he'd be well in three weeks. So I left him to sleep off the Nembutol. But an hour later the hospital called me and said that the impact had apparently caused serious internal injuries and he was having hemorrhages. He died before I could get back.

Please forgive the long-winded account but I feel better just telling someone about it. Tell mother that I won't write again. I'll leave N.Y.C. Wednesday and will be home either Sunday or Monday, depending on whether I spend a day in Chicago.

Love, Gil

Gil went to California in late summer of 1942 while the Thornhill band finished the summer season at Glen Island. The aforementioned film project never took place, and Gil joined the band on the road for a new series of theater and ballroom dates in Ohio, Indiana, and Illinois. The band's expense records for three weeks (from the week ending October 1 through the week ending October 15) reveal that the band, which numbered twenty musicians at this time, was getting a decent wage on the road. The total income was $5,057.04: the fee for the three one-nighters ranged from $350 for a dance in South Bend, Indiana, to $1,000 for a theater date in Lafayette, and the Palace Theater job netted $3,149.30 for three days. But considering that the band played three or four shows a day for theater dates, and the musicians logged many hours traveling, the average weekly salary of eighty-five dollars was not too good—and a fraction of what Goodman or Dorsey paid their top musicians. Thornhill himself was hardly getting rich—he received a hundred and fifty dollars per week, and Gil received seventy-five dollars. The band's numerous expenses included car rentals, railroad tickets, traveling (union) taxes for Gil and Claude, radio wires, etc. After the payroll and expenses, the band profited a big $1,213.93, which essentially gave them traveling money for the following week.

On October 26, 1942, the Thornhill band's touring came to an abrupt halt. Claude enlisted in the Navy at the lowest possible rank, apprentice seaman. According to *Metronome*, "The quietist entrance yet into the armed forces is that of Claude Thornhill. No fanfare about the band breaking up, no advance publicity of the great band to come in the Navy. For Claude Thornhill has entered the Navy as an ordinary citizen, with no strings attached, whatsoever—so far as he is concerned, he's not going to have a band, no great stars are coming to join him."[32]

Gil returned to the West Coast after Thornhill enlisted, doing odd musical jobs while waiting for his number to come up. He was drafted February 25, 1943, and his entrance into the service was even quieter than Thornhill's. No news items appeared in the music trades.

5 wartime

The United States government considered music absolutely vital for morale during World War II. Various military and government offices even discussed whether or not musicians were "essential" employees. But in early 1943, a year after the ranks of many bands had already been dispersed by the draft, musicians were officially deemed "nonessential" employees; as such they had to find "essential" occupations or face induction. String pulling for and among various prominent musicians was common and saved many of them from far more onerous active service. That was even the case for those who were not so prominent.

The guitarist Roc Hillman, a longtime member of the Jimmy Dorsey Orchestra, was drafted in late 1942. He was able to get into a Special Services unit at the headquarters of the Western Defense Command, located at the Huntington Hotel in Pasadena, California, with additional quarters for the servicemen at a nearby elegant estate. His "job" was to put together a small dance band. Hillman spent quite a bit of time in Hollywood finding out who was about to be drafted and in touch with the induction center. He found out from a friend that Gil was about to be called. "I called him up and said, 'We need you,'" said Hillman. "Gil thought it was a good idea and in a matter of a few days he was out there." Gil became the pianist for the Southern California Sector Headquarters "HQ" Band, a ten-piece outfit (three trumpets, four saxes, and three rhythm) that played three radio shows per week, played at daily and evening functions for every branch of the service, and performed regularly at the Hollywood Canteen.

"We started out with a good nucleus of a band," said Hillman, "and with Gil's help it became a much better band than it would have been otherwise. He was a fine arranger and a very good piano player and he knew what was going on in the current music world. Gil didn't consider himself a very competent piano player. He played good arranger's piano, good jazz solos, but he downplayed his reputation as a pianist. But he was sure a hell of an arranger. We'd play some Basie or Ellington tune and he'd know just what to do to make it sound legitimate."[1]

Hillman remembered the HQ band filling a lot of needs around the area. "We were busy 12 hours a day, seven days a week." In the spring of 1943, Skinnay Ennis, who was drafted in March, was asked to organize an army band at Camp Santa Anita, a new camp on the site of the racetrack in Arcadia, California, east of Pasadena. Ennis requested that Gil be transferred there, and he became second in command late that spring. A few months later, the headquarters of the Western Defense Command was relocated, and Gil returned Hillman's kindness, getting him transferred to the Santa Anita band.

The Skinnay Ennis band, officially called the 360th Ordnance Band, quickly earned a reputation as one of the best in the armed forces. It included a couple of Ennis's own sidemen and prominent musicians from other bands and the Hollywood studios. For the most part, Ennis and his musicians led a privileged existence compared to the rest of the armed forces. For instance, some of the noncommissioned officers—and Gil was now promoted to staff sergeant—did not have to sleep at the base. Ennis, Gil, and some of the other men took advantage of that, getting a respite from the inevitable restrictions of army life. Gil often slept at the home of another Ennis recruit, trumpet player Louis Mitchell, a cozy arrangement that allowed him to keep Zenith, his latest Great Dane, nearby.

The atypical military environment at Santa Anita came about due to the commanding general's initial directive: to start a first-class army band. The organizing was delegated to Bunny Edwards, the general's young aide, who was in charge of Special Services. Edwards, a non-musician, figured out quickly that the first logical step was to find a good bandleader, and he sought out Jules Stein, then music director at MCA, for advice. Stein knew Ennis as a professional and also knew he was about to be drafted. Edwards recalled, "it was arranged that Skinnay would be commissioned and head the band at Santa Anita, and that he would be informed when other great musicians were about to be drafted. Skinnay worked to get the guys he wanted, and he very much wanted Gil."[2]

The Santa Anita band grew into a star-studded twenty-one-piece jazz-oriented ensemble. Its members included Herb Stowe (initially one of Evans's boys from Stockton), Lou Mitchell, and Johnny Fresco, who had been Ennis's sidemen. Most of the others had been literally drafted from other name big bands. Trumpet player Chuck Peterson had been the high note artist with Tommy Dorsey and Artie Shaw. Joe Triscari, who had worked with Krupa, played most of the lead trumpet parts. Johnny Hamilton, who had been with Ozzie Nelson's band, played most of the tenor solos. A young pianist from Seattle named Jimmy Rowles, who had played with Woody Herman and Benny Goodman, "constantly knocked us out with his inventive piano solos," said Evan Vail, one of two French horn players with the band. Gil, in fact, was one of several seasoned arrangers: Skippy Martin (who'd written for Les Brown, Goodman, and others); Hal Mooney, who was Jimmy Dorsey's chief arranger; and Monty Kelly (Griff Williams, Skinnay, and others). According to Vail, Skippy and Monty wrote most of the flag-wavers while Gil tended more toward the ballads.

Other band members said that Gil did not actually do that much arranging for the Santa Anita band. Clarinetist Al Taylor, a Hollywood studio musician, recalled, "Gil was responsible—he was the responsible head of the band. We had a bunch of crazy people, and he was the one who made sure that the buses arrived and the guys got there and all that. And he was with Skinnay all the time. He didn't have time to write a lot of arrangements. Also, Gil was sober—he wasn't social, he was patient as hell, and he was in a situation where everybody was always flying off the handle. Gil was a problem solver."[3] Jimmy Rowles said that Gil hardly wrote anything new for the band; he might have reconfigured some of the things that he did for Claude. "All he did was copy his scores, or he got them from his head. It didn't make any difference what was going on—he could always write them, all the parts, without a score."

One of the last entrants into the Santa Anita band was clarinetist George Paulsen, who had been with Thornhill's orchestra until Thornhill joined the Navy. A chance meeting with Gil on a street corner in Burbank, California, "changed the course of my life," wrote Paulsen.

> I had been working with the Alvino Rey band at the Lockheed-Vega plant in Burbank... on the graveyard shift... that meant trying to sleep in the daytime. I hated that way of life.... Gil said he had two more spots to fill for the quota for the Army band. I enlisted immediately.... Billy May [another prominent arranger] was going to take the other opening but he got a 4-F rating and did not go into the Army. I could probably have avoided the Army too as I was on a limited service rating due to a hand injury. At the time the outlook for the US was very bleak.... the Japanese were beating us and Europe looked hopeless. I did not feel right about *not* being in the Army or some other service.... Gil was one of the most relaxed individuals I've ever met... always a big smile or grin, very friendly... just like his big great Dane dog.[4]

The Santa Anita band made its debut in June 1943 and, from early on, received raves for its performances at the Hollywood Canteen, the Hollywood USO, and anywhere else it appeared. The majority of the music they played was swing and jazz-oriented music rather than traditional military music. This was largely due to the remarkable musical influence that both Glenn Miller and Artie Shaw had achieved in a very short period with their respective service bands. Miller, after much persistence and wrangling, was made an army captain and authorized to form an Army/Air Corps band in the spring of 1943. At his insistence, his was the first army band in which the repertoire was largely based on popular music, which Miller firmly—and correctly—believed would be a tremendous morale booster. Ed Polic, author of a detailed account of the Glenn Miller Army/Air Corps Band, commented, "Almost everybody enjoyed the change, but there was some commotion.

Some military people opposed the change of musical styles, but all of that was pooh-poohed very quickly, and everybody agreed to it and everybody started doing the same sort of thing."[5]

Artie Shaw, who'd entered the Navy in April 1942 as an apprentice seaman and was then put in charge of a "pretty terrible" band, also prevailed with the military authorities. Shaw was granted permission to form a good navy band and to take it into battle zones. Shaw's celebrated Naval Reserve Band 501, known as The Rangers, landed at Pearl Harbor in late December 1942. The band, which briefly included Claude Thornhill on piano, toured Pacific bases and battlefronts under extreme conditions for almost a year, playing cherished hits from Shaw's book, such as "Begin the Beguine." Thornhill, perhaps chafing under the leadership of his old friend Shaw, asked for and was granted permission to form his own U.S. Navy Orchestra in February 1943, which, like Shaw's, toured the Pacific battle zones.[6]

By contrast Ennis and most members of the 360th Ordnance Band had it easy and never even made it overseas. These musicians did not make the transition to army life—not even the cushy Santa Anita army life—with particular ease, nor was there much incentive. The entire band were members of the "Special Services," rarely played military functions, and were barely taught military conduct, let alone basic training. Bunny Edwards recalled:

> A lot of the guys were pretty wild. At first everyone was so delighted with having all of them there, such great musicians and such a great band, that there was no problem. But finally someone said, "No! They have to have more basic training and go out to the rifle range!" Well, they went out to the rifle range, but most of them had gin in their canteens. I got a call from the rifle range, saying, "You've got to get over here! These guys are going to kill somebody!" There was never a dull moment— they were young and very wild, but wonderful guys.... The band played all over, they were in demand for war bond shows, and army camps for entertainment.[7]

Evan Vail, who played French horn with the Glendale symphony, remembered how much the band members hated to march. "They

were opposed to any kind of exercise. After marching down Broadway in Los Angeles for a War Bond parade, the guys complained so
much about how hard it was on the bod and chops that the next time
there was a Broadway parade we rode and played in 'ducks'—
amphibious jeeps."[8]

The Santa Anita Band toured up and down the coast—from
San Diego to Fort Ord, and out to the desert. Carmine Ennis and,
at times, Martha Tilton were the featured vocalists when the band
was on tour. The band also did some shows with songwriter/band-
leader Meredith Willson (composer of *The Music Man*) and made
several V-discs. On January 29 and 30, 1944, the band appeared
at a gala benefit concert at the Shrine Auditorium with the Los
Angeles Philharmonic and an array of stars that included Kay Kyser,
Lena Horne, Bing Crosby, and Dinah Shore. The proceeds were to
go to Armed Forces Master Records, Inc., which helped produce
the V-discs that were shipped to army bases around the world. Vail
thought that the band was, in fact, very special. "It was a far different band than any he [Skinnay] had led up until then. His was a
powerhouse jazz group that was a sort of culmination of big band
jazz prior to any be-bop influence. One reason it was so good was
its eclectic stable of arrangers, one of whom was Gil Evans."[9]

By summer 1944, Skinnay, then thirty-five and eligible to leave,
decided to get out of the army. Several others who were eligible also
left, and the remaining men were shipped to a distribution center,
Fort Lewis, Washington, for further orders. From there, sixteen of
them, including Gil, were sent to Camp Lee, Virginia. Gil became the
leader and sole arranger in that camp's Band Training Unit, or BTU.
After about three months in Virginia some of the Santa Anita men,
including Vail, were sent to Hawaii. Gil insisted they take the Santa
Anita book with them, which had over a hundred arrangements
when the band dispersed. Gil remained assigned to Camp Lee.

Camp Lee was an immense camp; between 1944 and 1945 there
were about 35,000 men undergoing training there. It had a far
more traditional and entrenched military environment than Santa
Anita. At first the Santa Anita men's privileges—and sense of enti-
tlement—held up. Page Cavanaugh, another Hollywood musician,
was sent to Camp Lee from the Signal Corps, and arrived a few
weeks after the Santa Anita servicemen did. "The Skinnay Ennis

band ruined it for every other musician that came in afterward, the whole damn band, because they were pretty much given carte blanche in the BTU. They were heavy players, important people, and some people were really abusing their privileges—sneaking in after curfew, or refusing curfew. So when we got there, things really hit the fan." Thenceforth, the band members were forced to taste conventional army life. "We were woken up at 5:30 in the morning and doing it all—people were saying, 'Hey, this is worse than training!'"

Gil received one of his regular letters from the Carpenters in July 1944, followed by a wire of money. Still, it took him some three months to get around to replying. The content and tone of Gil's response made it clear that army life was no picnic for Gil, nor was the foreign culture of the American South.

> Tuesday [in October 1944]—
> Three months after receiving
> your letter.

Dear Pete and Maybeth—

The promised "details to follow" are shamefully late, aren't they? I don't know what's the matter with me. I think of you kids all the time. I think of what I'm going to write & tell you about, but somehow it's like the arrangements. I never seem to be able to sit down and write them. Other fellows can sit on their bunks and dash off a few lines after lunch before we fall out or after supper before we go to a dance job or a rehearsal, but not me. I just sit and stare at the ivories or whatever the army equivalent may be at the time. It's really a nowhere groove to be in and it must make you feel like I'm a heck of a friend and an especially ungrateful one when I didn't even write and thank you for the wire for which I was really so very grateful. In short, I feel like a big heel and am very news hungry, so please write and I'll make l'effort supreme to answer sometime within the next thirty years.

By now you have probably seen Herb [Stowe], and any details that I could give on our sojourn in the rebel country would be strictly second-hand. So ah reckon ah'll wait till ah heah whetheh Herb came to L.A. on his fuhlough befoh ah paints you-all a little pictuah of mah life in the land of milk and honey chiles, heah?

I was supposed to leave last Thursday for Fort Douglas, near Salt Lake City, but nothing happened. The officer in charge of assignments from this place gets a little overenthusiastic in his promises to the men. He assures you upon your arrival here (if he is sufficiently impressed by your civilian musical background and he's about as difficult to impress as you would imagine an ex-3rd trumpet man from Mal Hallett's orchestra and an amateur opera singer who bellows everything he says at you from the very depths of his diaphragm would be) that BTU features "grand assignments at or near your home." After the introductions are over, his opening lines—with a typically gildersleeve delivery—go something like this: "Where did you say you lived, soldier? Brooklyn, eh?" (Accompaniment by the Metropolitan orchestra could come in anywhere along here). "We-e-l-l-l, we have a gra-a-and assignment for you *right* near your home!!"—But somehow the boy from Brooklyn finds himself (through some little slip somewhere along the line) in Wyoming & the boy from Seattle finds himself in Brooklyn and the boy who was to go to a hospital in Chicago to be in a band stationed there for the duration finds himself in a pup tent in Afghanistan or in a cave in the Himalayas meditating with the rest of the poor beggars on the mysteries of the universe. Or to put it all a little more exquisitely: C'est de la merde.... So I'll know where I'm going when I get there & in the meantime I'm forced to teach dance band playing & harmony classes here at BTU— which stands for Band Training Unit and not British Thermal Unit although there is a definite relationship. The British Thermal Unit is the amount of heat required to raise one pound of water one degree farenheit; while the Band Training Unit is the amount of heat required to raise your blood an incalculable number of degrees depending upon the length of your stay. With the exception of a few excellent musicians, the crows that run this place are a scandal to the jaybirds. It's run just like a grammar school with a frantic little ferret-faced captain as the principal and the non-coms as the faculty. The ugly part of it is that while everyone despises the captain, he is equally as feared because the good old fashioned knuckle wrapping with a ruler is replaced here by arrest & court martial or transfer to the infantry or threats of both....

Come with me now to Building T-652, 75th OM Training Company, 14th Battalion, 2nd group, just off 6th St. between Avenues A & B, Beautiful Camp Lee, Virginia, in the heart of the romantic Old South, drenched in the glory of history and tradition, bad beer (Red Arrow) and bad bourbon (Old American), bigotry and the blood of civil war soldiers. Land of chiggers and cockroaches, of soft drawls & loud brawls, of soft brains & loud mouths, of innumerable mementos of the distant ought-to-be forgotten but dishearteningly omnipresent never-to-be forgotten past.

Come then with me to Barracks T-652. Outside a military band is marching by, playing the thrilling strains of "National Emblem," and inside a nearby barracks another band is rehearsing for a concert. Their program includes a delightfully nostalgic Victor Herbert medley, a deliciously effervescent little arrangement of "Three Blind Mice" and, from Friml Favorites, an intoxicatingly whimsical little thing called "Rackety Coo." Inside our barracks I'm conducting a class in dance band harmony. Today, soldiers, according to our lesson plan M3-21-593A we'll take up the dominant chords. I give the rules for building the 7th, 9th, raised 11th & 13th chord. On the piano I strike a 13th chord. The legit musicians in the class are violently jarred out of their lethargy & look as though they might wretch; the military bandsmen blink, yawn and go back to sleep; the adolescent hep-cats emit little screams and gurgles of delight & approval and flood me with questions I can't answer. And me, I shudder, set my watch ahead 15 minutes, and dismiss the class—one step nearer to a severe case of battle (of the bands) fatigue.

Enough of this idle prattle. I'm falling back into that old letter writing groove of too much and too late, so I'll save the rest for next time. Please write real soon—although I don't deserve it—and tell me all the news. I really miss you all a lot. Give my best to everyone.

Love,
"39285745"

ı'ılıı

Jimmy Rowles was one of several colleagues who regarded Gil as a father figure and mentor, though the difference in their ages was hardly significant. Rowles was born in Spokane, Washington, in 1918 and was five years Gil's junior. He played piano around the Pacific Northwest as a youth, then went to Los Angeles where, in 1942 alone, he played with Lester Young, Benny Goodman, and Woody Herman. He first met Gil when Gil traveled with the Ennis band to Seattle and immediately idolized him—the word *guru* punctuated many of his conversations about Gil Evans ever after. Rowles had the luck to be stationed with Evans for a good portion of both of their military careers: Santa Anita, Fort Lewis, and on to Camp Lee. Rowles remembered Evans charming his superiors at will: "He called the commanding officer Cuddles, and the Captain would answer, 'Yes, Gil.' " But Gil still retained his slow writing habits.

Cuddles asked Gil to write a dance band arrangement, a nice pretty song, for a big inspection that was coming up, to see how the BTU was working. Weeks are going by. People are constantly asking him. Finally it got to be Friday and they were going to be here Tuesday and he hadn't written anything yet. So Sunday, he had a big record player that he took everywhere he went, with a bunch of Louis Armstrong records, Earl Hines, and some others. And he's sitting up there with a big jug, and score paper, and his pencils, and he's playing records, writing out parts, other people are mingling around, telling jokes and drinking, carrying on. He wrote it all out. No score, just all the parts. The next day we played it at rehearsal, he played an intro, the thing was written in 4 sharps. No mistakes, it was perfect. He counted it off, a ballad—it turned out to be "It Could Happen to You," so gorgeous. These things when you're in the army, a big orchestration that is so beautiful and has never been heard before—it was stunning. You realize you are with a real genius, this guy you've been living with, and on top of that an intellectual monster.[10]

Ralph Harden, a trumpet player who had been with Claude Thornhill's band, also thought of Gil as a mentor. "Gil was a great humanitarian. He was on a pedestal to us because of his musical genius. Camp Lee was a miserable place, you couldn't get a pass to leave the place. And Gil had a tremendous record collection. On a Saturday night, we'd sit around and he would play these records for us of Billie Holiday and all the jazz greats. I looked forward to those Saturday listening sessions with him. He gave us the good feeling that we were still players, not just soldiers."[11]

Evans and the Santa Anita musicians were "the stars around there with Gil leading the band," said Evan Vail, who was touched by Gil in his "young, impressionable years." But life at Camp Lee was far harsher than at Santa Anita, with stricter restrictions and a more entrenched military mentality. Being at a segregated army camp in the South (though the entire service was segregated) was an eye-opener for Gil; the inequities he observed stuck with him for the rest of his life. In his unselfconscious way, he broke through what barriers he could. Among the African-American soldiers at Camp Lee were musicians from the now-dispersed bands of Cab Calloway and Erskine Hawkins, who had their own orchestra. Though the higher-ups at Camp Lee would not allow the bands to "mix," Gil arranged a few "Battles of the Bands" between the Calloway/Hawkins group and the Santa Anita musicians. "They would play a tune and then we would," said Vail. "They were good, and had pretty good arrangements. They sounded better than we did—they had better soloists. We were better musicians—I mean, we could play in tune and the ensemble sound was always good."[12]

ı' ı‚ı ı

For the moment, the Camp Lee soldiers were in a sheltered position, but if the soldiers were physically fit, they were still eligible to become cannon fodder. Many of them were fearful of the battle-fronts and some—like soldiers everywhere else—were anxious to get out of the army. A few of them were desperate enough to try anything, and succeeded. Recalled Rowles:

> We were playing outside for a party for all the enlisted men. Joe Triscari [who'd played in Krupa's band] was there—he was a hell of a trumpet player.... Gil was conducting and all of

a sudden, Joe jumped up in the air and he started into his act. He was going to get out of the army right there! He went into a thing that was unbelievable—they sent for an ambulance and put him in a straight jacket and took him to the hospital. He was a very excitable guy to begin with, and he just carried it beyond a reasonable doubt. They put him in a padded cell. Gil was very cool and went along with it. Gil knew everything that was going on. He could see through a steel wall as far as personality is concerned.[13]

Gil's underclassmen were always asking him how they could get out of the army. Rowles recalled Gil saying, "I know you all want to get out of the army, but the way I feel about it is America is at war with Germany and Japan and all that. I just think that I should be here, and that's why I stay. I could get out tomorrow if I wanted to."

Everyone else said, "Yeah, we know *you* could." Because we all knew Gil is a guru. Even the dullest of us knew that, and that when asked a question, Gil would come up with a logical answer. So Gil said, "I heard about a guy in another company that got out the other day, and I'll tell you what he did. All of a sudden when it was roll call the other morning, everybody got up and fell out. Boom. He stayed in bed. The first sergeant came over and kicked his feet, and said, 'Come on.' And the guy referred to himself in the third person, 'I'm awful sorry but Private Jones just told me that he can't get up today.' And he stayed there. And they came and dragged him out of bed and they had to put his clothes on for him. They stood him up and he sat down. And he said, 'Sergeant, Private Jones just can't make it anymore. He just told me.' And they kept on with him and they fucked with him, and they took him over to the hospital and he stuck to his guns, and the son of a bitch got out. That day." And Gil said, "That's called passive resistance. And that's the quickest way to get out of the army there is. All you need to do is passive resistance."[14]

Gil continued to stick it out at Camp Lee, though some of his friends—including Rowles—were shipped out to other camps.

Despite Gil's vigorous promises to the Carpenters—and their sending him more letters, Christmas greetings, and more money—his next letter to them was six months later from Hotel Drake in Miami Beach, Florida, where he was now stationed. It was another voluminous catch-up letter (dated April 2, 1945) that rambled wildly while conveying the bizarre details of Gil's army life.

Any place, any
day, any month,
any year—they're
all the same
in the army.

Dear Pete & Maybeth:

I am rummaging thru' my footlocker—(a diabolically conceived combination dresser, kitchen drawer, bookcase, writing desk, liquor closet, icebox, cabinet behind the bathroom mirror, hope chest, rest haven for moths, roaches, etc)—in my usual schizophrenic fog, not remembering what I am looking for—when a very disturbing thing happens. Up to attention snaps my leather writing case flanked by two letters and one card addressed to me at Camp Lee, a Christmas note with a present that wasn't "dumb" at all, but wonderful and two letters—one enclosing ten for cigarettes which I finally sent but probably arrived long after the shortage ended, if it has—or if they ever arrived. The NCOICIPPI (army abbr. for non-commissioned officer-in-charge—the IPPI means nothing—I just put it in to add to the confusion) utters a clipped command & with their United States Army caliber .30 model 1903 type A3 (full nomenclature furnished upon request) rifles leveled menacingly & their accusing eyes boring in to me, they slowly but inexorably advance. Cursing myself for buying that white mule from the colored porter, I beat a hasty retreat and am now cowering in a corner at my writing desk, dashing off this little note under definite pressure.

Frankly, the only purpose of this letter is to get an answer, because after reading your wonderful, newsy letters I hate like hell to drag you with all the dull details of my life with Ares [Army Reserves]—a friendship that will always remain one-sided & has been up until now, as you know, purely platonic. But it may become a more personal affair any time as the big bad War Manpower Commission has been huffing and puffing around here lately looking for general servicemen—which means those physically qualified for active participation in the currently most popular of sports.

I neglected to mention in my last—and first—letter that during a particularly weak moment at BTU one day, I let myself be talked into taking up a band instrument—brother! All I can say about the experience is that I am the founder of the Society for the Extinction of the Baritone Horn, with local chapters in all major cities doing very nicely thank you.

About five days before leaving Camp Lee—Le Capitaine de la Merde, the character with the "gra-a-a-nd assignments right near your home" called me into his office and asked me whether I wanted to go to Ft. Douglas or Miami Beach. So naturally I told him Ft. Douglas (Jimmy Rowles, Johnny Hamilton, & Ralph Harden are there) & so naturally here I am in Miami Beach. When I got my orders to ship down here instead of Douglas, I fumed into the bellowing one who loudly denied having had any hand in the great double-cross. I gave him time to clear his throat which was a fatal mistake because, as I think I mentioned before, that incalculably short space of time is all he needs to cook up a whopper. I had been requisitioned (said he) by this 383rd outfit & the personnel dept. had cut my orders without his knowledge. He was helpless (with gestures) even though he had many other grand assignments for me. Well, my position in this military caste system is rather near the serf level, so, not being able to call him a goddamned lying, double dealing you-know-what & not wanting to incur the wrath of the powers that be at BTU & be banished to Bess-Arabia, I hypocritically thanked them for all they'd done for me, packed my belongings, got severely stinking, and dutifully entrained for this land of super-buildings, beaches, and breasts, in charge of eleven of the goddamndest squares it was ever the lot of a poor tolerant, altruistic, peace-loving soul to be associated with.

Of course my suspicions that the magnanimous one was lying about my being requested from here were substantiated.

No one knew me and the old warrant officer (band leader) was amazed that I didn't play flute and piccolo because that's what he'd ordered and I (a baritone horn man of no little virtuosity, I'll admit—but definitely no flautist—grande or petite) am what he got! I graciously consented to bow out & board the next train back to Camp Lee but the warrant officer (who himself out-classes me completely in preoccupation, indecision, lethargy, procrastination, or just plain punchiness—although he's had 25 more years to work on it—just give me time) refused my offer and made some vague reference to the forming of a large dance band which the fellows seemed to want for some reason incomprehensible to him, since the only beautiful music issues from a military band as any fool can plainly hear. Well, I wrote a few arrangements without the piano he promised to get (I sneaked into hotel lobbies, struck chords on the piano, and ran before the surprised clerks could recover themselves) & the band only sounded mildly horrible. But there is practically no use for a large dance outfit here because the places we play are so small & also because there are at least two jobs a night & usually three which necessitates breaking it up into small combos. The one I play with was never intended for human ears. The bass player couldn't hold down a job with Caleb Carson's Cactus-Eaters & the drummers name, so help me God, is Rolloff & that's exactly how he plays. And I, as you well know, am no rock of Gibraltar. However, after playing six nights a week for three months, I'm getting so I only get lost & leave out a bar here & there about twice a night.

Enough of this dull copy—needless to say, I have applied for a transfer & the C.O. has promised me that as soon as I get another—I mean *a*—piano player down here from Camp Lee—he'll O.K. the transfer & I'll be on my way to Fort Douglas. But first it has to go through many channels and much red tape during which I may get side-tracked into a tactical unit headed for the big game—but even that would be preferable to this rest home for the musically feeble-minded.

Gil then congratulated Pete and Maybeth for selling his broken-down car. At first he told them to keep the cash as partial payment for all he had borrowed from them—but then said he was due for a "pretty definite" furlough on the twenty-third of April and planned to visit them in California, and he asked them for "a C note" for the transportation. He spent the remainder of the letter complaining about his finances, saying that he had "still received no supersensory enlightenment on how to do the little extra things on $68.40 per month." He added, "But as you know, I've always been reckless at delicatessens." In conclusion, "Don't write as often as I do, *please.*"

In fact, Gil wrote the Carpenters twice within the next two weeks. The atypical short response time was due, in the first instance, to receiving the news that Maybeth was pregnant again, and in the second, to tell them that his visit to California would be delayed. It was written on crudely lined hospital stationary from the camp infirmary. "Due to a somewhat severe case of ringworm on the part of my anatomy that I'll be using the most on my trip home, I had to postpone the furlough until May 4th."

When the furlough finally came through, Gil tried to cram too much in too little time. He cut short his visit to California and managed to get on a flight to New York City, where he now had a place to stay: with the Maxwells and their two-year-old son in their one-bedroom apartment. The city—particularly the 52nd Street jazz scene—began to grab hold of him. Gil started going to New York as often as he could—though it ended up being only a handful of times—before his discharge in late February 1946. Jimmy Maxwell remembered:

> On his leave from the army he would come to visit us, and he slept in my son's bedroom. He'd sleep in his helmet because my son used to wake him up by throwing blocks at him. Gil would walk in the house and take over in the most charming way. He would totally disrupt your life, but you'd sit there smiling and so grateful.... One of the great parts of Gil's visits was we would play my collection of Ellington and Armstrong records. We'd start about ten at night and go until six in the morning, just punctuated by an occasional drink, and reassure ourselves that, "We're not bothering you, are we Gertrude?" And my wife would say, "No, no, it's fine."...Later he sent us a hostess present,

a suitcase full of gas masks, army boots, K-rations—little things he could pick up around the army post.[15]

During these visits, Gil also prowled 52nd Street, still a complete marvel to him (his first trip had been in 1941). He could go from club to club and hear some of the greatest names in jazz. It was undoubtedly on these trips that Gil first got to hear bebop performed live.

Gil was still stationed in Miami when he wrote his next letter to the Carpenters, in September 1945. It was another rambling catch-up letter, written over the course of several nights, in which Gil finally apologized for his unannounced and abrupt departure to New York during his last furlough. He had gotten hold of a Royal typewriter and was enthralled by seeing the crisp letters and discovering typological tricks (he changes the margins and pretends to begin the letter over several times). Under the influence of booze and doses of a Benzedrine inhaler, this letter also rambles on, full of faux jive, pseudo-philosophical ruminations, and the stream-of-consciousness of a stoned adolescent. Still, Gil's distinctively wry sense of humor, keen observations, and composerly building of a phrase stand out.

Not to be outdone by
yours of September the
13th, 1945, I'm back with
my little Royal (No
resemblance to the one
behind the fountain in
Balboa and
Valencia———) What in
the world made me
think of that? And the
hot roast beef sand-
wiches and hot fudge
sundae at the Santa Ana
Café on the way home to
old One Eyed Tom's
where dwelt that slightly

alcoholic couple who
raised those beautiful
Dalmations and the
Jaroso where, after une
pièce de resistance Itali-
enne à la Mère Maxwell,
there bloomed, before
eyes concerned only
with music, fans, and the
goings on of a pleasure
resort, what was—in
spite of the lack of med-
ical recognition—proba-
bly the purest form of
penicillin ever yet pro-
duced. And the 1935
jazzy de luxe phaëton,
and the early vintage
Plymouth tudor which
somehow lost its equilib-
rium, and Hubert's
Packard coupé that
Ralph—oh, well, let's
save all that for a future
get-together————Sep-
tember 17, 1945—4hrs
after mail call————

Dear Pete and Maybeth:————

Hello kiddies—this is just to show you that if you can do it,
I—hey wait a minute, I think I'm a victim of child psychol-
ogy————————anyway, what I want to say is:—— don't consider
that I'm one up on you because of this little note. . . .

For some reason or other, it seems odd to write at such short
length—especially since this week-end probably the most exciting thing happened since we've been here—a hurricane. But
somehow, without a lot of yapping and flailing of arms, a description would be impossible. . . .

Well anyway since it always seems that I must include a philosophical section for lack of something better to write about, I'll lay these few little pearls on you:—"A man is rich in proportion to the number of things he can afford to let alone"—Thoreau;—"It is wise not to try to thrust such moods on others, and stubbornly imply that here had occurred an era never again to be approximated. For each carries within his own memory a splendid golden age. Then, when he becomes old enough to seem secure against rebuttal, he tends to make a shining legend of that time. He feels ordained to go up and down like some tireless evangelist seeking to force the gospels and the virtues of his own mental treasure upon younger men properly occupied with enjoying their own present youth which, in its own ripening, will have become a golden age for them—one palsied day. Perhaps old men should be denied their clocks and calendars, their mirrors, and their writing tools."—Gene Fowler;—"The height of intolerance—a sober drunk's attitude toward a drunk drunk"—me.

I'll try to write something sensible soon. Still don't know where I'm going, but will let you know by the fastest correspondence; so if something colossal happens, such as Nancy or Gregory or Roger Simpson [evidently prospective names for the Carpenter's expected child], let me hear from you at this address. But if the scheduled seven weeks elapse, please don't wait that long. Listen to who's talking!!!!...

Love to all,
Gil

Dear Pete and Maybeth:

I am trapped alone in the band office on CQ duty without a crossword puzzle, which of late has become as serious as running out of cigarettes or sterno or laudanum or lemon extract, depending on one's taste. And so, fighting back my recurrent tic which you no doubt remember and which always seems to crop up at just such a tense moment as this, I give the room a quick casing for something to occupy myself with. The frantics disappear as fast as an EM's military courtesy toward a second lieutenant after VJ Day, because staring right at me and giving

me a shy little come-on is as pretty a little Royal Portable as
you'd ever want to see. Well, as you know, the things I don't know
how to do are numerous enough to make a 'light year' look
smaller than my bank roll and using a typewriter is definitely
no exception. But I figure that even though nothing or nobody
is lower than my self-confidence and xxx (whoops!) from past
experience I know I probably won't get to first base, my mascu-
line pride demands that I give it a fling—and besides, there are
a few characters around here whose I.Q's I wouldn't want to
bet on against an underprivileged sea-grupe, and they seem to
get quite a play from this little number. So maybe I'll get somewhere, even if it's only on a platonic basis.... And so to spare
my little chums the tedium of picking their way painstakingly
through reams of longhand, the expense of decoding experts,
and the final humiliation of having Petie decipher it—which he
will always be able to do as long as he himself never learns to
write, I set out with nerves aquiver, nostrils distended (from
overuse of Benzedrine Inhalors) to capture this little job with
all the gay repartée and subtle advances at my command.

SEVERAL DAYS LATER

Already yet I am completely discouraged with my progress on
this small night-mare of the MACHINE AGE.... And so before
typing any more letters I think I'll wait for the advent of the
Automatic Censor attachment which will prevent any such lit-
erary emetic as the preceding paragraph from ever getting into
print. What babble! What verbal dribble! What stupid flubdub-
bery! Quelle merde! (Maybeth! Don't you look that up!) Why in
the Ninety-nine Names of Allah the Merciful, the Compassion-
ate, instead of all that pure unadulterated junk, can't I just sit
down and write:—

Dear Pete and Maybeth:—
    I hope you don't think the delay in answering your two won-
derful letters is any indication of how I enjoyed them. As
always, they made me happy as hell, and the shock of hearing
from the Silent One was terrific. Be informed, O Master, as per

your instructions for our telepathic communication, that at 7:00 P.M. after several hours' dangling by my wrists in meditation from the rafters of an old deserted call-house, I was so completely suspended in my astral body that your call for a four-letter word for an East Asian enzyme came in very clearly, and, as I told you that evening, with the aid of several lieutenants whose cooperation and affability date from August 14th, 1945, I hope to find it for you very shortly. Holy Christ——I'm off again—well, nothing to do but give it another try:—

Dear Pete and Maybeth:—

When do you expect the wonderful event? You must be pretty darned happy and excited, because even I am, away down here. I'd give anything to be home with you kids, although I promise you I wouldn't be quite so prompt with my felicitations this time. I blush every time I think of it—imagine such naïveté at my age! Anyway, I would like to be there—just to smirk when my prediction comes true, because this time I'm not going to miss. Hold your breath, now———

IT'S GOING TO BE A <u>BOY</u>. The oracle I consulted this time is absolutely infallible.[16]

I started by contacting, through a supersensory medium, a dervish sect just outside in the hills behind Syrian Tripoli. They're called the Melewis and are an extremely———#$%&#$ brother———I mean, you know———I mean———this has got to stop—my little chums have been very patient in the past—but this—I mean—you know—one more try———

Dear Clancy and Maybelle—

If my mind seems a little unstable now, I wonder what it will be like at the end of this dashing, swashbuckling military career. Just dig a nice big hole in your garden and plant me there and keep me well watered, sprayed and pruned, and that ought to do it. (Brave little smile, lower lip tremblesvoicequiverswhileeyesblinkbackhotlittletearsoftheIllgetalongvariety).

I've heard from Rudy [Cangie] a couple of times since he's been at Crowder and believe it or not, have answered them both.... The poor kid is pretty miserable and I can full sympa-

thize with him. Camp Crowder is one of the acknowledged horror spots of the army, and that coupled with the sudden shock
of army life—the unbearable regimentation—the strain, both
mental and physical, of basic training—no familiar faces to share
and alleviate the misery—associations with feeble-minded
ciphers of the manswarm whose only language is obscenity
(pitifully lacking in color and disgustingly limited to a few
moronic clichés), whose only facial expression outside of the
vacuous is an occasional salacious smirk, and to whom art and
literature outside of the pornographic are non-existent—the
shocking loss of all sense of proportions by the non-commissioned and commissioned officers in charge of ridiculously
picayune portions of the war effort—and finally the discourag-
ing display of narrowness, pettiness, selfishness, ignorance,
intolerance, bigotry, prejudice that strain your faith and hope
for everlasting peace and all-prevailing justice to a breaking
point—these things make it really tough—and then one day
you suddenly find yourself faced with the greatest challenge of
your lifetime: can you ever attain tolerance of intolerance?

At the time this letter was written (September 1945) the war was
officially over, but the lengthy process of decommissioning soldiers—at home and overseas—was not. Gil wrote that he would
most likely be shipped out in the middle of October ("We've no idea
where we're going, but I'll let you know as soon as I find out"). The
Miami redistribution center would be folding, and some of the requisitioned hotels had already been returned to their civilian owners.

Gil then finally got around to writing about something that had
been weighing on his mind for some time:

One of the reasons I was so happy to hear from you was to know
that you weren't mad at me for dashing off without so much as
a fare-thee-well and especially after we had planned to ball it
up at the Bit of Sweden that evening. It was very impolite of
me—since I had planned to thank you then for the wonderful
furlough I had, and for putting up with mother and for all that
time, and the birthday party, and the use of the two cars for
which I characteristically neglected to apply for furlough gas

rations. The chance for a plane trip to NYC and a short visit with Gertrude and Jimmy was too much to resist, but I've had many an uneasy moment about it since—wondering what kind of an ingrate you must have thought me. That furlough taught me one good lesson and that's not to try and see everyone I ever know in ten days but to spend my time with my closest friends. I didn't see half enough of you kids before it was time to leave....

Clancy, I almost forgot to tell you that there was a snappy all-girls dance band—full sized (the instrumentation, I mean)—with arrangements by none other than Gene Gifford of the old Casa Loma band—that played down here at the local hot spot a few weeks ago—Ada Leonard and her orchestra [the first all-girl band officially signed by the USO]. Gene was here with them and seems to be completely recovered from his nervous breakdown of a few years ago. We had a couple of pleasant visits reminiscing about the old Casa Loma outfit and various other musicians, until he asked me to write a couple of arrangements for Ada. I didn't want to do it, but he was rather insistent; so I half-heartedly agreed, took the assignments home, and thus passed out of Gene's and his bosom friends' lives forever.

I have a hard enough time keeping arrangements practical enough to be playable by accomplished musicians of the superior sex, without getting involved all the more by trying to make it simple enough for a bunch of silly old girls. (A woman's place, you know————). Incidentally, Maybelle, I'm still pondering over that remark you made about your never being able to get too big for my old blue bathing suit. I'll bet it could stand a little letting out about now....

Love to all————

Gil

These last remarks were at least partly tongue-in-cheek. The letter was also addressed to Maybeth—a seasoned music professional herself. In later years, Gil hired and championed of several female instrumentalists, notably percussionists Sue Evans and Marilyn

Mazur, as well as innovative vocalists Flora Purim and Urzula Dudziak.

ı' ı, ı

In October 1945, Gil moved back and forth between Camp Lee and the 383rd ASF Band at Oliver Hospital in Atlanta, Georgia. The hospital was about ten miles from Fort Gordon, Georgia, where one of Gil's idols, the tenor player Lester Young, was serving his one-year military sentence in prison barracks for possession of a small amount of marijuana and barbiturates. Gil told Jimmy Maxwell and others that he smuggled booze and marijuana to Young while he was in the stockade. "Gil said the only thing he learned in the Army was how to smuggle four quarts of whiskey in his great coat to Lester," said Jimmy Maxwell. Anita Evans, Gil's second wife, said that witnessing how dreadfully Young was treated in the Army deeply affected Gil, leaving a lasting impression on him. Young's humiliating experience at Fort Gordon was sporadically alleviated by the fact that he was allowed to play music again, both surreptitiously and in "command performances." On Sunday nights, while Gil was stationed nearby, Young, Gil, guitarist Fred Lacey, drummer Paul Metz, and bassist Billy Goodall played dances for noncommissioned officers. Afterward, Young was escorted back to the prison barracks by two armed privates. Young was released from his sentence on December 15, 1945, two months early, and returned to Los Angeles, where he had been living and working before the war. [17]

Gil's final furlough came at the end of December. He decided to go to New York City again—this time at the beginning, rather than at the end, of his furlough. Rather predictably, he found it hard to tear himself away, and he never made it to California. Once again, he gamely handed out excuses to the Carpenters in a letter of mid-January 1946—handwritten this time—shortly after his return to Oliver General Hospital.

> After the wholesale discharge from this outfit—there are only ten left out of our original 38—I had told mother not to expect me home on furlough because they'd need me until replacements

arrived. In spite of this, however, I got my regular time—21 days—and being only one day's journey from New York City, I decided to go there first & say hello to Jimmy & Gertrude & then on to the coast to surprise Mother. It all sounded very simple but I hadn't reckoned with the Christmas transportation rush *plus* the 170,000 servicemen stranded out there & waiting for trains home. It would have been impossible. So I spent the whole time in NYC, except for a few days at Lake Placid where I found out: (1) that I can't ice-skate (no news to you) (2) that I can't ski (3) that bobsled runs at 70 mph scare the living daylights out of me. However, we did enjoy the droshky rides (sleigh & 2 horses) during which Maxwell insisted that, to be traditional, we drink vodka and throw bones to the wolves.———!!

Gil completed his three years in the service at the end of February 1946. He went back home to California for a couple of months. He spent most of his time resting, relaxing, and visiting—his mother, the Carpenters, and his old Hollywood friends, as well as various new friends he'd made who'd survived the army, such as Jimmy Rowles and Lester Young. Rowles recalled:

When I got out of the army, Gil and I got together almost immediately. I had borrowed a car, and picked up Gil. Gil had made an appointment with Lester Young, who was living with some family and we found Lester and had a few drinks with him. We were having a ball. He'd go out every now and again—he never liked for anybody to see him smoke shit [marijuana]. He lived on it—like Louis Armstrong, at least 15 joints a day. The best he could get. He just went around about that far off all the time, and he drank booze on top of that. And seldom ate. It's amazing he [Lester] lived as long as he did. We got in a fight with the family, because some man came upstairs and asked us to turn the record player off. Lester didn't like that, because we weren't really playing it that loud, but I guess we were a little too loud for them. But Lester really got into it with this guy. So he decided to move, and he was crying. So we moved him. He evidently knew some place with some woman or something. He just knocked on the door and started taking stuff in. We helped him make three trips.[18]

By late spring 1946, Gil felt ready to move himself. He packed up and got on a train with his treasured record collection and a few other possessions and headed for the city where he would spend the rest of his life.

6 52nd street annex

Today, if you walk along 52nd Street in New York City between Fifth Avenue and Avenue of the Americas, you'll pass several bland modern office buildings, four of which house banks. "Black Rock," the CBS Building, contrasts with the rest dramatically; an imposing monochromatic structure, it takes up a sizable chunk of the northwest corner. There's only one prewar brownstone building left on a block that once was lined with them: 21 West 52nd Street, housing the immaculately preserved restaurant the "21 Club," replete with its ornate wrought iron balustrade and decades-old snob appeal. "21" is the block's sole holdover from other eras. It was the city's most elegant speakeasy from 1930 to 1934, catering to the elite. After Prohibition's repeal, it retained its discrete perfectionism and legendary service and remained the only establishment without musical entertainment on a street that was quickly becoming the "Street of Jazz."

From the early 1930s until the late 1940s, 52nd Street was "Swing Street," the "Street That Never Slept," the "Montmartre of New York." Dozens of tiny shoebox-shaped clubs and restaurants, most with legal occupancies of only sixty or less, were housed in the basements and street levels of the nearly identical five-story brownstones. By day, the block—seedier than most—stayed relatively quiet. At night, it bustled. The sidewalks were packed with people choosing among the offerings. Rows of globe lights, streaming banners, and marquees outlined the club's doorways, and the blare of trumpets and saxophones spilled out into the street. Aggressive barkers hit on potential customers: "The world's greatest singer, Billie Holiday!" "The man with a thousand fingers, Art Tatum!"

By 1950 the Street was dead; most of the clubs had closed or turned into tawdry strip joints. But in the mid- to late 1940s, it was a bustling crossroads for jazz musicians. Many prominent white musicians, such as Jack Teagarden, Jimmy Dorsey, Charlie Barnet, Red Norvo, and Woody Herman, performed there from 1934 on, when the Street's many speakeasies were easily converted to night-clubs. All along, the 52nd Street clubs had also opened their doors to the phenomenal black musicians of the times: Sidney Bechet, Fats Waller, Roy Eldridge, Art Tatum, Coleman Hawkins, Count Basie, Lester Young, and Erroll Garner. Billie Holiday at the start of her career and Bessie Smith at the end of hers found employ-ment and a showcase there, far more readily than in other Man-hattan entertainment districts such as Times Square. Beginning in fall 1943, the exhilarating sounds of bebop, the complex and vir-tuosic new style that had been brewing in after-hours clubs in Harlem, found a welcome mat, too. Within a short time, the style's foremost creators—Dizzy Gillespie, Charlie Parker, Oscar Pettiford, Kenny Clarke, and Bud Powell—were a big draw on the Street. Bebop had officially moved downtown. The crazy quilt of clubs in close proximity, the nightly jam sessions, and the constant "sitting in" made 52nd Street a jazz paradise. You could hear the entire history of the music all within the space of a few doorsteps and a few drinks.

The clubs themselves weren't much to look at. Most didn't even have a real bandstand—the musicians just clustered together at one end of the room. The closely packed tables could barely hold two drinks. Miles Davis's reaction to the Three Deuces, upon see-ing it for the first time in 1944, vivifies one of the Street's most bla-tant contradictions:

> It had such a big reputation in the jazz scene that I thought it would be all plush and shit. The bandstand wasn't nothing but a little tiny space that could hardly hold a piano.... I remember thinking that it wasn't nothing but a hole in the wall, and that East St. Louis and St. Louis had hipper-looking clubs.[1]

The Onyx, the Downbeat, the Famous Door, the Three Deuces, and Kelly's Stables—all featured the very best jazz artists, teamed up on double and triple bills. During their intermissions, musicians and even whole bands would go from club to club, checking each other out. The allure, any night of the week, was incessant; anything new drew the jazz community—its black and white members—like a magnet. Dizzy Gillespie's innovative bebop big band, which opened at the Spotlite in spring 1946, immediately became a hot commodity. The band showcased Gillespie's extroverted virtuosity and the formidable talents of sidemen such as John Lewis, Milt Jackson, Kenny Clarke, and James Moody. It gave bebop's typical small-band setting an expanded context: the art of the improviser, within a framework of up-to-the-minute compositions and bop-driven arrangements.

In early spring of 1946, Gil Evans stepped off a train at Penn Station. After his discharge from the Army the previous month, he'd returned to California to visit his mother and catch up with some of his friends. He was contacted by Claude Thornhill in New York, who had reorganized his orchestra and wanted to hire Gil to resume arranging for him. Gil was thrilled—he knew that, musically, New York was the only place to be. He wanted to work for Thornhill, but also to "meet his heroes and make some contacts."

Gil arrived at Penn Station at night, after five days of crosscountry train travel. He knew exactly what he wanted to do. "I got off the train, got in a taxi and went right to 52nd Street. I threw my bags in the checkroom at the Three Deuces and walked up and down the Street between 5th and 6th, that's where all the clubs were." Even while reminiscing some forty years later, Evans resembled nothing so much as a wide-eyed, awestruck tourist, a fan enamored of his idols. "This whole thing on 52nd Street was fantastic! And exactly what I wanted to have happen happened. I met Bud Powell, Erroll Garner, Ben Webster and Prez [Lester Young] all on that first night—Dizzy had his big band. I didn't know anybody and nobody knew me. I said to Bud, 'Hey Bud, you're fantastic!' and he said, 'Yeah? Get me a job.' No thank you or nothing like that at all. Welcome to New York!"[2]

Welcome indeed. New York was to be Evans's home for the rest of his life.

At the time, Evans was thirty-four years old, a very attractive, personable man with no ties—except to music. He had met Lester Young in the Army, but most of his acquaintances in New York he knew through his work with Claude Thornhill's orchestra before the war. He contacted Jimmy Maxwell, his old friend and sideman from Stockton, California, and essentially moved into the Maxwells' small apartment. Maxwell had settled in New York City in the early 1940s after being swooped up in 1939 by Benny Goodman, fulfilling the young trumpet player's wildest fantasy. A year later, Maxwell fell in love with Gertrude Bernstein, the sister of Goodman's bassist Artie, whom he met while she was visiting the Goodman band during one of its periodic California stints. Maxwell was now well on his way to becoming one of New York's first-call studio musicians. Gil shared the one bedroom with the Maxwells' young son, while the parents slept on a Murphy bed in the living room.

Maxwell remembered:

Gil would come in and announce, "All a person needs is a little watercress and some yogurt, a few handfuls of raisins, maybe a few almonds. That's all you need." So we'd go out and buy watercress, yogurt and almonds. But I would also buy porkchops, roast beef and potatoes because that's what Gil wound up eating anyhow.

He would come in at three in the morning and have no trouble with my son David—who incidentally we named after Gil, David Evans Maxwell. Gil would be writing an arrangement, playing the piano and my son would be there helping him with his pastrami sandwich and a bottle of beer. This was a two-year-old boy. So, after a while, we sort of subtly hinted that we'd help him find another place to stay.[3]

Gil and Maxwell often stayed up late listening to records and talking, like they had done as youths in Stockton, or went out together to the clubs—*sans* Gertrude. Finally, after six weeks or two months ("I think my wife might have been checking a calendar off on the wall"), Gil managed to get his own place.

Early in the summer of 1946, Gil moved into a spartan basement apartment at 14 West 55th Street, next door to Jules' Barber

Shop and behind the Asia Laundry. Claude Thornhill had used the room for storage before the war, which was how Gil found out about it. The room, about fourteen feet wide and twenty-five feet long, badly needed fresh paint, and exposed pipes ran along two of the walls. The place wasn't as ill lit as most Manhattan basement apartments; light streamed in from the small windows that overlooked a courtyard behind the building. A makeshift kitchen area was equipped with a hot plate, a sink, and a small refrigerator. There was also a fat black cat named Becky, to whom Gil fed roast beef while he ate cheese sandwiches.

"It was one big room," said Gil.

> It had a piano and a bed and a record player and a tape player. In those days it was a weird tape machine, a great big thing you turned on and the needle vibrated on the vinyl and made a record for you, so it was more of a home recorder. Claude Thornhill bought it but left it with me because he never had any use for it. That's all there was in the place—and a sink. So I rented the place and then just left my door open for two years. I never knew who was going to be there when I got home and I didn't care.[4]

Gil literally did leave the door unlocked, though this was unusual for New York City, even in those safer, quieter times. As a result, within a few months Gil had a steady stream of visitors at all hours, on their way to and from 52nd Street. Almost all were musicians, and some became good friends and collaborators. A nonstop musical discussion developed among a small core of regulars, most of whom were aspiring arrangers and composers. Gerry Mulligan was then a lanky, hotheaded twenty-year-old baritone player and fledgling arranger, whose charts for Gene Krupa and a few other big bands had already earned him some attention. George Russell, also in his early twenties, had left his drummer's post with the Benny Carter band to move to the thick of the New York scene. Years later, when speaking about Gil's place, Mulligan always referred to Russell as the group's "resident innovator." Johnny Carisi, a feisty young Italian-American from Queens, was a trumpet player and composer/arranger. As a teenager, Carisi was one of

Ian Ernest Gilmore Green aka Gil Evans.
Courtesy Maybeth Carr Carpenter; Gil Evans Collection,
Delta Haze Corporation.

Gil Evans and His Sextet, California, January 1932. Front: George
Bucknam, tenor sax, clarinet; Laurence Heston, trumpet; Evan
Hencmann, trombone; Herb Crawford, third sax, baritone, clarinet.
Rear: Ciel McPherson, first sax, baritone, clarinet; Gil Evans, piano,
leader; Leroy Judd, drums, violin, vocal. Photo by Parker, courtesy
Mrs. Leroy Judd; Gil Evans Collection, Delta Haze Corporation.

Ryland Weston, Johnny De Soto, and Gil Evans at Lake Tahoe, Summer 1934.
Photo by Adrian Tucker; Gil Evans Collection, Delta Haze Corporation.

The Gil Evans Band, Stockton, 1935. From left: Ned Briggs, Herb Stowe, Gil Evans,
Jimmy Maxwell, Ryland Weston, Noris Hurley, Johnny De Soto, Ralph Liscom,
Abby Mattas. Courtesy Jimmy Maxwell; author's collection.

Gil Evans and His Orchestra, Rendezvous Ballroom, Balboa, California, 1936.
From left: Buddy Cole, piano; Jackie Pierce, Noble Lowe, vocalists; Clarence Ewing,
bass; Gil Evans, leader; Johnny De Soto, drums; Jimmy Maxwell, Ralph Liscom,
Sheldon Taix, trumpets; Pete Carpenter, Noris Hurley, trombones; Reuel Lynch,
Rudy Cangie, Ryland Weston, Herb Stowe, saxes. Photo by Musart; preserved by Ryland Weston,
courtesy Rudy Cangie; Gil Evans Collection, Delta Haze Corporation.

Gil Evans and His Orchestra, Balboa Beach, 1936. Front, from left: Ryland Weston,
Noris Hurley, Rudy Cangie, Sheldon Taix, Jimmy Maxwell, Elizabeth Tilton, Gil
Evans, Jackie Pierce, Reuel Lynch, Johnny De Soto; rear, Herb Stowe, Ralph Liscom,
Clarence Ewing, Buddy Cole, Pete Carpenter. Courtesy Jimmy Maxwell; author's collection.

Miles Davis *c*. 1948. Gil Evans Archive, courtesy Anita Evans.

Gil Evans and Miles Davis during a *Miles Ahead* recording session at Columbia's 30th Street Studio in New York, May 1957. Photo by Don Hunstein, courtesy of Columbia Records; Gil Evans Archive, courtesy Anita Evans.

Gil Evans during a *Miles Ahead* recording session at Columbia's 30th Street Studio in New York, May 1957. Photo by Don Hunstein, courtesy of Columbia Records; Gil Evans Archive, courtesy Anita Evans.

"Star on the Spotlite," another tremendous performance at the world famous Apollo Theater. Gil Evans at piano and microphone; Gil Evans Orchestra, top and bottom. New York, c. 1959. Photo by Doc Anderson; Gil Evans Archive, courtesy Anita Evans.

Gil Evans at the Apollo Theater, New York, 1959. Photograph © Carole Reiff.

a handful of white musicians who regularly checked out the after-hours clubs in Harlem, when bebop was just beginning to gel as a recognizable style. John Lewis, who cofounded the Modern Jazz Quartet, was a twenty-six-year-old pianist making his mark on 52nd Street as both player and writer for Dizzy's big band. Other guests included some of the more bop-oriented members of the Thornhill band: drummer Billy Exiner, guitarist Barry Galbraith, and—later on—a young, distinctive-sounding saxophonist from Chicago named Lee Konitz. Dizzy Gillespie and Max Roach stopped by frequently, and starting in the summer of 1947, Charlie Parker, who was playing at the Three Deuces, used Gil's place as a crash pad. Inevitably, Miles Davis, Parker's young sideman, would enter Gil's open door.

A few women were also drawn to Gil's place. Blossom Dearie, a gifted and individualistic song stylist who'd recently returned from Paris, participated in the musical shoptalk. So did Sylvia Gardner, a classical pianist, who completely disappeared from the scene a couple of years later and was never heard from again. Hortense Lambert, her husband Dave, and their baby daughter Dee ended up living at Gil's for stretches of time. Dave, a singer and arranger, formed two innovative vocal groups, the Dave Lambert Singers and, later on, the phenomenally successful Lambert, Hendricks and Ross. He left the Krupa band before the war to go out on his own. Now, he and his young family were truly scuffling. "It was a rough period for us for a while," Hortense recalled many years later.

> We were regular visitors at Gil's and sometimes stayed for days and even weeks. Gil was very gentle and paternal and just so forgiving of everything. He treated Dee just like everybody else—he just sort of let people be in his life in a way that was very special.
>
> It was his place. I don't remember anybody not being respectful of that fact. Everything was extremely casual, there were no ground rules. There was none of the communal spirit that came years later [in the 1960s]—nobody had any sense of moment. The reason we were all there was because we were all really involved in music and scratching out a living doing what we could. I don't remember anything abrasive, I don't remember

anything organized. I don't remember anything except this soft ambiance of mostly men, people coming over from the Street.[5]

Once again, quiet, mild-mannered Gil Evans was the unlikely ringleader. Like his first few months at Stockton High School, he'd gone from being a newcomer and an outsider to being a central, highly regarded figure without any self-conscious social climbing or maneuvering. Still a bachelor with no serious romantic involvements, his growing ties with some of his younger musician friends became his key relationships for the next few years. Meanwhile, his place was a 52nd Street annex, an informal musical think tank, and a hangout, a "scene" for the young, hip jazz cognoscenti.

The most obvious attraction to Gil's otherwise humble apartment was that it was within stumbling distance of 52nd Street, a slice of Greenwich Village sandwiched into midtown Manhattan, with a perpetual parade of colorful characters. Gil's unique personality and laissez-faire disposition was well suited to the locale. Friends coming and going constantly and people eating, sleeping, or talking at all hours was not a situation he found at all stressful. The round-the-clock activity felt very natural to him, part and parcel of the musician's life. He'd been traveling in a pack, sharing rooms, transcribing records in the middle of card games, and writing out parts all night since he was a teenager. Gil went about his business—writing music, traveling, and running Thornhill's rehearsals—without getting ruffled, no matter how many people were milling about or what time it was. He was generous and tolerant, without any sense of self-righteousness, and his place was a small oasis. A free-flowing collaboration sprang up between his musical companions, black and white. Gil hadn't had any African American friends before he moved to New York, but now he seemed at ease with all kinds of people, unfazed by extreme types or the "hipper-than-thou" attitude that ran rampant on 52nd Street.

"When I first met him, he [Gil] used to come to listen to Bird when I was in the band," wrote Miles Davis, describing his first impressions of Gil.

He'd come in with a whole bag of "horseradishes"—that's what we used to call radishes—that he'd be eating with salt. Here was this tall, thin, white guy from Canada who was hipper than hip. I mean, I didn't know *any* white people like him. I was used to black folks back in East St. Louis walking into places with a bag full of barbecued pig snout sandwiches and taking them out and eating them right there, right in a movie or club or anywhere. But bringing 'horseradishes' to nightclubs and eating them out of a bag with salt, and a white boy? Here was Gil on fast 52nd Street with all these super hip black musicians wearing peg legs and zoot suits, and here he was dressed in a cap. Man, he was something else.[6]

Gil's musicianship was what really attracted the other young musicians. He was at least ten years older than most of his guests and had a lot more professional experience. He shared his expertise with his younger friends, but he got a lot from them as well. Gil relished both their companionship and the constant conceptual woodshedding. "I was always interested in other musicians," Gil told Nat Hentoff. "I was hungry for musical companionship, because I hadn't had much of it before. Like bull sessions in music theory. Since I hadn't gone to school, I hadn't had that before."[7] In retrospect, Gil's place became a launching pad for ideas, when bebop itself began to give way to other developments. The music that eventually emerged from Gil's place—as played or written by Gil, Gerry Mulligan, George Russell, John Lewis, Johnny Carisi, and Miles Davis—gave rise to the "cool" sound of the 1950s. The work of these artists had and still has an enduring influence on "post-bebop" jazz. It was during this period that Mulligan started using the anagram for Gil Evans's name—Svengali. As Johnny Carisi said, "Gil was no doubt the focal point, but everybody that could do anything got to meet everybody that could do something. Like everybody knew George Russell and we all knew Bird and everybody certainly knew Diz. That was what being on the scene meant."

Gil availed himself of resources in ways that might not have occurred to his young friends, most of whom, like Gil, were essentially self-taught musicians. Johnny Carisi pointed out that Gil was the only person in that set to have a card to the music library—and he used it. "When you went to Gil's place, he was playing the latest recordings of twentieth-century composition—Stravinsky,

Ravel, Bartok, and so on," Carisi recalled. "As far as I was concerned, I was already into that, but to have a place where there was a group of guys listening to contemporary classical, that was special. Gil really had a lot of influence on all of us at the apartment because he was really stretching out musically in those years, and we started utilizing what we learned from him. In that sense, Gil was a mentor for a lot of us."[8]

Gerry Mulligan traveled in and out of New York frequently while on the road with Gene Krupa in 1946, when he became familiar with Evans's work for Thornhill. "I had a room on the air shaft [of the Edison Hotel] and I could hear the Thornhill band rehearsing in a studio right next door," Mulligan said. They were playing 'Buster's Last Stand,' one of Gil's arrangements, and every day they would play it over and over again. I loved it. I used to just hang out the window listening to the band rehearse. This was before I met Gil—if I'd met him by then I would have been at the rehearsals."[9]

New York in the late 1940s was a young musician's heaven, and Mulligan often spent whole days going from one rehearsal to another. Bands were everywhere. Mulligan settled in New York within a few months of leaving Krupa's band. In the course of scouring up new jobs, he befriended Gil, taking advantage of the older musician's generosity of spirit and open door policy. He tried renting rooms in a few places, but ended up moving in with Gil after a few months; he'd been virtually living at Gil's place anyway.

> It was great being around Gil because he was such a calm person—I wasn't calm and I'm still not calm. It's not my personality or metabolism.
>
> There's only one time I remember Gil getting mad at me. I wrote an arrangement for Herbie Field's band. Herbie asked me to write an arrangement for his singer and I did and brought it in to a rehearsal. Herbie liked the chart, but he wanted me to make some changes at the end. Well, my problem was I didn't know how to change it—I really didn't, because I wasn't that experienced as an arranger. I'd gotten a lot of experience writing for bands, but not really commercial bands. And I still wasn't

thinking that much about tailoring the chart to the individual needs of the band—I was still learning. I really didn't know what to do. So I just collected the arrangement and left. I'll never forget the look of stunned surprise on Herbie's face and on the band's. They must have thought I was crazy or a snob or was putting them down, although those things didn't occur to me at the time. I just felt a terrible sense of failure. When I went back and told Gil what had happened he was furious with me, just absolutely furious. 'How could you do that to them,' he said, 'and make those people feel like that?' I didn't realize that I had really let them down.

That was the kind of thing that Gil made me learn. He made me stop and think how other people felt. He helped me smooth off some of my rough edges because I was rough to people even though I didn't mean to be.[10]

In late 1947, George Russell, another regular at Gil's, achieved a lot of recognition on the Street for "Cubana-Be" and "Cubana-Bop," two pioneering and dazzling Afro-Cuban jazz scores he wrote for Gillespie's big band. He compared Gil's place to a school:

It was like an esoteric school and Gil was the school master. The key thing to come out of it was that we were all encouraged to reach for the impossible. That was the esthetic of the time and especially in that group. It was a centering place. A lot of us were scuffling hard, still are perhaps, and 55th Street was the place where you came and got centered and remembered to reach for the impossible, when you were there in that world. I think we all got a feeling from Gil that if you went along with art all the way, you would get some assistance from outside forces. He was a calming influence and seemed to have a kind of spiritual effect, not only on myself, but I think particularly on Charlie Parker. One would be lucky to see things through Gil's eyes. He just didn't seem to have many fears or anxieties.[11]

ı' ı, ı

In 1946, bebop was a powerful force—the impact of the new style on the rest of the jazz world was controversial and irrevocable. Bebop engendered a feeling, one that has persisted, that jazz was a music on the move. Its hallmarks—fierce tempos, advanced harmonic progressions, and long, searing, well-developed improvisations—were first thrashed out in the early 1940s by young, black musicians at Minton's and Monroe's Uptown House, after-hours clubs in Harlem. Thelonious Monk, Charlie Parker, Dizzy Gillespie, and Kenny Clarke formed the advance guard in pushing the music forward. Then in 1943, Dizzy Gillespie and Oscar Pettiford, who forged a way to play the new style on the string bass, opened with a group at the Onyx; the "new thing" (the term *bebop* came into regular use around 1945) was featured at a downtown club for the first time. A few months later, Dizzy and Charlie Parker co-led their own groundbreaking quintet at the Three Deuces, stunning the still-fresh 52nd Street audience with the dazzling fluidity of their music.

After World War II, musicians and jazz followers alike were startled by all the developments. There had been a tremendous lag in the presentation of bebop beyond the New York clubs, uptown or downtown. Some of this was due to the fact that the style itself was still fresh, still emerging from its inner-circle, musicians-only beginnings to being performed before an audience. The lag was also due to the myriad disruptions of the war: shellac rationing, for example, severely curtailed record manufacturing. That factor and a recording ban on instrumental music from August 1942 to November 1944 (imposed by the American Federation of Musicians to require record companies to pay royalties to union musicians) effectively stymied the documentation of early bebop by the major American record labels. The small independent labels didn't really start to pick up the slack until the ban and the war were over. No records meant no radio play. Whether or not the bop musicians would have the mass appeal of the big dance bands—kept aloft by the powerful radio medium—remained unknown.

But on 52nd Street in New York City, bebop was hot. From 1945 on the modern style was featured prominently in the clubs, and Parker's and Gillespie's influences among young musicians was unstoppable. The two literally turned the content and direction of jazz around: from big band music to small band music, from an eight-bar break in a big band score to a wild journey of improvisation, and from a dancer's music to a listener's music. Most significantly, bebop was an improviser's music, calling for a simultaneous grasp of complex harmonic, melodic, and rhythmic ideas expressed with virtuoso bravura. The music's "insider" aspects rekindled the long-running "entertainment versus art form" dispute among critics and jazz followers. The quirky introductions and endings that seemed to come out of nowhere and the relentless tempos startled even seasoned musicians. Bebop quickly established itself as the point of demarcation for "modern" jazz. Dedicated and accomplished jazz musicians suddenly felt compelled to reeducate themselves. "During the day you'd hardly see anybody," said John La Porta, a white clarinet and alto saxophone player who recorded with Parker in the late 1940s. "Everybody was holed up and practicing like mad, trying to catch up with Bird."

The new style called for different approaches to playing various instruments, in terms of both technique and musical conception. The alto saxophone, as played by Charlie Parker, was now the most widely copied voice; Gillespie's brash, extroverted style on trumpet was next. Bud Powell evolved his own dark-hued, dazzling hornlike style at the piano. The drummer's role, advanced by Kenny Clarke and Max Roach, was fast and light, the rhythm carried by the ride cymbal instead of the bass drum; their approach combined a swinging drive with provocative percussive effects that could complement the small combos and the improviser. The faster tempos required new techniques on the bass as well. Pettiford helped create the modern "walking bass": strong yet supple, harmonically sophisticated, and central to holding the ensemble together.

The music invited freewheeling experimentation and spacious improvisations but was very much tied to the composition at hand. A swing beat remained at the core of the new style. But bebop, as played by small groups of musicians, offered a release from the confinements of the typical big swing band arrangements—three-minute vehicles, which, with few exceptions, featured a soloist for a whole chorus, more likely eight bars. The thrill of playing with a powerhouse band like Ellington's, Basie's, or Earl Hines's no longer musically satisfied the current generation of jazz musicians. By the late 1940s, the big bands could no longer promise the career-building opportunities or steady employment of a decade earlier. For the young adept beboppers, a gig with a small group on 52nd Street was the goal.

The new style and all that went with it radically altered the role of the arranger, which was paramount during the Swing Era when arrangers were key in helping the best big bands establish a distinctive musical identity, by the way they apportioned the instrumental and/or sectional roles and shaped a piece. Audiences responded to this behind-the-scenes art; they latched onto the dramatic excitement of Fletcher Henderson's arrangement of Goodman's "Sing, Sing, Sing," the swinging unity of Duke Ellington's horns, or the Basie band taking a simple riff to a crowd-thrilling zenith. For the smaller bebop combos, arrangements—whether written or simply well rehearsed—had a different function; they provided the framework for the improviser. As such, except for the most faithful listener and the musicians, they could more or less be taken for granted. "Head arrangements," based on reinvented popular songs, emerged from bop's jam-session beginnings: the horns stated the theme in unison or octaves, the soloists improvised over the chord changes, and the ensemble restated the theme. However, in the hands of Parker or Gillespie (who was, in fact, a very skilled arranger), small combo arrangements such as the legendary "Koko" or "Dizzy Atmosphere" were miniature masterpieces. Unisons giving way to thirds or sixths and back again, spontaneous obbligatos, unexpected stop times, and the use of dynamics all helped build intensity in performance.

Musicologist Scott DeVeaux explained the syntheses at work in some of Gillespie's early bop arrangements for his small groups:

> Gillespie moved steadily toward the streamlined method of presentation that came to characterize bebop in particular: the convoluted melodic lines or heads played immediately before and after the improvised solos on familiar chord progressions.... The bebop head differs from the Swing Era riff in its unpredictability. Within its brief confines, bop musicians concentrated all that was most novel and disorienting in their new

musical language. By placing it *first*—before the listener could situate the improvisation within some recognizable context— the beboppers made it impossible to hear their music as a version, a "jazzing" of some other repertory. The effect was unnerving even to fellow professionals.[12]

Gillespie's restless journeys through the most progressive big bands of the day—led by Cab Calloway, Earl Hines, and Billy Eckstine—have been well documented, as have his attempts to inject them with his modern ideas. His overflowing imagination and musicality needed continual fresh outlets. Dizzy Gillespie's big band (whose second, 1946 incarnation was a smash on 52nd Street) was the first to make bebop its signature sound and style. The goal was not to please dancers but rather to express the concepts Dizzy had helped advance: extended harmonies, asymmetric phrasing, a driving percussive sense, and a healthy mix of improvisation and detailed arranging. Some of the arrangements for Dizzy's big band reintegrated the soloist with the ensemble to a much higher degree than the head-solo-solo-solo-head format of the small combos. The background lines on "One Bass Hit," for instance, have the entire band sounding like a Gillespie solo, while the soloist himself is urged on by the ensemble.

The agility and prowess of the beboppers invited a rigorous look at what the music really consisted of. What were all these flatted fifths and substitute chords? How did these elliptical phrases fit together? That's where the analytically inclined stepped in— Gil Evans, Gillespie himself, John Lewis, George Russell, and Gerry Mulligan. As arrangers and composers they were interested in examining the relationship between the written and the improvised, which had shifted radically from big band arrangements to the small combos of the beboppers.

George Russell once commented:

I think up to Bird's time it would be very debatable as to who had made the greater contribution, the composer or the improviser.... Now, when Bird came along with the small group, the contribution of the improviser became much stronger than the composed things.... So we moved into an era when the improviser became the dominant force. This was largely because there wasn't a compositional technique to really match the improvisation.... [The composer] may also write an idea that will sound so improvised it might influence improvisers to play something that they have never played before.... Everyone wants to preserve the intuitive nature of jazz, even the composer.... He wants his written lines to sound as intuitive as possible, no matter how much organization is behind them...if a composer writes a line that is so intuitive, one containing a feeling of improvisation so strong and so new, then I think the jazz improviser will turn to that composer to see what can be learned from that line.[13]

Gil in particular was interested in the possibility of a different kind of relationship between the improviser and the ensemble, especially since many of the endless blowing sessions that took place on the Street might have benefited from more structure: "Jazz musicians had arrived at a time when they needed a sound vehicle for ensembles, for working with larger bands, in addition to the unison playing between solo work to which they were accustomed."[14] Gil soon provided the "sound vehicle," furthering his own interests and development as an arranger and expressing his own churning musicality via the sound and textures of the Claude Thornhill Orchestra.

ı' ıı ı

Gil was one of the few people among his friends who actually had a steady job during this period—as an arranger and *de facto* musical director for the bandleader Claude Thornhill. The late 1940s was not the most auspicious time to reorganize a big band. Basie began to realize he needed to downsize to a small band (which he did in 1949) and the Ellington Orchestra was playing one-nighters. The top-selling records of the day—such as "White Christmas," "Peg O' My Heart," "Chi-Baba, Chi-Baba (My Bambino Go to Sleep)"—were by vocalists. The Thornhill band managed to work fairly steadily through most of 1948, riding on the popularity it enjoyed before World War II. It was frequently booked at the Hotel

Pennsylvania and the Strand Theater in New York City and at the prestigious Glen Island Casino up in Westchester, where it had enjoyed successful runs in the summers of 1941 and 1942. The band also traveled quite a bit, playing dances in Pennsylvania, Ohio, and Indiana, states where the band had also been well received in the early 1940s. The economics for big bands changed dramatically after the war; long engagements—even those of a week—became, for the most part, a thing of the past.

The war had taken a toll on the whole big band scene, and also on Claude Thornhill personally. He had been a petty officer in the Navy, and though he served as a noncombatant bandleader, being shipped around the Pacific war zones deeply affected him. After his discharge, he received electric shock treatments as part of some postwar psychiatric therapy. Always a bit of an oddball, the residual effects of the treatment, combined with his increasing alcoholism, made Thornhill more recalcitrant and peculiar than ever. He still cut an elegant figure on the bandstand in his tuxedo, but according to trumpet player Rusty Dedrick, who'd worked with Thornhill before and after the war, he stopped introducing songs altogether, often forgot his singers' names when attempting to introduce them, and would recite little poems he had written, apropos of nothing.[15]

The Thornhill band had always been an anomaly. Claude was never interested in creating another riff-based big band or emulating the swing units so popular during the Big Band Era. Instead, his was primarily a ballad band, and a romantic one at that; it attracted not jitterbuggers but "sweet" dancers who wanted an excuse to hang on to each other and move very slowly. Thornhill's dance book included original tunes that bordered on symphonic tone poems, such as his theme song "Snowfall," but the recordings that came closest to being hits were ballads such as "There's a Small Hotel" (which Evans arranged) and "A Sunday Kind of Love." Thornhill's repertoire had always been quirky. He attempted to make dance arrangements of popular classical themes, including Schumann's "Traumerei" and Grieg's "Piano Concerto." While these pieces had very little of the strong rhythmic beacon that dance music generally requires, musically they were *tours de force,* handled with care, intelligence, and great wit. "The harder the pianist and arranger Claude Thornhill tried to make a commercial success of his big band," wrote Whitney Balliett, "the more musical and original it became."[16]

Though the band skirted the edges of popular taste, never attaining the phenomenal success of a Glenn Miller or Artie Shaw, Thornhill's band had a lot of cachet among musicians. Much of this was due to its unusual instrumentation, which gave the band a lush, low-register sound, its studied lack of vibrato, and its custom-tailored arrangements. The band had a standard brass section, with trumpets and trombones often using derby mutes. The woodwind players doubled on all reeds and at times were augmented to feature a soaring seven-piece clarinet section. Claude was the first bandleader to use the French horn as a functioning part of a major dance band, and in 1947 he added a tuba. A typical Thornhill ballad arrangement featured two French horns playing the melody in unison with a clarinet double. The saxes—two altos, a tenor, and a baritone, or two altos and two tenors—were voiced below the horns, with the tenor or baritone also doubling the melody. The French horns lent the whole band a low timbre and forced the saxes, Gil said, "to play in a subtone and very soft."[17] Another of Thornhill's signature voicings was for five clarinets, three flutes, and tuba. All of this was a far cry from a standard dance band voicing, with a trumpet-sax-trombone-baritone sax stackup.

Thornhill was also a different breed of taskmaster. According to Evans, "His ear was infallible. When someone in one of the sections went out of tune, Claude would lead the musician through his part and play the correct note to get him back on pitch. He'd achieve the no-vibrato effect he wanted in the sections by telling the musicians to play with a vibrato; then he'd make them take it down until there was no vibrato."[18] He was a complete stickler for dynamics and intonation as well. Rehearsals regularly included several minutes' worth of playing long, sustained notes in unison, going from a *subito* to *piano* and back to a subwhisper. It was an eerie feeling—eighteen musicians all playing one note, as if time were coming to a halt.

These focused exercises paid off, especially for the musicians, many of whom considered the Thornhill orchestra a dream band. Years later, Lee Konitz remarked that "the whole experience remains very clear... when I talk about it long enough I get goose pimples."

Gil's reputation in New York was largely based on the arrangements he had done for the Thornhill band before the war, in keeping with Thornhill's conception and repertoire. "The writing of Gil's that people first paid attention to were things he had written earlier, his arrangements of Moussorgsky, Albeniz and Granados guitar transcriptions, things like that," explained Johnny Carisi,

> this business of taking classical themes and really retaining the original structure. Those were the first things people knew about Gil. He showed great respect for things done by pretty influential writers and didn't just do it for the sake of showing off his expertise. He really retained the feeling of the original. And what was also so special were his voicings, the way he'd apportion the instruments for that band. He'd have the brass playing without vibrato, and utilized a lot of things from 20th century symphonic writing. And from what I know, a lot of those voicings originated with Claude. All the other bands were generally more loud and raucous. Now here comes Claude's band playing without vibrato and the French harmonies and these mixed voicings. Gil would have a low clarinet reinforced by a French horn and get these strange timbres that really made you wonder what you were hearing. Everybody else had saxophones alone and then brass alone, and then saxophones and brass together, with a few *solis* thrown in. So Claude had been the mentor and Gil was the executor without Claude having to do any of the writing, like Ellington and Billy Strayhorn. Billy Strayhorn did Duke. Like I've often imagined Duke saying something like, "Yeah, Billy, you wrote it just the way I wanted it."[19]

ı¹ıｌ ı

Charlie Parker returned to New York in March 1947, after a sixteen-month stay in California that included his six-month sentence at Camarillo State Hospital. He was transferred to the hospital several days after his arrest on July 29, 1946, for arson and indecent exposure among other things while in the midst of an alcohol/-drug-induced breakdown following a disastrous recording session.[20]

Shortly after Parker's return to New York, he was offered a gig at the Three Deuces and brought in Miles Davis, Max Roach, and the relatively unknown Tommy Potter on bass and Duke Jordan on piano. Even after such a long absence from the New York scene, Parker remained an original and undeniable force. Mulligan recalled going to the Three Deuces frequently with Gil, George Russell, and the others to hear Parker's new quintet. That particular quintet—with Miles Davis—was one of Bird's finest. It was during this time that Gil and his friends started seeing a lot of Parker and became acquainted with Davis.

Between 1947 and 1948, Parker rented a room at the Dewey Square Hotel on 117th Street for himself and Doris Snyder, one of his most steadfast girlfriends, who had helped him recuperate from his breakdown in California. But Parker was everywhere—he had several girlfriends simultaneously, including the ultra-hip Chan Richardson (Parker's future wife), whose family's home on 52nd Street was a hangout for musicians and hangers-on. For Parker, Gil's place was a refuge with no women attached. Gil said that Parker often stayed at his place through the summer and fall of 1947 into early 1948. "Months after we had become friends and roommates, he had never heard my music, and it was a long time before he did."[21] Gil's recollection, typically, was charitable. Miles Davis had a different take on Bird as a roommate: "Bird never had time to listen to what Gil did, because for Bird, Gil only provided him with a convenient place to eat, drink, shit and be close to 52nd Street."[22]

Parker's presence at Gil's place made Jimmy Maxwell nervous: "Gil had one drawer there where he allowed people to keep their 'valuables,' so to speak. It used to terrify me. I told Gil if the police ever came they would send him away for a hundred years. But Gil never did anything with them, he was just very, very friendly. He'd accepted all these people as they were—he never lectured them and he didn't say 'don't,' and if you want to leave your things here, go right ahead. So you did meet a lot of interesting people." Both Maxwell and Gerry Mulligan mentioned that whenever they saw Parker at Gil's he was asleep.

Publicly, Gil never elaborated about his most notorious room-mate—what mattered to him was Parker's music. Parker's warm, glorious sound had captivated Gil like everyone else. So did the breadth of Parker's musicianship; he pulled off his capacious runs—marvels of harmonic, rhythmic, and melodic interaction—with ease and flair, making them sound like the most natural thing in the world. "What attracted Bird to Gil," Gerry Mulligan explained, "was Gil's musical *attitude*. How would I describe that attitude? ' Probing' is the most accurate word I can think of."[23]

Gil wanted to match up the sound and textures of the Thornhill band with Parker's bop-driven all-inclusive musicality. The circumstances were perfect. Just around the time that Gil decided to score a couple of Parker's tunes, Gil was essentially running the Thornhill orchestra. Over the course of 1947, Thornhill increasingly leaned on Gil and Gil let him—he wanted the experience. Gil wrote most of the band's new arrangements and scheduled and conducted the rehearsals. For the most part, Thornhill just showed up for the dates. Gil started to commission arrangements from Mulligan, Carisi, and Russell and hired progressive players such as Lee Konitz. He also hired Bill Barber on tuba, an instrument that Thornhill had long wanted to add to his lush carpet of horns.

Gil's sound and unique artistry fell into place with his arrangements of Parker's "Anthropology" and "Yardbird Suite," and "Robbins' Nest" by bop pianist Sir Charles Thompson. These scores, recorded in the fall of 1947, illuminate Gil's mastery of the sounds on the Street: he'd absorbed the current lingo, the idiom, and made it into something very much his own, transforming the fiery intimacy of bebop into a big band vehicle. The instrumentation—French horns and an array of woodwinds, and tuba—was his inheritance from Thornhill. These scores pointed bebop into the realm of the cool, adapting the quicksilver fluidity of bop to the low, lush sound of the Thornhill band. These arrangements were also designed to interweave the soloist's role with the orchestra, creating an environment from which the soloist could emerge and sustain a dialogue with the ensemble, dissolving the borders between the written and improvised from the listener's point of view.

Thornhill's French horns and tuba became part of Gil's palette for the rest of his life. But at that time, Gil used these instruments in a completely different manner from what Thornhill did or wanted to do. According to Bill Barber, "Claude wanted a sustained tuba part that filled out the bottom and helped support the bass, because the bass was not being amplified. Gil was much more interested in having me play the kind of parts he would write—scalar passages and 64th note runs! They were hard parts but we played them a lot, so you got used to them."[24]

Gil's bop-oriented arrangements reveal this remarkable feat for the tuba, as well as for the French horns. Gil maneuvered a linearity and lightness from the low brass that was completely unique in a jazz setting, let alone that of a dance band. The resulting sound, in combination with the other brass and woodwinds, was luminous and mystifying, a quality that grew ever more expressive as Gil refined his art over the next decade.

"The Parker things were a relatively late development in the band," said John Carisi. "Gil really had an affinity for bop applications, for that kind of rhythmic displacement in the music. Those scores were some of the best of Gil's things. He could really notate the way you would play them exactly. So if you could read them exactly, that's how they would sound, just as if you'd improvised a line, even if the whole band was playing it. Gil spent a lot of time just doing that."[25]

Evans's bop arrangements—which Gunther Schuller said "represent some of the most glorious moments in jazz history"—caused quite a stir in the jazz community. The noted big band enthusiast George Simon wrote: "By this time the band was so filled with good jazz sounds that none other than Thelonious Monk went officially on record as citing Thornhill's as 'the only good band I've heard in years!' "[26] More recently, Whitney Balliett cited these particular Evans scores as "the first fresh big-band inventions to come along since the great Ellington concertos of 1939–42. The best of Thornhill fed, directly and indirectly, the entire non-hot side of jazz— Miles Davis and Gerry Mulligan and the Modern Jazz Quartet."[27] Also like Ellington, the music already transcended any limiting stylistic definitions. Gil's new scores fulfilled George Russell's concept of the jazz composer's role: that the writer could lead the improviser, stimulating a fresh expression of ideas and a different kind of sound from both improviser and the ensemble. Gil was already beyond bop.

Thornhill himself was more skeptical about these pieces and eventually told Gil to stop playing them. "When the band started to run through my arrangement of Charlie Parker's 'Anthropology,' I saw Claude up in the balcony making faces. He was a night owl, and he finally came to my room at three or four one morning and told me he didn't want to play bebop anymore."[28]

Even though Thornhill disliked those arrangements, they represented a distinctive new sound inspired by bebop. By applying Thornhill's musical palette to the music of Charlie Parker, Gil—along with Mulligan, Lewis, Carisi, and Russell—was fusing a new sound. But the actualization of that new sound—the "Birth of the Cool"—still lay ahead. Its catalyst would be Miles Davis.

7 moon dreams

*Miles and I have a common interest in timbre, the
pure sound of the music. And sound is the thing
that's the most important to me of all the components of music. That's what got us together and
that's what keeps us together, always. And Miles is
a sound innovator, right? Nobody ever sounded
like him before, so we were attracted to each other
for that reason.*

—GIL EVANS, 1987

Sound, sheer *sound*—even more than melody or rhythm—guided
Gil's musical development. Gil pursued sound's ephemeral qualities and emotional resonance and found ways to blend instruments
to achieve overtones and confound the qualities of the instruments
themselves. This was what made his work as an arranger stand
apart and brought it into the realm of composition, or "re-
composition," to use the prevailing musicological term. Gil's interest in sound also brought him into contact with a unique set of
musicians throughout his career. It drew him irresistibly to New
York and brought about his first contact with Miles Davis.

The encounter with Davis came about, seemingly strangely,
by Gil's work for the Claude Thornhill Orchestra, a lily-white
orchestra. The orchestra's distinctive sound not only provided the
foundation for the musical affinity between Gil and Miles but—
as reworked and transformed through Gil—would become a signa-

ture sound for modern jazz during the 1950s. Miles Davis's trumpet would be its foremost voice. Gil took more risks than Claude in his use of certain instruments, especially tuba and French horn, and in his experiments with voicings or couplings, especially his mixed voicings for woodwinds and low brass. Gil's most adventuresome work for the Thornhill band took two very different paths. One was his reworkings of contemporary pieces, such as "Troubador" (based on "The Old Castle" from Mussorgsky's "Pictures at an Exhibition"); the other was his arrangement of contemporary jazz compositions, most notably his scores of some Charlie Parker tunes. Regardless of the compositional starting point, however, Thornhill's musical influence on Gil was profound and integral to all of Gil's scores: those he was continuing to write for Thornhill and those he was about to start writing on his own. That influence involved three key facets: orchestrations that had roots in classical and contemporary classical music, rather than in big band dance music; a constant refinement of specific combinations of sounds and instruments to express a mood; and the idea that sound itself was the primary element in music.

ı' lı ı

Through 1947, Gil continued to run the Thornhill band. The big band scene was withering, but Thornhill's band remained on the road, still playing the big hotel rooms and ballrooms in New York and other big cities. The band's status as a "sweet" band, excelling at the romantic ballads adored by many dancers, kept it viable. "A Sunday Kind of Love," for instance, which was recorded in November 1947 and featured vocalist Fran Warren, was the Thornhill band's biggest commercial hit ever. The Thornhill band also made the charts with three other features with Warren between 1947 and 1948: "You're Not So Easy to Forget," "Love for Love," and "Early Autumn" (not the Ralph Burns song).

"A Sunday Kind of Love" was arranged by Charles Naylor, one of Thornhill's other arrangers after the war. The lush use of woodwinds contrasts nicely with Warren's singing, which has a sultry, worldly edge to it. Hal Webman, then a young, influential *Billboard* editor and an ardent fan of Thornhill's music, recalled:

It was a hit—it gave Claude better money and the opportunity
to work better places. The early band was so advanced...[with
a] warm sound [that] was really the predecessor in terms of the
voicings to what Gil did with Miles. To me, Thornhill's band
was the most exciting musical band in the business, after you
remove Ellington from the whole competition, because Ellington stands on a plateau all on his own. A lot of the Thornhill
stuff was so subtle that it required a way of playing for each
chair, in order to create the kind of sound that he was really
after. "Sunday Kind of Love" gave Claude the opportunity to
put together the band of his dreams—the band at Glen Island
Casino he put together after the war. That band had nine woodwinds, two French horns and a tuba. There were 20-odd men
in the band instead of 15. But the popularity from "Sunday
Kind of Love" died out pretty quickly. It was not a very commercial kind of band, and Claude was a pixie kind of guy. I
remember their opening night at the Cafe Rouge at the Hotel
Pennsylvania. There was a song called "Near You," a big chart
[hit] song with a corny piano player, Frances Craig, a piano
record. All evening long people were dancing past Claude and
saying, "Play 'Near You,' play 'Near You'!" So about 11 o'clock,
after one last person walked by and said, "Play 'Near You,'"
Claude just got up and threw all the music on the piano up in
the air, like it was snowing, and he left.[1]

But even before this brief spate of fortune, Gil was already
thinking of leaving the band. He started writing some sketches for
a scaled-down version of the Thornhill band, stemming from the
ideas he and his friends had been tossing around. He discussed
these ideas—as well as some of his frustrations with Thornhill—in
the course of a series of eight numbered postcards written to Jimmy
and Dorothy Rowles, all postmarked on the same day, July 18, 1947:

1

Dear Jimmy and Dorothy:
Just a note to agree with you that after the big scene I made
about you never writing to me and your subsequent deluge of

correspondence, the least I could do would be to tell you I got your wonderful letters—but really—and the reason I haven't answered is because the things I have to talk to you about are too tough to write and

2

I've been on kind of a solitary kick these past few months trying to prepare myself for a new slant on things and even my mother has been screaming for a letter. The band has been at Glen Island Casino and is now on the road until September when they go into the Hotel Pennsylvania...

3

You asked me I think in one of your letters to tell you when Claude records with my arrangements. That's pretty easy to answer, because the answer is none since last year, because Claude decided he only wanted me to do standards, which was a compliment in a way, but from the angle of hearing your work

4

played occasionally, it's not so good because I stay in NYC all the time and don't get to hear the band very often and he's only been recording pop tunes so far. During the past ten days I've been loafing and getting around to the spots and talking to various cats in the trade and from what I gather things are kind of tough all around. I sure hope it hasn't been like that for you. What have you been

5

doing? Do you still play with Tommy [Dorsey] and record with Benny?...Are things cool enough for you to consider being a band leader? I'm starting to write in my spare time for a medium small band. I feel that the trend is away

6

from real big bands. So, I've set up the tentative combination of 4 rhythm, 1 alto (cl), 1 tenor (cl), 1 baritone (cl), 1 French horn, 1 trombone, and two trumpets. The success naturally depends on the individual performance and the writing, which could make eleven men sound deceptively large, small, loud or soft, frantic or cool, commercial or musical, etc., and the advantage of the

7

size of course, is in the booking. Agents are screaming for bands to cut down. I've got a lot of recording connections and that's where we'd start, with a very cagey selection of tunes and with a lot of thought about production and presentation. There is a way if you think about it carefully enough, to con the public into liking what we like.

8

It's too hard to discuss on paper but we'll talk about it some-time...

Love to all, Gil

Gil's next letter to Rowles was written two months later:

Peaks! For some unknown reason I woke up at seven this morning, got up and have been playing the piano for the past five hours (for some other unknown reason). Right now I'm try-ing to play Bud Powell's chorus on "Buzzy," but I guess you have to have muscles in your fingers or something. Then it sud-denly struck me that you're probably playing a lot like that and I wished the hell you'd wander in right now and sit down and say, "Let me see, now" and that would gas me...

Love to Dottie and Gary, your friend Gil

ı' ı, ı

In spring 1947, Charlie Parker and Miles Davis were among the "cats in the trade" Gil was hearing. Gil, Mulligan, and Carisi often went to hear Charlie Parker's quintet at the Three Deuces on 52nd Street, where it was playing opposite Lennie Tristano's quintet, when the innovative pianist/leader was still a relative newcomer to New York. Charlie Parker picked up in New York more or less where he left off before his ill-fated trip to California. Parker's new quintet—considered one of the best he ever had—included twenty-year-old Miles Davis on trumpet, Duke Jordan on piano, Tommy Potter on bass, and Max Roach on drums. Parker was back on a pedestal: idolized, emulated, and indulged despite his erratic behavior on and off the bandstand due to his increasingly destructive addiction to heroin.

Anyone who played with Parker earned almost instant respect and admiration in the jazz community, and Davis got his share of the limelight. He was one of four young trumpet players—along with Red Rodney (who played with the Thornhill band), Kenny Dorham, and Fats Navarro—who were considered the young lions of 52nd Street that spring. These four roved around from club to club during their breaks and engaged in the musical rivalry that has a time-honored place in jazz development.

Davis had actually started playing with Parker in 1945 and had followed him west. After Parker's arrest in California, Davis made his way back to New York with Billy Eckstine's big band. Davis was relatively easy to work with at the time; he had yet to adopt the aloof and abrupt stage manner that attracted so much notoriety in later years. His time with Parker was formative; years later Davis would readily admit to the extraordinary challenge, both musically and personally, of his nightly engagements with the legendary alto player. Davis played with Parker from spring 1947 through December 1948, a sustained creative period for Parker. Meanwhile, Davis was developing his own style and sound on trumpet—the spare midregister sound that became one of the most widely imitated in jazz. Recordings such as "Half Nelson," "Sippin' at Bell's," and "Little Willie Leaps" (Savoy, August 1947, which Davis led, with Parker on tenor sax) reveal both an undiminished Parker and a creative leap for Miles Davis as an improviser and composer.

In fall 1947, a musical swap involving the Davis composition "Donna Lee"—Davis's first recorded composition—brought Evans and Davis into more contact. "Donna Lee" is often incorrectly credited to Parker; the error first appeared on the Savoy side recorded by the Parker Quintet in May 1947 under Davis's nominal leadership, and was frequently repeated. The confusion is not outlandish given that the tune has a perfect bebop style, with all the sinuousness and quick-change harmonic substitutions of Parker's own compositions—qualities that had attracted Gil's interest. As Davis told Marc Crawford in 1961:

> He [Gil] was asking for a release on my tune "Donna Lee." He wanted to make an arrangement for a government electrical transcription of it. I told him he could have it and asked him to teach me some chords and let me study some of the scores he was doing for Claude Thornhill. He really flipped me on the arrangement of "Robbins Nest" he did for Claude. [2]

While "Robbin's Nest" is not an idiomatic bebop composition— it has a far less busy melody and a slower-moving harmonic rhythm than most—the relaxed attitude and special sound of Gil's arrangement appealed to Davis. In the interview with Crawford, Davis described the architecture of some of Evans's chord clusters and the way they produce intended notes as audible overtones, then added, "I was puzzled. I had studied the score for days trying to find the note I heard. But it didn't exist—at least on paper it didn't. That's Gil for you."[3]

By this time Gil had written a number of bop-oriented arrangements. In September 1947 the Thornhill band recorded Gil's arrangements of Parker's "Anthropology" and "Sorta Kinda" (a popular song by Trummy Young), and recorded "Donna Lee" in November. In Gil's arrangements of "Anthropology" and "Yardbird Suite," Evans treats Parker's complex melodies simply, as the beboppers usually did, and has the horns playing in unison or octave unison. The music is projected through the larger scale of the Thornhill band, with a variety of woodwinds, French horn, and tuba; yet the scale still fits the compositions because of the band's ability to play things down, to understate, and to sound as intimate as a chamber group. The "head" is followed by three or four soloists (accompanied by bass and drums only): Tak Tavorkian, trombone; Mickey Folus, tenor sax; Barry Galbraith, guitar; and a twenty-year-old Lee Konitz, alto sax, is prominently featured for the first time on a recording. Konitz takes the role that Gil might have envisioned for Parker in a refreshing direction. His solos were already oblique, edging toward abstraction in a thoughtful way. Gil then "takes his chorus," developing a kernel of a Parker improvisation into a full-blown orchestral idea, which manages to capture Parker's ebullience, spontaneity, and long-winded imagination. The results are still fresh and breathtaking.

One hears in Gil's writing before the war—his penchant for elliptical phrases and rhythmic displacement—the foreshadowing of these bop arrangements. Gil's approach contrasted starkly with the brash, brassy percussive big band arrangements Dizzy Gillespie was doing for his own big band at the time. It also stood apart from the arrangements of any of the other progressive bands of the day, such as Stan Kenton's, Boyd Raeburn's (which could border on the self-consciously complex), or Woody Herman's (which was more directly bop-oriented and aggressive). Evans achieved a crisp and light distillation of the fiery rush of bebop; the Thornhill band was no "Thundering Herd." The sound Evans coaxed from the band—fast and light with no vibrato—has a quality that Miles Davis made his own, and it would be widely emulated as the new sound of modern, post-bop jazz.

Evans's arrangement of Davis's "Donna Lee" differs a little from those of the Parker tunes. It starts with an abstract introduction by Claude, in another key with no thematic relation. The horns enter similarly—from out of left field; then after a quick modulation, cup-muted trumpets and woodwinds play the fast-moving sinuous melody in unison. After a second chorus and solos by Tavorkian, Folus, and Galbraith, a densely voiced *soli* kicks off the third go-round, veering off the melody with an improvised-sounding line. The arrangement ends on a resonant blue note after a "shout" chorus that finds its way back to the thematic material.

Charlie Parker didn't show much interest in Gil's arrangements of his own compositions at the time. But the jazz world, like any other, is full of people whose interests don't necessarily coincide;

when they do, it's not always at the most propitious moment. "When Bird did hear my music," Gil told Nat Hentoff years later, "he liked it very much. Unfortunately, by the time he was ready to use me, I wasn't ready to write for him. I was going through another period of learning by then."[4]

Miles Davis, on the other hand, *was* actively interested in Evans's music and in collaborating with Evans. Part of the attraction for Davis was Gil's skill at interweaving the soloist and the written material. Furthermore, Evans's work had an intellectual appeal that was lacking in the environment of small band bebop, where winging it was often the norm. "He [Miles] did what Charlie might have done if at that time Charlie had been ready to use himself as a voice, as part of an overall picture, instead of a straight soloist," Gil told Hentoff.[5] Davis also clearly wanted to arrange and compose himself, which can go hand in hand with developing new ideas.

Davis voiced his admiration for Evans's work early and frequently—the music of Claude Thornhill was the link. Through 1947 and especially during 1948, the friendship and working relationship between this odd couple—one age thirty-six, the other twenty-two, one white, one black—grew; both were interested in synthesizing various styles and influences to expand their range of expression. The musical ties and personal friendship between the two went on for another forty years, until Evans's death in 1988.

ı' ı, ı

At the time that Miles began spending more time at Gil's basement apartment, the New York scene was vibrant but also in another state of upheaval. Big bands were bailing out, and the 52nd Street clubs were closing one by one or converting to strip joints. Yet New York's jazz world, drastically shrunk now in its venues, was still innovating. The seeds of a post-bop direction were already in evidence, not just among Evans and his friends. Arranger/composer/pianist Tadd Dameron, who had written for Gillespie's big band, was fronting a medium-sized combo; his current music had a light, fluid approach that veered off from the more frenetic side of bop.[6] Dameron's music and working groups provided an alternative to Miles Davis's work with Charlie Parker in the late 1940s and had a formative impact on Davis's evolving style. Lennie Tristano was quickly making an impact in New York (in 1947 he was named Musician of the Year by *Metronome*) as a leader and teacher. Tristano was forging a style that also had roots in bop; it was characterized by angular, evenly accented long lines, with subtle rhythmic variances and advanced harmonic implications. His approach was expressed brilliantly in the work of his students/colleagues Lee Konitz and Warne Marsh but was simultaneously criticized for its intellectual nature and seeming lack of swing. The kind of writing that Gil was doing for Thornhill was one more stream that had been created in the wake of bebop.

At that time, Thornhill's own career and personal life did not show as much promise. Claude had grown increasingly unreliable through the course of 1947. His alcoholism, domestic problems, and the withering of the dance band world affected him. Ever more reclusive, he continued to rely on Gil for running rehearsals and taking care of the arrangements. Yet the band was still working fairly steadily, and Claude was quite aware of what the band was playing, how it sounded, and how it was received by the audience. He also remained interested in musical invention. Hal Webman recalled:

> Claude wouldn't have done the bebop things if he didn't really want to. He was 110 percent a musician. He undoubtedly recognized what the stuff represented so he took from it what he wanted to take from it. I think you could call it Claude's experiment—to show other musicians, "This is the way you could take care of bop. You don't have to play it like Max Roach plays it." This was taking it, smoothing it out, making it sound beautiful.[7]

Claude's experiment was in reality Gil's experiment; the members of the Thornhill band were the active participants. Claude's musicians, most of whom were not beboppers or even accomplished improvisers, played Gil's new arrangements willingly and enthusiastically; they made it possible. At this point, the band had some fine young jazz musicians in its ranks, among them Lee Konitz, Red Rodney, Mickey Folus, and Barry Galbraith. The band also had an aura of cliquish mystique that was a magnet for other young musicians.

Unfortunately, apart from their appeal in New York's jazz world, Gil's bebop arrangements did not help the Thornhill band much commercially, even taking into account the deteriorating climate for big bands. Gil's charts baffled the dancers who came to hear the band expecting to hear the lovely ballads that had brought Claude a degree of commercial success. "The better the music got, the worse the box office," said Webman.

Gil was in the process of moving on, both in his arrangements and in his conception of what kind of ensemble should play them. By spring 1948, Davis was an active participant in the running dialogue taking place among Gil, Mulligan, Johnny Carisi, John Lewis, and George Russell on the subject of what they called their "dream" band.

Months earlier, Gil had already sketched out some pieces for an eleven-piece band. The motive, which he shared with his younger friends, was to use the lush sonority of the Thornhill sound—still so unusual in a jazz context—in a smaller setting, allowing more flexibility for writer, improviser, and ensemble. Again, outside of Ellington or a few rare instances, this interaction had not been comprehensively explored either in a large or small setting. Mulligan recalled:

> [W]e were already talking about a dream band, the arranger's ideal band; that was what we were looking for. We finally came up with a cut down version of the Thornhill band, even though we didn't exactly start out thinking that way. The musical direction ultimately fell into place when Miles became interested because Miles was our choice to play lead anyway. And it's kind of fascinating that we loved the way Miles played, even though at the time he was *not* widely respected as a trumpet player. Most people thought that he didn't have his technical stuff together. Well, he didn't. He was approaching the trumpet in a different way—he didn't have that real trumpet sound that was the convention in the big bands or that kind of brass sound that Dizzy had—it was a totally different thing. Of course the thing we liked about it was his lyrical melodic sense, which a lot of people didn't really hear yet. Miles, hearing our conversations, started to think about how he could get it operating.

Miles made the move to materialize it and had all the relationships with people that he wanted in it that I never would have
thought of—Max Roach, for one, Max was perfect in that band.
And Miles was at a point where he wanted to do something on
his own. So he was the one that made all the phone calls and
called the rehearsals and that kind of freed the rest of us up,
especially me, because I was the one that did most of the writing.[8]

The aim was neither lofty nor commercial; it was simply to form
a rehearsal band, something for the group members to write for
and fool around with. The instrumentation Evans and Mulligan
came up with materialized as a nine-piece group, eliminating one
trumpet and one rhythm player (presumably guitar, since one
never appeared in the Davis Nonet or scoring) from Gil's eleven-
piece sketches of the year before. The horn lineup consisted of
four brass (trumpet, trombone, French horn, tuba) and two saxes
(alto and baritone sax), with a rhythm section of piano, bass, and
drums. As Evans would often remark later, "The instrumentation
was caused by the fact that this was the smallest number of instruments that could get the sound and still express all the harmonies
that Thornhill had used."[9]

In the summer of 1948 the Thornhill orchestra, foundering in
the woes of its leader and the dance band scene generally, temporarily disbanded. This freed up Gil and Gerry Mulligan, as well
as alto player Lee Konitz, bassist Joe Shulman, Sandy Siegelstein
on French horn, and the tuba player Bill Barber. Miles brought in
pianist John Lewis and drummer Max Roach and wanted to bring
in Sonny Stitt on alto but was convinced by Mulligan to use the
lighter sounding Lee Konitz instead. The nonet rehearsed at the
Nola Studios on Broadway and 52nd Street. Carisi recalled:

The nature of the writing we were doing was different from the
kind of Basie-style language most people saw at rehearsals.
That's not what they saw at these rehearsals and even though
we had good players, there were some monumental train wrecks
trying to play some of these things properly. Guys would be
yelling, "No, no! It goes this way!" I came to rehearsals, and most
of us did, knowing what I wanted to hear and being prepared

to sing all the parts and act them out. Gil was surprisingly good
at that too—surprisingly, because he was normally rather quiet.
But he'd bust out and sing things and he did a lot of things
with his hands, he was rather Italian at times.[10]

Mulligan found the rehearsals thrilling, their participants having few other interests or distractions besides music. He also
found Miles's leadership grating at times, especially when Miles
tried to override the strong collective sensibility that the writers in
the band felt they had already hammered out.

> Miles did get kind of imperious right away. He became the
> bandleader because he was getting the gigs. He ran into Mike
> Zwerin, who was then a young trombone player. Miles invited
> him to come and play at a rehearsal. Now that got into an area
> that John Lewis and I resented very much, that he'd bring
> somebody to a rehearsal without saying anything to anyone else.
> We felt that this was an arranger's band and he should have
> asked our consideration. So we weren't particularly pleased to
> have some young guy come in that we didn't know. His playing
> was kind of a nonentity, so it didn't mean anything to us. [11]

In the summer of 1948 Davis performed frequently at the Royal
Roost, a club on Broadway between 47th and 48th Street, with a
two-tier cover charge policy that made it a big attraction for fans
who flocked to hear the club's bop offerings. At the Roost, newly
nicknamed the Metropolitan Bopera House, young, hip, nondrink-
ing listeners could sit in a bleachers section for ninety cents, while
others paid a steeper cover charge for tables. The famous jazz DJ
Symphony Sid Torin broadcast from the club every Friday night,
lending it a "wanna-be-there" vibe. Miles often played at the club
that summer with Tadd Dameron's tentet, the house band, though
he was still gigging with Parker's quintet, which was to debut at
the Roost in September. Davis convinced Monte Kay, who handled
the club's bookings, to hire the nonet. The group was booked for
two alternate weeks in September. It was paired for its debut with
the Count Basie band; Parker's quintet was due to open during
the nonet's "off" week. The nonet, which just a few weeks before

was an informal rehearsal band, was suddenly about to be a performing unit at New York's most prominent showcase for bop. Gil
told Hentoff, "I remember that original Miles band during the two
weeks we played at the Royal Roost. There was a sign outside,
'Arrangements by Gerry Mulligan, Gil Evans, and John Lewis.'
Miles had it put in front; no one before had ever done that, given
credit that way to arrangers."[12]

Symphony Sid gave the band an unusual introduction: "Right
now we bring you something new in modern music, we bring you
'Impressions in Modern Music,' with the great Miles Davis and his
wonderful new organization."[13] Ten selections from the Nonet's
broadcasts at the Roost (two on September 4 and one on September 18, 1948) were recorded by Boris Rose (but only legally released
on CD in 1998[14]). They reveal a well-rehearsed outfit playing complex, subtle music. The Nonet's scores, by Mulligan, Carisi, Lewis,
and Evans, were not rewrites of pop songs, reharmonized for the
expanded language of bop. Several of them were extended forms,
with oddly shaped phrases; some of them were through-composed.
They required a deliberateness in execution and a different attitude from the soloist, who needed to respond to the entirety of the
writing—what the other musicians were playing—when improvising. Mulligan's misgivings about Mike Zwerin as an improviser
were painfully vindicated, as Zwerin bulldozed his way through
"Move." The group's star soloists, Miles Davis and Lee Konitz, handled their roles beautifully and with great imagination. On the same
tune, Lee Konitz's graceful solo bordered on the atonal, soaring
over the tune's difficult changes, with his own oblique sense of
purpose. Miles took the changes head on, more literally but with
equal fluidity and grace.

The group's efforts, rough edges and all, did not go unnoticed
by Pete Rugolo, Capitol Record's new musical director. Rugolo
had been the chief arranger and architect for the modern orchestral sound of the Stan Kenton Orchestra from 1945 until the band
temporarily broke up in 1949. Rugolo had recently moved to New
York and was anxious to put a roster of modern jazz artists in place
for Capitol; he ardently followed bop and what was emerging as
post-bop jazz. He wanted to rectify a lapse in the label's jazz coverage, which had been brought about by the two union recording

bans earlier in the 1940s, but remained intact for more subjective reasons, such as a general antipathy to bebop from the major record labels. Rugolo signed up several modern jazz artists for Capitol, including Tadd Dameron, Babs Gonzales, Lennie Tristano, Dave Lambert, and Buddy DeFranco. As an arranger himself, the Davis Nonet had particular appeal for Rugolo: "I liked all the composers, they were wonderful arrangements, and he (Miles) picked all the best players."

Rugolo attended almost every performance of the Nonet; but he was one of a few. After the Royal Roost engagement, the Nonet had no gigs and, as the fall of 1948 wore on, no prospects of any. Meanwhile, the Thornhill band started up again and reclaimed some of its personnel, while John Lewis and other Nonet musicians and colleagues landed other gigs. The group stopped rehearsing. Fortunately, Rugolo managed to convince Capitol to sign Davis to record twelve sides, specifically, to record the music of the Nonet along the lines of what the group performed at the Roost.

Three sessions took place, on January 21, 1949, April 22, 1949, and March 9, 1950 (in early 1949, the Nonet played for a few nights at the short-lived Clique Club on Broadway near 52nd Street, site of the future Birdland). The group's consistency of sound and purpose was remarkable in these three recording dates, which not only stretched out over more than a year but also had various personnel changes. Equally remarkable was the fact that these recordings, which sold dismally when initially released as singles, have long since attained canonical status, and their impact still looms large.

The sound quality, instrumental balances, and overall clarity of the studio recordings are far superior to their live counterparts. Also, the several personnel changes that occurred—mainly due to availability—were improvements. The struggling Mike Zwerin was out, replaced by two of the best young trombonists around. For the first session Kai Winding took the trombone chair, always intended for J. J. Johnson; Johnson finally participated in the second two dates. Since nonet cofounder and pianist John Lewis was not available for the first record date, bop pianist Al Haig lent the group an edgier sensibility on Lewis's own arrangements, "Move" and "Budo," as well as Mulligan's "Jeru" and "Godchild." The fact that the arrangements were *not* in the hands of a steadily working band may have kept them fresh; their execution was careful and pristine. The music's timeless quality is a testament to the writing, to the musicians, and to Rugolo himself, who supervised the sessions and who, in 1954, pushed to release eight sides on a ten-inch LP entitled *The Birth of the Cool.* It included "Jeru," "Godchild," "Israel," and "Venus de Milo" (previously issued as 78rpms), and the first release of "Rouge," "Deception," "Moon Dreams," and "Rocker."

Evans wrote only two of the arrangements: "Boplicity," which he composed with Davis, and "Moon Dreams," by Chummy Mac-Gregor and Johnny Mercer. "Boplicity" neatly serves up the months of discussions at Gil's place. The tune's meandering melody and Evans's closely voiced horns (minor seconds abound) are given breathing room by the relaxed rhythmic attitude—every twist and turn falls into place gracefully. The arrangement adroitly interweaves timbre (low and mid-range) and temperament (rigorously thought out but played with a casual offhandedness). "Moon Dreams," by contrast, is all Evans, and indeed a direct carryover from the Thornhill band. Gil had arranged this piece as part of a medley for Thornhill in 1947, and he scaled it down for the Nonet. Voices cross over, and the cloudy sonority of the horns has an added tension from each instrument playing, at times, at the absolute bottom of its range. The interlude, leading to solos by Mulligan and Konitz, and the coda reveal Gil as composer more than recomposer. His expansion of this poignant ballad results in a starkly experimental piece of writing—polyrhythmic, multitonal, and reaching for a luminous hovering quality that Evans expresses far more explicitly and with greater skill in his later work.

"Moon Dreams," recorded at the last session, March 9, 1950, was by far the most ambitious of the Nonet's repertoire and perhaps the least successfully executed. Yet all twelve of the recorded arrangements sounded of a piece, though they were written mostly by Mulligan and John Lewis, who each wrote five. The cohesiveness was a result of the unusual sonority, with its low emphasis, the way the instruments were played, and the relaxed attitude that the group—writers and players—used to convey their intricate and complex music.

The album's title, *Birth of the Cool,* boldly claims the genesis of a new sound. Rugolo recalled:

I'm credited with the title, but I have to be honest, I don't know who came up with it. I did create the album though. Those records took me over a year to finish. I spent a lot of time recording. We only did about three tunes a session because I wanted to get a good sound—I made the musicians like their solos, sometimes they weren't too happy with them. I told them to do another take, even if they were getting tired. I made sure that we played them back and that they were happy with them. I'm glad I spent a lot of time on it. When we put those out as singles, they bombed—nobody bought them and nobody outside New York knew about these. When the LP came out musicians outside of New York finally heard them, they loved them—they were the ones who bought most of them. Hardly any of the jazz singles they (Capitol) put out sold, they didn't know what to do with them.[15]

The sales figures hardly mattered to the musicians. They were very excited about what they were doing. They knew they were going off the beaten track, but they also knew that other groups were doing so as well. Bebop had become a jumping-off point. Mulligan recalled:

We had a very good idea, I thought, of what it meant in relation to what was going on around us—and whether other musicians were going to hear it and be excited by it. We were very conscious of the fact that we were doing something that hadn't been done, and it was our statement as young guys, and this coexisted in time with what was contemporary. Contemporary was what Dizzy was doing. Dizzy was working with his big band and that had a pronounced effect on everybody. We used to go hear his band as much as we could, and just felt that what we were doing was like another county heard from.[16]

"Another county heard from": Mulligan's remark is a reminder that the musical sound they were developing, now a landmark in the history of jazz, did not stand out all that much in the postwar experimental jazz world of New York. Jazz music and its shifting venues were in a state of transition. Just a couple of years earlier, jazz was synonymous with big band music: it was mass-marketed, overwhelmingly popular, and the dance step and heartbeat of a nation through the Depression and war. Now, jazz was on the margins, developing as a musician's music, a listeners' music—hip, elite, and more appreciated from a seat in a small club than by swinging along in a ballroom. Was it art or was it not? Could anyone enjoy it—beyond the insider musicians or knowing sophisticates, who now went to the Roost, Bop City, and Birdland to check out the new sounds? Was it palpable beyond New York? There were no easy answers to these questions. The musicians in Gil's group, at any rate, saw no need to address them.

On top of that, as Mulligan indicated, the Nonet was also but *one* "county" in the jazz world; its experimental spirit was not isolated. Other jazz artists of the late 1940s also inherited bebop's advances and veered away from what had become standard bop performance. They were looking for other ways to go with the newly enhanced language of jazz, but meanwhile wanted to avoid one of bop's worst tendencies: to be frenetic—all show, no content. Composers and performers such as George Russell and Lennie Tristano attempted to express the theoretical implications of modern jazz, some of which had begun to be codified. Their music explored a heightened sense of chromaticism, which at times leaned toward atonal or polytonal writing, a more deliberate use of modes and scales, and a varied rhythmic expression. All of these qualities were exploited with the jazz soloist, the improviser, foremost in mind. The Davis Nonet, therefore, offered a kind of musical oasis.

It was also an oasis in another sense; the group was relatively insulated from the largely segregated world of more mainstream musical events. Racially mixed bands no longer raised any eyebrows in New York's jazz world (though white musicians dominated studio work, which now included music for television), but they were by no means ubiquitous. An underlying precept, especially in the group that gravitated around Gil, was that everything was for the sake of the music. Gil thoroughly understood the racial and cultural melange from whence the music emerged. Racially, he acted as an equalizer, and he admired and gave credit to black and white musicians all along the line—Louis Armstrong, Jack Teagarden, Bud Powell, Claude Thornhill, Irving Fazola, and Lester Young. That didn't mean that racial or ethnic tensions disappeared from the hip and seemingly color-blind musicians surrounding him, or that there weren't territorial undercurrents. Johnny Carisi recalled an incident involving the pioneering bebop drummer Kenny Clarke, who joined the Nonet for the second recording session, April 22, 1949. Clarke had served in the Army in Europe during World War II and upon his return took a Muslim name (he would expatriate to Europe in 1955). Carisi recalled:

> At the date that "Israel" was taken up, Zoot Sims was there with me. The band had a couple of false starts, and all of a sudden Clarke stops playing and says, "What! Israel! Man, I ain't playing no Jewish music!" Pete Rugolo was in the control room, and he said, "Kenny, come on!" Zoot said to me on the side, "Hey, man, are you going to let him do that to your chart?" Finally, Zoot got me wound up enough so I went over to Kenny and I made a big point about his American name, "Come on now, Kenny Clarke, play the fucking thing!" And he played it, however reluctantly. I was always grateful to Zoot for that kick in the pants.[17]

Miles Davis's prominent position as the leader of a band with a fairly even racial mix provoked hostile remarks from black musicians who were not in the group.

> A lot of black musicians came down on my case about their not having work, and here I was hiring white guys in my band. So I just told them that if a guy could play as good as Lee Konitz played—that's who they were mad about most, because there were a lot of black alto players around—I would hire him every time, and I wouldn't give a damn if he was green with red breath. I'm hiring a motherfucker to play, not for what color he is. When I told them that, a lot of them got off my case. But a few of them stayed mad with me.[18]

Davis received similar flak at several points in his career—and his response did not change. But neither did he mince any words when it came to talking about racial inequity, and from the 1960s on, Davis's antiwhite remarks to the press were well publicized. Within the nonet, though, Davis's musical relationships and friendships seemed to bear no color line. That was particularly true of his relationship with Gil Evans.

ı¹ lı ı

The *Birth of the Cool* recordings received scant attention in the press when they were released as singles, aside from capsule reviews, and four "Jazz on Record" columns in *Down Beat* in 1950 and 1951 that analyzed Davis's solos. The recordings finally garnered the most widespread attention in 1957 when a second twelve-inch LP (entitled *Birth of the Cool*, as was the first ten-inch LP in 1954) was released. This album included three more tracks, "Move," "Budo," and "Boplicity," which had only previously been released on various Capitol anthologies. ("Darn That Dream," the remaining recording and only vocal selection, was released with the other selections in 1971 on a Dutch LP called *Complete Birth of the Cool*.) The attention from the LP was mostly due to and focused on the participation of Miles Davis, who was now fully established as a jazz star.

A "cooler" sounding jazz indeed permeated the decade, and the music of the Nonet was a profound influence in terms of musical conception and performance style. Successful spinoffs were formed by members of the Nonet itself. In 1954, John Lewis, Milt Jackson, Kenny Clarke, and Ray Brown formed the Modern Jazz Quartet (after recording and working together for two years as the Milt Jackson Quartet). J. J. Johnson and Kai Winding organized a quintet that "employed counterpoint while stimulating a vogue for trombonists."[19] After settling on the West Coast in the early 1950s, Gerry Mulligan formed his own tentet (which he reformed from time to time), but it was his pianoless quartet with Chet Baker that gave him worldwide acclaim. Lee Konitz did not garner the box office success of the Modern Jazz Quartet or Mulligan, but he was the first alto saxophonist whose sound and approach came out from under the influence of Charlie Parker. Konitz's style caught on, particularly with West Coast saxophonists Art Pepper, Bud Shank, and Paul Desmond, a member of the phenomenally success- ful Dave Brubeck Quartet, another group with decidedly "cool" underpinnings. Indeed, the Nonet inspired a close-knit group of West Coast jazz musicians during the 1950s. Performers and com- poser/arrangers such as Shorty Rogers, Shelly Manne, Art Pepper, Bud Shank, and Jimmy Giuffre were prominent among L.A. stu- dio musicians who sought to further explore the written/impro- vised balance the Nonet expressed in their records. The music of the mainly white "West Coast" school, though, has often been maligned (at times with good reason) for lacking spontaneity and swing and using complex contemporary compositional devices for their own sake. In 1962, with the release of the single "Desafinado," Stan Getz, another Lester Young–inspired tenor player, would become the foremost voice in the most commercially successful "cool" spinoff of them all, the bossa nova.

Meanwhile, every subsequent reissue of the *Birth of the Cool* recordings has raised the ante of their "classic" musical status, with Davis and Evans getting the lion's share of credit. Two other major contributors, John Lewis and Gerry Mulligan, who did the bulk of the arranging, continue to be shortchanged. So does the person who, soundwise, was the fundamental link—Claude Thornhill. Early on, Evans acknowledged the influence and impact of the Thornhill sound on the Nonet—and essentially what Evans was attempting to do with it:

> I would say that the sound was made ready to be used by other forces in music. I did not create the sound; Claude did. I did more or less match the sound with the different movements by people like Lester, Charlie and Dizzy in which I was interested. It was their rhythmic and harmonic revolutions that had influ- enced me. I liked both aspects and put them together.... Jazz musicians had arrived at a time when they needed a sound vehicle for ensembles, for working with larger bands, in addi- tion to the unison playing between solo work to which they were accustomed—the sound of the Thornhill band became common property very fast...but that sound could be altered and modified in many ways by the various juxtapositions of

instruments. If the trombone played a high second part to the trumpet, for instance, there would be more intensity because he'd find it harder to play the notes. But you have to work these things out. I never know until I hear it. After those records [with the Nonet], what we had done seemed to appeal to other arrangers. There was, for one thing, a lot of tuba-type bands.... It got to be traditional awfully fast to do a date with French horn and tuba.[20]

When the first *Birth of the Cool* LP was released in 1954, commentary about "cool" jazz began in earnest; some of the concerns raised in the 1950s are still being debated. To several jazz writers, the music of the Nonet represented a new and significant benchmark in jazz styles—one that advanced the ability of jazz to absorb influences, thus to expand its language. To others, the more pronounced European elements—the use of symphonic instruments, the deliberate purposefulness of the writing, its subtlety, its very quietness—overrode the African American elements of the jazz mix and eroded its value as jazz music.

The French jazz critic André Hodeir, an early champion of jazz as art music, wrote one of the first comprehensive articles (1954) about the Nonet's recordings and the nature of "cool jazz":

> For a long while, [Lester]Young was believed to have given the tenor sax a new style; actually what he did was to give birth to a new conception of jazz.... This new style has been labeled "cool," undoubtedly in allusion to the hot jazz of 1925 to 1935. Personally, I can credit the movement with only two incontestable masterpieces, "Israel" and "Boplicity," both by the Miles Davis band.... Chronologically, the cool movement represents the furthest point reached to date in the evolution of jazz.[21]

Hodeir also, however, noted the danger of too much deliberation, pointing out what would become the most common criticism of "cool jazz." "It is also possible to believe that music so essentially intimate and excessively polished may lose some of jazz's essential characteristics and cease to be anything but a devitalized successor."[22]

British jazz writer Max Harrison similarly regarded the Nonet's music as a landmark in modern jazz development and also red flags the music's very subtlety. He traced a "cool" tendency among some prominent jazz musicians—black and white—stretching back to the early 1920s.

> For this was a new stylistic development, the first in jazz since bop, and the music was both progressive and backward-looking.... This fresh initiative, while finding plenty of room for solos, always made them parts of a greater whole.... This was almost uniquely a jazz movement started by composers (and one recomposer).... Jazz that may be described as cool had been heard from such players as Benny Carter, Lester Young, Teddy Wilson, Frank Trumbauer and Arthur Whetsol all the way back to Johnny O'Donnell with the Georgians in the early 1920s. Cool jazz was not introduced by Davis, Evans or even Thornhill. Yet the history books have decided that the nonet and with it cool jazz were almost entirely Davis–Evans initiatives.[23]

The Nonet's coolness also invited, then and now, complete antipathy. Stanley Crouch underscored certain "cool" elements in Davis's pre-Nonet (bebop) recordings before proceeding to trounce Davis and the Nonet.

> This style had little to do with the blues and almost nothing to do with swing. That Davis, one of the most original improvisers, a man with great feeling for the blues, a swinger almost of the first magnitude, should have put "cool" in motion is telling. Indeed, it is the first, promontory example of his dual position in jazz. Heard now, the nonet recordings seem little more than primers for television writing. What the recordings show us, though, is that Davis, like many other jazzmen, was not above the academic temptation of Western music.[24]

It is difficult to fully swallow Crouch's criticisms and his barbs at Davis. A fresh listen to "Move" or "Godchild" can refute the notion that the nonet "did not swing." And according to John Szwed's new research, Miles Davis was more classically literate than most writing about him has revealed. As a youth Davis regularly attended the opera and the symphony with his family, and his studies at Juilliard included a Hindemith seminar. Finally, just what is this detrimental temptation of Western music? The use of symphonic instruments, the very act of writing music? Do people accuse Ellington or Charles Mingus or, for that matter, Jelly Roll Morton of such transgressions?

More specific were Bill Cole's comments in his 1974 biography of Miles Davis. Cole found fault not so much with Davis's explorations but with the imitators who indeed followed and fell into the potholes Hodeir warned of.

> For this literate music, the band was built on musicians who were strong readers. It did launch a line of other bands whose intent was to play complicated written lines rather than spontaneous improvisations, but what Miles himself was trying to do in this band was to perform amidst a sound.... The consequence of all this was a long line of imitators who were not really interested in improvisational music, but rather needed a mechanism to exploit African American music. The so-called 'cool' period cropped up to give jazz its unemotional, literate guise.[25]

"Cool" as a term has become problematic itself, as has "swing" or "the blues," musical descriptions that many people use but that are not easily defined and have taken on loaded implications. Krin Gabbard wrote:

> Consider an NBC program from 1958 called "The Subject is Jazz—Cool." Gilbert Seldes...introduces a group of jazz musicians as if they were members of the Budapest String Quartet. Led by Lee Konitz (also sax)...the band plays lively versions of "Godchild," "Half Nelson," "Move," and "Subconscious Lee" while the camera pans over photographs of Miles Davis, Lennie Tristano, Lester Young.... Toward the end of the program Seldes quotes the French critic Andre Hodeir on the nature of "cool jazz" and then asks Konitz to explain what Hodeir means. Not entirely comfortable with Seldes's (or Hodeir's) approach

to jazz, Konitz says he doesn't know. Then, shrugging a bit, Konitz says that he always thought that Louis Armstrong's Hot Five recordings were cool.[26]

Putting aside the dubious nuances of "cool," the foremost legacy of the Nonet was Gil's doing—what got transformed from the Thornhill band through Gil to Miles Davis and then back to Gil. That was the attention to sonority, sound itself, and the desire to use it as a medium for the emotional content of the music. That was what brought Gil and Miles together.

Ironically, much of the intense deliberation that took place among Gil and his friends about the instrumentation and size of their "dream band" may have been unnecessary. "We found out the hard way that we didn't need the French horn, or even the tuba," said Mulligan. "The sound was in the conception of the lead player mostly. Miles dominated that band completely; the whole nature of the interpretation was his. That was why we were always afraid to get another trumpet player." [27]

ı' lıı ı

The late 1940s and early 1950s were years of great cultural and musical flux. Bebop managed to remain a force and become passé simultaneously, rhythm and blues and jump bands stirred up dust in the Southeast, and rock and roll was not far behind. A new media, television, was quickly becoming the latest form of American entertainment, one that could be enjoyed at home.

> The dance places disappeared, and each time a place closed down it was another place for a band not to work. The business itself—the whole idea of social dancing was becoming less, and that was even before rock had entered the picture. All the postwar changes were reflected in the music business as well. Everything came out of the pecking order. The bands had been the dominant thing and suddenly they were slipping away a little bit at a time, and what replaced them was television. By the time Presley came along guys like Claude were put into a box somewhere quietly. They had nowhere to go.[28]

Meanwhile, it seemed as if Gil had nowhere to go either. In the aftermath of the Nonet's short performing life, Miles Davis was very much a man on the scene, playing with several groups, but Gil was betwixt and between. He continued to work for Thornhill when the band regrouped in the fall of 1948, and he was able to get Mulligan hired as arranger and Carisi as a trumpet player. Carisi recalled:

> When I joined the band in 1949 it was reassembling again. I remember Gerry rehearsing us a lot at the Nola studio. We were still playing out of town quite a lot. We were playing the Schribman circuit in New England—Bridgeport, Pottstown, towns in Massachusetts, New Hampshire, and also in Pennsylvania. I really don't know how much writing Gil was turning out by this time. Claude was living out of town, so he wouldn't show up at a rehearsal until Gil informed him that the band was in decent shape, especially for the kind of charts Gerry was writing. Then he'd come and work a couple of rehearsals and we were off on the road. Every once in a while, Claude would whip out one of those early scores of his—they were fantastic! But we never really played them on the job because we never really learned them. Also they were written for the full clarinet section, which we didn't have anymore. Claude had to give that up for economic reasons.[29]

Gil went through an intense period of personal transition as well. In 1949 he became involved with a woman named Lillian Grace. Although Gil undoubtedly dated here and there, this was the first serious romantic relationship of any duration since his move to New York. Lillian had been living with Jack Ferrier, a clarinet and alto player who'd been with Thornhill before and after World War II. Though she never worked as a professional, she thought of herself as a singer, and Anita Evans said she looked like one of the Andrews sisters, all "done up."

Gil wrote to the Carpenters in April 1949, informing them that he and Lillian would be visiting soon:

> Dear Pete and Maybeth: A note to tell you that we're on our way to California via Pittsburgh, Cleveland, Akron, Detroit,

Chicago, Milwaukee, Indianapolis, and St. Louis, where we'll
be in about two weeks and then on to L.A. for a nice vacation
and visit. These two weeks "on the road" are for the lamp company Lillian works for. It reminds me of traveling with a band—
only I get more arranging done this way.... Life is wonderful,
Love, Gil.

During this same period, though, Gil suffered a deep depression and personal crisis. As anyone who knew him well would
attest, Gil had a dark side, a brooding melancholy that—later on—
would be profoundly expressed in much of his music. Referring to
this crisis, George Russell wrote, "Gil had reached the point of
mental exhaustion from having been everybody's friend, hero, saint,
analyst and counselor."[30] Many years later Gil described what he
experienced as a nervous breakdown, brought on by numerous
experiences, not the least of which may have been the stress and
internal pressures of being a creative artist:

> When one is a child, one learns the world through ideals. When
> one grows up, you realize that these ideals can not be realized
> and experience a period of shock. One day I was sitting on the
> lawn in Central Park. The top of my head was very hot, it was
> not because of the sun. I was experiencing a huge change in
> my mind. I was in a state of great confusion, it was before I was
> married—before 1950. I had friends who accompanied Peggy
> Lee. To avoid my going to Bellevue, they took me with them on
> a six-week tour and took care of me. When I returned, I was in
> much better shape. Then I got married. It was a completely dif-
> ferent experience. I had to learn to live with someone else.[31]

The crisis passed, with help, and Gil and Lillian were married.
This was a welcome change, yet a dramatic transition. Gil had been
living with a host of people, albeit in a collegial fashion, for most of
his adult life. George Endrey, a fellow musician and counselor/
mentor to Gil, George Russell, and others on the scene, felt that Gil
was ready to embark on a different, more balanced way of life.
Endrey wrote:

About 2 A.M. one morning, in a cafeteria, Russell and others there, Miles Davis, Gerry Mulligan, John Lewis, Charlie Parker, etc., we stopped for watermelon to cool off the heat of a summer night.

"George," Gil turned to me, "I want to give my life a chance. I'm thinking of a girl I like. What is the right thing to do? You know...marriage can change your life, children, steadiness. I'm ready for it. How long can I go on like this? I make plenty of money but where is my life going?"

Gil wanted to retire into marriage, to live like other people— Lillian and Gil disappeared...although we all knew where they lived, we thought we were letting them...live.

Gil also retired to study—music! He wanted to do two things, listen and study from someone.[32]

Gil was thirty-eight years old when he and Lillian got married in 1950. They eventually settled at the Whitby Apartments at 345 West 45th Street, a large building in midtown where many musicians lived. (Lillian continued to live in the building until 1992, when she became incapacitated by encephalitis and meningitis and was placed in a nursing home.) According to some friends, Lillian was not eager to have musicians rehearsing or talking all night in her living room, but others remember her as a genial hostess who offered food and drinks whenever they visited. But hanging out endlessly at Gil's place was no longer an option for his friends and colleagues. Gil later said that during this period, he practiced a lot in his apartment, "but it didn't add up to anything. I wasn't really in good shape, aside from the fact that my first wife was not really interested in what I did. I knew almost nothing aside from the music that I loved. I didn't know how the world worked."[33]

In the early years of his marriage, Gil did various musical odd jobs.

I did a lot of dates like club work. A singer would want an arrangement that would sound fine with five men or fifteen men, so I would write some stock arrangement type things for singers. Not the greatest work by any means, but.... There was a vocal coach named Sid Shaw, and he had me and a piano player named Jimmy Lyons, and we would go around to these different people's houses, and Sid would pick out things that he felt they should sing in their act, and we would write the music for them. So I did quite a bit of that.[34]

Between 1950 and 1951 Gil worked at a strip club in Greenwich Village called the Nut Club with a drummer and a tenor player. "I would play the bass part," Gil recalled many years later. "It was a good experience for me. Seventy-six dollars a week. Incredible."[35] Gil occasionally worked with name musicians; he played a gig at Basin St. West with Mulligan and Al Cohn. He did some arrangements for Billy Butterfield, a popular jazz trumpet player in the Bobby Hackett–Louis Armstrong vein; "Singin' the Blues" has the kind of chorus Gil liked to reserve for himself, with long elliptically phrased lines and a bop feel. Evans indeed wrote for singers, and several obscure recordings have resurfaced only recently. In 1950, Gil arranged four songs for Pearl Bailey, which were released on two Columbia 78s. In 1951 he arranged "Ev'body Clap Hands" and "Do That to Me" for a promotional single featuring Claire "Shanty" Hogan, a singer who worked with the Jimmy Dorsey band in the late 1940s. The arranging is straightforward with only a few signature Gil touches. The most noteworthy thing about this record is that "Gil Evans and His Orchestra," a huge band of twenty or so pieces, was mentioned on the label. He also wrote some arrangements for Peggy Lee and Tony Bennett in the early 1950s, but no recordings of these have emerged.

The painful truth is that in less than two years Gil had gone from being in the thick of things to nothing. The club scene was much tinier than it had been when Gil settled in New York in 1946, and the decline of the Big Band Era left jazz arrangers such as Gil scuffling. Some arrangers, such as Manny Albam, Neal Hefti, and Johnny Mandel, latched onto lucrative arranging work for television, radio, and records. As the 1950s progressed, Gil did occasional jobs for hire, but he was by no means a fixture in the studio world.

The trumpet player Jimmy Maxwell, Gil's old friend from Stockton, seemed to have had no major obstacles in becoming an A-list New York studio musician. In the 1950s he was on staff at the NBC Orchestra, on call for record dates of all description, and still played with a variety of jazz groups. Maxwell said that Gil was not on the "short" list for studio arrangers; people did not automatically think of him, and he had a terrible reputation for being slow and delivering things late.

Maxwell recalled:

> He was sort of freelancing and I was doing the Patti Page Show. He said that he'd like to write some arrangements, and I told him I was sure they'd be thrilled. So I spoke to Patti Page and her manager. They said great, and they gave him an assignment. It came time for the rehearsal and they said, "Where's your friend Gil?" And I said, "What do you mean?" They said that he never brought the arrangement around. I said, "Oh God, I didn't tell you this, did I?" "Tell us what?" they said. "I don't think he's going to." So I called him up, and Gil said, "Was that today?" And I said, "Yes, the broadcast was today." "Oh darn," he said, "I haven't even started it yet." This happened with two or three people, until I thought, "Oh, just forget it."[36]

Gertrude, Maxwell's wife, recalled that it used to drive Lillian crazy—Gil did get many offers, would always say "sure," and then he would mess them up somehow. "Tommy Dorsey brought charges," Maxwell remembered. "He said he'd do an arrangement and didn't do it on time."

Gil went through a lengthy spell of scuffling, much of which was self-imposed. He was not at all a self-promoter and was a terrible businessman. He may also have felt that he'd put in plenty of years being a pen for hire and was following his own interests, which included doing a lot of musical research and listening, some writing for rehearsal bands, and other pursuits, such as studying the work of the controversial psychoanalyst Wilhelm Reich. Life was cheaper in those days—one could get by carefully and follow one's muse. Gil recalled in 1957:

> As for jazz dates, one reason I didn't do much was that nobody asked me.... I've also been trying to fill in gaps in my musical development in the past year. I've been reading music history,

biographies of composers, articles on criticism and listening to
records from the library. And I'm working as much as I can.
There are other reasons for my not having done too much jazz
writing in the last few years. As I said, I have a kind of direction of my own that seems to cross three things—pop, jazz and
sound. Now I feel ready to do more jazz.[37]

Something else may have held him back, in unpredictable ways.
The Maxwells, Carisi, and others have said that Lillian was a heavy
drinker. In those days, people, especially in the entertainment
world, tended to downplay drunken episodes, but Lillian's behavior was questionable at times. For instance, Gil and Lillian house-
sat for the Maxwells and took care of their four cats and two dogs
in Great Neck when the family accompanied Jim to Florida to play
with the *Perry Como Show* and the *Tonight Show*. Gertrude recalled:

They were supposed to pick us up at the airport; we were coming off the plane with two children, not terribly small, but you
know. And there's no Gil. We took a cab and came home. The
house was immaculate, the animals were fed, and there wasn't
even a word from them. That was so typical—they left two or
three days before we were due home, and the neighbor fed the
animals. Lillian was a natural housekeeper, the place was immaculate. But there was never a word of explanation. And after-
wards we found out Lillian was a lush. She used to get drunk
and call you [Jim] up, and tell you about Gil and complain.[38]

Jim added:

After that Gil and I weren't so friendly. I always thought it was
because when I returned a suitcase to his wife, I put a bottle of
gin in it and didn't say anything—meaning it was an insult to
her, because she was drunk the whole time they stayed here.
She went around to the neighbors telling them what slobs we
were and lots of terrible things. Gil would never in a million
years have any part of that. He liked the piano and was probably at the piano the whole time, which was probably why she
was drunk.[39]

In the spring of 1953, Gil stumbled back into the periphery of the jazz limelight. He was asked to write some arrangements for a Charlie Parker session. The timing was not optimal. This was probably the period that Gil described to Hentoff: "by the time he was ready to use me, I wasn't ready to write for him." Furthermore, Parker at this time was hopelessly unhealthy, unreliable, and unpredictable, but he was still a tremendous draw as a performer. He had worked intermittently for Norman Granz as a "Jazz at the Philharmonic" artist since 1946 and was a big attraction at Granz's concerts. Granz, in his role as Parker's record producer for Clef Records (then distributed by Mercury), allowed Parker plenty of leeway in terms of recording direction.

In a *Down Beat* interview published in January 1953, Parker said that he was interested in recording with "five or six woodwinds, a harp, a choral group and full rhythm section. Something on the line of Hindemith's 'Kleine Kammermusik.' Not a copy or anything like that. I don't ever want to copy. But that sort of thing."[40]

Whether this remark was casual or not, Granz took Parker seriously. On May 22, 1953, Parker recorded with an ensemble that included one French horn, four mixed woodwinds (flute, clarinet, oboe, bassoon), Tony Aless on piano, Charles Mingus on bass, Max Roach on drums, and a vocal quartet. The vocal arranging and contracting fell to Dave Lambert, a friend of Bird's and a former roommate of Gil's. Gil was hired as the instrumental arranger, and he also conducted the session.

Parker's legendary stature as a soloist makes it easy to forget that his rise to fame took place in big band settings. His ease in large ensembles is palpable on a slew of recordings made in the late 1940s, including several outstanding dates with Machito's Afro-Cuban jazz orchestra. In 1949 Parker realized a longtime dream in recording with strings; "Just Friends," from a November 1949 session for Verve, was Parker's biggest hit single, and all six sides were released as an album, which was also quite successful. Parker's bluesy, earthy sensibility kept the recordings from sounding overly sweet.

Gil's outing with Parker didn't fare nearly so well. The session reportedly was a disaster. Only three tunes were completed: "In the Still of the Night," "Old Folks," and "If I Love Again." The first two tunes required many takes, eating up the meter-driven studio

time. The rehearsals took place at the recording date, and, in this
case, additional rehearsals might have helped considerably. The
recordings reveal the incongruity of the vocal and instrumental
parts—these two components never mesh, and the sonorities of
the voices do not work well with either Parker's sound or those of
the woodwind quintet.

According to Phil Schaap, who oversaw the reissue of these
recordings in 1988, "Granz was so discouraged that he stopped the
session before the fourth title could be taped." There were at least
seven attempts of "In the Still of the Night," resulting in four complete takes, and even the issued version has major flaws. The melody
and lyrics are very active, rendering the vocal parts extremely
busy. There is no sonorous meeting ground on any of the arrangements, as there is in the first Parker-with-strings undertaking.
Furthermore, Gil's woodwind parts are too subtle to come off, and
the winds never establish a meaningful presence. When Parker
finally has a solo chorus, accompanied only by the rhythm section,
everything else seems superfluous. This is in dire contrast to any
of Gil's work to this date, in which—no matter what the setting or
size—a mutual and natural-sounding commingling takes place
between the soloist and the rest of the ensemble. One can sense
that Gil was reaching for something elusive with the backgrounds—but never found it. These are probably the most ill-con-
ceived recorded arrangements Gil was ever involved with.

A couple of weeks after the session, Granz sent the reference
records from the sessions to Evans to select two titles for a single
release. Schaap wrote:

> Evans decided to get together with Lambert for a listen. It was
> a hot day in the early summer of 1953. To keep cool, they put
> the speaker in the window and went outside to listen on the
> stoop. Gradually their spirits brightened as their appraisal of
> the session's worth grew. It wasn't the music or the perform-
> ance that was flawed—the engineer's balance was wrong. The
> voices drowned out the ensemble, the jazz rhythm section was
> lost. (In deference to one of Gil's last wishes and to the extent
> this could be compensated for, I tried to remedy this in the
> remastering.) Gil Evans and Dave Lambert went to Charlie

Parker with this insight. Then the three of them went to Granz. All three were willing to do the date over for free if Granz would put them back in the studio, an action that would have rescued the fourth title. Granz refused.[41]

Granz was right. It would have taken far more than correcting the instrumental balance to make any of these recordings a hit on the level of "Just Friends," or to ameliorate the flaws in the arrangements. Chances are, if Gil had been the sole arranger, he might have come up a nonet-styled setting, from which Parker's alto could have soared forth. If Gil's recordings with Bird had been successful, the arc of his career in the years when he seemed to be barely working might have been quite different.

Gil's career from 1947 to the mid-1950s was erratic—but perhaps no more so than that of other talented jazz musicians in those years. With the Davis Nonet, Gil had achieved a unique sound and direction, but it was overlooked at the time—except by similar-minded musicians. He finally got to write some arrangements for Charlie Parker, but the too-many-cooks factor undid the project. Gil's equanimity carried him through the vagaries of his life and career in these years, as it would in other periods of extreme ups and downs. Music making is often a messy affair with no guarantees: things didn't always come out the way Gil heard or envisioned them, records did not always sell. Gil's constant pursuit of refining the sounds in his mind was what ruled his life, whether there was a job at hand or not.

8 jambangle

*He started listening more to Ravel, Debussy, and
some of the older classic writers. And he would
stick a little bit here and a little bit there and it
would seem like a wonderful recipe of how to be a
great musician. The only thing is that at a certain
point he'd learned all he could about voicing this
and voicing that, and where the others may have
gone off this way, he went that way, straight into
the music we all know. And unfortunately what he
did is not the formula to become a genius, because
it didn't work with me and I know a lot of other
people it didn't work with.*

—JIMMY MAXWELL

Gil's professional dry spell continued until early 1956, but there it
ended, and in a big way. He then entered the most prolific phase of
his recording career and finally regained visibility in the jazz world.
By the end of 1956, he began planning a large-scale project with
Miles Davis. It would turn out to be the first of three groundbreaking albums that would link Gil's name inescapably with Davis's.
Their collaboration on *Miles Ahead*, *Porgy and Bess*, and *Sketches
of Spain* was the music for which Gil would become best known.

The early 1950s, in the aftermath of the end of the Big Band
Era and the collapse of the 52nd Street scene, brought difficult

times for many New York musicians. There was little work. The shriveled-up club scene had shifted: to Broadway in midtown, where the Royal Roost, Bop City, and Birdland were all within a few blocks, and to Greenwich Village, home of the Village Vanguard and, from the mid-1950s on, other clubs that sprouted up, such as Café Bohemia. The recording industry was beginning to warm to the marketable possibilities of rock and roll, although pop vocalists still dominated the charts. Charlie Parker's death on March 12, 1955, cast a pall over an already dispirited jazz world.

Gil and Lillian were still living on West 45th Street, in a far more upscale dwelling than Gil's basement pad. At Lillian's urging, Gil had ordered professional stationery—with envelopes to match:

Gil Evans
Music Arrangement

But the apartment and the stationery could hardly disguise the fact that, from 1950 to 1956, Gil was at loose ends. In interviews much later in his life, he claimed to have done some radio and TV scores during this period. Though there is little documentation to support this, it may well be true; the busier studio arrangers often farmed out work under the table. He also continued to do various work for vocalists, though he never considered himself a true vocal arranger—despite the numerous vocal arrangements he had done for Skinnay Ennis, the Hope radio show, and Claude Thornhill's band, both before and after the war. "I learned about the pacing of singer's songs. My pacing up until then had been orchestral, not vocal," he told Nat Hentoff in 1957. Gil didn't seem to find this work musically challenging, except in a trade sense. "I learned to cross voices so that an arrangement that was good in Erie, Pennsylvania, for five voices could be used for 20 musicians on TV."[1]

Personally, too, Gil seemed a little at sea. Some close friends felt that his relationship with Lillian was difficult, though everything appeared to be fine. While Gil constantly worked on his musical development, his avid curiosity led him into many other areas, including psychoanalysis and the other arts. He saw himself as always learning, though the path was not always straight.

There are two extremes in character structure as far as learning is concerned. Some people learn how to do something but they don't need it then; they put it away until the time when they need it. Others, like me, they only learn to do something when they need it and can't store it away. If I suddenly need something, I'll just stop everything and read about it for two or three weeks—steady, steady, steady. I have to have it then. That's the way I work—the way I am.[2]

In the late 1950s, for instance, Gil became interested in the work of Wilhelm Reich, a controversial psychoanalyst whose books were banned in the United States in 1954 and who died in a federal prison in Maine in 1957. Reich's proactive body-centered approach to therapy fascinated many artists and intellectuals, including actor Orson Bean, writer Saul Bellow, and artist William Steig.[3] "I was so amazed with his [Reich's] writing and all," Gil said, "that for three weeks I sat down in my place and read everything he ever wrote. I couldn't do anything else. I had to have it."[4]

ı' Iı I

Starting in early 1956, some opportunities came Gil's way, and his professional life began to improve. Some were for arrangements for instrumental jazz albums, but most of his work that year was still for vocalists.

George Avakian asked Gil to do some arrangements for a then unknown singer named Johnny Mathis. Avakian was then head of two departments at Columbia, Popular Albums and International. He first heard the nineteen-year-old singer at a San Francisco theater in the summer of 1955. He spotted star quality right away and signed Mathis immediately, but told him he needed much coaching. Mathis, who also happened to be an Olympic-class high jumper, was torn between a career in sports and one in entertainment. The following year Avakian scheduled the singer's first record dates in New York.

Avakian had first met Gil when the Thornhill band was recording for Columbia in the late 1940s, and they struck up a friendship. Knowing Gil was scuffling, Avakian hired him among a few other arrangers to work on material for Mathis's first album. Avakian knew

Gil could write for singers and—hoping to save money—also knew
that Gil could arrange for a small band so that it would sound like
a large ensemble. When the Olympic trials for high jump and hur-
dles conflicted with the recording dates, Mathis skipped the trials
and came to New York for the first session, on March 21, 1956. Gil
arranged and conducted three songs—"Love, Your Magic Spell Is
Everywhere," "It Might as Well Be Spring," and "Easy to Love"—
which appeared on Mathis's first album, *Johnny Mathis,* the singer's
most jazz-oriented album. By the next year, a string of popular hits
with lush backgrounds, starting with "Wonderful, Wonderful," made
Mathis the biggest-selling male vocalist after Frank Sinatra. As Mathis's star rose, Gil failed to capitalize on the connection—or couldn't.
As the episode with the Patti Page show revealed, hustling in the
studio world was neither Gil's forte nor his interest. The Mathis
recording, however, did put Gil back in contact with George Avakian.

Gil's next opportunity, an instrumental jazz arrangement, was
for an album inspired by the Miles Davis Nonet.

The recording came about in part because of the revitalization
in the jazz record market that followed the standardization of the
twelve-inch high-fidelity LP, with stereo LP technology waiting in
the wings (stereo tape for recording was now available, and most
record labels were using multitrack recorders). Jazz and classical
music were natural genres for long-playing pieces that suited the
extended format, and the major record labels—particularly Columbia and RCA Victor—were suddenly on the lookout for new voices
and new ideas. "Concept" albums—hot and easily marketable—led
to a surge of recordings by jazz artists, many hardly known outside
of New York.

One such artist, vibraphonist and composer/arranger Teddy
Charles, recorded his debut album for Atlantic in January 1956.
Charles, a member of Charles Mingus's Jazz Composers Workshop
(another member was Teo Macero, later Davis's producer at Columbia), had recently done all the arranging for a Miles Davis album
produced by Mingus. He fronted a tentet for his Atlantic album,
an expensive proposition that testified to the label's willingness to
go out on a limb. Charles admired Gil and hired him to arrange one
selection. Gil chose the standard "You Go to My Head" and completely reharmonized the song, taking advantage of the spectrum

of overtones created by the vibraphone. He used upper structure chords to play off those overtones in a way that stretched out the harmonies until they bordered on the atonal—except for the bass line, which basically followed the song's original harmonic structure. The breadth of the harmonic structures, the serpentine boppish background lines, and the oblique washes of color were essential qualities of Gil's writing even then.[5]

Two months later, alto player Hal McKusick, an active studio musician who expressed bop-generated ideas with the even-tempered sound of the "cool," asked Gil to write arrangements for yet another Nonet-inspired album, the debut LP in RCA Victor's Jazz Workshop series. Again, Gil was hired not through his own hustling but because McKusick admired his work.

The RCA Jazz Workshop series, begun by producer Jack Lewis, was in much the same vein as Pete Rugolo's for Capitol and likewise the result of the industry's hunger for fresh product. Lewis chose "cool" musicians whose subdued, chamberlike music had proved so popular, as played by the Modern Jazz Quartet and Gerry Mulligan's pianoless quartet. Jack Lewis's choices were not "name" artists. Like Rugolo's, the recordings did not succeed commercially—most (including McKusick's) are out of print.

McKusick's album, recorded on April 4, 1956, featured an octet and included two original compositions by Evans and three by George Russell, with arrangements by the respective composers. McKusick's alto sax was the predominantly featured voice, though Art Farmer on flugelhorn played a prominent role. The rhythm section consisted of two guitars, bass, and drums. Bill Barber's tuba, as previously in Gil's work, played several roles: it bubbled up with the bass at the bottom of an ensemble line, or added a surprising counter melody.

"Gil was extremely important to all of this," McKusick said. "I had taken Lee Konitz's chair in Claude's band in 1949, and that was where I got to know Gil and Gerry. Those rehearsals were really something. Gil would start to rehearse us and then he'd go lie down at the other end of the hall; he'd go into some kind of reclining meditation and let all that sound just sink in."[6]

"Blues for Pablo," written in tribute to a fallen fighter in the Spanish Civil War, successfully uses alternating themes and rhyth-

mic feels—in this case, Spanish bolero and swing—a practice that
would become more common in jazz as the 1950s progressed. The
composition juxtaposes a Spanish-inflected minor theme and an
extended major blues, swinging loosely from a half-time feel to
straight 4/4 and back. The opening theme, complete with tremolo,
derives from the opening measures of Falla's *Three-Cornered Hat*
(this theme also appears, somewhat altered, in the ending of
Evans's arrangement of "La Paloma"). A Mexican folk song
inspired the other main theme. To Gil's astonishment, the musicians found the quirky rhythm difficult for improvisation. "Now,
the kind of rhythmic changes that tune went through are very
common in jazz. But at that time, I remember bringing in a number in 3/4 and someone said, 'I couldn't improvise in *three*'—my
goodness!"[7]

Evans's "Jambangle" has an AABA structure with some odd-
length transitional phrases. In performance the song sounds sim-
pler than it is—very reminiscent of some of the writing for the
Davis Nonet. It opens with a blues-based ten-bar AA section,
played with a jaunty boogie-woogie feel that might have sprung
from Gil's days playing for strippers at the Nut Club in Greenwich
Village.

Neither the sound quality nor the overall performances are
optimal on this album. The Evans pieces sound charming but
have a slightly ragged quality. Nonetheless, the significance of the
album lies in the writing, which exemplifies the kind of struc-
tural development that Gil and George Russell were after. Their
work balances the written with the improvised and strives for a
spontaneous feeling in the scored ensemble passages to lend them
an improvised quality as well. It is particularly interesting to com-
pare these Evans arrangements with the expanded versions he
wrote the following year, which feature Miles Davis and soprano
saxophonist Steve Lacy in much larger and more complex orchestral settings.[8] They evolved from sketches to polished, finely
honed large-scale works.

Jack Lewis also recorded two other musicians whose work was
directly linked to the Nonet: Johnny Carisi and George Russell.
Carisi's Workshop album (which was never released) includes his
own version of "Israel" (one of the most lauded recordings by the

Nonet) and "Springsville." His octet plays the latter piece in a deliberate medium tempo, cleanly delineating the score's layered entrances, ambiguous tonality, and winsome theme. "Springsville" would, a year later, become far more celebrated as an Evans arrangement for *Miles Ahead*, the first collaboration by Miles and Gil for Columbia Records. Russell's contributions to McKusick's record led to his own Jazz Workshop LP, an excellent recording and a vivid sampling of Russell's theories in practice.[9]

Gil's next project was for an album by Helen Merrill, the first album he arranged in its entirety.[10] An up-and-coming twenty-six-year-old nightclub singer in 1956, Merrill projected an image of ultra musicality, intimacy, and sophistication: a cool-inspired vocalist. Gil clearly conceived of the album as a cohesive whole, a natural extension of his own tendency to paint on as large a canvas as was available. It was a professional turning point: from now on, he would work on an album scale.

Merrill, who had spent countless hours as a teenager checking out the rehearsal bands at Nola studios, was friendly with several prominent young jazz players, including Clifford Brown and Miles Davis. She was thus picky when it came to sidemen. On her second album, she had insisted on using Clifford Brown to head up a sextet, for which Quincy Jones was the arranger. For her third album, *Dream of You*, she insisted on having Gil Evans arrange the entire album. Bob Shad, Merrill's producer, strongly resisted. Aware of Gil's slow working habits and penchant for large ensembles, he dreaded going over budget and allotted recording time and pressed Merrill to accept a piano trio accompaniment—at most a sextet—instead. She refused, and Gil got a guarded carte blanche.

Shad's fears did come to pass—Gil's arrangements for *Dream of You* required up to four horns and five strings plus a four-piece rhythm section, a total of thirteen sidemen, among them such first-rate artists as trumpeter Art Farmer, guitarist Barry Galbraith, trombonist Jimmy Cleveland, pianist Hank Jones, and bassist Oscar Pettiford. The extravagance was unheard of for a young vocalist who had yet to score a hit. And while the recording was scheduled for three sessions in June 1956, it required an extra session, though the fault was partly Shad's. He interrupted a session that was going very well to tell the musicians about Clifford Brown's death, and the musicians found it impossible to continue. "Gil was very upset with him about that," recalled Merrill. "He [Shad] could have waited to tell us, so we could continue with our work."

Gil's arrangements for *Dream of You* drew out the best in everyone's sound. Merrill's clear voice, with its dead-on intonation and phrasing, is the featured instrument, the focal point. Each lyric phrase is accompanied by a fine stroke of color from the ensemble, underscored at times with a hint of rhythmic uplift or a tremolo in the strings, but without becoming too cute or literal. Gil recycles a few of his pet sounds, textures, and motifs. In "Where Flamingos Fly," he reuses the Spanish rhythm accented with tambourine from "Blues for Pablo." Four years later, Evans rearranged "Where Flamingos Fly" (a field song from Alabama) as an instrumental; this piece became a staple in Evans's repertoire, performed with wholly different orchestras and instruments over the years.[11]

On *Dream of You* Gil approached every piece afresh. Gil meticulously articulated almost every note of the string parts, as he did for Thornhill's musicians; these strings could swing, and their phrasing is perfect. Remarkably, it was the first and only album on which Gil used strings, though he later used Harry Lookovsky on tenor violin for other projects. Gil allocated to himself at least a few bars in each song to stretch out or fool around with an idea—this was his chorus. The entire album fits together like an elegant silk glove, with artfully designed crooked stitches here and there.

Merrill was never a commercial headliner, and *Dream of You* was not a commercial success. Still, she had—and still has—a devoted following. After work on the album was completed, she went to Europe as part of a jazz package tour that included Miles Davis's quintet and subsequently made three more albums for Mercury/EmArcy in the 1950s. Years later, she finally became aware that Evans knew she had insisted on Shad's hiring him. Evans never forgot the favor. What she didn't know was that at the time Gil had also stuck up for himself, which he—at times—shied away from doing. "The day that this guy tried to keep me from making that album with her, I called him all day long until I finally cornered him. I said, 'Listen, if you don't want me to make this album with Helen Merrill, you just try to stop us, because Helen really wants me to make it.' She stuck up for me, and she just insisted that he use me. Otherwise I would never have gotten that job. He was just being awful."[12]

Dream of You, now on CD, is still in print. A few months before Gil's death, Merrill and a more enthusiastic producer were able to fulfill a longtime fantasy of reuniting Merrill and Evans. In 1987 they rerecorded *Dream of You*; the arrangements sound as fresh and contemporary as ever, Merrill's voice deeper and stronger.

ı' ı,ı ı

Miles Davis's career, meanwhile, took a different path, one that has been thoroughly documented and scrutinized. Gil and Miles had last worked together in 1948 during the formation of the Nonet, though Gil was not present at any of the Capitol recording sessions. In the next few years, Davis worked with several notable musicians, black and white, including Tadd Dameron, Thelonious Monk, Sonny Rollins, Lee Konitz, and Stan Getz. But by far the most significant development was that Davis—who had performed, traveled, and hung out for years with addicts Charlie Parker and Dameron without becoming involved with hard drugs—was now hooked on heroin himself. The addiction took its toll on Davis, as it did on many other musicians during this time, including Gerry Mulligan, Stan Getz, Chet Baker, Anita O'Day, and several members of Woody Herman's band. The press loudly trumpeted each arrest, magnifying the damage to careers. Davis was soon gigging only sporadically; by 1952 his behavior and performances had become so erratic that his recording contract with Prestige was, for the moment at least, not renewed.[13]

Meanwhile, Clifford Brown's rapid emergence as a new star on trumpet seemed to herald the decline of cool and to revitalize the language of bop (Clifford was also held up as a new role model—a "clean" virtuoso). By 1954 many people thought Davis was washed up, personally and musically.

That year, however, Davis underwent a dramatic turnaround. In a much-told story, he went cold turkey on his own, moved back to New York, teamed up again with Prestige, and recorded an innovative and well-received album called *Walkin'*. Davis made a thrilling appearance at the first Newport Jazz Festival in summer 1955, at

which Aram Avakian urged his brother George to sign Davis to a
Columbia contract immediately.

Musically, Davis had matured. Davis liked to profess baffle-
ment when interviewers confronted him with questions about his
supposed new directions, and would tell them, "I always play the
same." Yes and no. His sound had gelled—his spare use of notes,
deliberate emphasis on sonority, and tonal nuance added up to the
essence of cool. He was actively working at a new aesthetic with
his new quintet, with John Coltrane on tenor saxophone, yet these
changes were anything but disingenuous or chameleon-like. Davis
had an insatiable musical curiosity and could comfortably play
blues and soul, hard bop or cool, pursuing his own intuition and
ignoring the boundaries that so obsess music critics. Davis was on
the road to becoming a bona fide star, both for his musicianship
and for his demeanor. As writer Gary Giddins put it:

> Thus the warring subcultures, West Coast jazz (cool) and East
> Coast jazz (hard bop), had the same midwestern parent: one
> Miles Dewey Davis of Alton, Illinois. And though Davis rejected
> cool jazz, he came to personify jazz cool. Miles looked cool,
> dressed cool, and talked cool—in a guttural, foul-mouthed sort
> of way. His posture was cool as he approached the mike or
> turned away from it. His notes were cool fat voice-like plums
> sustained in a siege of meditation or serrated arpeggios ripped
> into infinity. Cool, too, were his rests, those stirring oases
> enacted with flashing eyes and shrugged shoulders. Miles was
> an ongoing musical drama. In the world of Marlon Brando and
> John Osborne, he was the angry young trumpeter: handsome,
> unpredictable, and smart, driving fast cars and squiring beauti-
> ful women. Miles was the first subject of a *Playboy* interview.
> Miles didn't need a last name. Miles was an idiom unto himself.[14]

In 1956, the year he reunited with Gil, Davis was not yet an
icon, not yet the jazz musician people who didn't even like jazz listened to, not yet a national symbol of cool or the prince of darkness written up in *Playboy* and *Esquire*. Davis was still tied to a
contract with the small jazz label Prestige, though Avakian did
succeed in signing him to an exclusive contract with Columbia in

fall 1955. This was a coup for Davis. While small labels such as Prestige offered musicians the opportunity to record, the low budgets sometimes brought painful restrictions. "We used to call Prestige the sausage factory," said George Avakian. "They'd just cram all this music into a session, cut the musicians off after three hours, and see what they got."

According to the terms of Avakian's deal with Prestige, Columbia Records could not release any recordings by Davis until 1957, when Davis's contract with Prestige was up. But Avakian already knew the powerfully cool image that Davis could project and had in mind what Davis's debut recordings on Columbia would be like.

Avakian had two ideas. The first was obvious—to record Davis's working quintet, which, he hoped, would stay together long enough to showcase at least some of the recorded music live when the album came out. Eager to get his new star into the studio, he organized the first Columbia session for the Davis quintet in October 1955. This material was included in 'Round Midnight, Davis's first Columbia LP, released in 1957. The title track, recorded in September 1956, has long been held up as one of the greatest ballad performances in jazz. Jack Chambers, in his biography of Davis, dated that September session as the musical reunion of Gil and Miles; he credits Evans as the arranger for " 'Round Midnight."[15] It's a hard call—it might as easily have been Davis's idea; both he and the members of his quintet quite adeptly came up with more than the standard "head-solo-solo-solo-head" small-combo arrangements.

Avakian's second idea was more farsighted and ambitious—to place Miles in a large ensemble setting. This idea, eventually to materialize as the album Miles Ahead, had several sources. One was Avakian's admiration for the music of the Miles Davis Nonet. A second was Avakian's genuinely eclectic taste and his experience in producing a wide variety of music, from mainstream pop to contemporary classical—he had been the first person to record the music of John Cage. A third was Avakian's involvement with "third stream music," another example of his open ears. In the mid-1950s Avakian lived near Gunther Schuller on Manhattan's Upper West Side. Schuller and former Nonet member John Lewis had formed an orchestra called the Brass Society (later to become Orchestra

USA, eventually managed by Avakian) to commission and promote new compositions that attempted to fuse elements of jazz and classical music. The Society also dedicated itself to thoroughly rehearsing any music it performed. Schuller convinced Avakian to produce an album of music commissioned by the society and asked if Davis was interested in performing two pieces requiring a jazz trumpet soloist. Davis agreed. Avakian said, "Another musician might have said, 'Ah, I don't want any of that crap. It's so phony!' Miles was interested in all kinds of music. He was the perfect person. He certainly surprised me by bringing out a flugelhorn, because I'd never heard him play flugelhorn. He was very effective on it."[16]

Today, the "third stream" idea has become mainstream—musical borrowings of all kinds have become commonplace. Much of the music on *Music for Brass* and its successor *Modern Jazz Concert* holds up as imaginative and compelling twentieth-century music. One of the reasons Avakian was inclined to produce *Music for Brass* in the first place was because he knew that the Brass Society had indeed rehearsed this music well beforehand, in preparation for a concert that never took place. Miles's brilliant performance, both as ensemble player and soloist, in John Lewis's *Three Little Feelings* and J. J. Johnson's *Poem for Brass* solidified Avakian's concept of Davis's expansive abilities. Avakian was, typically, both artistically and commercially motivated; his dual-edged sensibility made him successful. He was convinced that setting Davis's trumpet in a large ensemble—with music that was even more jazz-oriented than the above compositions—would attract a whole new audience for the trumpet player.

Avakian approached Davis with the concept of recording in a large orchestral jazz setting for his next Columbia project. Davis, though intensely involved in the work of his quintet, was still interested in the Nonet style of improvised/structured music with its rich array of textures; he liked the idea. A large ensemble called for a first-rate arranger. As far as Avakian was concerned, the only conceivable candidates were Gil and Schuller.

With no hesitation Davis chose Gil. Even during Davis's "down time," the trumpet player professed to Nat Hentoff and others that Gil was his favorite writer. Coincidentally, Helen Merrill, while touring with Davis in Europe in June 1956, had raved about Gil's work on her own new record and suggested that Miles—now in a more prominent position and with more leverage—use Gil as an arranger.

By late 1956, the record's concept was approved by Columbia's bigwigs. Avakian met with Gil and Miles to discuss the project, which Avakian had already entitled *Miles Ahead*. "I told Gil, 'Anything goes,'" said Avakian. "He looked at me as if I were crazy. He'd gotten so used to being told that he couldn't use more than eleven musicians!"

ı' ıı ı

Gil and Davis had had very little contact since the conception and formation of the Davis Nonet. Years later, each would say that they continued to be friends during the period from 1950 to 1956, but they did not see one another socially and had nothing to do with each other professionally, though Gil occasionally showed up at Miles's gigs. Yet Gil exerted some influence over Davis. Miles, at a certain point in his struggle to kick his heroin habit, thought of the boxer Sugar Ray Robinson as a role model because of Ray's extraordinary sense of discipline and competitive edge. Davis knew that Robinson, in turn, had a mentor of sorts, a father figure spirit guide whom the famous boxer called his "soldier."

> Ray was cold and he was the best and he was everything I wanted to be in 1954. I had been disciplined when I first came to New York. All I had to do was go back to the way I had been before I got trapped in all that bullshit dope scene. So that's when I stopped listening to just anybody. I got myself a soldier just like Sugar Ray had; and my man for talking to was Gil Evans. Of all the people I knew, Gil Evans was one of the only ones who could pick up on what I was thinking musically. Like when he would come to hear me play, he would ease up next to me and say, "Miles, you know you have a nice open sound on your trumpet. Why don't you use it more?" And then he'd be gone, just like that, and I'd be left thinking about what he had said. I would decide right then and there that he was right. [17]

The making of *Miles Ahead* offered an opportunity for Gil and Davis to reconnect musically and personally. Late in 1956, the two started meeting regularly to discuss the choice of music, the sidemen, and so forth. Avakian confidently left the major artistic decisions to them; his only condition with respect to the repertoire was that there be a composition entitled "Miles Ahead," to promote the album. At Columbia, the extra-musical nuts and bolts of an album were extremely well thought out: the title, the concept of the repertoire, the cover, and so forth, all had to be decided upon months before anyone set foot in the recording studio.[18] Avakian's title embodied the image he wanted to convey: that Miles was ahead, way ahead of everybody. This was both a sincere musical judgment and a sign of Avakian's record-industry savvy.

Once the recording dates were set, for May 1957, Gil set to work with a rapidity that astounded everyone who knew him. Avakian felt the seemingly smooth progress may have been in part because "Gil must have had a lot of pent-up ideas.... I got to feel that in the back of his mind he'd wanted to do something like this one day."

The opportunity dovetailed with Gil's maturity as an artist and with Miles's maturation of sound and style. Skilled and creative though he was, Gil's life as an arranger thus far had been essentially as a pen for hire. This was different. The artistic direction was his and Miles's but mainly his: he had a green light on the number of musicians and on the repertoire. Moreover, working for Columbia Records had distinct advantages: state-of-the-art equipment; the use of the 30th Street Studio, an old church refurbished as a recording studio, whose sound and spatial quality were consistently excellent; the best engineers—the works.

One can't underestimate the significance to Gil of working with "sound" innovators such as Davis. Evans was almost a complete romantic in this respect—he idolized, followed, and had longed to write for the Armstrongs, Lester Youngs, and Miles Davises of this world. Gil's surge of rapidity may have been due to his desire to hear the sound world he was creating for Miles as soon as possible.

A more tangible reason is that Gil selected three compositions for which scores existed: "Springsville" by John Carisi, which Carisi had arranged for his own octet; Delibes's "Maids of Cadiz," which Gil had arranged for Thornhill but which was never recorded; and his own "Blues for Pablo."[19] He reworked the existing material completely, but the fact that it already existed on paper gave him a slight edge. So did using Ahmad Jamal's composition "New Rhumba"; Evans essentially transcribed pianist Jamal's trio version for Miles and the ensemble, including Jamal's solo. (Davis, then an acknowledged Jamal admirer, chose this piece himself.) The remaining selections, by Dave Brubeck, Kurt Weill, and J. J. Johnson, were all contemporary, giving the entire album an up-to-the-minute feel.

Miles composed the title track, "Miles Ahead," though one might presume that Gil had input. Indeed, of all the selections on the album, it is the most reminiscent of the *Birth of the Cool* recordings, particularly of "Boplicity," Davis's and Evans's first jointly composed work.

The resulting eclectic mix of compositions/composers was a stretch for a jazz album, or anything resembling a big band album. The album broke ground in several ways, though its musical and technical innovations sound commonplace now.

For one thing, Gil conceived of the entire album as a suite and wrote segues for each piece, including a seamless transition between the original LP's side breaks, one that was never heard until the first CD of the album was released in 1987. Avakian thought Gil's idea for a continuous performance might have stemmed—at least in part—from his awareness of a couple of albums from Columbia's *Piano Moods* series in which the material was programmed like the old radio shows, on the basis of two related fourteen-minute segments. "It wasn't an idle idea," said Avakian. "Surprisingly, he didn't tell me in advance."

A technical innovation on *Miles Ahead* was the use of overdubs, a rarity in 1957. An entire session was devoted to them. Avakian was one of the first producers to suggest this option to instrumental soloists, and Miles was happy to take advantage of it. His solos were overdubbed on four selections, and one can hear him varying his approach on the numerous rehearsal takes that were issued as part of the 1998 box set *Miles Davis–Gil Evans: The Complete Columbia Studio Recordings*. The option to overdub his solos freed Davis up considerably and allowed the ensemble to concentrate on getting the basic tracks down, which meant some very demanding performances by the orchestra.

The album was so well performed and recorded that it is easy to forget that the studio bands for this and the Davis–Evans collaborations to follow were essentially pickup orchestras. The musicians involved, however, were the best studio musicians in town, worked together frequently, and were a mix of classically trained ("legit") players and versatile jazz musicians. All were crack sight-readers, and the reed players were expected to double on several instruments.

These were not cookie-cutter musicians. Gil assigned each musician his part for each tune and wrote that person's name on each part; he clearly visualized who would play lead or what doubling instrument at all times. When talking with journalists about these sessions years later, Gil often understated how difficult the sessions must have been, even for such accomplished professionals.

> In the old days, you used to be able to make a record in three three-hour sessions. I made the one with Helen Merrill, the ones with Miles, with no rehearsals. We made the *Miles Ahead* album in three sessions. We could do that because everybody had that idiom under their fingers. The actual notes were different, but the idiom was so much the same that they could play it right off. A man like Ernie Royal—he could just play it right off because he was so experienced in that.[20]

Again, this is Gil's modesty talking—and his kind memory. The most recent discographies for the Davis–Evans albums list all of the Davis–Evans LPs as having four recording sessions, not to mention countless hours editing tape the old-fashioned way, with razor blades. This was new music not being performed anywhere else; the only rehearsals took place at the recording sessions. Early on, Avakian started "sneaking takes" because of the time pressure in the studio and because he felt Gil wore the musicians out. "He [Gil] didn't have to be as meticulous as he was—in the writing or execution. He drove the musicians crazy on *Miles Ahead* by rehearsing them constantly on the troublesome places. The trumpet players in particular would pull me aside and say, 'Tell him to hold off, my chops are gone.' There were one or two sessions

where we didn't get that much done because he spent so much
time rehearsing."[21]

Trombonist Joe Bennett, who played on all three of the Davis–
Evans albums, recalled the sessions actually being double dates,
or two three-hour sessions a day.

> It wasn't because the guys couldn't play the parts. It was because
> Miles's guys [Paul Chambers and Philly Joe Jones] wouldn't
> show up until two or three hours after the call. They had to call
> standby guys. Jimmy Cobb actually played more drums on
> *Porgy and Bess* than Philly because he was there. And Milt Hin-
> ton was called to cover for Paul Chambers.
>
> Conducting, he [Gil] was very precise. He wasn't mean, he
> was very particular. His idea of intensity was not loud—most
> players think when something gets intense it gets loud. Gil's
> idea was just the opposite. He'd want you to *think* you were
> playing loud, but play soft. And his harmonies were so compli-
> cated. You'd be playing an F natural, the guy next to you would
> be playing an F#—you'd swear there were wrong notes, and
> he'd say, "That's *exactly* what I want." [22]

The rehearsal takes reveal Gil's assertiveness and perfectionism: his insistence on the score's dynamics ("Is that as soft as you
can play?"), and articulation (bah-de-dah-*dah*). There are numerous instances of Gil striving for a better sound, playing around to
see what worked best; experimenting with the use of piano on
some selections, for example, or deleting certain passages or test-
ing out alternate background parts.

The original LP is a remarkable composite, having many more
splices than most albums at the time because of the surfeit of takes.
Gil kept meticulous track of every take and solo. He knew which
source he wanted to draw from in every instance, and he directed
the entire editing process, which was more extensive than usual
for a jazz recording. In addition, some of the edited material was
drawn from tapes recorded on a new three-track machine that
Ampex had lent Columbia for the engineers to check out; tape ran
on the Ampex machine for part of a couple of the sessions. Consequently there were even more editing options and more confusion

when the first CD was issued in 1987, under Teo Macero's direction. At that time the three-track tapes could not be located in Columbia's files and Macero had to edit the material using alternate sources.

The suitelike nature of the album was achieved through Evans's dual long/short focus. He saw each selection on its own and as part of an extended work with an overall dramatic rhythm; the orchestral colorings help tie things together. The performance quality is crisp—fast and light with no vibrato—and the dynamics have the stop-on-a-dime dynamic precision Gil insisted on, with full *forte* sections by the entire orchestra a rarity. The textures and instrumental combinations shift as soon as a listener begins to decipher them; at times one has the impression of hearing a far more intimate ensemble—a small combo headed up by Miles. The fact that Miles play on flugelhorn adds a burnished luster to the entire album.

"Springsville," the opening selection, remains true to composer John Carisi's melody and form. Its far brisker tempo gives it a propulsive lift through the tune's chromaticized shifting tonalities. It has a musical urgency lacking in Carisi's own recording, and it goes against the "cool" veneer of much of the album. Likewise, Delibes's "Maids of Cadiz" is treated counter to the feverish Carmenesque interpretation it usually receives and is slowed down to a sensual stasis. The other ballads—Kurt Weill's "My Ship," J. J. Johnson's "Lament," and Bobby Troup's "The Meaning of the Blues"—evoke a palpable yearning quality, one that would run through a good deal of Evans's and Davis's work in the future.

Gil reached an elevated artistic plateau with the album *Miles Ahead* in several concrete ways. First, his penchant for mixing unusual combinations of brass and woodwinds was exploited to wondrous effect on this album, an effect that was only enhanced by the superior ensemble and Columbia's recording facility.

More significant, Evans's ability to orchestrate a mood—his legacy from Thornhill—was heightened by Davis's ability to respond to the ambiance Gil created for him. This was the essence of their artistic symbiosis. To the degree that Gil would be tailoring the compositions and arrangements for Miles, an operatic term might best apply: *puntature* (plural), from the verb *puntare*, which means "to point." Verdi and other Italian composers used the term to refer to arias or portions of arias that had been changed to optimally serve or "point" to a particular singer. Gil often did exactly that with aspects of his arrangements, especially for Miles Davis; his scores were molded, pointed toward Miles. In doing so, Gil recomposed the compositions—or good portions of them—and crafted them into new, cohesively structured works.

ı¹ Iı I

The new level of mastery Gil achieved on *Miles Ahead* permeated the next six albums, all recorded in the next two and a half years, that Gil scored in their entirety, including two other large-orchestra albums with Miles and four albums recorded under Gil's sole leadership. Each album would explore different themes, different sources, and different content.

But the three collaborations with Davis—*Miles Ahead, Porgy and Bess*, and *Sketches of Spain*—all share another operatic feature. Gil's arrangements convey a story, with Davis's plaintive trumpet as the voice of every lead character, male and female: Porgy, Bess, the lover, the wanderer, the toreador, the dancer, the Pan Piper.

Porgy and Bess, Miles's and Gil's second large-scale collaboration, was recorded in August 1958. At the time, George Gershwin's folk opera was enjoying a comeback. The original 1935 Broadway production had closed after 124 performances—a successful run for an opera, but a Broadway flop—and a brief tour. Written by a white composer/songwriter strongly influenced by black music and jazz, it received rough treatment at the hands of some critics. Gershwin crisscrossed several sacred boundaries, creating a netherworld between opera and show music, symphonic jazz and Gullah spirituals. *Porgy* also provoked controversy among black critics, artists, and audiences: set in a lowdown wharf called Catfish Row, it raised troubling questions about authenticity and appropriation.

Though some of the songs, particularly "Summertime" and "It Ain't Necessarily So," became standard jazz and pop repertoire, the opera did not inspire a great deal of interest until 1943, when its revival on Broadway was hugely successful. From this time forward, in performance, a good deal of Gershwin's incidental music (between the songs) was often cut. The opera received a new surge of interest in 1952 when another revival (which launched the career of soprano Leontyne Price) toured internationally—including Russia—through 1958.

One spinoff was a Hollywood film with a sterling cast of black stars—Sidney Poitier, Dorothy Dandridge, Sammy Davis, Jr., Pearl Bailey, and a young Diahann Carroll—accompanied by a sea of advance publicity. The film's production and release (June 1959) coincided with the rapidly growing Civil Rights movement. Once again *Porgy* attracted criticism in the black community due to increasing sensitivity to racial stereotyping in the world at large and particularly in the entertainment industry. Still, for many black actors—including Miles Davis's then girlfriend, Frances Taylor—a role in *Porgy and Bess* was an enviable job. Whatever the political climate, the music never lost its luster with jazz musicians, especially in the wake of Miles's interpretation.

Capitalizing on the buzz surrounding the film and the success of *Miles Ahead*, which made a follow-up logical and viable, Calvin Lampley at Columbia approached Miles about recording an interpretation of *Porgy and Bess* with Gil.[23] (Avakian had left the company by this time, and Lampley was his successor.) Initially, Davis was reluctant to do so; he knew that several other jazz interpretations were in the works. Years later, Davis said that it was *his* idea to do *Porgy and Bess*; he attended the City Center production several times because Frances was in it ("that's where I got the idea to do the music").[24] At any rate, Davis and Gil eventually decided to make it their next collaboration.

Gil reconstructed *Porgy and Bess* both narratively and musically. He reordered Gershwin's songs almost completely, stayed close to some, considerably recomposed others, and left out those that didn't fit well in this rendering. Gil's version opens with the ominous "Buzzard Song," which sets a brooding tone for the entire album, in striking contrast to Gershwin's opener, "Lullaby/Summertime." The ballad "Bess, You Is My Woman Now" is now the second song, effectively condensing the development and impact of the love story. Abandoning the narrative structure of Gershwin's song sequence, Gil reinforces his own by fusing together various melodies, fragments, and incidental motifs of Gershwin's, or using them as developmental motifs for his own arrangements. Evans omitted "I Got Plenty of Nuttin'" but used the bridge as the introduction for "It Ain't Necessarily So"; a woodwind motif from "Requiem" became the basic motif for Evans's "Summertime" (this version would be popularized even more in the early 1960s by the vocal group Lambert, Hendricks and Ross). Gil included one composition of his own, "Gone" (later retitled "Orgone"), a bristling uptempo jazz number, with a lengthy improvisation by Miles and a crackling drum solo by Philly Joe Jones. It is the emotional inversion of its inspiration, Gershwin's dirgelike "Gone, Gone, Gone," in which Gil's full use of the ensemble makes it sound like a symphony orchestra. Gil created a cohesive new story that, despite its lack of plotted narrative, retained and even intensified the pathos of Gershwin's original—an extended meditation on love and loss.

Gil's *Porgy and Bess* is a marvel of post-bop modern jazz arranging. As symphonic as some of the writing is, a bluesy quality still permeates it thanks to Miles's playing. Furthermore, the harmonic language Gil used in a good portion of *Porgy and Bess* was prescient of the modal harmonies that Miles was starting to inject into his small band music. The score's drift toward modal writing—hovering around a particular scale and tonal center— and Gil's tendency toward polytonality gave the music a moody ambiguity that was becoming an ever more refined aspect of Evans's art. Some of the elements he used to accomplish his harmonic colorings, such as ostinato figures and pedal points, had their roots in his work for Thornhill.

A sustained pedal point streams through "Buzzard Song," unifying the harmonically complex vocal part with the lengthy modal vamp over which Miles improvised. Gil used this unifying device similarly in "Arab Dance" (1942). The tremolo that introduces "Prayer" thrusts this piece, a masterwork of call-and-response, into a modal dirge that builds into a cry of tragic proportions as the orchestra swells and fades in contrary motion. Gil explores a similar range of sound and emotion in "My Man's Gone Now." He uses tremolos, glissandos, and out-and-out swoops and hollers to extraordinary effect. The "cry" is what Evans sought to orchestrate, a universal cry. In his later work, the cry steers the music to the verge of chaos before its resolution.

The orchestrations are remarkable. The tuba is often doubled with Paul Chambers's bass, or improvises over a Greek chorus of three flutes, one an alto. The four trombones pops off chord clusters—including half-step intervals—like a jazz pianist. Flutes and trombones often play together, the inner voices filling themselves in with the overtones emanating from the low brass. Miles himself uses a battery of sounds—open flugelhorn, muted trumpet, and cracked notes; as in *Miles Ahead*, he sporadically joins the ensemble to play lead. In certain sections, Cannonball Adderley's alto is the very discernible voice leading the woodwinds.

The brooding quality of the Davis–Evans interpretation of *Porgy and Bess* invited the charge that Evans's arrangements did not swing. John S. Wilson wrote:

> The Davis–Evans collaboration is colored by the now familiar slowly shifting panels of sound of Evans's arrangements and the plaintive, occasionally uncertain trumpet playing that Davis affects in this context.... the steady accumulation of slow, mournful sounds added to Davis's shaky breathiness results in dullness. One begins to suspect that Evans is determined to dig the same musical grave for himself that he and Claude Thornhill dug for Thornhill's band. [25]

Jazz historian Martin Williams went even further. Though "Evans has frequently provided a fascinating and effective setting for Davis's improvisations," Williams wrote, he "does not utilize the rhythmic idiom of modern jazz."[26]

But on up-tempo or mid-tempo portions of this album, drummer Philly Joe Jones and bassist Paul Chambers uplift the entire orchestra, delivering the light yet insistent swing that characterized Davis's small band records of the 1950s and epitomized modern jazz swing. Jones has his own cameo on "Gone," a crackling solo with a rhythmic motif that is echoed in Gil's finale, "There's a Boat That's Leaving Soon for New York." (Gershwin's finale was "Oh, Lawd, I'm on My Way.") In addition to the propulsion the ensemble gets from Jones and Chambers, each piece has a multitude of inner rhythms, its own momentum, its way of unfolding.

Bassist Paul Chambers was a mainstay on all three of the Evans–Davis albums (as well as in Davis's quintet from 1955 to 1962) and fulfilled an important role in Gil's writing. The bass provided a harmonic color base as well as a rhythmic one, a foundation for the shifting polyrhythms among the brass and woodwinds. Evans's opinion of him was sterling:

> There was nobody ever before or after Paul Chambers, he was such a glorious player. When he played up-tempo it was never the least bit choppy—he could hang onto the preceding note as long as possible before the next note so it was all connected, so smooth. And as far as the bow was concerned he was a natural. Most other jazz players, when they start to use the bow, their pitch would get touchy. Not Paul—he'd just pick up that bow like a swashbuckler.[27]

The recording of *Porgy and Bess*, like that of *Miles Ahead*, had its problems. One was created by the newness of stereo recording. Columbia Records had jumped on this new technology quickly, before various kinks had been worked out. Trombonist Joe Bennett remembered, "It was at the beginning of stereo recording. There were separation problems, they [the engineers] really didn't know much about how to set the band up. We were at that old church down on 30th Street. They had us sit in some kind of semicircle, and they placed the rhythm section in the middle. No matter what, there were always time lags from one side of the band to the other."[28]

The most serious problem, however, was due to the strange status of Miles's and Gil's collaboration within the recording world. Gil and Miles did not have a working nineteen-piece band or the luxury of playing this music before an audience regularly like Ellington, who had written several extended works in the late 1950s, or Charles Mingus, whose Jazz Workshop ensemble played his challenging material constantly. Gil's music was heard for the first time in the studio and was rehearsed one piece or a section at a time until a take could be made. The musicians were allotted little more than a one-shot opportunity to rehearse and record extremely complex music. Though Evans's musicians for the date

were among the world's best sightreaders, it was still daunting.
Said Bennett,

> I was so busy trying to stay out of trouble because Gil's writing
> was so difficult. The way he notated would push your talents to
> the limit—we were just trying to get through the parts. He'd
> hear all this stuff in his head and then he'd go ahead and write
> it and he'd go stark-raving out.
>
> It was an experience. There was no piano on these dates, so
> he'd [Gil] have two pages of trombones just playing comp
> chords behind Miles playing a jazz chorus. There'd be a dotted
> 1/16 rest coming on the upbeat, and pretty soon your eyes
> would cross, and some guy would come in wrong and you'd
> have to go back. At that time, there was no punch in, punch
> out—you went from the top to the bottom, or that part of the
> section. They didn't know that much about taking one guy's
> note out. You'd play from this number to that number, and it
> had to be correct before you'd go on to the next section.[29]

Several musical and technical problems become apparent in the
1998 Columbia remastered version and the alternate takes: uncertain
entrances, flubbed voicings, instances of stereo "time-lag," abrupt
edits. Gil was aware of these and once remarked that "one more
session would have cleared up most of the clinkers. Looking back
on it, I'm outraged at myself for not sticking up for my rights."[30]

Miles alone saw Gil's scores ahead of time. On all of the Davis–
Evans projects, the two met regularly to discuss the music—both
in the initial planning stages and as Gil was writing the arrangements. Even so, Davis had some bad moments in the studio and
later said that this was the most difficult thing he ever did. Joe
Bennett recalled, "Gil also had to deal with Miles, and Miles had
his own ideas about how the arrangements should sound and be
played. But my estimation of him rose greatly through those sessions. I remember walking by Miles's stand and just looked at his
part—just the chord symbol part was so complicated, and Miles
made sense of the whole thing."[31]

Still, the recording flaws on the Davis–Evans *Porgy and Bess*
album are negligible compared to the grandeur of the work. The

album, like *Miles Ahead*, fulfilled Avakian's initial vision of Davis's ability to become a crossover artist. People were starting to buy his albums whether they liked jazz or not. According to Jack Chambers's biography *Milestones*, *Porgy and Bess* was the biggest-selling Miles Davis album (one hundred thousand before the reissues on compact disc) until the release of Davis's *Bitches Brew* in 1971, which sold a phenomenal four hundred thousand copies. Working together on the album cemented Gil's and Miles's sense of themselves as collaborators. Their working rapport was easy, natural. People were already asking what the next project would be.

ı' Iı ı

In the two years since Davis had started recording for Columbia, the company realized it had hit upon a winning formula with its two albums a year featuring Miles Davis, a small band album and an orchestral collaboration with Gil Evans. *'Round Midnight*, *Miles Ahead*, *Milestones*, *Porgy and Bess*, and *Kind of Blue* are all synonymous with the best expression of modern jazz. The level of creative intensity that both Miles and Gil maintained during this period was an artistic coup. As Amiri Baraka wrote, "During the fifties years, Miles in a bop or hard bop context, and finally in his symmetrically exquisite quintets and sextets with Trane, later with Trane and Cannonball (1957–59), and in the fresh and lyrical Gil Evans collaborations created music at a level very few people ever approach, anywhere, anytime on a scale that needs a Duke or Billie or Armstrong or Monk to equal for aesthetic influence, length, and consistency."[32]

By 1958 Miles had become a full-fledged celebrity, a status that suited him and that the publicity and marketing machinery of Columbia Records helped him achieve and maintain. Goddard Lieberson, then president of Columbia Records, was an unusual CEO, a cultivated man who cared about artistic standards and culture. He was as committed to developing his jazz roster as he was to his classical artists, who at the time included no less a charismatic star than Leonard Bernstein. The jazz program at Columbia in those years was equally stellar: Duke Ellington, Billie Holiday, Dave Brubeck, and Erroll Garner were all Columbia artists, most of

whom had been brought in by Avakian, who left the label in early
1958. Miles was Columbia's coolest, hippest modernist. "The Black
Prince," Amiri Baraka notes, was his irresistible soubriquet. Said
Dan Morgenstern:

> Columbia was really willing to invest in Miles and he really
> benefited immensely from all the publicity. A woman named
> Debbie Ishlom was the head of publicity at Columbia. She did
> a whole "I Like Jazz" campaign, and she was brilliant at help-
> ing promote Miles's image. He was going the way of sports cars
> and elegant clothes anyway, and she took it and ran with it.
>
> If Gil had been a different kind of person, interested in
> promoting himself, he could have hopped on that Miles band-
> wagon, but you don't even see him on the album covers. That
> didn't concern him. *He* certainly wasn't concerned about
> publicity.[33]

Although Gil was never the subject of magazine articles in *Playboy* and *Esquire*, his work with Miles brought him long overdue
recognition in the jazz world and enabled him to record as a leader.
(The albums he made sans Miles during this time, discussed in the
next chapter, had a totally different ambience.) Even more important, Gil's enhanced reputation helped him to form and maintain a
twenty-piece rehearsal band that met fairly regularly at Nola Studios for about a year, which allowed him to expand his experiments
in musical border crossing. An eleven-piece version of this band
performed at Birdland for ten days in late 1958 and was part of
an eclectic lineup (Dinah Washington, Thelonious Monk Quartet) at the Apollo Theater in 1959. The band's main purpose, however, was as Gil's workshop. Soprano saxophonist Steve Lacy
recalled:

> Some of the scores were based on things he did for Thornhill—
> the Moussorgsky, Rimsky-Korsakov, an Indian folk song called
> "Punjab." These were very exciting arrangements and played
> by some of the best musicians in New York, who at that time
> could be coerced into coming and rehearsing for nothing because
> the music was so good. Of course there were standards too,

but mostly I remember those classical things. Indian music, classical music, jazz—it was all just music to him, really.... [For Gil], there were no departments in music.

Gil painted with his players. I felt like a color—a ribbon in this great spectrum. I'd never felt that before, and not much since then. It was a unique experience, to be a strand of color—there's no more you, there is just *it*.[34]

Gil may have wanted the rehearsal band to play his older scores, especially the "classical things," to refresh the orchestration ideas he had worked out with the Thornhill band over ten years earlier. Some of these, such as "Troubador" and "La Paloma," directly link to the textural ambiance, voicings, and harmonic language Gil incorporated into *Porgy and Bess* and would soon use on his next collaboration with Miles. Gil's innovations with Miles Davis did not appear full blown out of nowhere—he'd been working out his ideas for a long time.

Sketches of Spain, the third of the three ambitious albums in which Evans constructed an entire sound world for Miles Davis, reaches farther outside jazz territory than either *Miles Ahead* or *Porgy and Bess*. The impetus came from a recording Miles heard while visiting a friend in Los Angeles. The music was a little-known concerto for guitar, the *Concierto de Aranjuez* by Joaquin Rodrigo, a contemporary Spanish composer. Gil explained the evolution of the new record:

[W]e hadn't intended to make a Spanish album. We were just going to do the *Concierto de Aranjuez*. A friend of Miles gave him the only album in existence with that piece. He brought it back to New York and I copied the music off the record because there was no score. By the time we did that, we began to listen to other folk music, music played in clubs in Spain, where you could hear the glasses crashing and the guitars playing along, not paying any attention to all the racket. So we learned a lot from that and it ended up being a Spanish album. The Rodrigo, the melody is so beautiful. It's such a strong song. I was so thrilled with that.[35]

As it turned out, Miles and Gil ended up using only the second movement of the piece, the "Adagio," with a new middle section composed by Gil. The rest of the repertoire for *Sketches* consisted of "Will o' the Wisp" ("Cancion del Fuego fatuo"), an excerpt from Falla's sung ballet *El Amor Brujo*, and three compositions by Evans, inspired by flamenco music and South American folk music.

A Spanish-flavored album by a prominent modern jazz musician was novel at the time, decades before the record industry had latched onto "world music." Gil's tastes, however, had been all-encompassing for many years, and Miles was open to anything. Gil started listening to the music of Manuel de Falla as a twenty-year-old and had already expressed his interest in Spanish composers with several works. A recording has recently surfaced of Falla's "Ritual Fire Dance" (from *El Amor Brujo*) by the Santa Anita Army band, which was almost certainly an Evans arrangement (Gil was stationed at Santa Anita in 1943–44).[36] Gil arranged at least two other works by Spanish composers for Thornhill after the war: "La Paloma" by Sebastian Yradier and "Spanish Dance" by Enrique Granados. Evans's own "Blues for Pablo" (1956) takes its opening theme from Falla's *Three-Cornered Hat*.

Listening to a literal treatment of Rodrigo's "Adagio" (from the *Concierto de Aranjuez*), one can sense the attraction the piece held for Miles and Gil. The wavering melody for guitar has an improvised quality, and the "voice" of the guitar is beautifully interwoven with the orchestral writing—soloist and orchestra interact, converse.

The first section of Evans's arrangement has Miles playing a fairly faithful rendering of the guitar melody, but set in Evans's quasi-symphonic, quasi-jazz world of sound. Evans dressed up Rodrigo's more traditionally written orchestral voicings and spiced them up with dissonances, but he took his greatest liberty by inserting "his chorus" into the middle of the "Adagio." He constructed an interior vamp, which was far more connected to his own pieces, which come later in the album, than to the Rodrigo. This becomes more apparent as the motifs and other elements from this addition echo throughout the album. This section is propelled rhythmically by castanets and brushes, and finally builds back to a restatement of Rodrigo's main theme, with far darker colorings

and a deeper majesty than the original. It ends differently, disso-
nantly, in a staggered fashion, with traces of Rodrigo's work drifting
in and out.

Falla's *El Amor Brujo* (*Love, The Sorcerer*) is based on an Andalusian gypsy tale of a love triangle in which new lovers are thwarted
by the jealous ghost of the woman's former lover. In Falla's concert
version (of 1916), only a small portion of the orchestra accompanies
the vocalist on "Will o' the Wisp," imitating a guitar accompaniment. Gil transcribed the song for Miles and his ensemble, and for
the most part he used only small groupings of instruments. These,
once again, are mysterious, forming whole new sounds and voices.
The lead voice is muted Miles, coupled with bassoon, French horn,
and, at times, another muted trumpet that crosses parts with him.
Percussion, harp, arco bass, and tuba repeat a flamenco-styled
ostinato figure throughout, which ebbs and flows with the intensity
of the music. The woodwinds—clarinet, oboe, bassoon, bass clarinet,
and clarinet—all stretch to the extremes of their ranges, sounding
like Mideastern bagpipes rather than guitar.

Here, as in *Porgy and Bess*, Gil is the ultimate translator, trans-
ferring music and lyrics composed for the human voice to instrumental soloist and ensemble. It is the challenge of the soloist to
evoke the poetry of the lyrics, and this was Miles's particular talent. On "Will o' the Wisp" we hear his muted trumpet convey
the lyrics: "Woe to those black eyes that desired to see his flame at
play. Love is a will o' the wisp. You flee from him, he pursues you;
you call him, he runs off." Gil stays faithful to the song's original
form and brevity—a full two AABA choruses, with a brief interlude between them. However, instead of ending on Falla's optimistic major chord, Gil's ending vamp becomes more and more
dissonant and eerie, befitting the ghost's demise rather than the
new lover's triumph.

By filling out the rest of the album with his own compositions,
Evans was not really doing anything that he had not done
before—his consummate originality as a "recomposer" transformed
a fragment or motif into a fleshed-out musical idea. In this case,
the material that he deconstructed and reconstructed for Miles
and his orchestra was based on the flamenco and folk music he'd
been steeping himself in for months to research material for *Sketches*.

"Pan Piper" is based on a Peruvian street vendor's song Evans heard on an anthology of folk music. Nat Hentoff wrote that it was a morning song, and on the folk recording, the melody was "played on the penny whistle by the local pig castrator who was whistling up business." Here, Evans takes the modal tendency of *Porgy* even further. This short piece (less than four minutes) is built on one mode, one chord, and a repeating melodic and rhythmic motif, foreshadowing the minimalist compositions and ethnic borrowings of Philip Glass and Steve Reich that would become so popular in the 1980s. Miles, the sole trumpet on this piece, takes up the street vendor's cry, meandering between shifting palettes of woodwinds (flute, oboe, flute, piccolo, and oboe) and low brass (French horns and trombone), while the harp, percussion, and bass carry the rhythm.

The emotive heat of the album rises with "Saeta" and "Solea." "Saeta," one of the oldest types of Andalusian religious music, is the "arrow of song" sung on Good Friday by a woman standing on her balcony "aiming" her song of grief to an image of the crucified Christ or Virgin Mary being carried in the street procession below. A bassoon opens Evans's "Saeta," intoning a Moorish prayerlike chant that overlaps in an Ivesian fashion with the trumpet fanfare (that traditionally signals the procession to halt or to move along) and then Davis's entrance. Evans's mix is cultural and musical— the mingling of the Moorish, Christian, and gypsy that is deeply flamencan, the jazz man as supplicant or fallen conquistador. Again, in this story the plot remains unclear, but the "cry" is ever present.

The album's finale is Evans's "Solea" (from the Spanish *soledad*—solitude), based on the traditional flamenco form, which is a song of sorrow or loneliness—a multicultural blues. Again, it is built primarily on a melodic and rhythmic vamp. The three-piece percussion section is a brilliant amalgam itself: Jimmy Cobb holds forth a driving jazz swing on brushes, while Elvin Jones and another percussionist (probably Jose Mangual[37]) create a roving procession of shakers, tambourines, and terse drum rolls. The music intensifies to a white heat as the orchestra's inner voicings thicken. About midway through the piece, during a lull, a new theme is introduced, leading the piece ever more sensually toward chaos. Miles's solo is grippingly sexual, climactic, and yet grief-ridden, as befits the Andalusian form. After a return to the original motifs, the music finally subsides and fades to a close.

As Davis himself explained, his role—that of the singer—had to express joy and sadness:

> Now that was the hardest thing for me to do on *Sketches of Spain*: to play the parts on the trumpet where someone was supposed to be singing, especially when it was ad-libbed, like most of the time.... What really made it so hard to do was that I could only do it once or twice. If you do a song like that three or four times you lose that feeling you want to get there.... What I found I had to do in *Sketches* was to read the score a couple of times, listen to it a couple of times more, *then* play it. For me, it was just about knowing what it is, and then I could play it.... After we finished working on Sketches of Spain, I didn't have *nothing* inside of me. I was drained of all emotion and I didn't want to hear that music after I got through playing all that hard shit. Gil said, "Let's go listen to the tapes." I said, "*You* go listen to the tapes."[38]

The recording process for *Sketches* differed significantly from the previous two albums. Miles and Gil were given a lot more studio time due to the insistence of Teo Macero, who had risen up through the ranks at Columbia under Avakian and was now the A&R man for Davis's recordings. Through Macero's varied roles at Columbia and his ken for recording technology, he also became a pioneer in stereo recording. In *Sketches* Macero utilized advances in stereo recording techniques and his own skills in innovative overdubbing and fudged multi-tracking. A composer and musician himself, he fully appreciated the musical vision of Davis and Evans and was willing to run interference with the Columbia hierarchy to help them realize their ambitions. Under Gil's direction, Macero had done the final editing and assembly of *Porgy and Bess*; he also produced Davis's *Kind of Blue*. Macero was a key figure in the recording process of *Sketches* and later Evans–Davis collaborations and also in most of Davis's recordings for Columbia through the mid-1970s.

The need for more rehearsal and recording time became clear at the very first session, which took place November 10, 1959, from

2:30 to 5:30 P.M. Gil's precisely notated articulations, the music's frequent meter changes, and its underlayers of polyrhythms made the execution of *Sketches* the most daunting project yet. The lead trumpet player, Ernie Royal, complained that the trumpet parts looked like flute parts, and Davis himself made several comments that this was the most challenging music he had played to date.[39]

Several factors contributed to the stop-and-start recording process for the *Concierto de Aranjuez*. Miles did not arrive at the first session until after five P.M.; meanwhile Gil rehearsed the *Concierto* with the ensemble, and a first tentative take of the orchestra was made without Miles. According to some accounts, Miles had the flu that November and several sessions were cancelled. Finally at a fifth session on November 20, the entire sixteen-minute work was recorded in sections—with Miles. In the liner notes to *Sketches*, Nat Hentoff captured the difficult atmosphere of the session he attended: "The rhythms were complex and several of the musicians found it hard to keep their time. Gil stopped one take as the rhythms became tangled. 'The tempo is going to go,' he waved his arm in an arc, first to the left and then to the right, 'this way and then that way. Just keep your own time and let the rhythm *go*.' "[40]

By the end of November, the recording of the *Concierto* was completed and Miles was due to go on the road. Gil did not finalize the other arrangements until Davis returned, and the other recording dates took place on March 10–11, 1960. These sessions apparently went a lot more smoothly. Useable takes were made for all remaining four tracks—"Will o' the Wisp," "Pan Piper," "Saeta," and "Solea," as well as for "Song of Our Country," which was not included in the album. All told, it took approximately fifteen three-hour sessions to record the album and many hours of editing and post-production work by Macero and Gil. Again, the amount of studio time was unheard of for a "jazz album." Macero's insistence and persistence, and Goddard Lieberson's faith that the project was worth all the time and effort, carried the work forward. Indeed the record stands as an artistic monument, but it was also a commercial success.

With *Sketches*, Gil finally addressed a fundamental financial problem with his chosen work as an arranger. In 1957 he'd admitted to Nat Hentoff that arranging was a "loser's game," because

arrangers do not receive royalties for their arrangements, as composers do. By including three of his own compositions, though,
Evans finally "wised up," doubtless at Lillian's urging. She had
formed Gillian Music as their publishing company in the mid-1950s
to maximize any composer royalties Gil received. *Sketches* was
destined to be a big seller because of Miles Davis, and Evans's royalties were bound to accrue.

As with the previous two albums with Miles, Gil was paid a flat
fee for his arrangements. Rumors have persisted for years that Gil
was paid approximately four or five hundred dollars—total—for
each of the Davis–Evans albums. A handwritten memo on lined
yellow legal paper from Gil to Macero listed the charges for Gil's
arrangements and the copyist's fee. It included payment for some
arrangements that Gil wrote for that project that have never come
to light, presumably based on folk and flamenco themes. The
copyist William Frazier was due $453.48; $239.10 of this was for the
sixteen-minute *Concierto for Aranjuez* and included all instrumental parts, conductor parts, numbering, rehearsal-night rate, and
materials.

Gil's own fees were grouped as follows, but there is no mention
of the *Concierto* on this memo:

    1. Song of Our Country $900
    2. Will o' the Wisp
    3. Zortziko[41]

    1. La Vida $500
    2. El Amor
    3. Los Juegos

    Love in the Afternoon $500
    Solea $500
    Pan Piper
    Will o' the Wisp

Whether Gil actually received twenty-four hundred dollars is
unknown. Perhaps his fees were not quite as pathetic as legend
would have it.

"Song of Our Country" remains a bit of an enigma (Bill Kirchner called it an anomaly in his notes for the 1998 Davis–Evans box set). Presumably, it was intended for *Sketches,* but it was not released until 1981 as part of *Directions,* a Miles Davis compilation of quintet recordings made during the 1960s. "Song of Our Country" was reissued for the 1998 box set, which also includes one alternate take. In all of these instances, Evans is credited as composer.

This attribution is incorrect, which after all these years is a mystery itself. Evidently no one consulted Macero's 1960 session notes, which clearly state the composers for both pieces recorded at that date: "Song of Our Country" (Villa-Lobos); "Pan Piper" (Evans). The noted twentieth-century Brazilian composer Heitor Villa-Lobos was indeed the composer of "Song of Our Country"; it is the second movement of *Bachianas Brasileiras, No. 2.* However, the scarcity of examples of Gil's compositions that have been recorded—especially at that time—makes it difficult to pin Gil down to a compositional style; by contrast, his arrangements have an indelible signature style—no matter what composition they are based on. The error may have been compounded by the fact that not everyone who is working on archival jazz projects—or is well versed in jazz repertoire—is knowledgeable about classical or contemporary repertoire. The composer credit error may simply have been sloppiness on the part of the record company, hardly unusual; Evans's "Gone" (on *Porgy and Bess*) was long credited to Gershwin. More egregious is the fact that Evans's highly original work as a "recomposer" or arranger could not have earned him more royalties.[42]

For "Song of Our Country," Gil's arrangement is based only on the slow section of the second movement, and there is no ambiguity about Gil's faithfulness to Villa-Lobos's work. Evans wrote a sketch for "Song of Our Country" in 1957, showing that yet again, his interests were way ahead of the pack. It is possible that he was inspired by the first recording of the entire *Bachianas Brasileiras,* released in 1957 and conducted by the composer—years before Villa-Lobos's *Bachianas Brasileiras* series, particularly *No. 5,* became better known.

"Song of Our Country" sounds completely different from any of the pieces on *Sketches.* The most obvious difference is that it is played with a modern jazz swing rhythm throughout—no Spanish or flamenco feel here, nor any added percussion. Further, it uses none of the Spanish/Moorish scales or motifs that characterize the other selections. Thus, it is easy to understand why it was not included on *Sketches*. However, its circular development, tonal ambiguity, and brooding majestic sense of mystery as conveyed by Davis are very much in line with the growing Davis–Evans *oeuvre*.

ı' lıı ı

The three Evans–Davis collaborations introduced a new sensibility, ambiance, and sound into modern jazz arranging and composition. Gil and Miles comfortably hopped over several boundaries—classical, jazz, ethnic, racial, big band/small band—as if they were nonexistent.

But jazz criticism is largely about boundaries: jazz critics keep themselves busy by noting them, tracing them out, and praising or condemning the musicians who respect or transgress them. Unsurprisingly, the jazz critics who first reviewed these Evans–Davis albums, whether enthusiastic or hostile, found them difficult to discuss meaningfully.

Those who raved about the albums often found themselves tongue-tied, at times using the kind of heated, hyperbolic language one resorts to when one can't find the right words. Ralph Gleason, awarding the album five stars in *Down Beat*, wrote that "this is some of the best mood music produced since Duke."[43] Bill Mathieu, writing in *Down Beat*, called *Sketches of Spain* "one of the most important musical triumphs that this century has yet produced."[44]

Other critics were not nearly as receptive. *Miles Ahead*, the least boundary crossing of the three, got off easy, though John S. Wilson wrote that "there are times when Mr. Evans seems to move out of the proper realm of jazz." *Porgy and Bess* straddled boundaries in other ways. There was the genre problem: was it opera or Broadway? Was it high art or pop culture? Jazz or something else? Then there was the racial politics. *Porgy* had originally attracted criticism by virtue of being written by a white author, DuBose Heyward, with music by a white composer strongly influenced by spirituals and jazz. Now it had been redone by a white arranger, also strongly influenced by black music and jazz, who—with Miles as the omni-present lead—translated the opera into a color-blind musical world even as Evans stayed true to Gershwin's drama and pathos. The star, meanwhile, was a preeminent black jazz musician whose roots were not exactly Catfish Row and who likewise ignored boundaries, both racial and musical, that seemed so obsessively important to critics. Davis expressed scorn when black musicians told him that he should play more "black" and suggested that his hiring of white musicians amounted to commercial sellout and racial betrayal.

Sketches, another boundary crosser, also encountered hostile criticism. Martin Williams called the *Concierto* "something of a curiosity and a failure," another manifestation of Evans's tendency to provide "a succession of beefed-up, quasi-impressionist color harmonies and background for Davis's horn."[45] More recently, some of Evans's arrangements for Davis have been analyzed rigorously, using some traditional musicological methods and others developed for the jazz idiom, but adapted specifically for Evans's work. Gil's "harmonic world," according to Robin Dewhurst, had to be examined in its own realm; Evans's chord structures and harmonic progressions had an internal logic that was his creation.[46]

Amiri Baraka was and remains one of the few commentators able to respond to the Evans–Davis collaborations with both the requisite musical and cultural sensitivity. In an article about Davis, Baraka showed he had no problem whatsoever with "the mix," with Davis's heedless crossing of boundaries, be they racial or musical.

> Recently Miles has received some criticism from certain black circles for hiring so many white musicians, thereby depriving some black musicians of some well-paying prestigious gig.... But interracial bands are nothing new to Miles. So talk of Miles's eye to the buck as being the principal reason for using white musicians doesn't really wash. Though it is my own feeling that Miles knows always almost exactly what he is doing around the music—form and content, image and substance. There is something in the mix Miles *wants* [us] to hear. It might be commercial, to some extent, but it is also social and aesthetic....

Davis, Baraka wrote, was going after a new musical fundament that Baraka called a "bottom," and Davis had been put on the path to this bottom by Claude Thornhill.

Those cool lush harmonies that Evans gave to Thornhill, and even the innovative use of brass and Dukish (reeds, winds) scoring had a heavy effect on Miles.... He said he was drawn to Thornhill's music because there was "something to relate to." Not just the flying fury of Bird's aerial wizardry. Aside from the reemphasized Africa of new Bop rhythms, the reassertion of the primacy of blues and improvisation in African-American music. Miles wanted a music with more melodic access and a "cushion" of harmonies that made his own simple voice an elegant, somewhat detached "personality" effortlessly perceiving and expressing. It is this harmonic cushion or bottom, the Evans/Thornhill (quasi-Dukish) music parallels; the "something to relate to" that Miles described that speaks to the kind of *lush* sensibility Miles has, essentially melodic floating in relief above shaded chromatic harmonies.[47]

Davis finally found his bottom, Baraka wrote, in the "fresh and lyrical Gil Evans collaborations" that produced music "at a level very few people approach, anywhere, anytime."

[T]he hugely successful pieces with Evans are symphonic tone poems, to a certain extent summing up midcentury American concert music. *Miles Ahead* was the giant step, replaying yet extending even further the Evans/Thornhill *Birth of the Cool* concept.

   Sketches of Spain and *Porgy and Bess* are high American musical statements; their tension is between a functional impressionism, serious in its emotional detail, versus mood without significance. It is the bluesiness of the Davis conception even submerged in all the lushness that gives these moods an intelligence and sensitivity. There is yet a searching quality in Miles's horn, above, beyond, below, inside, outside, within, locked out of the lushness, the lovely American bottom. It is a searching, a probing like a dowser, used for searching out beauty.[48]

If Davis's horn is like a dowser searching out beauty, it explored and discovered treasures in a territory created by Evans. His arrangements had created that fundament, that bottom. Evans, fully as much as Miles, knew what he was doing in his explorations of Gershwin, Falla, flamenco, and those other musical territories. He, too, wanted to share that mix.

ı' ıɪ ı

In June 2000, *Porgy and Bess* and *Sketches of Spain* were performed in their entirety at Carnegie Hall as part of the JVC Jazz Festival. Maria Schneider, an assistant to Evans during the last three years of his life, conducted; jazz trumpet virtuoso Jon Faddis, who worked with Evans on and off in the 1970s, took on the daunting role of playing the Davis parts. Three other members of the orchestra, including Gil's son Miles on trumpet, Bob Stewart on tuba, and Warren Smith on percussion, had worked with Evans extensively during various periods of Gil's career. The remaining musicians included members of the Carnegie Hall Jazz Band (directed by Jon Faddis), several not-so-well-known jazz musicians, and classically trained woodwind and French horn players, who may or may not have had extensive exposure to Gil Evans's work.

The performance, not without a few small problems, was a tremendous success. Evans's music could finally be heard live, played by a new group of sensitive professionals—with all its trickiness and all its glory intact. What became most apparent is how plastic and resilient the music is. Gil's unusual instrumental doublings—alto flute playing along with tuba and string bass, or muted trombones and French horns stretched to the top of their ranges in unison—and use of symphonic instruments—bassoon, harp, piccolo—seemed ever more remarkable heard in the flesh. It was also a revelation to realize how much of Miles Davis's parts Evans had actually written.

More than anything else, though, the concert brought the music into the world of performed repertoire. As Evans's work becomes performed more frequently, there are bound to be inevitable comparisons to Miles's performance, or the outstanding contributions to the original recordings by musicians such as bassist Paul

Chambers. Under Maria Schneider's direction, the music—the utter poignancy of Evans's *Porgy and Bess* and the Andalusian fantasy of *Sketches*—took hold. The musicians latched onto Gil's art, both its intimate and subtle details and its vastness.

To a listener in the late 1950s, the music it might have sounded overly impressionistic, the textures at times densely chaotic, its formalism overriding the "jazz" part of its mix. But to a listener in the year 2000, one steeped in contemporary jazz, what was astounding was the opposite: the depth of the music's jazz roots is intensified by the music's very structure. The richness of the mix and its finely wrought expression allow these Evans scores a rightful place alongside cherished contemporary American orchestral repertoire; they are Evans's own *West Side Story*, his *Appalachian Suite*, his recomposed *Porgy*.

9 out of the cool

*Back then you didn't have to be paid to play, and
you didn't have to pay to get in to hear other people
play. That was a golden age. Music was accessible
and all the giants were on the scene, and there was
a truth—the menu was much smaller than now.
Everybody—all the different schools of players
were active and in their peak. I worked with
people from New Orleans, from Chicago, from
Kansas City. These people were in their 50s and
60s, and then there were the young radicals, the
experimentalists, and the traditionalists. You
couldn't get away with any funny business. If there
was a new bass player in town all the other bass
players would come check him out. Everybody
knew who could play and who couldn't. Now it's
just a sort of flim-flam going on—most of the
giants are gone really. But back then, it was a very
beautiful time.*

—STEVE LACY

While Gil worked on his masterpieces with Miles, he continued to
attract a growing cadre of musicians and artists as friends and collaborators. He had his own corner at Charlie's Tavern at 55th
Street and Seventh Avenue, where friends congregated to shoot

the breeze or talk music or shop. His marriage to Lillian, calm and stable on the surface, began to grow stormy. Friends who knew them as a couple perceived that Lillian in fact had a difficult time living with Gil the artist—a person so rapt in his work, who needed to spend endless hours at the piano, whether he had arranging jobs to complete or not.

Gil stayed in touch with his old West Coast friends, the Carpenters, who had also befriended Lillian. Pete was now an established studio arranger in Los Angeles, and in the spring of 1957 the Carpenter's son graduated from high school. Gil wrote them a cheerful letter for that occasion, and, true to form, did not get around to actually sending it until mid-September.

> Dear Pete and Maybeth:
>
> Petie's graduation announcement was unbelievable.... Please tell him that upon request, or even not upon request, I will gladly pass along to him any of the worldly wisdom I have picked up during my (ahem) 40 years on this globe. For example: 'New ways to prepare the lowly minor seventh chord' and other related formulas are his for the asking, so please tell him to feel free—
>
> All the very best to all of you from us here in the Apple, Gil

Also true to form, Gil doesn't bother to mention his own accomplishments, the imminent release of *Miles Ahead,* or the fact that, just days before, he had finally recorded his first album as a leader.

Gil Evans & Ten was recorded September 10, 1957, at Rudy Van Gelder's studio in Hackensack, New Jersey, for Prestige. For this project, Gil created a wholly different sound environment than that of *Miles Ahead.* He had to scale back to using eleven musicians again, a number that took on almost mystical significance for him; eleven was the maximum number of musicians hired for a tight-budget recording that aimed at a big sound. Gil eluded the strictures of this adeptly and viewed the number limit on personnel as a creative challenge. Evans lined up an unusual combination of five brass and three woodwinds (plus rhythm—piano, bass, and drums): two trumpets, trombone, bass trombone, French horn, soprano sax, alto sax, and bassoon. The resulting sonorities are startling and lush, with the extremes of the bass trombone and the upper reaches of the soprano sax creating a spacious breadth.

The album features a fresh-sounding instrumentalist: Steve Lacy, a twenty-three-year-old soprano saxophonist (three years before John Coltrane repopularized the instrument). Gil hired him after hearing him only once, five years before, playing with a Dixieland group on the radio on the Major Bowes Amateur Hour. Gil was so dazzled by Lacy's sound—he played in a style inspired by jazz pioneer Sidney Bechet—that he called the station on the spot to ask his name. When Gil began thinking about his new album, he remembered Lacy and decided to give him a call.

Lacy was then eking out a living in Greenwich Village with various Dixieland bands while artistically committed to exploring an emergent "free jazz" with pianist Cecil Taylor. Though a well-schooled musician who had been professionally active in New York since he was a teenager, Lacy did not know everybody in town. When he received a phone call from someone who identified himself as Gil Evans, he had no idea who that was. The phone call began a profound musical and personal friendship that lasted, like Gil's friendship with Miles, until Gil's death.

In *Gil Evans & Ten*, Evans broke away from the star-centered approach of *Miles Ahead*. Lacy was often the soloist, but trombonist Jimmy Cleveland was featured as well, and the individual voices and surrounding textures enhanced one another in a shifting series of focal points. Gil mixed and matched not just unusual combinations of instruments but strong musical personalities. Lacy said, "He knew how to combine certain people that would never have played together, old and young and different styles, different schools.... He had Jimmy Cleveland next to this old bass trombone player, me and Lee Konitz, and Jake Koven and Louie Mucci. These were unheard of combinations but they worked."[1] Evans paired Cleveland, a young post-bop trombonist with a gorgeous sound, with Swing Era veteran trombonist Bart Varsalona; Mucci and Koven were paired similarly. Their differences, expressed through phrasing, intonation, and the use or lack of vibrato in their sound, created a richness in the mix.

Lacy also appeared as the lead voice in several ensemble passages, an unusual role for soprano sax. The quasi-piercing cry of

his instrument cut through the ensemble, feeding off the arrangements. Gil took a risk letting the twenty-three-year-old loose. This
was one of Gil's strong tendencies, both as a bandleader and col-
laborator. He trusted those he hired to come up with the right
stuff—be it as a strong improviser, unique instrumental personality, or, in his late career, assistant arranger (Maria Schneider became
Evans's assistant right out of graduate school, in 1985). In this
case, he trusted Lacy to carry much of the album.

Lacy had no idea his role would be so large or that the music
would be so challenging. "At that point I couldn't read music very
well, and I was the worst one in the band. They had to do things
over and over again because I kept messing up the reading. It
wasn't that the notes were so very hard, it was the rhythms—they
were very precise and very subtle, they were like speech rhythms.
The other guys in the band were very accomplished readers, and
that experience forced me to learn to read as fast as I could."[2]

Another fresh instrumental voice on the album was Evans's
own—he was heard prominently on piano for the first time on
record. Technically he was no rival of modern jazz piano masters
such as his idol Bud Powell or his friend Jimmy Rowles. Still,
Evans's playing, as a soloist or accompanist, expresses all the
beauty, economy, and individualism of Basie's or Ellington's. Like
them, he's a helmsman. By playing certain harmonies, or melodic
or rhythmic riffs, he steers the music in the direction he wants
the ensemble to go; one can also hear his conception of the music
in its entirety. Evans's playing confounded his low opinion of
himself as a player, which some friends thought bordered on
neurotic.

The compositional sources for this album are all American and
African American. Evans's arrangements pay tribute to the work
of Irving Berlin, Leadbelly, Leonard Bernstein, Rodgers and Hart,
Cole Porter, and Tadd Dameron. Also included is a new arrangement of Evans's own "Jambangle," expanded to great effect from
the McKusick recording of the previous year. (The opening bars of
"Jambangle" were reworked in the late 1960s by the rock group
the Doors as a main motif for "Light My Fire.")

Two key things inspired Gil's selection of thematic material
for his arrangements: the emotional quality and the "sound" ele-

ment—how he envisioned the sound of the piece as played by a particular musician or group of instruments. He was always attracted to a certain melancholy, pieces that had an inherent "cry," such as Kurt Weill songs or the Charles Mingus tunes he wrote arrangements for later on ("Orange Was the Color of Her Dress, Then Silk Blue" and "Goodbye, Pork Pie Hat"). He loved the songs of strong melodists like Rodgers and Hart, and the quirky angular melodies of Thelonious Monk. He was inspired by folk music, ethnic music, and twentieth-century composers. At this stage in his career, his thematic choices also had to align with his vision of the album as a whole—how moods and textures would vary through the course of an album, as well as an individual arrangement. Jimmy Cleveland once said that Evans always called him to make sure he liked the tunes on which he would be featured; this was true of other musicians as well.

Gil typically took liberties with the material. Berlin's "Remember," originally in 3/4 time, is now in 4/4. Leadbelly's blues, "Ella Speed," turns into a modern jazz swing number with an *arco* passage by Paul Chambers. One can hear Gil's love of bass sonorities: his rich voicings for low brass, conspicuous use of bass and tuba, and duets for trombone and bass trombone. He played with textures that he would reuse and expand in *Porgy and Bess*. This is particularly apparent in his treatment of "Nobody's Heart."

The producer constantly pressured Gil about time and money in the making of the album. Years later, Evans said:

> You'd have thought it was the most expensive album in the world. It cost $2500 at the time, but Bob Weinstock thought that was a lot. He was used to having groups come out in a van, and every time they'd practice a little bit, he'd get so uptight. He'd say, "Okay now, play a blues!" In one afternoon, he'd expect to get a record out.
>
> We went out there with a 10-piece band, and after the sessions were over, he wouldn't even let me take the time to clean it up. So what happens—years later I start getting statements from the Bahamas, because they don't have anything in New York anymore, that the album cost $2500 in 1957 and I still owe them $800![3]

Evans's innovations on this record—his unusual choice of instruments and couplings, his scrambling of tempos and themes, and his elongated phrasing—are obscured by the album's blithe spirit and breezy swing. This album should not be evaluated alongside those Gil did with Miles, rather, it should be viewed as the first document of Gil's work on his own. In it he was liberated from the exigencies of writing for Claude Thornhill, the constraints imposed by various singers, and the ambitious challenge of creating a "setting" for Miles Davis.

ı' ıı ı

Gil's musical interests constantly expanded, and he shared them with others, acting as a kind of musical gateway for new ideas in the often narrow-minded jazz world. He gave Lacy a Ravi Shankar record, initiating what would become Lacy's lifelong interest in Indian music. He turned Lacy on to the work of Harry Partch, a brilliant and offbeat composer who experimented with intonation and microtones and who became a friend of Gil's later on. They went to see Partch's performance piece *The Bewitched*, for voice, dancers, koto, Partch's invented instruments, and cloud chambers among other things. "Gil took me up to Columbia to see "The Bewitched"—we went twice," said Lacy. "I met Partch and that was rare—it was really important for me. Then Partch heard that first record [*Gil Evans & Ten*], and used the soprano sax himself."

Gil was an early admirer of Thelonious Monk and Cecil Taylor, when Monk was yet to be widely respected and Taylor was regarded as an oddball avant-gardist who evoked derision more often than respect. Lacy recalled:

> Gil had no barriers, he had perfect taste and he was unafraid, no matter what anyone else thought. Almost everybody was against Cecil. Club owners would close their pianos, drummers would run out the door. People at jam sessions would see him coming and say, 'No, no, no, no, no!' But Gil liked his playing. Gil was always open to hearing something that he hadn't heard before, thinking thoughts he'd never thought before, reading things he'd never read before. He was intellectually curious,

non-stop. I've never met anybody like that. He was really an intellectual mentor for me.

He gave me a lot of books. One of them was a biography of Wilhelm Reich. Gil was interested in many things like psycho-analysis, some of which I wasn't interested in, but he turned me on to what he could. Gil and I shared an interest in the other arts—in painting and literature, and theater and cinema, song and dance, and all those things. He furthered that in me a lot.[4]

Wilhelm Reich's ideas were in vogue among several New York artists in the late 1950s and early 1960s, partly because Reich advocated an active therapy that was less introspective and cogni-tively oriented than others; the therapist used cues from and encouraged expressive body movements. The painter Kenneth Noland, a friend and fan of Gil who was involved in Reichian ther-apy himself, recalled:

Art is not made without some kind of contact with something. Gil was always in contact with music when he was making music, and that's a Reichian kind of concept. Reichian therapy gets very expressive; I mean it is *actually* expressive. The aim is to get a person active, expressive—to breathe, to get angry, to get frightened, to cry. It runs through the gamut of all of the expressive feelings. And they [Reichian therapists] know how to use that therapeutically, so that it has parallels in all kinds of creative work. [5]

ı' lı ı

Meanwhile, Gil got more offers for commercial work, thanks to the current commercial trends in jazz and pop music. Andre Previn's jazz trio treatment of *My Fair Lady* had been a bestseller on the pop charts since its release in 1956, and its success caused a surge of spin-offs. Jazz now could be marketed as mainstream in a com-pletely accessible way that had not been possible with bebop, and record companies hustled to exploit this opportunity.

In 1957, Gil arranged a jazz album featuring the multi-instru-mentalist Don Elliot (on trumpet, mellophone, vibraphone, marimba, and bongos) performing some of the songs from the hit show *Jamaica* composed by Harold Arlen and Yip Harburg. The music is clever, cute, and sparkly—jazz-lite. It was one of the very few albums Gil worked on in which his signature style is almost completely absent. The album was significant mainly because it revealed that Gil Evans could indeed write commercially if he felt like it.[6]

Gil's other arranging work at the time better reveals his versatility and craftsmanship. He never completely severed his ties to big band swing music, for instance, nor his love of early jazz innovators. He periodically did some arranging for trumpet player Billy Butterfield, whose big band recorded Evans's arrangement of "Singin' the Blues" in 1950 and again in 1956. On the latter date it also recorded an obscure Evans composition entitled "Again and Again and Again"—a solid swing tune harkening back to the era, though the lackluster arrangement (probably by Bill Stegmeyer) has nowhere near the drive or drama of Evans's "Buster's Last Stand" (1942).

In the late 1950s, Benny Goodman, still actively touring, commissioned Evans and several other arrangers for new, modern-sounding scores—a full twenty years after he had first asked Gil for some arrangements. Goodman quickly found out that his audiences preferred his old standards, and the new arrangements went unplayed. But Gil had changed his opinion of Goodman since the days when Gil was a young bandleader and flattered by Goodman's interest. Gil told Helen Johnston:

> He kept me sitting up there in the Essex House one night, all night long. He wanted this arrangement from me and he wanted to pay me fifty dollars, and said that was the market price. I said that I didn't care what the market price was, it was worth $150.00, and I wouldn't do it for a nickel less. And I sat in that bar all evening and wrangled around with him while he probed me.... He was trying to find out whether I was trying to get this extra money out of him, you know, what my circumstances were. Finally, he realized I really didn't do anything else at all, but I wanted to get paid for that arrangement. Then he came through. [7]

As Gil had discovered all too well, arranging music was one of the least paid skills in the music industry. The only exceptions were for A-list studio arrangers who could crank out an album in seventy-two hours straight, or for advertising arrangers who received residual payments on nationally aired jingles. A jazz arranger like Gil was either paid a flat fee or paid according to the union's fees for orchestration, a byzantine computation based on the number of measures, the number of instruments, and so forth. There were no royalties for arrangements, and no producer's points for an album's profit, which entrepreneurish arranger/producers such as Quincy Jones learned to insist on years later. Though Gil was now sought after—thanks to his work with Miles—he was still not well compensated.

For Gil's next recording project under his own leadership, George Avakian again became a key figure. Avakian left Columbia in early 1958, warned by his doctor to slow down. His eight-year tenure as A&R director for jazz and international pop albums at Columbia Records had been literally gold-plated, and he left the label with a star-studded jazz roster. But Avakian seemed unable to stay out of the recording business. He was invited to form a partnership with West Coast producer Dick Bock, owner of the World Pacific label, with tempting conditions: fewer recordings, less bureaucracy, and the freedom to make quick decisions. Avakian accepted. World Pacific (Pacific Jazz), flourishing from the success of its recordings by the Gerry Mulligan Quartet with Chet Baker, now had an active on-the-scene jazz producer on both coasts. Shortly thereafter, Avakian ran into Gil, who said that he had some ideas for an album along the lines of *Miles Ahead*. Gil wanted to feature Cannonball Adderley, an alto saxophonist with a joyous sound à la Charlie Parker, who had been getting a lot of attention as a sideman with Miles Davis; Cannonball was also between labels. Avakian suggested they could do something for World Pacific. The result was *New Bottle, Old Wine*, which was recorded in New York in four sessions in April and May 1958.

The album, subtitled "The Great Jazz Composers Interpreted by Gil Evans and His Orchestra," romps through jazz compositions by some of Gil's favorite composers and performers. It moves chronologically through pieces by W. C. Handy, Jelly Roll Morton,

Fats Waller, Louis Armstrong, Lester Young, Thelonious Monk, and
Dizzy Gillespie, and ends with Charlie Parker's rousing "Bird Feathers." Its buoyant mood contrasts starkly with the brooding beauty
of *Miles Ahead*. The rhythm section—bassist Paul Chambers with
Art Blakey or Philly Joe Jones on drums—delivers a powerful
swing to the mid- and up-tempo numbers.

Cannonball runs away with the album; his voice predominates.
The scores sound like what Gil might have written for Charlie
Parker if he had been unencumbered by the mishaps that occurred
in his work with Parker in 1953. Gil tailored the arrangements to
Cannonball's strengths—his warm sound, his bop-oriented cas-
cading improvisations, and his unflagging energy. The arrangements were written for three trumpets, three trombones, French
horn, and tuba; Cannonball, two other woodwind players, guitar, bass, and drums completed the fourteen-piece ensemble. Gil
plays piano on Waller's "Willow Tree" and Monk's " 'Round Midnight." The transition from " 'Round Midnight" to "Manteca" renders the two pieces a suite, the latter performed with a relentless
drive reminiscent of Gillespie's own late 1940s big band. Gil's
arrangement of "Bird Feathers" by Charlie Parker opens with a
unison-with-a-twist—flute, muted trumpet, and brushes, in this
case—which brings out new facets of the composition.

In 1959 Evans recorded a sequel for World Pacific, *Great Jazz
Standards*, produced by Dick Bock. (Avakian had moved on to start
a pop division at Warner Brothers Records.) This album included
some musicians new to Gil's work on record, notably drummer
Elvin Jones and veteran tenor saxophonist Budd Johnson, who,
along with most of the other musicians—Steve Lacy, Johnny
Coles, Bill Barber, Jimmy Cleveland, Louis Mucci, and Al Block—
would play and/or record with Evans frequently over the next few
years. As a group they added as much substantive personality to
Gil's music as did long-term members of Ellington's band. Gil, like
Ellington, wrote expressly for his players, targeting them for certain pitches and effects, certain nuances. Their unique voices were
inseparable from the character of the composite sound Gil was
after.

Great Jazz Standards was recorded in February 1959, shortly after
Gil played at Birdland for two weeks with approximately the same

personnel. Gil again used "great jazz composers" to tie the album together and wrote arrangements for compositions by Bix Beiderbecke, Thelonious Monk, Don Redman, John Lewis, and Clifford Brown; the album includes one Evans original, "La Nevada" (Theme). This album, like *New Bottle, Old Wine*, was marked by a strong rhythmic drive not often associated with Evans's work, delivered on most selections by Elvin Jones's drums.

The highly improvisational "La Nevada" had been worked out onstage at Birdland. It was one of several pieces that would remain in Gil's book for years, serving as a fluid exploratory vehicle for improviser(s) and the ensemble. The arrangement of this modal piece, built largely around a minor ninth chord that turns major (Gm9-G), includes several orchestrated motifs and riffs that were cued in and out by Gil's piano, to guide the soloist in forging the musical drama. This kind of arrangement—requiring a sensitized participation from all the musicians and not just the soloist of the moment—would become increasingly common in Gil's work.

By 1959 Gil could easily assemble a working band for the sporadic gigs that came his way from a loyal pool of high-caliber musicians. He led a twelve-piece band at a show at the Apollo Theatre that included nearly the same personnel who had appeared at Birdland. The show was typical of the Apollo's eclectic programming: Dinah Washington was the headliner, and the other acts were Thelonious Monk, The Axidentals, Gil Evans and His Band, and Dinah's two sons "in their debut as the Queens' Jesters." On April 2, 1959, Gil and Miles reassembled most of the personnel from *Miles Ahead* for a taping of the *Robert Herridge Television Theatre*, a prestigious local New York TV program dedicated to the arts (the Davis–Evans program was broadcast July 1960). The program, entitled "The Sound of Miles Davis," opened with the Evans Orchestra and the Davis quintet (John Coltrane, Wynton Kelly, Paul Chambers, and Jimmy Cobb) playing Evans's orchestral prelude to "So What," the now-classic modal tune that had been created by Davis et al. in the recording studio just a month earlier. The prelude, though brief, is a striking arrangement developed from an introductory motif on bass by Paul Chambers. Anita Evans said that Gil may have been inspired to write the prelude by hearing Paul Chambers fooling around with this piece; the two were very good friends at the time.[8] The quintet took over after the introduction, then folded itself into Evans's orchestra for the remainder of the program, in which the entire ensemble performed three selections from *Miles Ahead* ("The Duke," "Blues For Pablo," and "New Rhumba") with Evans conducting. A video of the broadcast shows the orchestra seated in a recording studio set-up—an elongated "U," rather than concert-style. The verité look—no glitz—was part of the appeal of Herridge's shows; the focus was all music. "Blues for Pablo" gives a great glimpse of Gil's conducting style. He's often intent on the score, tapping his foot, bobbing his head, but he moves into action to articulate the trickiest entrances and exits, and to help the orchestra sustain sounds, textures, and his implied polyrhythms.

Gil left no corner of his musicianship untouched. Even as he was constantly working out voicings and thinking about orchestrating for large ensembles, he was also seeking to improve his piano playing. Since, in the late 1950s, he performed more often, he felt anxious about it. Lacy remembered a period of "many months when Gil was very interested in getting his piano playing together. So he would rent a studio, and we would jam, with Dennis Charles on drums, and a blind bass player, Dick Carter [both of whom played on *Great Jazz Standards*]. We would jam for hours on standard tunes so Gil could practice."

ılıı ı

The Carpenters visited the Evanses for a few days in the summer of 1960, cementing the friendship between Lillian and Maybeth to the point that Lillian took over as the correspondent between the two couples. Lillian's chatty letters, handwritten on stationery edged with seagulls and sailboats, were usually filled with gossip and household hints—though at times they revealed deeper glimpses of her life with Gil.

Dear Maybeth and Nancy [the Carpenter's daughter],
 "Our" career is still up in the air and there is nothing to report at present. As James Haggerty put it, there may be an announcement in a short while. Meanwhile, however, we aren't

feeling too perky about the way things are—or are not—going. The smiles are still on though, and we both took our Pollyanna Pills this morning....

Best love from Gil and Lillian

Just over a month later, *Sketches of Spain* appeared in the stores, and Gil and an eleven-piece band (drawn largely from his rehearsal band) were about to start playing at a new, already prestigious jazz club in the Village. Lillian finally had more substantive information to relay to the Carpenters.

Sept. 26, 1960
Dear Maybeth and Carpenters All,

Our big news here is that Gil is taking himself and ten men into a place called "The Jazz Gallery" on Oct. 18. How about that. I was a little upset about it for awhile because of a number of bogeys I'd let get the better of me.... You know he has never, repeat, never quite overcome the siren song of having an orchestra so he might as well have jolly fun while he can. This place asked him to form the group and want him in for six weeks to start. That, among other things was the inducement really. He will have enough time to build it and hear something out of it. Not like going to a place for a week or two.... You might notice that I didn't call this new venture a "band." Gil doesn't want to have it called that, or orchestra or group..or? He wants a new name for the "thing" but doesn't want it to sound snobbish or pseudo intellectual.... You've got those two smart kids there; ask them the numerical prefix for "eleven." Lord help us, Maybeth.

That Columbia Records deal fell through with a bang.... That's out for now. Actually it will be better in the long run but it sure looked like emergency here for awhile, Gil binding wounds with me on the changing dressings shift. Boy were we MAD.... They just didn't act like men up there. They had no intention of acceding to what Gil wanted but they kept stringing him along until he lost another session on Mercury (a one-time shot), they released an announcement that Gil had signed with them when he hadn't. Oh, the list of infractions is endless.

So Gil told the guy handling (Handling???) it to hang up. That's all, just HANG UP. That's really the reason why he had to start this personal presentation thing going. There seemed nothing else to do.

So now Gil is writing his head off and I am in the kitchen and things seem to be jumping. Like orchids, we are living on air. It agrees with us, however, because we really do have fun talking about all the many things to think of....

Have you heard the "Sketches of Spain," the album Gil and Miles did? The reviews have been terrific and I understand it is selling like mad. I'm very glad because Gil has three originals on it and his wife is the publisher. Well your money-hungry, greedy New York Democratic friend has come to the end of her saga for today...

Toodle-ooo, Love Lillian

Throughout their ten-year marriage, Gil and Lillian scraped by, with Lillian holding various jobs to help support them. She formed Gillian Music, their music publishing company, to acquire as much a percentage as possible on royalties from the handful of Gil's original compositions that were recorded during this period. (Gillian Music also published compositions of some of their friends, including Johnny Carisi's "Springsville.") Lillian clearly thought that Gil's work with Miles was going to dramatically improve their tenuous finances.

Thus it came as a huge blow when an all-but-executed agreement between Gil and Columbia fell through—the deal she mentioned in her letter—just as *Sketches* was released to immediate acclaim. Earlier that summer, the label had drafted an exclusive artist's contract for Gil, which could have begun as early as June 1, 1960, had Gil signed it. The contract's boilerplate reflects how abysmally the record industry treated its artists.

You will not perform for the purpose of making phonograph records for any person other than us, and during a period of five years after termination of this agreement, you will not perform any musical composition recorded for us for any person other than us for the purpose of making phonograph records; and you acknowledge that your services are unique and extraordinary.

...All compositions written or composed by you shall be licensed to us at the rate of 1 cent per side on basis of 90% of all records sold. Arranged versions of musical compositions in the public domain shall be free of copyright royalties.

...For your services we'll pay you within 14 days at union scale, in advance of royalties.... We shall specify your accompaniment, arrangements, and copying, and pay costs.

...We will pay you a royalty of 5% of suggested retail list in respect of 90% of all records sold by us and any subsidiary; and 2 of such percentage so manufactured and sold....

The contract would have been for one year with options to extend it. Handwritten on one of several copies of the unsigned contract, the composer's royalty had been increased to 2 percent for original compositions.[9]

Gil never signed. Other Columbia Records correspondence from this period suggests that Gil balked at the outrageous terms involving royalties and use of composer's material, standard though they were. Typically, he did not have a manager, lawyer, or agent (with the exception of MCA during his California days, he never had a business representative of any kind) and was attempting to negotiate for himself.

June 16, 1960
From: Irving Townsend
To: Teo Macero

I spoke to Gil Evans today and he asked what was happening with his contract. I have heard nothing and I hope you will push it along so that we can get it signed and started. He will be calling you the first of the week for news.

This is one we shouldn't lose.

July 6, 1960
From: Walter Dean
To: Teo Macero
Subject: Gil Evans

This will confirm my telephone conversation with you regarding the proposed contract with Gil Evans. In view of your conversations with him last week about the financial arrangements which he would be willing to accept, I would appreciate it if you would follow up with him to ascertain the best deal that can be made under the circumstances. If you will then send me a memo setting forth the best terms that you have been able to obtain from Evans, together with your records regarding acceptance of such terms, I will forward your memo to Mr. Lieberson for approval.[10]

As Gil's proposed A&R director, Teo Macero wrote up a first—undated and unsigned—Request for Approval, Talent Term Contract—a precontract agreement that was to commence immediately and specified two albums over a twelve-month period. Arranging costs per session were pegged at one thousand dollars (probably payment for two or three arrangements), and it was not specified whether this was part of an advance or not. A second agreement was amended in Gil's favor (and addressed to Gil Evans c/o Miles Davis at Davis's Tenth Avenue address). This one was an eighteen-month contract commencing September 1960; the arrangement cost per session a more generous twenty-five hundred to three thousand dollars, with a copying fee of five hundred dollars per session. Macero signed it on July 28, 1960, but his superiors Al Lorber and Goddard Lieberson did not. The deal fell through somewhere along the line over the summer.

Office Communication, Columbia Records
September 8, 1960
From: Walter Dean
To: Teo Macero
Cc: Kavan and Talbert
Subject: Gil Evans

In accordance with our recent discussions, I am returning to you your requisition for Gil Evans. No further action will be taken regarding this pending further word from you. Should you hereafter have any renewed interest in signing this artist, please let me know by forwarding a new requisition indicating the terms of the proposed contract. If you decide that we should make another effort to sign Evans, but you want to negotiate some of the terms with him, please leave these items blank in your requisition and I will try to conclude these on the best possible basis.[11]

Thus the Jazz Gallery gig of October 1960 came as welcome news for Gil and Lillian. The nightclub had opened earlier that year as an alternate space to its sister club, the Five Spot, run by Joe Termini and his brother Iggy. The Gallery was in a small theater that seated about two hundred and fifty people. It was already notable among serious jazz fans for hosting the debut of John Coltrane's first quartet in May and June of that year. Gil stayed at the Jazz Gallery for six weeks that fall; it was the longest running gig of his New York career until the early 1980s, and he and his band were well received. One review notes:

> So far John Q. Jazzbuff has remained relatively aloof [to Evans and his Orchestra], but boniface Joe Termini, who talked Evans into assembling the band for the engagement, is a determined man. He's returning two of the Gallery's topdraw headliners in support of Evans, hoping the faithful will go away with a new allegiance. Diz Gillespie comes in tomorrow, followed by Thelonious Monk for the final two weeks of Evans' stand.
>
> By all standards of the popular arts, Termini's double-headliner gambit should work, because the Evans band is the freshest sound on the jazz scene since Ornette Coleman busted the formula barrier at the Gallery's sister club, the Five Spot. Evans' catalog, due to his own progressive arrangements, has the excitement of a new era.... Execution is perfect, which is a boost to the band's commercial value. [12]

Soon after the six-week engagement ended, Gil recorded an album, *Out of the Cool*, for the newly formed Impulse! label, founded by producer Creed Taylor. Years later Gil told interviewers that he made that album in an afternoon. In a sense, he did—but this illustrates yet again how oral interviews can be misleading. The album was recorded at Rudy Van Gelder's studio in December

1960. The useable takes only came after three previous sessions that were essentially rehearsals.

Gil used mostly the same personnel for this recording as had performed at the Jazz Gallery, adding Elvin Jones on percussion. The music has a molded ambiance, a plasticity that came about because the group had worked so intensely together at the club. Taylor, in the uncomfortable position of a producer hoping to get useable tracks as the clock ticked, recalled:

> "La Nevada" was not only original but was totally sponta-neous—we had gotten nothing until the fourth trip out to Rudy Van Gelder's. Gil started noodling at the piano for awhile, and he started this thing, and the rhythm section started doing something and then something sparked in Gil. And he walked over to Tony Studd, the bass trombone player and said some-thing to him. Then, he wrote something down on a match book. Literally! I know it sounds like an exaggeration, but that's what he did. Then, he showed it to Tony, who started playing that figure, and then Gil passed it around to the other horn players. So it was arranged on the spot without anything except Gil Evans suggesting these notes, and then he went back to the piano. Then it proceeded for quite awhile—it [that tune] was not edited.
>
> The other pieces were a little more arranged. But we didn't get any of them down [as useable takes] until he got whatever it was on "La Nevada" out of his system. That session let the dam loose; he was struggling with the musicality until then. There was nothing to do as far as I was concerned except patiently sit and wait. I knew it was going to happen at some point, but I sure hoped it would happen soon.[13]

The musical breakthrough that took place with *Out of the Cool* can be dramatized by hearing the first recording of "La Nevada" (made less than two years earlier) alongside this newer version. On the earlier recording, the soloists are urged on by riff-driven background lines conventionally played, though the figures and Gil's phrasing are original; it has the feel of a standard hard-bop performance. The later recording reflects an important transformation; there is a new, floating quality imparted by the rhythm section. Gil's piano enters with a moody, urgent riff. Jones follows on shaker, which he plays with an unshakeable rhythmic constancy through the track's entire eighteen minutes. Ron Carter plays an *ostinato* figure on bass, a stark contrast to the more boppish approach Tommy Potter took on the previous version. Gil recalled the band and album some twenty years later.

> Six steady weeks, six days a week. We knew that music. The way we played "La Nevada" was different than we had ever played it before, but we always played it differently. The only change from that record was Elvin. Charlie Persip was the drummer and Elvin came in and just played shakers for the whole fifteen minutes. It's all he did and he just kept it together, letting Charlie spill over all he wanted. The form—we didn't plan it. I think I just gave the order of the solos.

The other selections on *Out of the Cool* are equally compelling, though Gil defined their development more specifically through the course of the arrangements. "Where Flamingos Fly" is based on Evans's arrangement of the tune for Helen Merrill; here, Jimmy Knepper plays the poignant melody on trombone. This tune is also set afloat by a repetitive motif initiated by Gil and passed around the ensemble. Trumpet player Johnny Coles, who worked with Gil from 1958 to 1964, plays a prominent role on this album and delineates Gil's ambiguous nuances. Though Coles's playing recalls Miles's in some ways—spare, with a meted-out intensity—Coles has a sound all his own. An otherworldly vibe pervades the album and is perpetuated by the rhythm section: Gil himself, Carter on bass, Jones on percussion, and Persip on drums provide steady support but with unconventional chords and bass lines and the use of percussion instruments. The music has an elastic unpredictability that is not at all standard jazz fare.

Impulse! was intent on making a splash with its Evans LP and the three other jazz albums that the new label released at the same time; they all had elegant gatefold covers and high-quality production values. The sound quality on *Out of the Cool* is pristine, spacious, and the instruments are balanced well. The care taken in this regard far surpassed that on Gil's previous LPs as a leader.

Out of the Cool represents another important leap in Evans's artistic expression. Pieces like "La Nevada" were Gil's response to the jazz of the early 1960s—most notably the fiercely probing improvisation of John Coltrane, whose music profoundly affected Gil. More venturesome than previously, Gil's new work integrated the written and improvised, at times allowing the balance to shift imperceptibly. He created an altogether different "sound world" from the one he built with and for Miles Davis, and from his two previous albums of standards—now so tame in comparison! He was reaching—however subtly—toward the loose, bordering-on-chaotic music that would comprise a great portion of his later work.

The album won over the jazz press—even John S. Wilson, who had panned Gil's albums with Miles and his work for Thornhill. Wilson awarded this one five stars:

> Here we see Evans plain—not concerned with creating suit-able settings for Miles Davis, not reworking old jazz standards, but expressing himself with his own band. And it's quite a musical sight. For Evans is a full-fledged member of that select group of composer-arrangers who have completely instinctive musical personalities—a group in which Duke Ellington still remains head man and which includes, at the very least, Jelly Roll Morton and John Lewis.[14]

The dark emotional landscape that Evans sculpted here is a terrain that he seemed compelled to explore. From it comes a "cry"—like that first heard in *Porgy*—that would resonate in almost all of Gil's work to follow.

ı¹ ıı ı

Miles Davis was now a cultural superstar, featured in *Playboy*, *Esquire*, and *Ebony*. He continued to top the jazz polls, but he became canny and protective about how much recording he would do. In the early 1960s, he began an unusual financial arrangement with Columbia in which the label provided him with "loans," which were really advances on LPs he'd just recorded. Columbia was still flush with the success of Davis's albums to date, and the higher-ups were quite willing to accommodate him, as revealed by the following memo from Irving Townsend to Goddard Lieberson:

> November 8, 1960
> From: Irving Townsend
> To: Goddard Lieberson
> I talked to Miles Davis this morning and he asked if his current earning status has improved enough so that he can get another loan.... I pointed out to him that from our standpoint the only way this financing makes sense was for him to record and that the album pacing that I originally worked out with him of one large band per year and a couple of small group albums would make his earnings rise on Columbia and justify future loans much more readily. He promised to do something about this immediately.
>
> I would appreciate your having his situation reviewed in New York and contacting him if a loan is possible.[15]

While the loans helped Davis's cash-flow problem, they actually kept him in debt to the company—especially after his sales began flagging in the mid- to late 1960s. No matter how well his records sold, Davis complained to Columbia executives almost daily.

There were several reasons Miles was reluctant to record in the early 1960s. He felt burned by the way Prestige had handled his recordings, for one thing. The label had amassed reams of material it had acquired from him in the 1950s, which it was still slowly releasing as his popularity soared. For another, from 1960 to 1963 Davis had difficulty maintaining a group whose collective creativity came up to the level of his work with Bill Evans, Cannonball Adderley, and, above all, John Coltrane. In the spring of 1960, Coltrane finally left to form his own group and received immediate critical acclaim. Coltrane's shoes were hard to fill; his searing abstractions and virtuosity were fantastic counterpart to Davis's spare, honed lyricism. None of the tenor player's successors—including talented musicians such as Hank Mobley, Sonny

Stitt, Sam Rivers, and George Coleman—lasted more than a few months. In 1963, Davis's longtime rhythm section of Wynton Kelly, Paul Chambers, and Jimmy Cobb all left to go out on their own.

Davis was also in some physical and psychological turmoil, which affected his willingness to record and/or perform frequently. He had been diagnosed with early stage sickle-cell anemia and was in pain a good deal of the time. Biographer Jack Chambers speculated that Davis was traumatized after getting beat up by the police outside Birdland in October 1959, a month or so before the sessions began for *Sketches*. Furthermore, Davis's intensely creative pace of the previous five years was hard to sustain. Davis himself remarked that both *Porgy* and *Sketches* were the most difficult recordings he'd ever made and left him drained.

Throughout the 1960s, Miles played cat-and-mouse with various Columbia executives anxious to keep up the flow of product. This situation made several Columbia executives uneasy, even though Townsend fully appreciated what he knew of the reasons. He did what he could to encourage Davis, especially on a promising idea for another recording with Gil, and counseled the Columbia higher-ups to be patient.

Feb. 16, 1961
From: Irving Townsend
To: Goddard Lieberson
Cc: Al Lorber, Frank de Vol, Teo Macero
Apparently we are all involved with our poll-winning friend Miles Davis.... I think the best way to handle him is by keeping in touch mutually with what we hear.... Miles tells me that he plans an album in March with Gil Evans. I hope this is true. He also is willing for me to record him out here in Hollywood on location....

Miles' delay in recording is based on nothing else but his feeling that only when he has something new to say musically should he make a record, but without at least 2 albums a year from Miles his earning capacity will not continue.[16]

Townsend did convince Miles to record with the quintet at the Blackhawk in San Francisco that April, resulting in two albums

(*Live at the Blackhawk,* volumes one and two) that have long since become classic bestsellers. Indeed, Miles's entire Columbia "product" with his quintet during 1961 was all drawn from live dates, but the attempt to record another studio album with Evans never materialized.

Gil and Miles continued their friendship and working relationship and often discussed possible recording projects. Gil sketched out many fragments the two had hummed, played, or sung to each other over the phone. They began to establish a pattern. Columbia would ask them to do a new album; Davis would tell Townsend or Macero that he and Gil were "almost ready," that they had plenty of material. Through the rest of the 1960s, though, the few recordings they made together were rarely on the level of their earlier masterpieces.

On May 19, 1961, shortly after Miles returned to New York from San Francisco, he and Gil appeared in concert together for the first time. The concert was to benefit the African Research Foundation, a group that sought to provide emergency medical and food supplies for Tanganyika and Zanzibar (what is now Tanzania).[17] The concert took place at Carnegie Hall; this was the first time Davis appeared there as a headliner and Evans's debut at the hall. They played to a sold-out house.

In the weeks prior to the concert, Teo Macero, who felt strongly that this would be a historic musical occasion, set about getting the requisite authorizations and reserving the portable equipment to make a live concert album. At the eleventh hour, Miles objected. Most of the program was already available on record, and he didn't want to compete with himself.

Teo cancelled the portable equipment for the night, but unbeknownst to Miles, Gil, and the other musicians, he secretly set up a monaural seven-and-a-half-inch recorder while Gil was rehearsing the band just before the concert. Also unbeknownst to Davis, Gil, and the other musicians, a small group of protesters was picketing the concert out on the street; they believed the African Research Foundation perpetuated colonialism.[18] Picketing was not unusual at the time, in New York or anywhere else in the country. The growth of the Civil Rights movement and the initial stirrings of the Black Power movement spurred on protests of all sorts,

large and small, that accompanied similar cultural events. Gil
recalled:

> The concert was packed. During the intermission Max Roach
> and some friends dropped by and we talked. After the inter-
> mission was over, Miles played "Someday My Prince Will Come."
> Out on the stage comes Max, who sits down on the floor and
> holds up a sign which says, "Give Africa Back to the Africans."
> Well, he wouldn't get up. And Miles is not one to get upstaged,
> so he stopped playing and out came these burly stage hands
> and just picked Max up and carried him off.[19]

After Roach was physically removed from the stage, Miles came
back out and resumed playing with an increased intensity that
carried through the rest of the program. His performance was what
one thinks of as "classic" Miles—that tightrope walk of an artist in
control of an enormous range of expression.

Macero's instinct to record the concert was on target. He clearly
knew that a live "Miles at Carnegie Hall" was a marketable historic
event and wanted to release the album as soon as possible. Shortly
after the concert, Macero confessed to Davis that he had recorded
the concert after all, saying he had "just made the tape for myself."
When he played it for Miles, Miles said, "Put it out," though Davis
insisted that the "Adagio" from *Concierto de Aranjuez* not be
included because it was still newly available on the *Sketches of
Spain* LP.

Macero then set about trying to convince Columbia to release
the tape. Although the recording quality was monaural and not
up to Columbia's usual standards, he got approval to release the
material, and in September the tapes were transferred to larger
tape for mastering. The Carnegie Hall album was released in early
1962 and was a smash, despite the poor recording quality. It was
voted *Melody Maker*'s "Jazz Record of the Year," among other
awards.[20]

Miles and the orchestra performed two unfamiliar arrangements
at the concert. These scores—like others—were Gil Evans's nod
to other musicians: pianist Bill Evans and bassist Paul Chambers.
Musical borrowing—developing fragments of a solo or expanding

upon someone else's harmonic concept—was very much part of Gil's working method. The concert opened with Gil's orchestral prelude to "So What," Evans's reply to Paul Chambers's introductory passage to this piece. Miles and the orchestra also performed a new Evans arrangement of the ballad "Spring Is Here" by Rodgers and Hart. It was based on Bill Evans's chordal reharmonizations of this song, exploring the upper reaches of the harmonic spectrum. This arrangement also provides another striking example of Miles's ascerbic lyricism couched in the "lush bottom" described by Amiri Baraka.

The concert closed with the "Adagio" from the *Concierto de Aranjuez*. The recording (finally released in 1987) reveals that, in some passages, Gil drew forth different emphases from the orchestra; it soars with Davis's entrances, and he ad libs more freely with his part, most of which was written. Gil's unusual scoring came to life in concert: the bass doubled with the tuba and the clatter and glitter of castanets, tambourine, and harp. Again, Davis and Evans conjured a world and story of mythic grandeur.

The experience inspired new musings between Gil and Miles regarding another joint album.

> From: Irving Townsend
> To: Teo Macero
> May 24, 1961
>
> Miles discussed with me yesterday the advisability of recording with Gil Evans two or three pieces they now have ready, in releasing a single before enough material is ready for an album. I am in favor of this, for, as you know, I think we have sadly neglected the single possibilities of our strong jazz artists, and also I think if we do this sort of thing now, we will get more product out of Miles than we would if we have to wait until an entire album is ready for recording.[21]

But 1961 ended without any new collaboration between Gil and Miles; each was soon distracted by other matters, both musical and personal. It wouldn't be until the summer of 1962 that they would reenter Columbia's 30th Street studio together.

ı' Iı ı

In 1961, Gil and Lillian went their separate ways. Many of Gil's friends found her difficult, a scene-maker. "She gave him a tough time," said Steve Lacy. "She threw a cocktail glass at him at a party once. She didn't favor him the way he needed to be favored. He was relieved to get out of her life."[22] Gil had tolerated the unhappy relationship; Lillian initiated the breakup and divorce proceedings. She stayed in the 45th Street apartment, where she remained until the onset of an incapacitating illness in 1992 (she died in 2000). She revealed some of her feelings—without mentioning Gil once by name—in a guarded letter to Maybeth Carpenter in February 1962.

> Dear Maybeth:
> This is directed to you as nominal head of the Western Clan. I cannot thank you enough for your letter and card.... From this disaster area there seems to be very little to relate since it all involves personal discomfiture and an extensive readjustment to a new routine. It may be understood that only time takes care of this and it cannot, rather refuses, to be pushed. It is a slow, painful process....
> I've managed to ramble on without saying most of what I wanted to say. Let me do say this though. I deeply appreciate your wonderfully sweet thoughts and expressions of friendship. I certainly include you in all this. I would always want to be in touch with you and my dearest wish right now is that I can be the kind of person you would want to call a friend. Confidence of friends can be of as great assistance as professional help. People have been grand to me and I feel that only by my actions can I assure them that they haven't misplaced their judgement.
> Please take good care of yourselves and give my very best regards to anyone you might see who remembers me....
> All best love, Lillian

Gil found another apartment, this time on the Upper West Side, at 86th Street, right near Central Park. Friends say he was not at all devastated by the breakup and took it with equanimity. Characteristically, as alimony, he gave her the rights to Gillian Music, which included the compositions that appeared on the Davis–Evans LPs, those that produced the most royalties.

Years later, Gil spoke cheerfully of moving to his new place, as if the move was not precipitated by any big life change: "I had a ping pong table, a basketball net, a grand piano!" Once again people could traipse through at all hours. Paul Chambers was a neighbor, as was Dan Morgenstern, whom Gil invited over to listen to Louis Armstrong records. But Steve Lacy said that Gil was uninterested in rebuilding the bachelor musician's lifestyle that he first enjoyed in New York, and that Gil spoke about "shopping for a wife."

He soon found her. Anita Cooper, then in her twenties, was an engaging, beautiful African American woman who lived for jazz, painting, and the creative ambiance of early 1960s Greenwich Village. After separating from her first husband she had taken an apartment on West 12th Street. She left for Europe in the summer of 1962 after completing a masters in social work at Fordham University. In Paris she befriended Bud Powell and Francis Paudras (the pianist's self-appointed caretaker) and became a familiar figure in the Parisian jazz scene, which consisted of expatriate American musicians and their French friends and admirers. Cooper returned to New York that fall, motivated by the news that John Coltrane would be performing again in the city. She resumed living in her Greenwich Village apartment.

In October 1962, around the time of her birthday, Anita received a tape in the mail from Paudras. She suspected that Paudras had sent her a recording of Bud Powell as a birthday present, but she was unable to listen to it because the tape had been recorded on a professional quality European machine at an unusual speed. She asked around trying to find someone who owned a similar machine, and someone suggested she contact Gil Evans, who had various tape recorders at his home. She gave him a call; he did have the right machine, and they both listened to Powell deliver an unusual transatlantic birthday tribute to Anita. The two quickly started spending a lot of time together.

Cooper found Gil reluctant to talk about his past, especially about his marriage to Lillian. She recalled:

Gil wouldn't ever mention her name, or speak of her or answer
the phone when he sensed it might be her calling. When I first
met him, the phone would ring all the time and he wouldn't
pick it up because he knew it was her calling. He was away
from her—he didn't have whatever it took to tell her to just
stop calling.... To me it was very peculiar, and I thought, poor
thing. It was humiliating that she would keep calling this person who obviously didn't want to hear from her.[23]

Gil and Anita quickly established a close romantic relationship,
and he moved in with her within a few months. Among a certain
circle of musicians and friends, Gil was in demand—women pursued him, they fell for him. A couple of women told Anita that she'd
made the "catch of the year."

Gil had no money as usual and was living hand-to-mouth,
despite the fact that he was a jazz star at the time—in his own
right and because of his work with Miles. He was honest with
Anita about his finances. He told her he was broke and had no
bank account (though somehow he had managed to help support
his mother while she was still alive). It didn't faze her, though she
had a far more conservative attitude when it came to money. Anita
recalled:

I had work and got some scholarships, and had a little money
from my family. I'm very bourgeois-minded about money in the
bank and so forth, which made it possible. Otherwise, I don't
know what would have happened to Gil if he hadn't bumped
into me—which was also what *he* said.

He also said if that if we had a band, it would be my job to be
the brains and take care of the business—that he didn't have
those skills. That was laid on me instantly. It was out front and
I accepted it.[24]

Anita and Gil shared several strong interests: modern jazz, painting, and other arts. They both passionately followed John Coltrane
and went to hear him whenever they could (Gil said they "bathed
in Coltrane"). They also shared a compelling interest in the phil-
osophies and writings of Wilhelm Reich. They agreed with Reich's

perception that in modern society most people lived an "armored" existence, which obstructed them in their personal lives and artistic endeavors. Reich developed a body-centered psychotherapy intended to help people break through that armor. Various kinds of bodywork, such as bioenergetics, were founded on principles and experiences Reich explored in the late 1920s while he still an active member of Sigmund Freud's inner circle in Vienna. Reich moved to the United States in 1939, where he established a clinical center in Forest Hills and later in Maine that attracted a close circle of therapists and researchers.[25]

Gil had begun Reichian therapy in the 1960s with a therapist, Dr. Oscar Tropp (who with his younger brother Simeon had joined Reich's circle in Maine in 1946). The vocalist Jon Hendricks once dropped in on Gil and found him about to leave for an appointment with Tropp. Hendricks expressed surprise that Gil was in therapy. Gil explained that it was because he didn't think anyone liked his music, which surprised the singer even more.

Despite his avid interest in Reich, Gil began Reichian therapy almost by accident. Dr. Oscar Tropp had an office around the corner from Gil's 86th Street apartment, and John Carisi, who knew of the therapist's work, insistently recommended him to Gil. Gil described aspects of his therapy to Helen Johnston:

> I went to a therapist but he didn't do analysis—it wasn't intellectual. He thought it was a waste of time to analyze dreams and that it was a waste of time to find out who and where, when and how you were first brutalized into this condition of so-called civilization. He thought you would get more out of it physically. So I would have these breathing sessions—he would press me all over while I breathed—you know, slow breathing, when you're lying on the couch. He would have me breathe, maybe a hundred and fifty, or two hundred times. And by that time, you usually have some kind of breakthrough, you start laughing or crying—you have to.[26]

Gil saw Tropp for about three years until the therapist died suddenly. Gil then saw Oscar's younger brother Simeon, but he, too, died. Gil, who could scarcely afford therapy in the first place, then gave it up. Anita Evans recalled that Oscar Tropp's death devastated Gil: "It was like he'd lost a hundred of his best friends."

Gil's career continued to advance slowly. The collaborations with Miles Davis had helped Gil win some jazz polls, but, lacking Miles's celebrity status and interest in self-promotion, Gil did not acquire the same household name recognition. Like Miles, Gil was not always anxious to record, but his situation was different from that of other bandleader/arrangers. He did not have a steadily working band whose appearances would, among other things, necessitate a steady flow of new arrangements, as in the glory days of the big bands. He did not have a drive to churn out "product" for recording purposes, or to keep record companies happy. His work, never formulaic, was not easy to crank out.

In 1961, Gil did not record a new album (with the exception of the Carnegie Hall Concert), but this was not due to lack of opportunity. *Out of the Cool* had met with rave reviews, and he was under contract to record another album for Impulse!, but he backed out. For one thing, Creed Taylor, who had produced Gil's first Impulse! album, was leaving the company to head up the Verve label. Gil, having found a producer he thought suited his recording style, wanted to follow him. Because of this, and also because Gil might not have had a new LP's worth of material, he handed over his Impulse! session dates, in September and October 1961, to Johnny Carisi and Cecil Taylor, each of whom recorded half a side. Impulse! put out the resulting album, *Into the Hot*, with a cover similar to that of *Out of the Cool,* including Gil's photo; the label printed the two covers at the same time to save printing costs. But the album—Carisi's side an outgrowth of his early work, Taylor's more percussive, motivic, an aggressive form of "minimalism"— was not at all a Gil Evans album. Gil did not perform on it, nor did his orchestra, nor was there any of his music on it. When asked why he chose Carisi and Taylor for this windfall, Evans, who'd admired their work as composers, said that was the only way he could hear their music.

Columbia, meanwhile, was still trying to lure Davis back into the studio, and Irving Townsend and other Columbia executives hoped for another Miles–Gil studio album. Miles must have dropped some hints to lead them on, because on January 3, 1962, paperwork began rolling in the form of a recording authorization for Miles Davis with arrangements by Gil Evans for twenty-six musicians, at an estimated recording budget for musicians of nine thousand dollars. The concept was "A Latin-American album w. large dance band."

The resulting album, *Quiet Nights*, has long been considered the stepchild of the Evans–Davis oeuvre. It was finally released in March 1964, and in the eyes of Gil and Miles, it should never have seen the light of day.

Miles, Gil, and the Evans Orchestra spent four sessions during July, August, and November 1962 getting less than twenty minutes' worth of music on tape. No further sessions were held under Gil's supervision, either for recording new music or for editing what existed, part of the post-recording process with which he normally involved himself. In late 1963, without Gil's and Miles's knowledge or approval, Macero cobbled together just enough music to fill an album by adding the track "Summer Night," which Miles and a "fill-in" quintet had recently recorded on the West Coast. This upset Gil and infuriated Miles so much that he cut off his working relationship with Teo Macero for several years.

Quiet Nights received tepid reviews; it was not the musical blockbuster Columbia had hoped for. One problem was that the label marketed it as a bossa nova album when the airwaves had long been oversaturated with this maligned Brazilian–"cool" jazz fusion. The idea of Gil and Miles "doing the bossa nova" has a certain attractive irony—because Antonio Carlos Jobim, João Gilberto, and other Brazilian bossa artists idolized Gil and Miles, the concept might have lead to a kind of reverse fusion. But the album is not all bossa nova music, and the selections are poorly sequenced and edited. Finally, the album does not feel like a cohesive musical whole, something people had come to expect from Gil and Miles.

"Song #2," a bossa composed by Gil and Miles, opens the LP. Though the piece and the arrangement are cool and light, true to the bossa nova spirit, it may be Miles's and Gil's least interesting work on record. Gil's arrangements of "Aos Pes da Cruz" and "Corcovado" (Quiet Nights) are only slightly more interesting musically, with Miles and orchestra capturing the bittersweet quality so present in the music of the bossa's originators. The title track is curious; Gil may have never completed the arrangement. About 1:18 minutes into the selection, the cyclical vamp from "Aos Pes da Cruz" was clumsily edited in, extending the piece by another one and a half minutes.

The remaining three Evans arrangements on the LP defy musical pigeonholing. "Song #1," an Evans–Davis composition, is the album's standout. It opens with a through-composed passage, dark in feeling, which leads into a sorrowful melody—like a Brazilian *saudade*. The piece is underscored with snatches of bossa rhythm that give way to a slow swing, as the sounds of Willie Bobo's bongos intensify along with a series of ascending brass figures. A theme and variations, "Song #1" is strung together with deliberate precariousness; Miles's strength of will was the glue. The piece segued thematically into the next, "Wait 'Til You See Her," an obscure tune by Rodgers and Hart. The two pieces together form a suite as mystery-laden as any of Davis's and Evans's finest work.[27]

Quiet Nights was the last album Gil and Miles worked on together for Columbia, though they did several more studio sessions for the label in the 1960s. Evans's and Davis's working relationship was not based on what was or was not going on at Columbia. They actively and reciprocally exchanged ideas until Gil's death. Sometimes this resulted in music on tape or on score paper; but the habit of bouncing ideas off each other was integral to their friendship.

In October 1963, Gil and Miles had another full-fledged joint studio date, at Columbia Studios in Hollywood.[28] They had been hired to write and record incidental music for a play entitled *Time of the Barracudas*, a black comedy by the fledgling British playwright Peter Barnes. The play was to debut in San Francisco, starring Lawrence Harvey and Elaine Stritch, and then move to Los Angeles. The play's producers flew Gil, Anita, and Miles out to Hollywood to record the music and arranged hotel suites equipped with grand pianos for all of them, including Anita.

Columbia, hoping that the music eventually could be released as an album, paid for two studio dates, and Irving Townsend was the producer. Gil and Miles treated the project ambitiously, and some of the cues were arranged for fourteen musicians. On the first date, Davis recorded the orchestral cues with members of his new quartet—pianist Herbie Hancock, bassist Ron Carter, and drummer Tony Williams—as the rhythm section. On the second date, Davis recorded with the quartet alone. This became the first recording by the group that would soon be thought of as the creative equal of Davis's late 1950s group with John Coltrane, Cannonball Adderley, and Bill Evans.

The ten musical cues recorded for the play, which add up to about twelve minutes and forty-five seconds of music, are startlingly original. At least some fragments were probably written by Davis and Evans before they were commissioned for the play, part of their cache of material that was always "almost ready" to record. Gil further developed "Time of the Barracudas" (later known as "General Assembly") and "Hotel Me" (later known as "Jelly Roll") a few months later and recorded them with his own ensemble (sans Miles) for Verve. These two tunes became standards in Gil's repertoire. Gil based "Hotel Me" on a riff by blues pianist Otis Spann; Miles plays the tune counter to his usual style, with a gutbucket earthiness. "Time of the Barracudas" is more elegant, a surging modal piece in 6/8. The shorter incidental cues have their beauty, too. Brief abstractions of sound, Miles's trumpet rises out of a density that presages by several years the sound and textures Gil and Miles would explore further with their own groups, enriched with synthesizers and electric instruments.

While the Evanses were in Hollywood, a couple of incidents occurred that made them realize that their life in New York City was easier than it might be elsewhere. As a black and white couple in Greenwich Village, involved in the jazz world, Gil and Anita were living in their own scene. When they first started going out together in New York, people, even among Gil's friends, made more of an issue about their age difference than about their racial difference. A few years later, Gil recalled this trip to L.A.

One of the reasons Anita and I don't like the idea of living in Southern California—Hollywood—is because they are very peculiar out there. Every time I looked in the rear vision mirror in the car we rented the police were following us because we were an integrated couple. It's fantastic, really fantastic.

We were out in front of a club in Los Angeles where Miles was playing...it was a neighborhood club, it wasn't a chic place. So I parked the car across the street. When I came out it was about four in the morning and there had been a dark red stripe that had been painted there. You couldn't even see it. But a cop gave me a ticket.

Well, that ended up with him wanting to search everybody and he's saying to me, "What do you do?" And I said, "I'm a composer." And he said, "Well I hope you don't write jazz!" Imagine a cop bothering to say that to me.

He's got Harold [Lovett, Davis's lawyer] up against the car, turned around—over nothing. It was because we were all mixed together, that was it.... Lawrence Harvey was there, too. It was a mixture like that and that policeman took it upon himself to be the cultural dictator besides the social director of the city [laughter].[29]

Time of the Barracudas was panned in San Francisco and quickly closed. Ralph Gleason said in his column for the *San Francisco Chronicle* that the music was the best part of the play. "The trouble is that, as director Anthony Page frankly said before the opening, 'Miles' music is too good.' You get to hear it, played from a tape made in Los Angeles, in tiny bits.... Little as it is, it is a distinct delight to hear the Miles Davis–Gil Evans music coming through."[30]

Gleason must have been one of the last people to hear the taped music. The show was supposed to move to Los Angeles, but the Los Angeles Musician's Union forbade the use of taped music for a live theatrical performance. Their ban was moot, because the play did not generate enough interest to open in L.A. anyway. The tape lay in Columbia's archives for over thirty years before it was finally released in 1998 as part of the Davis–Evans Columbia box set.

ı' lı ı

Shortly before Gil and Miles went to Hollywood, Gil held his own first recording session for Verve with Creed Taylor as producer in September 1963. Gil lucked out with Taylor (founder of the Impulse! label and producer of *Out of the Cool*). Arriving at Verve not long before, Taylor made an immediate splash as producer of the first wildly successful bossa nova records (with Stan Getz, Antonio Carlos Jobim, and João and Astrud Gilberto), including "The Girl from Ipanema." Verve gave Taylor carte blanche, which he passed along to Gil. Gil was allowed the number of musicians and recording time he wanted. He was even able to record some sketches on studio time—an unheard-of luxury for a composer/arranger. Gil was also allowed to record one or two pieces at a time, whenever he had something ready, instead of conceiving of an entire album beforehand. Taylor was confident that an album would eventually materialize if he gave Gil free reign.

At the first session, Gil recorded two of his own compositions, "Flute Song" and "El Toreador." It wasn't until April 1964 that he recorded another two arrangements; then, in the following six months he recorded six new arrangements for large ensembles and several sketches with a quartet. The resulting album became *The Individualism of Gil Evans*, released in late 1964.

The album contains some of Gil's best music on record. Selections include Kurt Weill's "The Barbara Song" and four Evans originals: "Las Vegas Tango," "Flute Song," "Hotel Me," and "El Toreador." Several of the musicians, including Johnny Coles, Steve Lacy, Al Block, Jimmy Cleveland, Tony Studd, Bill Barber, Elvin Jones, and Paul Chambers, played on all the sessions, preserving a consistency in the textures, mood, and overall sound. Other stellar personnel—Eric Dolphy on various woodwinds, Wayne Shorter on tenor, Phil Woods on alto, and Kenny Burrell on guitar—were on hand for some sessions and recorded with Gil for the first time. Gil plays piano on every track, and his performance, particularly on "The Barbara Song," functions as an indicator of his conceptual direction. On the Weill song, the mood is full of pathos, with Wayne Shorter's tenor sax taking up the cry. "El Toreador," built on one chord, sounds like a development of one of the *Barracuda* cues; Johnny Coles's plaintive trumpet is the foremost voice, cutting through the rumblings of the low brass and three acoustic basses and a whirring tremolo in the high reeds.

The musicianship on all the Verve sessions is of the highest order. The musicians dig deeply into the music, both as soloists and as ensemble players. Again there is an Ellingtonian parallel;

the musical personalities are so strong on these recordings that horn voicings and ensemble passages are characterized by the collective sound of the people playing them. It's not a minor ninth chord, per se, but rather Steve Lacy, Phil Woods, and Eric Dolphy singing a sound together.

Gil and Creed Taylor went on to different things in the late 1960s, and the remaining orchestral tracks were not released until the early 1970s, under the title *The Gil Evans Orchestra with Kenny Burrell and Phil Woods*. That album includes three full-scale arrangements from the 1964 sessions: "Time of the Barracuda," featuring Wayne Shorter; "Concorde;" and an edited take of Willie Dixon's "Spoonful," featuring Phil Woods. It also included two tracks by a quartet with Gil on piano—"Cheryl" by Charlie Parker and "Ah Moore" by Al Cohn. The latter were only sketches and Gil never intended them to be released.

In 1988, Verve issued most of the material from Gil's 1963–64 sessions on compact disc. The disc had been compiled under Evans's supervision the year before he died. It includes two previously unreleased big band arrangements, "Proclamation" and "Nothing Like You," which were recorded at Gil's last session for Verve as a leader, October 29, 1964. The quartet sketches and an orchestral sketch of "Punjab," which Lacy remembered so glowingly, were not included, as per Gil's wishes.

Over the next two decades Gil recycled arrangements such as "Time of the Barracudas," "Hotel Me," "Proclamation," and fragments of his other pieces from this period again and again. From this time on, he used these works to cast an increasingly wider net. Without sacrificing his carefully calibrated "sound worlds," he conceived of ever more flexible arrangements—and relied increasingly on the collective sensitivity of his musicians—to spur on improvisation and to use those improvisations as ideas for new work.

ı' ıı ı

Meanwhile, Gil and Anita got married in the spring of 1963 and soon started a family. Gil became a father for the first time at age fifty-two. Noah was born March 21, 1964, and Miles followed sixteen months later, on July 5, 1965. Since Gil worked at home, for the most part he was able to spend a great deal of time with his sons, sitting at the piano while they crawled around at his feet. He really enjoyed being a parent and having the chance to "relive" childhood. "I did nothing for three years except carry those kids around—one in front, one behind."[31]

By now Gil was a prominent musician—in the jazz news at any rate. He and Miles received a Grammy for *Sketches*, and Gil became a poll winner himself—he beat out Duke Ellington, by a wide margin, for best composer in the 1960 *Down Beat* Reader's Poll and in *Melody Maker*, the British jazz journal. He won the International Jazz Critics Award in 1962 and the *Down Beat* reader's poll in 1964, and *Individualism* was nominated for a Grammy.

At the Grammy reception, held at the old Astor Hotel, Gil met Louis Armstrong, who had been nominated for *Hello, Dolly*. This was the only time Gil ever met the legendary trumpet player, who was a lifelong hero and musical inspiration for him. Gil went down a hallway, offstage near the bandstand, to a table where drinks were set up, and Armstrong was standing there having a drink.

I told him that I was the world's number one Louis Armstrong expert. He had bought *Miles Ahead*, the first one we made, and he told me he liked it very much. And after we talked for awhile he said, "We could make an album!" And I said, "That's right, we could!" Then he said, "Now, I don't want to hear any of those funny chords of yours, forget them. But go see my man Joe Glaser."

So I did, and he said, "Well, in the first place I've never heard of you, and in the second place you have to know that Louis is a very, very friendly man. You have to realize that sometimes he says things that he doesn't mean."

I was outraged, of course. But he did ask me to come back in a couple of days. I did, and then he said, "It's a funny thing, I had never heard of you before, and here on my desk is a music magazine with your picture on the cover." ...So he said he'd look around and see what he could do.

Later, when I contacted him again he said that he couldn't get anybody interested. So we never did do it, which was really a drag. And when I tried to get some information from him, like who was the guitar player that played the intro on "I'm Confessin' that I Love You"—whoever it was played it on a slide guitar—he said, "Oh, don't ask me about *that!*"

I tried, you know. But sometimes I think I didn't push hard enough.[32]

Gil longed to write for Armstrong, and also for Lester Young, another of his heroes, but these wishes never came to pass. In this case, the fault was mainly Glaser's; he could be quite antagonistic at first encounter. "You *could* reason with Joe Glaser," Dan Morgenstern once said, "but that was not in the cards with Gil."

As far as Gil was concerned, when his sons were young toddlers, he was all domestic. He told several interviewers that he did very little in the three years after the birth of his children. Jazz writers often accept the remarks of their heroes at face value. For instance, in 1967 Leonard Feather wrote: "Between the 1960 band and the one he [Gil] formed for West Coast appearances in the fall of 1966, there seemed to be a long period when, except for his work with Miles Davis, he wasn't doing any writing at all. Instead he seemed merely to be contemplating." Gil conceded.

That's right. I knocked off for a couple of years. For me, it was a question of a total life, a whole life, which has priority over any one of the things you do in the course of living. They are all part of it, but sometimes they have to wait a little while. Emotional development with me is like that. If I feel the need for some emotional development, well, I think about music and play and even write. But as far as the product is concerned, there is no product.[33]

Yet it was an intensely creative period for Gil. Aside from the projects already mentioned, Gil worked on two other albums for Verve (with Creed Taylor as producer), *Guitar Forms*, featuring Kenny Burrell with a large jazz orchestra, and *Look to the Rainbow*, featuring Brazilian vocalist Astrud Gilberto. Gil was also still actively involved with Miles, and the two had enough ideas at any given time that Miles kept tantalizing Columbia execs with the possibility of another Evans–Davis record. Anita Evans recalled Gil working on music constantly: "There are twenty-four hours in the day and Gil worked on music for at least seventeen of them." Sometimes that meant working on one chord for hours at a stretch; sometimes it meant scoring for an upcoming session.

The years from 1965 to 1967 saw no albums with Gil on the cover, to be sure. As his young sons played nearby, though, he experimented and explored at the keyboard and moved toward yet another innovative phase of his career.

10 svengali

For all my life I'd been sitting in front of that piano
trying to figure out another way to voice a minor
seventh chord. For thirty years I was sitting there.
I sat there for so long, I had calluses on my ass.
One on each cheek. I hadn't even realized it until
my wife said to me, "You've got calluses on your
ass.' So I thought, 'You're right.' I'd been sitting
there and I was so tired of it, so bored from doing
it for so long. It was such a lonesome thing that I
decided that I needed adventure and the only way
to get adventure was to get a band together.
—GIL EVANS, 1981

Gil's music took unorthodox and experimental turns in the late 1960s, resonating with the rapidly changing music of the times. Accomplished rock improvisers such as Santana were influencing jazz musicians and vice versa. Groups such as Blood, Sweat and Tears, with their tight horn arrangements, brought together an energetic blend of jazz-inspired soul-rock; so did the music of singer/songwriter Laura Nyro. Aretha Franklin, James Brown, and a new wave of R&B and soul musicians became tremendously popular. Their music, especially the instrumental arrangements, had roots in swing, the blues, and "jump" bands. Young jazz musicians such as Tony Williams, John McLaughlin, Herbie Hancock, Larry Coryell, and Chick Corea fed on this energized, electrified musical culture. The rocker with the most impact on the jazz scene was the guitarist Jimi Hendrix. His music was freeform, riveting, improvised, sophisticated; it revolutionized the sound of the guitar. A new sound innovator had emerged.

All the new artists, the sounds, the energy, and the more up-front rhythmic base of rock, soul, and pop interested Evans and Miles Davis. They continued to collaborate, their new work colored by what they heard; it was electrically tinged with flexible structures and forms and used even eighth-note rhythms that bordered on rock, but had more of a "floating" sense of time. Miles's small group (with Wayne Shorter, Herbie Hancock, Ron Carter, and Tony Williams) took up most of his energy. Gil still needed the larger canvas of a big ensemble with a variety of instruments. In the late 1960s, Gil put together bands for a handful of special occasions. During the 1970s, after a faltering start, he created and maintained a large ensemble that became one of the most vital artistic incubators in New York City. With it, Gil once again reshaped the arranging of large orchestral jazz pieces.

ı¹ ıₗ ı

After his final Verve sessions for Astrud Gilberto in 1965, Evans's recording activities slacked off for a couple of years. During this period—"all domestic," he once described it—his daily routine mainly consisted of working at the piano at his 15th Street apartment with his two young sons underfoot. In 1967 Gil applied for a Guggenheim Fellowship, intended for mid-career artists and scholars, in order to write music for what he called a "symphonic jazz orchestra." Though he had recommendations from Duke Ellington, John Hammond, Gunther Schuller, and Harry Partch, he was turned down. At that time no jazz artists/composers had received a Guggenheim.

Generally, it took a concrete paying proposition to spur Gil to complete new arrangements. An invitation from Jimmy Lyons, director of the Monterey Jazz Festival, in spring 1966 spurred a spate of activity. Lyons invited Gil to put together a band to perform at the festival and also at the Pacific Jazz Festival in Costa

Mesa, down the coast near Newport. The invitation was parlayed into a small California tour that would wind up in L.A. for a few nights at Shelley's Manne-Hole, the popular L.A. jazz club, and a concert at UCLA.

Evans wrote sixteen new arrangements, but the band was still not fully prepared as the tour neared. Despite receiving an advance, Gil couldn't "buy" enough rehearsal time, and he and the band managed to polish only a few of his new arrangements. The most polished was Eddie Harris's "Freedom Jazz Dance," then a popular jazz recording, which was the most enthusiastically received.[1] At Costa Mesa, the band was scheduled to play a matinee with the Stan Kenton Orchestra. Lyons had billed it as a "Balboa revisited" event, knowing that both Evans and Kenton had led bands in Balboa Beach three decades before, and that Kenton had subbed on piano with Evans's band. If people came expecting nostalgia they were disappointed. Gil's new musicians—tenor player Billy Harper, and multi-instrumentalist Howard Johnson—were hardly Swing Era veterans; born in the early 1940s, they came from an entirely new generation of jazz artists. Neither Evans nor Kenton played any Swing Era music, with the exception of "King Porter Stomp," which Gil told the crowd he'd played at the Rendezvous Ballroom in 1936.

The tour had problems. One of the new trumpet players fell apart due to his drug addiction and began to disrupt the other musicians onstage. Evidently Gil was the only one in the band unaware of the situation—until the musician broke down during a performance.

By the time Gil and the band wound up at Shelley's Manne-Hole, both band and music had begun to shape up. Gil was ecstatic to be playing with his own band again. While the results were a little ragged, Gil wasn't aiming at the sound of a perfectly rehearsed big band playing a perfect arrangement. "We didn't have enough time to get everything really ready," he said, "so we stretched the ones we did play.... I didn't have control of the soloists—that was a problem, because sitting at the piano I felt like I was just one of the musicians, and it's very difficult to play the piano and then jump up and direct the band and then go back and play the piano. This was my first time out since 1960."[2]

After the tour, Evans would have liked to do more with this band, but offers never came.

ı¹ Iₗ I

The late 1960s were also a turning point for Miles Davis. Columbia grew worried about Davis's record sales. Clive Davis, now Columbia's CEO, began to liken Davis's appeal to that of a classical musician such as Vladimir Horowitz—someone with a devoted following, but who no longer nabbed big and instant record sales. Clive Davis was willing to subsidize the trumpet player, up to a point, but also looked for ways to put Davis back on top. The label tried a new marketing tack with *Miles Smiles* (1966), presenting Davis not as the cool black prince but as funky, warm, and psychedelic. Davis remained fairly impervious to the label's machinations. Musically he pursued, as ever, his own direction. His music was abstract, expressionistic free jazz with no pretenses and with a patina of elegance. Albums such as *ESP* indeed gained Davis a new generation of fans but not the mega-sales of the rock groups.

Davis and Evans continued their musical exchanges. Gil often went to Miles's brownstone on West 77th Street, or, if Miles was on the road, the two frequently spoke by phone. Columbia kept hoping for a new Davis–Evans album that seemed always perched on the horizon. These hopes were always dashed.

May 4, 1966
From: Howard Roberts
To: Jack Wiedenman
Cc: Gallagher, Dean, Townsend

Miles cancelled his sessions.... Perhaps suspensions should be considered. Evans, Miles's arranger, demanded an additional $1500 advance which would represent a payment of $500 per arrangement, which in itself is very high, coupled with the $3000.00 he has already received, plus whatever additional arranging monies would be forthcoming. It would make the arranging bill astronomical. After a discussion with Bob Ciotti I informed Gil that it was practically impossible to advance any more money. It was after that that Miles cancelled the sessions.

I understand that Columbia is $40,000 in the red as of now with Miles Davis, but Teo informs me that there is enough in the can to put out one or two albums. Perhaps we should take that route.

I certainly would appreciate hearing your thoughts on the entire matter.

P.S. By the way, I was under the impression that Miles and Gil had been working on the concept of that album for over a year. However Gil told me flatly that only three tunes were ready and they still had to decide about the rest of the material.[3]

It is unclear what "that album" was or even whether Evans and Davis themselves had a firm "concept" of it. Still, the Columbia brass persevered.

From: Irving Townsend
To: Walter Dean
March 17, 1967

I'm sure you're tired of the MILES DAVIS problem, but I would like to tell you what I know of it as of now.

On the album with Coltrane, I discussed this with Bob Thiele and after I found out that involved our participation as well, including an advance, I told Bill Gallagher that I thought it was a poor idea and I also told this to Miles. Miles then said he would just as soon not record with Coltrane if we would do something with him where he'd get some money. He apparently has an album ready to go with Gil Evans and wants to record.

I have conveyed all this to all concerned in New York. If he calls me again, I will tell him that you will pay him an advance for his new album when he has made it. I think he will then do it. I will urge him to get going, but I want you to know that I did not convey to anyone concerned that I was in favor of the Impulse deal.[4]

Months later, Macero wrote a note to Clive Davis to keep him up to speed:

To: Clive Davis
From: Teo Macero
Oct. 13, 1967

The other day I discussed the possibility of doing a Miles Davis–Evans album with Miles and, as of the moment, it's only a possibility. They have been working on this possibility for three and a half years.

Clive Davis jotted a handwritten reply: "He is one of the few giants who appeal to the youth—we must keep after him."[5]

Just three days after this exchange, Teo proposed to Davis an album based on the music from *Dr. Doolittle,* a film released earlier that year. While the movie was popular, what the two artists might have seen in the music is impossible to fathom. Nevertheless, Macero jumped at any chance to bring Evans and Davis back together.

To: Clive Davis
From: Teo Macero
October 16, 1967

I have just had the pleasure of being with him this morning. He is very enthusiastic about doing a *Dr. Doolittle* album with the possibility of doing something from *Camelot,* with arrangements by Gil Evans.

It's difficult in a few paragraphs to discuss the value of his work and the scale and scope of it in terms of the present market...would appreciate meeting with you.[6]

This project remained stillborn, like virtually all the others Gil and Miles discussed in the late 1960s. Anita remembered frequent occasions when Gil and Miles would talk excitedly about some piece or bounce a riff off each other, then Gil would rush home and write out a few bars. "[W]e have so many new numbers half-finished now," Gil told Leonard Feather. "I talked to Miles just the other day, and we decided to put all the music together and get going on another album as soon as we can." Nothing ever gelled.

In January 1968, Gil attended a recording session of the Davis quintet plus George Benson. Herbie Hancock, Wayne Shorter, and

Miles himself wrote the material. Gil showed up with a pile of
music and told writer Martin Williams, who was at the session,
that he had "midwifed" a couple of the pieces. Miles had become
interested in experimenting with electric "sound"—which was
new, especially in jazz—and had Herbie Hancock playing celeste,
electronic piano, and electric harpsichord; Gil helped lay out the
new instrumentation for performance. The session resulted in
"Teo's Bag" and "Paraphernalia," which ended up on *Miles in
the Sky.*[7]

A month later, on February 16, 1968, Gil attended another
recording session with Miles supported by a large ensemble and
Davis's quintet. They recorded a piece entitled "Falling Water," a
tentative stab at a largely improvisational work using electric instruments, with a floating, rock-inspired rhythm. It was clearly unfin-
ished, a musical sketch—as experimental as the music for "Time of
the Barracudas," the last large ensemble piece they had recorded
together (in 1963), but nowhere near as cogent. It is not surprising
that the music was never issued until the 1998 Davis–Evans
Columbia box set.

Two months later, on April 19, 1968, Davis and Evans played a
concert together, their first since the 1961 Carnegie Hall performance. The occasion was the second annual Berkeley Jazz Festival,
where Davis had appeared with his quintet the previous year. The
quintet opened the program, then folded themselves into Gil's
orchestra. They played three new Evans arrangements: an unti-
tled raga (possibly a recycled "Punjab"), Aretha Franklin's mega-
hit "You Make Me Feel Like a Natural Woman," and Wayne Shorter's
"Antigua." Evans continued to expand his colors and instrumental
combinations, with two and three electric guitars, mandolin, harp,
marimba, three French horns, two bassoons, and an arsenal of
woodwinds. For once Evans stole the show. A *Down Beat* reviewer
described Davis's playing as "unsteady as a drunk on fast runs"
with a "fog-drenched" sound; Evans, by contrast, was "the Boswell
to Davis' Johnson: illustrating journeys, underlining anecdotes,
revealing Davis' personality in full."[8]

With these sessions and the concert, Gil began to emerge from
his "all domestic" retreat. That May, he was invited to perform
with his band at a new Tuesday night series at the Whitney Museum

consisting of four concerts featuring improvised music by jazz and contemporary classical musicians/composers. Each event was set amid Noguchi sculptures and selected works from the museum's collection—all for fifty cents' admission. "Art and music, experienced together, will enhance each other," the concept ran.

Evans's assemblage of instruments that evening was not at all standard—tuba, piccolo, and bassoon along with his mainstay of woodwinds and brass—even in the days of free jazz, when musicians often experimented with a variety of instruments. His need to express certain sounds and timbres was very specific; that guided his choices. (Unlike some of the free-jazz experimenters, his musicians were adept on their respective instruments.) His band gave a performance that would become typical in the ensuing years—a program of loose arrangements that juggled improvisation and detailed scored passages. The mixed review was also typical of many to come. John S. Wilson wrote:

GIL EVANS LEADS JAZZ AT WHITNEY
Arranger-Conductor Ends a 7-Year Absence Here

Evans the arranger and conductor who has been part of the jazz underground for most of the last 20 years, surfaced last night at the Whitney Museum of American Art to give his first concert in New York since 1961. More than 1300 people jammed into the museum's third-floor gallery to hear his 13-piece orchestra.... This was an audience that came to see the musicians as well as listen to them, and the more distant galleries were virtually empty.

Mr. Evans has a loose flowing approach to orchestral jazz. Using his rhythm section as a vital core, he builds ensembles and solos that swirl around it and ride on its pulsating power.... As the momentum built, tuning-up was blending with the beginnings of section developments and suddenly the whole band was diving into Mr. Evans' piquant and swinging "La Nevada."...

As the evening wore on it became apparent that it was not yet ready to function up to its potential as an orchestra. It was, most of the time, a rhythm section accompanying individual soloists.... The need for more preparation was evident (the group had been together for only two and half hours before this performance) because Mr. Evans, as he has shown in the past, has much more to offer than a setting for whatever soloists he may happen to round up.[9]

Evans worked on other projects in the late 1960s and early 1970s, including three film scores. In 1967 he composed incidental music for *Fragments*, a Danish film that he later described as "Peyton Place in Copenhagen." In 1969 he scored the music for *Parachute to Paradise*, a documentary short, and the following year for *The Sea in Your Future*, an educational documentary. At that time, he professed interest in doing more film scoring, but he was clearly conflicted about it; he did not have an agent, but neither did he actively promote himself. He refused to do jingle work ("if you're a professional jingle writer, when the phone rings, you can't say what, you must say yes"); he didn't like the constraints or the deadline pressure. It wasn't until the 1980s that he allowed himself to get involved in two big, star-studded movies—but even then, he had to be persuaded to do so by people involved whom he actually liked working with.

Meanwhile, back at the Columbia label, the brass still pursued its quest for another Evans–Davis collaboration.

CBS Memorandum
From: Edwin Mathews
To: Teo Macero
August 5, 1968

It has been brought to my attention that Miles Davis and Gil Evans' sales are superior to anything Miles has done singularly. Three LPs sold over 225,000 and continue to sell as catalogue. It would be most helpful if you would please take an opportunity to get another album from Miles and Gil.

Cc: Jack Gold, Bruce Lundvall[10]

The always determined Macero sent the memo back with a handwritten note: "We have been working on it for the last 5 years. Good luck. Will keep trying. Teo."[11]

Meanwhile, in June 1968 Gil got involved with the Davis quintet's next studio sessions, which resulted in the album *Filles de*

Kilimanjaro. The high-level improvisations on the album reveal a creative peak for this quintet (Davis, Shorter, Hancock, Carter, Williams). The album also shows a stylistic shift, with Hancock's electric piano and Carter's electric bass, and a rhythmic base that is founded on slightly funky grooves, neither modern swing nor rock. The album represents a planar shifting between abstract jazz, electric rock, "free" acid-rock, and the blues—the stirrings of a jazz-rock fusion.

Around this time, Evans and Davis listened frequently to Jimi Hendrix records. Davis had recently befriended the innovative young guitarist through his new girlfriend (soon-to-be wife), Betty Mabry. "Mademoiselle Mabry" is Evans's and Miles's direct nod to Hendrix; the opening chords are an inversion of Hendrix's hit song, "And the Wind Cries Mary." There is no doubt that Gil shaped this piece as well as others on the album. He was co-composer of "Petits Machins," though he received no credit, then or on subsequent Davis reissues. This piece is built on a fragmentary scalar phrase in an up-tempo 11/4 that repeats five times, building in intensity before opening up improvisationally. Gil developed it orchestrally and structurally when he formed a new band a couple of years later. Retitled "Eleven," it became a standard in Gil's book, and Davis was listed as co-composer when the piece was included on subsequent Evans albums.

Gil's involvement in *Filles de Kilimanjaro* raises some thorny issues about his work with Miles and his perception of the originality of his own work. Years later Evans admitted, "The last one [Davis album] I really worked on was *Filles de Kilimanjaro*—I really should have a credit on that one."[12] Gil's attitude—as always—was that working with Miles gave him so much pleasure that he didn't care about the credit. Another issue was Gil's reverential idea of what a composer or a composition was. He did not really consider himself a composer, even though his arrangements at times were such complete reconstructions that they were new compositions. Music was for everyone, he felt; his reworking (e.g., the Hendrix fragment) was a natural part of an ongoing process that did not, in Gil's eyes, amount to composition. Yet his composer or co-composer credits, especially on albums with Miles, produced valuable royalties. Miles did not single Gil out in this way—Wayne

Shorter and Herbie Hancock had to go after Miles for credit for their own compositions on Davis's LPs. But Gil's friendship with Miles was a factor. Anita Evans said that Gil would never go after Miles, nor even raise the subject with him. Gil would occasionally go after people at Columbia instead, claiming that Goddard Lieberson had said that Columbia would always take care of him. Lieberson, no longer at Columbia, had never really taken care of Gil as an artist in the first place. And by the late 1960s, it was a new era—rock ruled the record biz.

Down Beat voted *Filles de Kilimanjaro* Record of the Year in 1968. It had Gil's imprint and input, and poised both Gil and Miles toward further boundary pushing. From here on, each musician produced original and controversial work that was eclectic, electric, and energetic. Many critics charged that their new work had gone over the edge to the point where it was "not jazz." But Evans and Davis no longer did large-scale works together. With *Filles de Kilimanjaro* the Evans–Davis Columbia collaborations came to a close—after several years' worth of dashed possibilities.

Though *Filles de Kilimanjaro* was a critical success, the openness of jazz artists such as Evans and Davis to other influences, once considered their strength, was now deemed a betrayal. When Leonard Feather dropped in on Davis in his Hollywood hotel room he was aghast: "I found strewn around the room records or tape cartridges by James Brown, Dionne Warwick, Tony Bennett, the Byrds, Aretha Franklin, and Fifth Dimension. Not a single jazz instrumental."[13] For Evans and Davis the potential musical mix could be richer than ever, with elements from rock, soul music, and the new electric sounds.

This is evident on *Gil Evans*, an album Gil recorded in 1969, his first new LP as a leader since *Individualism* was released in late 1964. The album was one of the first releases by the newly formed Ampex label, a venture into the recording field by one of the leading producers of stereo tape.[14] It was also one of the first sixteen-track recordings ever produced. The recording came about through Albert Grossman, the notorious manager of Bob Dylan and Janis Joplin. Grossman was a great fan of Evans, and though they had no contractual agreement he helped Evans out from time to time.

Gil's use of electric instruments on this album (electric piano, bass, and guitar) signaled a new era in his sound. Some of Gil's unisons—electric piano and electric guitar playing single lines together—sound like a synthesizer. The electric instruments enrich Gil's multi-textured sound, which he would soon explore further with synthesizers. On pieces such as "So Long" (Gil's tribute to John Coltrane, who died in 1967) and "Proclamation," the whirling density of sound create a vortex, which is at the heart of Gil's most successful experimental music.

The fourteen musicians on this album form a typical Evans combination: black and white, old and young, ace studio musicians and experimentalists. Snooky Young, Ernie Royal, Johnny Coles, Billy Harper, Howard Johnson, Elvin Jones, and Joe Beck rose to the challenge of Evans's new set of syntheses. Here as elsewhere, Evans's choice of thematic material ranges widely: Billy Harper's "Thoroughbred" fuses jazz, soul, and rock; Evans's "Spaced" is a through-composed piece built on "sound" elements; "General Assembly" is a rocked out reworking of "Time of the Barracudas"; and George Russell's "Blues in Orbit" is typically complex. The variety underscores the fact that Gil's choices of material for arrangements were come upon one by one; no one compositional style ever dominated. He used some tunes because he fell in love with them—he discovered them viscerally. He used others, and updated many arrangements, because it gave him the chance to explore the material with specific musicians in mind, or a new array of sounds (e.g., "Proclamation").

Coincidentally, while mixing the album at the Record Plant, Anita and Gil met Jimi Hendrix, who was rehearsing in the studio next door and who shyly introduced himself. "There were a few dates when we were there simultaneously," Anita recalled, "but it didn't get personal. He came in a few times to hear what we were mixing."

Gil Evans never became an emblem of visionary jazz-rock fusion like *In a Silent Way* and *Bitches Brew*, Davis's next two LPs, yet Gil's album is equally pivotal to the new directions in jazz. Herbie Hancock, whose own work in this vein was much admired and emulated, more than once referred to Gil Evans as the "father of jazz fusion."

ı' Iı I

In 1970, Gil and his family moved into a spacious two-story loft in the Westbeth Apartments after living in the Vermeer Hotel at Seventh Avenue and 14th Street for much of 1968 and 1969. The Westbeth complex, a converted Bell laboratory overlooking the Hudson River in the West Village, was the first subsidized building for artists in New York City. The Evans family members were among the first residents and Gil became Westbeth's first official artist-in-residence. Gil's sons still live in the same sixth floor apartment in which they grew up.

Gil's erratic career, whose vicissitudes mirrored those of other struggling creative artists, took a toll on Anita. Commercial work did not interest him, except for the rare offers that coincided with his interests. Other talented New York arrangers, including Don Sebesky, Manny Albam, and Bob Brookmeyer, wrote their share of jingles, film scores, and jazz arrangements to order, jobs that kept them afloat and even well off financially. They paid a different price: constant deadlines, frantic clients, their time, and—at times— their pursuit of music that was *not* attached to any product to sell.

Gil was not tempted and was given to rail against the music business when the subject came up. Anita recalled many times when the family had no money and no food in the house, yet their sons had a rich childhood. They had a father who was always around, interesting people dropping in and out, trips to Europe and Japan with the band, and excellent private school educations for which they received scholarships.

At the most desperate times, with no gigs in sight, Gil might finally turn to Miles for some cash, or Anita to her family. Anita, in the frustrating position of being Gil's business manager, convinced Gil to apply for grants; she did all the information gathering and writing. In 1968, Gil reapplied for a Guggenheim and was granted the award: a nine-thousand-dollar fellowship for composition for the period from April 1, 1968, to March 31, 1969. Evans and George Russell were the first jazz musicians to receive this prestigious award. In 1972, Gil received a grant from the Creative Artists Public Service Program (CAPS) to create new work and to participate in community services through his performances and artists-in-residence programs. He also received several additional honors: in 1971, he was named one of the Founding Artists for the Kennedy Center in Washington, D.C.

For all their financial difficulties, Gil and Anita made deliberate choices about basic life issues. They were still very much influenced by Reich's ideas about child rearing, and those of A. S. Neill, founder of the Summerhill School and a close friend of Reich's. Their sons went to progressive schools with child-centered approaches to learning and development—the City and Country School in the Village and the Open Community School in Claverack, about an hour from the city. Anita Evans said:

> The boys started at City and Country when Miles was three and Noah was four. The school was founded by Caroline Pratt, a great educator to this day, and was also influenced by John Dewey—it was very '30s liberal. For instance, there was no formal teaching of reading until age seven, because their research had shown that the eyes of children weren't really ready to focus on print and in books until then. So they could read if they wished and go to the library, but the formal reading training didn't start until age seven. They'd have a half hour of compulsory reading for pleasure, that was one of the very few compulsory things, and they had clay work every day.... I thought they were going to be sculptors, and actually I wanted them to be architects. I didn't want them to be in this business. But they had other things in mind.
>
> Then, when they were eight or nine they went to the Open Community School up-state in the country for a year. The director patterned that school on Summerhill as best he could, so that was an interesting experience for them.[15]

Since moving to New York in the late 1940s, Gil had lived in a diverse, artistic community. His musical heroes, his profession, and his questing nature drew him there. He was fiercely anti-prejudice, and he had many theories that people were far more racially hybridized than anyone would care to admit, especially if they were white. But he refrained from explaining too much about racism too soon to his young sons.

Once in a while Gil and Anita mused about moving out of New York City. From a few experiences they had, though, they realized it was easier living where they did than in many other places in America. "We have nowhere to go right now, that's the problem about where to live," Gil told an interviewer in 1974.

I was here [in New York] for all the reasons you come here, to learn more about whatever your trade is, and to possibly help iron out some of your emotional problems. And when that's over and you've got what you need from the city, then I think it's time to move on, but I don't know where to go.

We can't live on Long Island or hardly anywhere else because of the racial problem.... A [billionaire] friend of ours lent us his chauffeur and limousine and we went out to Long Island to look for a house. And even with the chauffeur and limousine as soon as they saw Anita's brown face they would say they didn't have anything or the owner wouldn't want to rent to us.

The children haven't really had to face the problem too much yet.... They know they are considered black. And I tell them it's a political nomenclature and I'll explain it to them in more detail as they grow up and need to know. Why I'm called white and they are called black.[16]

Gil loved his wife, and, Anita said, he also loved the attention they sometimes got as a couple. He liked causing people to question. "It was fun for him," said Anita.

He loved to be outraged about anything having to do with it [race issues]—he was just waiting for something to be outraged about. He always felt like an outsider. In California his mother was the maid, and meanwhile he was friends with all these rich kids. So to me—the pop psychoanalyst—he really felt more comfortable when he could be with the "outsiders"—he felt more at home.

But he was crazy about white jazz musicians too, people like Jack Teagarden. He [Gil] was really color-blind. And in true reality, he was also blind. He couldn't see much. He felt people more on an energy level. He'd get attracted to people with the speed of light, there wasn't a whole lot of logic to it.

He called himself an armchair terrorist. He loved thinking of himself that way—sitting there, gripping the arms of the chair, growling—wanting to change things by violence or something, but sitting there quietly. It was kind of a strange place to be really.

Meanwhile Anita did all the information gathering and grant writing, and took care of applications for Westbeth and for schools and scholarships for the children.

Gil was the genius, but I had to write them. That really wore me down but I did it, the Guggenheim and getting the kids into the schools and saying the right stuff, and it worked. I was a social worker—I knew how to get what we needed. We wouldn't take just anything, though, it had to be exactly what we wanted.

So, we got scholarships, and the children didn't know we had no money in the bank or hadn't paid the rent for three or four months. They had no way of knowing, except that I was really stressed out. There was no regular income. I had to look at the little money I had and say how long was it going to make it until when. [17]

Nonetheless, Gil found the music business revolting and insisted that he was not *in* the music business. He kept thinking that the record companies should just let him do what he wanted; the companies had plenty of money and they ought to subsidize his work. Anita also said he was sometimes unable to accept work when it did come along. "I took on the job, right? Yet, if you don't get any cooperation with your plan about how to make things better, it could be pretty frustrating. Although I did admire Gil's way of being, I tell you—this square bourgeois mind of mine. Sometimes my jaw just dropped at how loose he could be about things. I was really impressed."[18]

As their finances were so tenuous, their most serious disagreements usually sprang from what Gil was or was not willing to do.

These two strong personalities both got along and struggled with each other. They inspired each other, too. Anita was a songwriter and actress who worked on her own material whenever she could. For Gil, she was a bit of a muse and extremely supportive of his work. "He was always at the piano. He was a compulsive worker— he'd stay on the same chord until his mind went nuts. I just compensated by working on my own music. And he said that when I was cooking, he would use the rhythms of what I was doing in the kitchen. 'Anita's Dance' and 'Makes Her Move' are based on cooking things, so it worked for us musically."[19]

In the early 1970s, things did appear to be looking up. Between 1971 and 1973 Gil managed to get enough gigs so he felt that he had a working band. A nucleus of musicians formed, including Howard Johnson on tuba and other instruments, Sue Evans on percussion, Herb Bushler on electric bass and slide guitar, Billy Harper on tenor saxophone, and Hannibal Marvin Peterson on trumpet. All of them, except for Peterson, had already been involved with Gil for a few years. This corps began to get a grip on Gil's new modus operandi: highly improvisational music with room to be individualistic and the goal to create something together.

Sue Evans, a classically trained percussionist, was the first female musician who worked with Evans (no relation) for a substantial duration—about ten years. Gil asked her to join the band in 1969, when the Ampex album was being recorded. She had been a student of percussionist Warren Smith, who worked with Gil sporadically from the late sixties through the seventies. She and Gil started practicing together at Warren Smith's studio, where they frequently crossed paths to use Smith's studio when he was out of town. Sue Evans recalled that at first she didn't realize "how great he was. I wasn't intimidated and I was able to just sit and practice with him for hours. If that had happened years later, I would have tried to second guess what he wanted."

In the summer of 1971, at the age of fifty-nine, Gil and the band went on their very first European tour; they performed in the Netherlands and several Scandinavian cities thanks to the Netherlands Jazz Foundation. That November, he returned to Europe to conduct the annual "dream band" of the Berlin Jazz Festival in a program of his own works. The program was broadcast, and he and a small band (including Howard Johnson, Lew Soloff, and Steve Lacy, who had lived in Europe since the late 1960s) toured Germany for a week.

In fall 1971 Evans recorded an album for Capitol; Albert Grossman was instrumental in getting Gil the deal. The album was produced by John Simon, a member of Grossman's loose circle of Woodstock music professionals and also the producer of The Band (formerly Bob Dylan's accompanists). This was the first recording in which Evans used synthesizers and was one of the first "jazz" albums to include the new instruments. Evans knew the work of Morton Subotnik and other electronic music composers, and he had also been playing electric piano onstage and in recordings since 1968. Gil had been given one of the first mini-Moogs by Robert Moog, and he also experimented with ring modulators (electronic devices that, when used with electric piano, emit metallic bell-like sounds).

Although Evans played some of the electronic instruments, he left most of the experimentation and expertise to his musicians. He used the instruments in his band increasingly throughout the decade; some of his recordings and performances called for three and even four synthesizers. He was interested in exploring the endless new sound possibilities that the new wave of instruments opened up, plus those created by combining them with acoustic instruments. On the Capitol recording, the synthesizers were played by Don Preston, formerly of the Mothers of Invention, and Preston's friend Phil Davis—both soon to become in-demand studio synthesizer musicians. Preston and Davis lived in Hollywood, and Davis, who really wanted the experience of working with Evans, came to work with Gil in New York (and went to Europe with him) for no pay. He was hardly alone in this. Over the next decade, several of Gil's musicians would at times turn aside more lucrative work or work for free in order to play with Gil.

The album included new versions of "Where Flamingos Fly" and "Hotel Me," tailored for Gil's new musicians and instruments. The synthesizers are used tastefully, never overwhelming anything else, but they add to the already mystifying doublings and unisons and give the ensemble sound a greater depth. The Brazilian percussionist Airto had come to Evans fresh from working with Miles Davis, and he brought his own set of exotic colors. Gil also hired Airto's wife, vocalist Flora Purim. This was the first time Gil used a vocalist in his own work, and Flora's five-octave ranged voice functioned wordlessly as an instrument—yet another color.

Unfortunately, just as Gil completed the recording, a new administration came in at Capitol and cancelled many projects, including this one. The album was finally released ten years later as *Where Flamingos Fly* on Artists House. Like the Ampex record, it is an excellent measure of Evans's exploratory work at the time. When the album came out in 1981, jazz fusion was big business—over-commercialized and often deserving of its pejorative reputation among jazz purists.

Most significant, the making of this record came during a period in which Evans wanted to have a working band again. The band performed at a range of venues, from seedy Village clubs to elegant concert halls. In January 1972 the band played for a week at Slug's in the East Village; this was Evans's first jazz club engagement in New York since his stay at the Jazz Gallery in 1960. On March 19, 1972, Evans and a fifteen-piece band performed at the newly inaugurated Kennedy Center in Washington, D.C. In April the band played for a week at the Westbeth Cabaret, an informal club seating about 125 people in the basement of the artist's complex where Gil lived; the band then played there on Saturday and Sunday nights for the rest of the spring. This busy season culminated that summer in Evans's first trip to Japan.

The Kennedy Center concert was tied to Evans's status as a founding artist. The founding artists each presented a concert during the Center's inaugural year. The artists crisscrossed the wide spectrum of American musical life; they included Cannonball Adderley, Leonard Bernstein, Beverly Sills, Merle Haggard, B. B. King, Leopold Stokowski, Dionne Warwick, and Count Basie. A description of Evans's work in the program is particularly apt: "Evans has been involved in intensive study, research, and experimentation in timbres, including both the emotional and mechanical aspects of instrumentation." Accolades poured forth for events such as this, when artists and politicians mingled, but the most surprising event occurred after the concert. The Evanses and the musicians stayed at the Watergate Hotel the very night of the Watergate break-in, the beginning of the undoing of President Nixon.

Evans expanded the band to sixteen pieces for the Kennedy Center event. The personnel included Snooky Young and Hannibal Marvin Peterson on trumpets, Howard Johnson on tuba, and Joe Henderson (substituting for tenor player Billy Harper) and Trevor Koehler, who were both new to the group, on sax. The rhythm section rivaled the horns in number, a tendency on Gil's part that would continue: Gil on acoustic and electric piano, Dave Horowitz on synthesizer, two electric guitarists; electric bass; and Sue Evans and Airto on percussion. Vocalist Flora Purim also appeared for the event. As the performance stretched to three and a half hours, the house gradually emptied to a set of diehard admirers, among them Martha Sanders Gilmore, who wrote up the event for *Down Beat*:

> All manner of sound-makers, from whistles to gongs to rattles, popped up at the proper moments and the miracle was that the pieces all seemed to fit together like a massive musical puzzle, intriguing to watch and creating a panoramic, three-dimensional sound. It was extremely moving to watch the group operate. They worked hard, never seeming to tire, compelled by the joy of creation.... Has the magic of Gil Evans created an entirely new genre of music? Certainly his conception is unique. [20]

Throughout the 1970s, new musicians started to filter into the band through recommendations and Evans's openness to try new people out. These included Pete Levin on French horn, Dave Bargeron on trombone, and Bruce Ditmas on drums, all of whom remained with Gil on and off through the 1970s and into the 1980s. Like Phil Davis, the synthesizer player Dave Horowitz offered to play with the band for no pay in order to work with Gil and gain the experience of performing with a synthesizer in a live setting. The trumpet players Woody Shaw and Jon Faddis (then nineteen and a newcomer to the New York jazz scene) played with Evans on and off over the next couple of years while en route to becoming major jazz figures on their own.

Around the same time, Evans acquired his first portable cas-
sette recorder, and he made use of it constantly, keeping a mirror
on the band and its developments. He taped rehearsals, his own
practice sessions at the piano, recording sessions, and performances. He always felt that anything at all might be useful for
musical development. He taped music from radio and TV, but he
also taped his own phone conversations, lessons, and visits with
people. Many hours of tapes that the Evans family catalogued in
the past few years were of Evans's conversations with Miles Davis
both over the phone and in person. Some of them have moments
of inspiration, with Davis playing Evans's riffs over the phone,
but for the most part they are just Gil and Miles, two guys hanging out. While the televison, stereo, and radio blared simultaneously, Evans and Miles talked about their kids, sports, and new
pop songs. Their conversations also included long stretches of
silence.

ı¹ lı ı

Slug's was a wholly different scene from the Kennedy Center.
Kenneth Noland, a well-established painter, was one of a handful
of non-musicians who went to Slug's. "Very few people went over
there—it was a rough neighborhood. You had to know what you
were going to hear when you went over to Slug's. Because only
musicians who were pretty much out of work played there and
went there to listen. There was no money involved—we all knew
that. It was just a get-together rehearsal band. Gil was playing
catch-as-catch can, wherever he could find a place to play."

Noland and Evans became close friends around this time. The
fact that they had both been influenced by Wilhelm Reich and had
been in Reichian therapy gave their friendship a "kind of cement."
Noland, Peter Bradley, his friend and fellow painter, and a few
other artists followed Evans devotedly. They painted to his music,
caught his performances whenever they could, and appreciated
the increasingly wild direction of Gil's music. The improvisational
nature of Gil's work and his need to revise his own arrangements
resonated with Noland's own artistic experiences.

It [his writing] needed to be performed, not just performed once, but a changing continuing performance of the same material—and it became re-arranged, reinvented every time it was performed again, which I thought was wonderful. It was a continual invention process. Musicians loved it, they loved to play it. He never had much trouble getting really good musicians, because they loved to play with him, they liked the creative ambience.[21]

ı' ı, ı

Gil's band continued to be very active through the fall of 1972 and into 1973. It played at the Bitter End, Henry Street Settlement House, the Whitney Museum, and the Village Vanguard as well as churches and community centers. In late June 1972 Gil was invited to Tokyo for the first time, and he gave a concert at Koseinenkin Hall, at the time Tokyo's most prominent concert hall, on June 27. The promoter also set up a record date for Gil to arrange an album of jazz standards for Kimiko Kasai, a Japanese singer. For the concert, Gil brought only two of his regular musicians, Hannibal Marvin Peterson and Billy Harper, his foremost improvisers, who carried the weight of the performance. The rest of the orchestra was composed of nineteen Japanese musicians organized by Masabumi Kikuchi, a pianist, keyboardist, and composer who went on to become a close friend and working associate of Gil's.

On July 5, 1972, Gil, Harper, Peterson, Kikuchi, and the Japanese orchestra made a studio recording of the concert program. The Japanese orchestra performed the music with amazing spirit and crack precision. The challenging repertoire was no different from what Gil and the band performed in New York: Gil's arrangements of Carla Bley's "Ictus," "Thoroughbred" and "Cry of Hunger" (both composed by Harper), and the Evans–Davis "Eleven" ("Petits Machins"). Evans also arranged a piece by Kikuchi, "Drizzling Rain," a dark impressionistic ballad, which later became part of Gil's book, as did several of Kikuchi's compositions. Peterson, Harper, and Kikuchi (on electric piano) handled the solos, while Gil conducted and played ring modulator.

Kikuchi has an active career in Japan and the United States; he played with Gil on and off through the 1970s and 1980s, was in a rehearsal band of Miles Davis's from 1978 to 1979, and has often worked with Gary Peacock and Paul Motian. Gil became both a mentor and an "uncle" to Kikuchi. Years after the fact, Evans told Kikuchi that when he was first reforming his band in the early 1970s, he had gotten "tired of notation."

He wanted the orchestra to play beyond notation—nobody talks about this. That's why he started hiring people who have unique sound and vision, like Hiram [Bullock], Howard Johnson, George Adams, George Lewis. I had been watching him working, and I realized that was what he was trying to do—go beyond notation. When I was in the band he didn't care if I could read or not.

Later on, I joined George Russell's orchestra, when Russell came back from Scandinavia and started a band. He loved my playing. We had rehearsals for a week, and then started performing at the Village Vanguard. After the first night, I couldn't do it. His [Russell's] music is all very scored, and you can't do anything else. He really wanted a certain thing. I didn't want to do that, so the next morning I called him to tell him I quit. He was so upset. Nobody ever said no to him.

When I was in Gil's band, I didn't really appreciate it. But after being with Russell I realized how much freedom Gil gave me.[22]

In 1972 and 1973, additional musicians joined Gil's band, again resulting in juxtapositions of strong musical personalities. Virtuosic, versatile players such as Lew Soloff were in-demand studio musicians; David Sanborn would become a jazz-fusion star. Still others, such as George Adams and Arthur Blythe, nurtured their art from a different base, the expressionistic avant-garde of the sixties. George Adams worked with both Gil Evans and Charles Mingus until the latter's death in 1979. "I always said that Gil was more of a gentleman, Mingus was more street life," said Adams. "With Gil, you can see the history of the music right in front of your eyes and be a part of it."

At that time, Gil Evans and Charles Mingus were the foremost leaders of large ensembles who gave their musicians such a great degree of freedom. Their band members became collaborators in a continual give-and-take with the score and the improviser, with the added possibility of substantive group improvisation. With both leaders, the key to the music's success was familiarity—with the arrangements and also with their band mates. However, neither Evans nor Mingus shied away from the messier aspects of such collaborative music-making, the times when the collective execution didn't come off. Evans later paid tribute to Mingus's music with his arrangements of "Orange Was the Color of Her Dress, Then Silk Blue" and "Goodbye, Pork Pie Hat" (both were played frequently by his band from the late 1970s on).

Meanwhile, Miles Davis was suffering severe physical problems. In October 1972 he ran one of his sports cars into a concrete embankment. The impact smashed up the car, and Davis broke both ankles. He was immobilized for almost three months, then in casts and on crutches for another few months, which further exacerbated his deteriorating hip joint. Other difficulties cropped up over the next few years such as bouts of pneumonia, ulcers, and a hernia.

Davis had been relentlessly creative since 1968, forging the fusion trail with electronic instruments, a "wah-wah" pedal for his trumpet, and an assortment of grooves. His newest thing again forced people to query: "Is it jazz?" His music was dance-oriented below, abstract and free on top—"Barricuda," electrified and with a strong backbeat. In the first half of the 1970s, his musicians were not just jazz adepts, but included sitar, tabla, and funky bass players. Davis's latest albums, creatively assembled in the editing room by Teo Macero from hours and hours of tapes, made his most fervent *Bitches Brew* fans blow hot and cold: *Jack Johnson*, yes; *On the Corner*, no. The urbane sleek, Italian suit–clad star now wore sequins, leather, tassles, and fringes. He got flak from all sides.

Davis and Gil kept in touch. Now there was no pressure to create a masterpiece, no A&R schedule. In 1974, Gil did some arranging on *Nasty Gal*, Betty [Mabry] Davis's album. He and Miles continually tipped each other off about musicians. Tony Williams ended up recording with Gil in the mid-1970s. Airto (who made his reputation with *Bitches Brew)* drifted in and out of Gil's band when he wasn't working with Davis. Guitarists John Abercrombie and John Scofield spent time with both bandleaders, as did saxophonists Bill Evans and Steve Grossman and keyboardist Masabumi Kikuchi. This continued to be an active facet of Gil's and Miles's musical relationship.

Miles could afford to pay his sidemen well and often kept them on a retainer even when he wasn't performing much. For Gil, the finances of having a big band never added up. Once he had paid his musicians for a given gig or concert, he rarely had much left to pay himself, even when the band was working a lot. If he did have extra money he would use it to hire additional musicians, feeling the need for a third French horn or trumpet, another woodwind player, a second percussionist, or a third bassist. Help came from painter Kenneth Noland, who became an active financial supporter of Gil's work until he moved to Vermont in 1975. Noland lent Gil money and gave him instruments, including an electric piano and vibraphone. He recruited a friend, an amateur sound engineer with his own equipment, to record some of Gil's performances and gave the tapes to Gil. These tapes were an important source of feedback for Gil. Noland recalled:

> The musicians made $15.00 a night, and that just didn't amount to anything. And we're talking about excellent musicians. Anita was a force that helped keep all of that together. Jazz has always been hard-pressed to survive. It's almost in the nature of jazz that it *can't* be popular entertainment, because it's so inventive and so improvised. It's almost in the nature of jazz *not* to be good entertainment, because entertainment is something that by definition is expendable, self-eliminating. That's what it's wanted for, to pass time and not have any residual value.[23]

Noland, increasingly convinced of the worth of Gil's work, took a giant step and decided to help finance a record by Gil and his orchestra. Noland was friends with Ahmet Ertegun, founder of Atlantic Records. The painter persuaded Ahmet to release the prospective album on Atlantic. Anita recalled, "He had a huge gorgeous loft on Spring Street, he invited us over. He said he had somebody that really wanted to meet Gil. It turned out to be Jobim [Antonio Carlos Jobim] with Ahmet Ertegun. It was really something—the loft was such a large space. Jobim came all the way across the floor on his knees to kiss Gil's feet. It was an incredible thing—he treated Gil like a god!"[24]

Gil and the band booked several noontime concerts in late May at Trinity Church near Wall Street and the Community Church on East 35th Street in Manhattan. They were also scheduled to perform a George Wein event at Philharmonic Hall on June 3. With Noland's encouragement and backing, Gil and Anita decided to record these events, hoping that there would be enough album-worthy material. By doing so the recording process would be less expensive than a studio album. Plus, the three of them valued the "live" ambiance for its own sake—to preserve the on-the-spot nature of Gil's music at this time.

Noland put up all the money for the project, paying for the musicians, the engineer, the rented recording equipment, and the many incidental expenses, such as lunches and cartage, that go into such an endeavor. He gave Ertegun a painting—Noland's paintings were then selling in the fifty- to sixty-thousand-dollar range—to cover the costs of recording. Atlantic covered the manufacturing and distribution costs, and—theoretically—advertising, publicity, and promotion.

Anita and Gil essentially self-produced the record, lining up the dates, musicians, etc. This do-it-yourself route continued for almost every recording Gil made for the rest of his life. There was no producer or A&R guy, no George Avakian, no Creed Taylor, no Teo Macero—no one to expedite things, move things along, or, on the other hand, to expect things. There would be no more album "concepts"—the content would be whatever music the band was prepared to play.

The sound quality of the new recordings, particularly in the churches, was not always good. Noland recalled that a lot of great music never got recorded: "Each time the band played they created something. It was very real, quite extraordinary." For all the problems, the resulting album, called *Svengali*, is one of the finest examples of Gil's band during the 1970s. All the tracks were taken from the Trinity Church date except "Zee Zee," which came from

the Philharmonic Hall concert. The band had been living with
the material for quite some time. Their sound was at times plastic,
molded, as on "Zee Zee" or "Summertime"; at other times it crack-
led with precision—"Eleven" and "Blues in Orbit." With this band,
Evans created yet a new "sound world" from which emerged some
inspired solos, such as Billy Harper's on "Cry of Hunger" and Hannibal Marvin Peterson's on "Zee Zee."

Noland felt certain that this album would be a hit for Gil. It
gained critical success, was nominated for a Grammy, and *Down
Beat* gave it five stars. It is still being reissued (though not by
Atlantic) and continues to sound contemporary. Atlantic, however,
did nothing to promote the album and sales were average, even
for a jazz record of that era. Furthermore, Noland, who thought
he was making an investment, never received any straightforward
accounting or royalty statements. Nonetheless, the painter remains
proud of the fact that he was able to help get *Svengali* produced.
"It's a shame that there was not more opportunity for what Gil
did. It was difficult then, and would be practically impossible now.
Everything is put in a commercial context—it has to sell."[25]

Anita recalled Ahmet telling Gil that he knew *Svengali* would
be an artistic success but a commercial failure. "What an honor,
having the prophecy fulfill itself. 'OK, you can make this record,
but don't expect to sell any'! But that was his *job!*"

Even before the album's release Anita and Gil had decided to
put the band on the road—to let the world know, in effect, that Gil
Evans had a working band. Gil had been invited to appear at Newport Festival West in Los Angeles at the end of June 1973, and
Anita wanted to build a tour to wind up there.

She knew that this time she would need extra help, but she and
Gil were wary of managers and booking agents. Anita's friend and
Westbeth neighbor Maxine Gregg (later Gordon), who had been
around the jazz scene her entire life, had recently acted as a liai-
son for the Berlin Jazz Festival. Anita approached her about working for them and Maxine agreed. Together, they lined up bookings
in Cleveland, Dayton, and Chicago. Maxine was the road manager.
This meant helping to manage things at home as well, not an easy
task. "Gil's concept of when he needed something—it could be at
any hour, day or night. He worked at night and said the only cre-

ative time was an hour before sunrise. The rest of the time was for rewriting, the only time he would get original ideas was in that one hour or so."[26]

Gil was not practical or well organized. Working on music and performing took precedence over anything remotely connected with business. When it came to the upcoming tour, he was uninterested in the travel logistics, wanting, as Maxine put it, to "just get transported there."

> Gil was very difficult, in terms of the everyday. You couldn't say, "Gil, we have to talk about the gigs, the contracts—do you want to sign this, do you agree to it?" He often wouldn't deal with business until it was a last minute emergency, which is hair-raising for people who are trying to be organized. And this was during the time that he agreed he *wanted* to have a band. It's not like anybody forced him. I can only speak for that period, but in that period it was very *very* hard.[27]

Things came to a head the night before the tour began. Gil, Anita, Gordon, and the band were to leave on a tour bus the next morning. Gil suddenly announced to Maxine and Anita that he wasn't going. "I changed my mind," he told them. "I don't want to go on the road. I want to stay home and write. I don't want to be a bandleader, I don't want to play the piano. I'm not going. Cancel it."[28]

Maxine and Anita were incredulous. At last they had a major opportunity, and Gil was about to upend it entirely. For the moment they were dumbfounded. Then Maxine suggested that the three of them take an hour or two to think about alternatives.

About an hour went by. Then Anita called everyone together, saying that she'd figured out a solution. "We'll make a cardboard cutout of Gil," she said. "We'll prop it up against the piano. Nobody cares if Gil's there anyway; they just care about the music. We'll take the arrangements and Howard Johnson will conduct. We're leaving tomorrow."[29]

It was Gil's turn to be incredulous: "You'd leave *without* me?!?" But the women were adamant. He backed down, grudgingly.

The *Svengali* tour, whose venues ranged from small clubs in Dayton and Cleveland to the festival in L.A., was not easy to manage.

This was not just a read-the-parts big band; the highly improvisa-
tory music required the band to put in a lot of hours together playing. Like previous Evans ensembles, this one consisted of people
who would not have ordinarily played together. Musical tension was
generated by people playing against style, or by the juxtaposition
of wholly different musical personalities. Gil loved what the tension
lent the music, but it took a toll on some band members. "If you
listen to Billy Harper with Gil and you listen to him with his own
group, it's totally different," said Gordon.

> This band gave Billy Harper migraine headaches. There were
> so many conflicts—with the personalities and the styles of music,
> and bringing in the synthesizers, and a jazz drummer that Billy
> might not normally have wanted to play with.
>
> If you didn't know Gil, if you could be stressed being on the
> road, then being with him would not be good. Some people
> organize their stuff—they are very calm, they meditate, they
> want things to go smoothly. Then there's other people that
> attract problems that have to be solved—that was Gil.
>
> There was often high drama. Once Hannibal got arrested in
> the airport. He was carrying something, like a Japanese instru-
> ment or a sword that set off the alarm. Then they [security
> guards] came to search his things and he made a sarcastic
> remark like, "If it was a gun you'd let it through, or if I was a
> terrorist...." So more security guys came running and took him
> away, and I had to get him out of it.
>
> The whole thing lasted a few weeks, which aged us consider-
> ably. But the music was fabulous. When you take people away
> from the problems of home—the every day problems of being
> a musician in New York—all they can do is play, they really
> focus on it.[30]

After the tour ended, Maxine continued to work for Gil and Anita
for about two years, helping them out with sporadic gigs and solv-
ing numerous organizational problems. Gil came to rely on her and
took it for granted that he could call her anytime.

In 1973 the band played Monday nights at the Village Vanguard
(while the Thad Jones–Mel Lewis band was on tour), then spent

most of October at the Bitter End. On March 21, 1974, Evans performed at Carnegie Hall in one of the first concerts presented by the New York Jazz Repertory Company, a short-lived organization founded by George Wein. Gil, Stanley Cowell, Sy Oliver, and Billy Taylor were the company's musical directors. The company consisted of "over 100 musicians capable of playing the earliest traditional jazz to the most contemporary or avant-garde jazz music of today. For the first time jazz has its own permanent institution which hopefully will become as renowned as the great symphony orchestras of today." The Evans concert was billed as "An Evening Devoted to the Music and Career of Gil Evans." A homemade program noted that the concert also celebrated Noah Evans's tenth birthday. The first half included Gil's earlier works: "Concorde," "Bilbao," two pieces from *Porgy and Bess*, Thornhill's "Snowfall," and an updated "King Porter Stomp." The second half consisted of the band's more recent arrangements.

Maxine had to make sure that the copyists got everything finished, always a last-minute affair in Gil's case because he often kept rewriting until moments before a performance. For a band of this size—expanded to twenty-two musicians for the occasion—this meant loads of work. "The copyists would make thousands of dollars. He made nothing of course," Maxine recalled. "I had to find people who could read his stuff. The copyists would call up and say, 'We can't read this! You have to talk to him.' Then, of course, he'd be asleep. 'Well, wake him up.' 'No, I can't wake him up.' You had to wait until *he* woke up. You couldn't wake him up. There was no way to wake him—it was like he was dead."[31]

The Carnegie Hall concert solidified the direction Evans had been taking since the late 1960s. The music was exploratory, rocked out, electronic, and dense. It was wild and shocking compared to the pristine beauty of his arrangements of the fifties and sixties. Despite some raves, traditional critics had traditional criticisms— Gil was too loose, too free, and too close to leaving jazz.

Gil periodically complained about his band's performance style—the tendency to get too loud, or for some musicians to hog the solo spots. But he did not think he was betraying himself or his talents with his current work. The band constantly inspired him and led him into the unexpected. "I've had people come up to me and say, 'What are you playing that stuff for—I want to hear *Porgy and Bess*! They'd go hear Miles and want to hear 'Green Dolphin Street,' and all that, but they haven't listened to the gradual development that led to where the music is now."

John S. Wilson of the *New York Times* commented that this was one of the band's better performances, but the aim of the concert— "an evening devoted to the music and career of Gil Evans"—"left a lot to be desired." There was

> a total lack of any information either in the printed program or from the stage about what Mr. Evans was doing. Listeners were left on their own to try to piece together whatever rationale the program had, finding a clue here and there when phrases of "King Porter Stomp" or "Jumping with Symphony Sid" peeked through Evans' sounds, or a fully formed projection of Thornhill's theme, "Snowfall," suddenly appeared. The performances were superior Evans, but the presentation left all but the most knowledgeable elements of the audience out in the cold....
>
> In a program this long, one appreciates any handles, any respites from the unknown one can get. But this is essentially quibbling about what I believe to be the most adventuresome, exciting regularly working large ensemble we have. [32]

If that concert was hard for the jazz cartographers, Gil's next NY Jazz Repertory concert, on June 8, 1974, was still harder. This one was devoted to the music of guitarist Jimi Hendrix, arranged by Gil and members of his band.

The idea for a collaboration between Gil Evans and Jimi Hendrix had sprung up in late spring of 1970, a few months before Hendrix's death. Miles Davis was an intermediary; both he and Gil had already been influenced by Jimi's music. They had utilized a harmonic motif from a Hendrix tune for one of their own, and both bandleaders now employed strong and inventive guitarists in their bands. Davis, who often hung out at Jimi's studio, kept suggesting that Jimi do something with Gil Evans.

Hendrix wanted to expand his own musical horizons with his new group, the Band of Gypsies. Theatrics aside—such as igniting his guitars onstage—Hendrix was a risk taker, an accomplished impro-

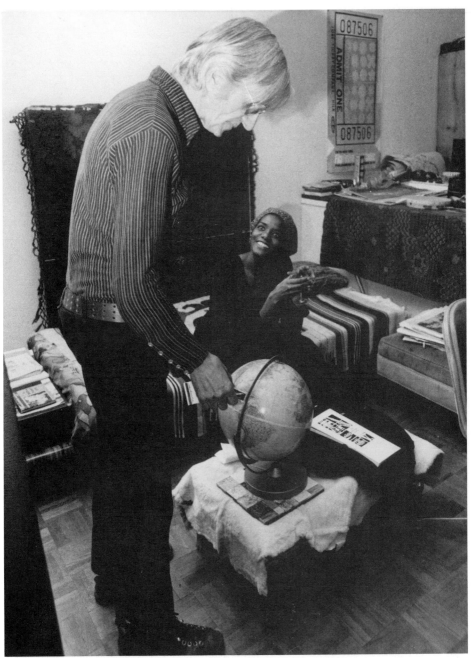

Gil and Anita Evans at home, New York, 1972. Photo by Ichiru Shimuzu; Gil Evans Archive, courtesy Anita Evans.

Noah and Miles Evans outside of Westbeth, New York, 1972. Gil Evans Archive, courtesy Anita Evans.

The Gil Evans Orchestra in rehearsal, *c.* 1973. From left: John Clarke, French horn; Tom Malone, trombone; tuba, trumpet, unknown; David Sanborn, alto sax; George Adams, tenor sax; Howard Johnson, bass clarinet. Photo by Gerard Murrell; Gil Evans Archive, courtesy Anita Evans.

Noah, Gil, and Miles Evans at home, New York, 1972. Photo by Ichiru Shimuzu; Gil Evans Archive, courtesy Anita Evans.

Masabumi Kikuchi and Gil Evans; first row, far right, Billy Harper; third from right, Hannibal Marvin Peterson. Tokyo, July 1972. Photo by Ichiru Shimuzu, courtesy Masabumi Kikuchi.

Lew Soloff and Miles Evans, Montreux, 1974. Photograph © Luisa Cairati; Gil Evans Archive, courtesy Anita Evans.

Gil Evans at the Village Vanguard, New York, September 20, 1976. Photo by Fred Dubiez; Gil Evans Archive, courtesy Anita Evans.

Gil Evans at the office-studio of Artists House, West 37th Street, New York, 1978.
Photograph © Carol Friedman.

Tony Bennett, Gil Evans, and Lee Konitz, Greene Street, New York, 1980.
Photograph © Carol Friedman; Gil Evans Archive, courtesy Anita Evans.

Sting, Anita Evans,
and Gil Evans at the
Umbria Jazz Festival,
Perugia, Italy, July 1987.
Photograph © Mimmo Rossi;
author's collection.

Gil Evans and Steve Lacy, Paris, 1987. Courtesy Steve Lacy.

The Gil Evans
Orchestra at the
Umbria Jazz
Festival, Perugia,
Italy, July 1987.
Front: Gil Evans,
Chris Hunter,
George Adams,
John Clarke,
John Surnam.

Photograph © Mimmo
Rossi; author's
collection.

Gil Evans at the Umbria Jazz Festival, Perugia, Italy, July 1987. Gil Evans: photo by Larry Simpson; author's collection.

viser who revolutionized the sound and approach to electric guitar, qualities that attracted Gil and Miles whatever the musical genre. Hendrix had already spent considerable time in New York jamming with jazz musicians such as British guitarist John McLaughlin, Tony Williams, and organist Larry Young.

Alan Douglas, Jimi's engineer and de facto manager in the last year of his life, encouraged Hendrix to collaborate with Evans.

> I was recording Jimi at the time, and Miles was always around. We knew Gil was crazy about Jimi's stuff through Miles, and I just made Jimi sit down and listen to some of Gil Evans' music—I played all the Miles stuff for him. Everybody was trying to move Jimi out of the whole rock-'n-roll bag into more sophisticated things.
>
> Nobody was dealing with arrangements in those days in pop. The music was so free and the kids were writing their own tunes—everybody had moved away from structured arrangements. It seemed like you would have to move back into it, and Gil was the guy.
>
> So I thought a lot about Gil. Before Jimi went on his last trip, which was August of 1970, we agreed that we should do an album with Gil. We wanted to base it on "Third Stone from the Sun"—we conceived of that piece as something Gil could make something beautiful from. And "Little Wing," and the blues-oriented songs. It was supposed to be basically an instrumental blues album with big band—with strings, woodwinds, whatever it took to deal with the material. We were going to tell Gil what we wanted, but essentially leave it with Gil.[33]

Douglas had two or three meetings with Gil while Jimi toured in Europe. He gave Gil a list of songs that Jimi wanted to do. The three planned to get together when Jimi returned in the fall and work out the basic material, making sure to allow ample time for give and take between Jimi and Gil, and for rehearsals.

Hendrix never returned. On September 18, 1970, he died in London of complications from a drug overdose. The project was aborted.

Four years later, as the date for Gil's next Jazz Repertory concert approached, he told the band he wanted to include some Hendrix tunes. Several musicians wanted to write the arrangements, and Gil told them to go ahead.

The concert did not go smoothly. Trombone player Tom Malone said that it was utterly chaotic and the acoustics horrendous. Electric and amplified instruments do *not* sound good in Carnegie Hall—and Gil was using three electric guitar players, an electric bass, and three synthesizers plus electronic keyboards. "The sessions were just as crazy," said Malone. "There was no way to get a headphone mix, it was a total mess. But even so, Jimi's music had certainly never sounded quite like that before."

Gil had a two-album contract with RCA Records at the time. A few days after the concert the band recorded the Hendrix charts at RCA's Studio B, on June 11, 12, and 13, 1974, with nineteen musicians, including Gil. Only two arrangements were by Evans himself, "Castles Made of Sand" and "Up from the Skies"; the others were by Tom Malone, Warren Smith, Howard Johnson, Trevor Koehler, and Dave Horowitz. The album is a mixed bag. Translating Hendrix's singular voice and style into Gil's orchestral terms is challenging, and most of the album sounds more lightweight than either Hendrix's or Gil's music did on its own. The album had neither Hendrix's tossed off "complexity cloaked in nonchalance," as one reviewer described it, nor Gil's band at its most transcendent.

Nonetheless *Down Beat* awarded it five stars. Peter Occhiogrosso, who reviewed the album at length in the *Village Voice*, wrote that Gil "admits he made this one to show the pop-top middlemen with the Top 40 that his chronically unemployed band can get it on, baby." Gil's admission is uncharacteristic, but he said the same to the British journalist Brian Priestley in London a couple of years later. Occhiogrosso thought that the album was

> commercial in the sense that it should sell records and get airplay.... Tom Malone's version of "Crosstown Traffic" ... shows the kind of high-powered pizzazz the Orchestra could get up at the drop of a high-hat, if Gil wanted to go that way... if God's in his heaven, then the album will sell (not to Gil Evans fans), the band will get some work for a change, and we might get a real Gil Evans album next time instead of this rather elegant curiosity.[34]

But this album suffered the same fate as most of Evans's others—high hopes, not much airplay, mediocre sales. The hoped-for massive purchase by non-jazz fans did not materialize.

Still, Gil had become enamored of Hendrix's strong melodies and the resonant "cry" of the guitarist's music. The Hendrix arrangements became an integral part of his work. From 1974 on, almost every performance by the band included at least one or two Hendrix numbers, which would typically go on for a good twenty minutes. With time, the Hendrix pieces became more and more Gil's own; a 1986 recording of the Evans band playing "Voodoo Chile" is a great example of the band totally inhabiting the material.

The following year, in June 1975, Gil made another album for RCA, which fulfilled his two-album contract. *There Comes a Time* is one of the rare studio albums Gil made in the latter part of his career. He finished his business with RCA with a bang—*There Comes a Time* sounded even wilder than the Hendrix LP, more ambitious and far less commercial.

Part of the wildness is due to the size and the nature of the orchestra. Some selections have as many as twenty-five musicians; at times Gil used two tubas, two percussionists *and* two drummers, three french horns, three or four synthesizers, tympani, celeste, gongs, a wide range of percussion instruments, and koto (a Japanese stringed instrument). The personnel is mostly the same as on the Hendrix LP, but the addition of tenor George Adams (who had recently worked with Charles Mingus) and Tony Williams on drums renders the feeling of the arrangements inimitable.

For these sessions Evans again updated his scores, tailoring them for certain musicians and instruments. "King Porter Stomp," featuring David Sanborn, is set to a Latin boogaloo. The theme of "Joy Spring" is first stated by xylophone, electric guitar (with a "wah-wah" pedal), and electric bass, then expanded by the horns in a wildly warbling unison. With George Adams as featured soloist, "The Meaning of the Blues," so delicately treated on *Miles Ahead*, becomes a metaphor for creation; Evans redrew the tune's slowly ascending harmonies for these musicians, who responded with brilliant bursts of group improvisation. It may be one of the best examples of a collective sensibility on record.

Over ten years later, Evans almost entirely re-created *There Comes a Time* in the studio while preparing it for reissue on compact disc. He altered the repertoire dramatically; "Joy Spring," "Buzzard Variations," and "So Long," previously unreleased, were included, and "The Meaning of the Blues" expanded from six minutes to twenty ("Little Wing" was reissued on the Hendrix CD, and "Aftermath the Fourth Movement Children of the Fire" was omitted). In the process of remixing and re-editing, Evans cast new instrumental emphases on some selections, allowing lighter textures to come through the density of sound. On both editions, the performances achieve the idea of "going beyond notation" that Evans wanted to express.

On May 13, 1977, Gil turned sixty-five. He was in the rare position of being a senior citizen in jazz. He was thrilled to get his senior MTA (half-fare) pass and considered it a badge of honor. Even more amazing than his new status was the continued youthfulness of his outlook and his openness to new ideas.

Gil's celebrated his birthday with a concert at St. George's Church on East 16th Street. The concert also served as a benefit for City and Country School in the Village, which Miles and Noah attended. The previous December, all of the school's musical instruments had been stolen during the holidays, and Evans hoped to use the concert's proceeds to replace them. By coincidence, producer John Simon (who had produced Gil's Capitol recording in 1971) was now a school parent. Simon helped organize the event and, with Gil, decided to record the concert for an album.

Priestess, culled from the two-and-a-half-hour concert, was the only album Gil recorded in the United States in the latter half of the decade. *Priestess* is far more mainstream than *There Comes a Time*; it has nowhere near the latter's swirling density and extensive group improvisations. It is a beautifully produced album; the sound is luminous, and Gil's textures come through clearly. The concert's biggest surprise was Gil's announcement that this was the orchestra's last appearance because he was going to resume working with Miles Davis. He would become the arranger and a keyboard player for Davis's latest small group, which had already begun rehearsing some of the new arrangements.

In his review of the event, critic Gary Giddins welcomed this information:

The news that Gil Evans will once again be working with Miles Davis can only be cause for rejoicing. It's their fourth reunion in four decades: there was *Birth of the Cool* in 1949–50; the peerless collaborations of 1957–60,... and *Filles de Kilimanjaro*, for which Evans was strangely uncredited, in the late '60s. Davis would seem to have his fill of Motown funk, and Evans is ready to bring another decade of discoveries to the greatest solo voice he has ever worked with. So if the concert is a farewell, it was also another prelude to another embarkation.[35]

Gil had struggled hard to maintain his big band. The gigs had gotten increasingly sparse, and he could not always afford to pay his musicians for rehearsals. Though several of them did not mind working for free, they couldn't continually turn down paying jobs. Miles's invitation came at a good time.

Gil often dropped everything when Miles asked him for help, and the trumpet player seemed ready to start performing again. Davis had been virtually living in seclusion since late 1975, following hip replacement surgery. By his own account, Davis's pain management for his health problems resulted in serious substance abuse and other personal excesses. Gil had been one of his steadfast friends and supporters through this period. At this point, Gil had high hopes—for his friend and for himself.

Davis's new group had thus far been a rehearsal band, with Masabumi Kikuchi on keyboards, Pete Cosey on guitar, Sly Stone on electric bass, and Jack DeJohnette on drums. When a tour offer came along, Miles decided to take it.

Kikuchi remembered, "Miles told me that he was going to hire Gil as arranger. And I said, 'Why don't you let Gil play keyboards too?' He said, 'Gil's not a keyboard player!'" Miles must have relented. Gil would never have made that announcement lightly; he still lacked confidence in his own playing.

But once again the possibility of Davis and Evans working together evaporated. Said Kikuchi:

Miles had a tour job lined up and he really wanted to go. We were waiting for Sly to show up. We waited for two days at Miles's house, Pete, Jack, and me, and Sly never showed up.

Then, Miles got an infection in his knees, and had to go to the Hospital for Special Surgery. The tour never happened. After that Miles said he wanted to be a pop star. The KIX concert in Boston, that was a pop band. What we were doing was jazz-rock, very dark. I wish it had happened—the music was great.

Once, Gil said to me, "Your music and my music is so melancholy, it can't sell. But Miles's sold a lot. Why?" Gil was complaining. "Miles's music was melancholy, too. Why can't ours sell like his?"[36]

Gil picked up where he left off. In February 1978, he regrouped the band for a British tour that culminated in a sold-out concert at Royal Festival Hall in London. Evans returned to Europe that summer and again in the fall (first to Spain and Italy, then to West Germany) with smaller ensembles. He and the band recorded on all three trips, making three albums in five months—unheard of for him. The Royal Festival Hall concert resulted in two critically acclaimed volumes, which are the best of these live recordings. The second trip, a two-week tour to West Germany, the Netherlands, Spain, Antibes (which was a George Wein event), and Rome, was a financial disaster. Evans got "nicked by a European promoter for $7,000." In Rome, Evans was ripped off by a record producer and was paid only five hundred dollars of the ten-thousand-dollar fee he had contracted for recording the album. The financial arrangements for a tour of West Germany in October were more above board; but *Little Wing*, a live album from one of the concerts, included all of three tunes.

In later years, Gil was often asked why he didn't make more studio albums. "Nobody asked me," was his stock reply. People presume that studio albums are better because one has more control over any given sound or instrument, as well as the overall sound balance of the band. In a multi-track recording, one can alter, edit, adapt any single element or parameter, or redo a solo. Naturally, this has advantages. Gil was extremely discriminating when it came to mixes and balances, but he also went after high performance quality; some of Evans's live albums fell far short of what he wanted (e.g., the *Live at Sweet Basil* recordings made in the mid-1980s). Yet, for a musical experience as vibrant as that of his band's, recordings would tell only a piece of the story.

With the exception of a few nights at Lush Life in the Village and occasional other New York gigs, Gil seemed to be receding into oblivion again. His personal troubles were also mounting. The complexities of Gil's life could not always have been easy to cope with. His neighbors at Westbeth kept trying to get him evicted because of his constant practicing. "This was the weird part of living in an artist's building," said Anita. "The walls are thin, it's horrible! The neighbors wanted to kill him. You play one chord and they're banging on the walls. He'd go as far as he could before they went nuts." When electric pianos came in, he practiced and wrote as much as he could with headphones on, but that was far from ideal. He was always looking for other places to practice.

During 1978, the stresses of the Evanses' intense creative life finally got to Anita, as did the challenge of living with two teenage boys. She needed space, mentally and otherwise, to work on her own music and acting. Over the years, Gil wondered "why she didn't run out of here screaming." Anita remembered:

> In a way, to me it was such an adventure. I grew up so normally—you go to work, at the end of the month you pay your bills. You have money to pay for what you need. It was so wildly bohemian to not know where the money was going to come from to pay the rent. It was like going to Coney Island or something.
>
> I guess, in the depth of me, I couldn't really believe that this person whose music and work I admired so much could be penniless! The music that I was so heart and soul involved with! I figured it *must* be some eccentricity, that he had a closet full of bucks somewhere. I guess I had to think that. I also knew I could always get a job, I had a graduate degree.
>
> There was a time when it seemed like a bad dream, but not now—now it just seems like a dream.[37]

Anita moved into her own studio apartment nearby. Gil told John Wilson that he was now "the chief cook and bottle washer." Meanwhile, she was in and out of the loft constantly; though she

and Gil had indeed separated, they maintained a tight family unit
with their sons. She continued to manage the band, and Gil relied
on her completely. He refused to travel on tours without her.

Gil lived in the apartment with the boys and practiced when
he could at other peoples' studios or homes. The family's financial
fragility continued. Gil, as always, refused to promote himself. This
frustrated Maxine, who remained a close friend and spoke with
him about business matters at length, though she no longer officially worked for him. She was outraged that he would turn things
down. She thought that if he took some of the lucrative offers that
popped up, it could subsidize his work with his own band. She
found some of Gil's attitude disingenuous:

> It would appear that Gil is quiet and restrained, and stays out
> of turmoil, but he creates all this anarchy around him. And he
> was very aware of it. There seems to be this impression that his
> life went on despite him, that he just kind of followed his life
> instead of being aggressively involved, and that makes him
> seem very weak.
>
> His relationship with Miles Davis had a lot of negative aspects
> to it, but he sustained that relationship, in a way. We'd have fights
> about why he didn't take credit for things he did with Miles, or
> why he couldn't go to Miles for money. He'd tell me, "Well,
> Miles needs the money. It makes him feel good. He needs the
> car, and the big house and clothes and money to make him feel
> good about himself. I don't need those things. I don't need any-
> thing." But he did have a wife and two kids.[38]

As the 1970s drew to a close, so did Gil's prospects. In 1979, the
band hardly worked at all. His main sources of income were his
Social Security checks ($330 per month), approximately two thou-
sand dollars a year from BMI royalties, and loans from Local 802's
Credit Union to tide him over when he needed it.

What Evans had told Robert Palmer two years earlier was still
true: "Having a band has been more or less an illusion for me. We
worked about eight weeks last year.... I've been lucky with such
excellent players, lucky they were available when I had work."[39]

The band, which he had hoped would sustain his enthusiasm and creativity, lost all momentum. Over the course of ten years Gil had recorded thirteen albums and made trips to Europe almost annually, where he and the band were feted royally. He was twice honored in Washington, D.C., once as a Founding Artist of the Kennedy Center (1971), and then again by President Jimmy Carter, who held a Tribute to Jazz Musicians in 1978 ("Jazz Musicians Are National Treasures"). His working band had given him the adventure he sought, personally and musically. The more improvisational nature of his arrangements through these years fed his process. Opportunities for the band had seemingly dried up. Gil's process, by default, came to an impasse.

11 sweet basil

I haven't been a hard worker in music. I had a hard time getting along in the culture. I had to maneuver around, be an Artful Dodger. It took energy that I could have put into my music. The problem with this civilization is that it's next to impossible to have any kind of business reputation without being a chiseler or a crook. You can't just take your fair share and go away. I don't mind decent rivalry, but I'm not made for a competitive-type life.

—GIL EVANS, 1980

The last two years of the 1970s seemed a downward slope for Gil. He had some glowing moments, such as the triumphant trip to London in 1978, but in 1979 he didn't work at all. His band had no gigs, at home or abroad. He was enlisted on yet another project with Miles Davis—a trio with Paul Buckmaster, an old friend of Davis's who was Elton John's arranger. (Buckmaster was also a cellist; earlier in the decade he had spent quite a bit of time with Davis in New York, turning him on to Stockhausen and Bach.) Gil started to rehearse with them and felt the group had a good rapport, but he never received the money promised him. He told John Wilson, "Miles is cheap."[1]

During this time Gil made several trips to England for eye therapy to avoid having surgery for cataracts. He was at loose ends again after his last trip. But for once, new work possibilities soon arose. In November 1979 producer John Snyder asked Gil to do a solo piano album for his new label, Artists House, a boutique label with albums by Ornette Coleman, Dave Leibman, and Paul Desmond. Snyder, like Kenneth Noland, was extremely helpful in a non-assuming yet productive way. He gave Gil a ten-thousand-dollar advance for the album and allowed him to use the company's 37th Street loft office as a practice studio when no one was around. It was equipped with a small Steinway grand and a tape recorder. Evans ended up spending a lot of time playing the piano there to prepare for the album. He shared the space with another creative genius who happened to be down on his luck at the time, Ornette Coleman, who had been evicted from his East Village loft. Coleman slept at the office and Snyder rented an adjacent space from the building so that he could store his belongings there. The two musicians did not end up collaborating, and Coleman rehearsed elsewhere. (At the time, Coleman was regrouping his original quartet with Billy Higgins, Charlie Haden, and Don Cherry, as well as getting his new electric group, Prime Time, off the ground.)

Evans's intense work at the piano coincided with another totally unexpected offer. The owner of Greene St., a new Soho restaurant/nightclub, invited Gil to play piano there. Gil, feeling that he would probably need at least one other musician to carry the performance, asked alto saxophonist Lee Konitz to join him. Konitz, no stranger to the vagaries of a career in jazz himself, had been playing solo concerts recently; he agreed.

The two shared a long history together: the Thornhill band, the *Birth of the Cool* sessions, *Miles Ahead*, and Gil's own 1957 album *Gil Evans & Ten*. Konitz had also played on a couple of Gil's dates in the late 1960s, the Kenny Burrell album, and one of Gil's film scores. Both musicians were still restless musical explorers, though Konitz stayed acoustic, unplugged. They rehearsed ahead of time, concentrating mostly on standards. Gil was skeptical about being so exposed on the piano, but he was broke. He took the gig, saying that for 1980, he was "accepting all offers."

Gil and Konitz proved to be a draw for the small new club, and John Snyder recorded the duo there live on January 11 and 12, 1980. Their playing has an oblique rapport, reflective of their very uniqueness as musicians, as does their unpredictable repertoire: jazz standards, such as "All the Things You Are," bump up against "Moon Struck One" (by Robbie Robertson of The Band), a tune that Gil had fallen in love with. On pieces that Gil had written arrangements for—"Orange Was the Color of her Dress, Then Silk Blue," "Copenhagen Sight," and others—one can hear Gil's orchestral conceptions beautifully exposed.

In the long run, the duo setting was tougher on Gil than he thought it would be. When he played with his own band, he was not so exposed. Now, he was thrust as a player into the spotlight—all night every night. He wasn't used to it. "I wasn't fluent enough. It was all right sometimes, but you know, every night I'd go home bloody, and the next night I'd be ready to do it again. I haven't had that kind of experience. So I figured I'd better go home and woodshed for a year or so before I did it again."[2]

The two did do it again three months later. Konitz lined up a small tour in Italy and asked Gil to go along. It coincided with an invitation Gil received to conduct a program of his music with the Rome Radio Orchestra, the kind of invitation he was now more inclined to accept, though it meant re-orchestrating his arrangements for a more standard big band instrumentation.

Lee and Gil played ten concerts in ten days, and Gil made five hundred dollars a concert, which he found astonishing. Gil never put himself on the spot in this way again, in concert or at a club, but he got spoiled. Though he and Lee reportedly had some spats, the logistics stayed simple with just two. Gil didn't have to listen to the usual chorus of complaints from sixteen musicians about transportation and hotels.

The first few months of 1980 were busy. Gil performed with his band at the Public Theater in New York on February 8 and 9, 1980. The concerts were to be recorded for a Japanese label, Trio Records, a deal that Masabumi Kikuchi helped to arrange. Gil quickly reorganized his band for the occasion (fourteen musicians this time), using some of his favorite heavyweights: Hannibal, Lew Soloff, Jon Faddis, George Lewis, Arthur Blythe, Kikuchi, Pete Levin. The new voices were Hamiett Bluiett on baritone sax, Tim Landers on bass, Alyrio Lima on percussion, and Billy Cobham on drums. Before the concert Gil cautiously told one reporter that the band was reassembled just for the Public Theater concerts and the recordings. There was no mention of trying to get the illusion up and running again.

The albums, *Live at the Public Theater, Volumes 1 and 2*, which Kikuchi produced, show the band playing at a fantastic level. The repertoire was material the band had frequently played during the 1970s, except for two new arrangements, "Alyrio" (dedicated to Gil's new percussionist) and the rarely performed "Sirhan's Blues" by Gil's old friend John Benson Brooks. These albums includes a greater concentration of Evans's original compositions than previously. One thus finally hears Gil's compositions as a cumulative body of work—a full portion of the Electric Evans, when the band is playing at its best. Evans achieves a synthesis with elements of modern jazz, rock, funk, and electronics. Electric guitars and basses, synthesizers, ring modulators, kotos and cuicas all have their place: contemporary pop, rock, and jazz meet the avant-garde. In an Ellingtonian way, Evans found musicians who could participate in his synthesis and add to it with their individuality.

Yet in an interview a few months later, Evans said that he hadn't written any new arrangements for a long time. He was back in a domestic period. Anita was living in her own apartment, but was very much in their lives, and the boys were growing up—Noah was going on sixteen, and Miles, fifteen. Gil told one interviewer, "Right now, since I've never had teenagers before, and my teenagers have never been teenagers before, we're going through some funny changes.... I didn't really know what to expect. Now they are at an age where they don't want you to run their life and yet they don't want you *not* to run their life." When asked if he was experiencing the generation gap, Gil replied, "What does it mean? It might mean that you don't get high the same as your kids, right? I've been smoking grass for forty years, so it's no new thing for me. The drug scene is not a gap between us there, you know."[3]

ı' Iı ı

Gil lapsed into low visibility again, though he'd helped instigate some of the big-selling jazz-fusion sounds of the last decade. Now, jazz fusion was big—but the innovation had disappeared. It had become a genre, a market, predictable—with all the pejorative

associations that the termis still laden with. To all but the most
diehard jazz fans, acoustic jazz was a throwback. Gil's own music
was neither one nor the other; it was never in sync with the marketing forces at work in the music business. Gil seemed to have
long since put aside concerns about this; he always went his own
way. But he often said regretfully that "being an arranger is a
loser's game."

Gil had no plans to reactivate the band, but it rehearsed fairly
regularly. He spent hours a day at home listening to music and at
the piano, reworking scores and writing sketches. Plans for an
all-electric album with Kikuchi fell through, but Gil and Kikuchi
cowrote an arrangement for an album by Terumasa Hino, a prominent Japanese jazz trumpet player. In 1981, Gil re-formed the
band for the Kool Jazz Festival and received tepid reviews. Right
afterward, though, the band went on one of its biggest tours of
Europe; they played eighteen concerts in twenty-one days in the
Netherlands, France, Italy, Austria, Finland, and some other coun-
tries, and were enthusiastically received everywhere. In terms of
performing, though, that was it for the year. During the fall of 1981
Evans received an unusual invitation. He was being honored with
a STAR Award (Stockton's Top Arts Recognition) by the Stockton
Arts Council. Their salutatory dinner would be in January. At first
he accepted the invitation; a couple of weeks later, though, he told
the Council he couldn't afford to go. The organization came up
with a paid round-trip ticket and lodging, but Gil never showed
up, and didn't really give them a reason. He had occasionally been
in touch with Abby Mattas, one of his old Stockton friends, but he
may have gotten cold feet. He was also scheduled to perform at
the Public Theater in February. He had to regroup the band and
the music yet again.

In the fall of 1982, Gil accepted what was for him an atypical job.
He ran a master class series for the college band at the City University of New York, conducting some of his arrangements; the
band then performed a concert at Aaron Davis Hall. He had had
similar invitations in the past but always shied away from them—
a mixture of self-effacement and a misconception about what the
work might entail.

I never used to take jobs like that, because of being a non-academic person. But...at CCNY and the students were so good and it was all so much fun that I realized I could do that. They were all players, and they were good, too. We rehearsed once a week for six weeks and played a concert. I treated them just like professional musicians, the only thing different was that by the time the next week rolled around they'd have forgotten some of what we did because they were so busy with their other school work. But it worked out really nicely. They paid me something like $3000; it seemed like a lot to do that. So it wasn't academic—I didn't have that problem at all.[4]

He really enjoyed the experience because it was practical—it wasn't delivering a lecture about his arranging methods, something he *never* did. He participated in similar programs in Canada in 1984 and in Brazil in 1987.

In the spring of 1983 Gil Evans was seventy-one years old. Though he was working all the time, he was out of the public eye; as Anita said, working did not necessarily mean earning. New jazz fans couldn't quite place Gil: "That older guy who worked with Miles once?" Some people thought he was dead.

He remained a familiar figure in the Village. He walked daily through the cobblestone streets near Westbeth, constantly exchanging greetings with storekeepers and neighborhood kids. At times, he looked like a caricature of his former self—the dapper, attractive man in a suit huddling over scores with Miles Davis. Now, deep furrows etched his thin face, and he often wore a beaded headband to keep his long white hair out of his eyes. He dressed in jeans, moccasins, and a faded T-shirt from one jazz festival or other, layering up in inclement weather.

In April 1983, his visibility suddenly took an upward arc. He and the band started playing regularly on Monday nights at Sweet Basil, a Greenwich Village jazz club.

Mondays are traditionally off nights in New York City, when theaters and concert halls are dark. Some jazz club managers, thinking they had nothing to lose, took a chance on less well known musicians on Mondays. The premier example was the Vanguard Orchestra, which began on Monday nights at the Village Vanguard in 1966 as the Thad Jones–Mel Lewis Orchestra. With members who were some of the best jazz and studio musicians in the city, the band had great arrangements and a polished urbane sound, and it soon gathered a following.

In the early 1980s, one of the co-owners of Sweet Basil on Seventh Avenue South hoped for something similar. In the late 1960s, Horst Liepolt, a German, had moved to Australia, where he promoted artists such as Cecil Taylor and the Art Ensemble of Chicago. Liepolt later moved to New York, and in 1980, he and two partners opened Sweet Basil, with Liepolt handling the bookings. At that time, the club's atmosphere was unique among New York City jazz clubs; it was above ground, fairly well ventilated, and had a halfway decent menu and wine list. Liepolt nurtured a relaxed yet attentive atmosphere—the club always seemed poised for a good night.

New York's active jazz loft scene of the seventies seemed to have petered out. Sweet Basil filled a void. Top-notch mainstream groups, such as Art Blakey's Jazz Messengers, followed a week's worth of Cecil Taylor's fierce solo piano improvisations; the eloquent Benny Golson/Art Farmer Jazztet might succeed a run by David Murray, then touted as Coltrane's true successor. Sweet Basil became the Vanguard's rival as a jazz lover's haven. At that time, with the exception of a few scattered concert series and festivals, these two clubs consistently presented the best jazz offerings in the city.

In early 1983 Liepolt decided to take a chance on Gil Evans. He knew that Gil had kept up an experimental, highly improvisational band whose music was to his liking. Also, Gil still had the whiff of legend, and Liepolt hoped to cash in. The bottom line wasn't much: nine hundred dollars a week guarantee against the door for Evans's entire band of fifteen or sixteen people. The pay was cheap, even for Monday night, and the band members essentially played for little more than cab fare.

Liepolt's instincts were sound. The legendary Davis connection attracted some people; others were curious about what Gil was up to now. Still others could not pass up the opportunity to hear someone of Gil Evans's stature in an intimate club setting no matter what he was doing.

Opening night, Monday, April 17, 1983, was packed. Half an hour before the first set was scheduled to begin, the audience squeezed around the club's forty tables. All the barstools filled up, with onlookers crowded alongside them. All in all, about two hundred people jammed the long narrow room. Meanwhile, a line streamed outside around the block.

At 10 P.M., one person appeared on the bandstand—Gil Evans himself, less than a month shy of his seventy-first birthday. He seated himself at the piano—relaxed, informal, alert—and leafed through parts and scores.

Soon several other band members began tripping over extension cords and inching across the crowded stage to get to their seats. The stage at Sweet Basil couldn't really accommodate anything larger than a sextet, and Gil's fourteen musicians had to make do. By ten-twenty or so, all had finally assembled. Visually, the group was arresting. David Sanborn, the jazz-fusion star dressed neatly in a plain white T-shirt with a black Armani jacket, sat next to George Adams in resplendent African garb. Pete Levin's bald pate glistened as he leaned intently over a small bank of electronic keyboards. Three burly guys who played the largest horns—trombonists Dave Taylor and Dave Bargeron, and Howard Johnson, tuba—sat just inches away from the first row of tables. Guitarist Hiram Bullock strutted provocatively in what little aisle was left at the side of the stage.

Gil did not introduce the personnel, himself, or the songs: the band simply started playing. It opened with a wild version of "Orgone," based on "Gone," written for the *Porgy and Bess* album in 1958. The current arrangement maintained the taut brass statement of over two decades earlier, augmented with synthesizer, electric guitar, and electric bass. The band took the piece at a fast swing tempo, giving way to an explosive outburst among the brass instruments and then to a dramatic trumpet solo by Lew Soloff. The piece ended on an emphatic clipped high note. The band then launched into "Short Visit," featuring alto saxophonist David Sanborn, urged on by rumblings from the other horns. The third piece was Evans's arrangement of the Charles Mingus ballad "Orange Was the Color of Her Dress, Then Silk Blue," with a slowly building, virtuosic solo by George Adams. The audience responded with a standing ovation as the band ended the set.

The club stayed packed for the second show, which lasted until after two A.M. Through all the selections, the music juxtaposed the individualistic styles of the musicians. George Adams's tenor playing was earthy, abstract, and deeply passionate. His robust sound soared up alongside that of Sanborn's warbling alto sax, which by this time had graced hundreds of pop albums. Some of the musicians—Adams, Levin, Tom Malone on trombone, trumpet marvels Lew Soloff and Hannibal Peterson, and John Clark on French horn—had by now played with Evans, on and off, for about fifteen years. Others, like drummer Adam Nussbaum, had joined him more recently. The energy continued to gel as the night wore on.

Within weeks, Monday nights at Sweet Basil belonged to Gil Evans. For the last four years of his life, he and his orchestra performed there when they were not on tour. To everyone's surprise, including Gil's, this engagement became the longest-running gig of his entire career. Word spread quickly. The line outside the club on Monday nights became unwieldy; it usually extended all the way around the block by nine-thirty. Crowds even flocked to the late set, which began around midnight and often lasted until two A.M. Celebrities such as Gerry Mulligan, Mick Jagger, Michael Caine, and the jazz bassist Jaco Pastorious could be spotted in the audience. Cecil Taylor often dropped by. These evenings were also a family affair. Anita Evans presided over a central table or two, surrounded by friends, fellow musicians, spouses, significant others, and occasional business contacts. Miles Evans played trumpet, and his elder brother Noah was the band's sound engineer.

Gil usually arrived on time, going over scores as other band members straggled in. Usually by 10:30 someone would begin the strains of a tune; the other musicians would pick up. Momentum gathered quickly. Synthesizers and saxes, electric guitars reeling, horns bristling with Charlie Parker riffs—a wild tumult of sound would begin to soar. At other moments through the night, weightless washes of music, reminiscent of a much earlier Evans, hung over the room.

The band typically played from two to four songs a set. Stretched out with improvisations, some pieces lasted up to twenty minutes.

Each evening usually included "Orgone," a Jimi Hendrix tune, a Mingus or Monk composition, and one of Evans's own. For a while the band's closing theme was an Evans original called "Bud and Bird," an upbeat segue of themes by the bop masters.

Many of the people who started to flock to Sweet Basil on Monday nights were surprised by what they heard. Gil Evans playing Jimi Hendrix? Freeform blowing? Rock and roll drumming? None of it was new. For the young, hip twenty-something members of the audience who helped turn Monday nights at Sweet Basil into a scene, the mix-and-match aspect of the music was no big deal, it was just "cool."

The steadiness of the gig allowed Gil and the band to deepen the experience Gil had begun with his band in the seventies. Some of the arrangements were far more detailed than others, but all were flexible, geared to explode improvisationally—for individual soloists, collectively, or a combination of both. "Orgone" is a classic case in point; in the latest version, one can hear an electronically expanded palette of sounds, and an array of rhythms that strays far from the 4/4 swing of the older version. Other arrangements were new—the music sounded like Charles Ives with a jazz feel, with two or three wholly different melodies and rhythms superimposed on one another.

Gil's current scores continued to give the musicians considerable freedom, and the interchange between soloists and band members often took on a life of its own. To nudge this along, Gil used an approach akin to Ellington's—he wrote with particular musicians foremost in mind. "Short Visit," mentioned earlier, was a prime example: Sanborn threw caution to the wind; with Gil he played with a ferocity lacking on his own recordings.

"What Gil liked to do was to think of the person," Lew Soloff explained. "He didn't think of a tuba, he thought of Howard Johnson. He didn't think of a saxophone sound, he thought George Adams. And that's the way you hear it.... He didn't want you to play like a machine or a perfect band playing a chart; that wasn't what he was after at all. He was after the particular people he hired to sing this thing together in their own very individual manner."[5]

The Monday night gig was a godsend for Gil and his musicians, some of whom frequently passed up better paying gigs in order to

work with him. Gil had been a musical magnet since his early days
in New York City, and this was still the case. His current crop of
musicians felt honored, handpicked. They knew the experience of
working with Gil was something they couldn't get from anyone else.
Furthermore, playing regularly in front of an appreciative audience
heightened the band's sense of being a unit, sharpening the musicians' intuitions about what they could expect from each other. In
his quiet way, Gil knew how to push them to get the most emotional
impact from a performance.

Tom Malone, who had been playing with Evans since 1972,
described one aspect of Gil as a bandleader:

> Gil always gave the musicians ultimate freedom in that band.
> Sometimes that baffled people. A musician was playing with
> the band for the first time one night, and he was a little con-
> fused as to what was going on and finally he asked Gil, "What's
> happening? When do I play a solo?" Gil told him, "If you feel
> like playing, stand up and play. If you don't feel like playing,
> don't stand up and play. If you feel like playing a solo, just
> stand up. If somebody else is already standing up and playing a
> solo, and you feel like playing, stand up and play. If the band is
> playing the melody of the arrangement, and you feel like stand-
> ing up and playing, stand up and play." Artistic considerations
> were always the foremost thing in his mind, the *only* thing in
> his mind.[6]

Gil's considerations did not always guarantee a great performance. At times, the music on Monday nights dissolved into messy,
uninspired playing with no focus. Sometimes a soloist would get
greedy and hog the solo spot, disrupting the interaction. In response,
another musician would try to grab back the tune, and sometimes
this worked, but at other times it felt like an argument. For the most
part, Evans remained untroubled by such evenings. "I love this
band," he once said. "We've been playing together for so long that
we can improvise, get by with it and land on our feet. Some nights
are better than others. We teeter on the edge of formlessness a lot
of times—then someone can't stand it any longer and will do
something definite and we all move on."[7]

The band's performances transcended any notions about what jazz is or is not, a familiar refrain with respect to Gil's music, even in the days of *Porgy and Bess* and *Sketches of Spain*. The music had no boundaries, Gil concocted his own late-twentieth-century impressionism. When the band was tight, on a good night, it was great performance art—spontaneous and bursting with life.

ı' Iı ı

More than anything else, Monday nights at Sweet Basil helped give Gil a new prominence. He was finally on the biggest roll of a career that now spanned over fifty years.

The band had been making a splash at the club for six weeks when it went to Japan for a sold-out, eight-concert tour on a double bill with Miles Davis's quintet. Though Gil and Davis shared billing, as they would several times over the next two years, neither musician put in even a cameo appearance with the other's group. It was a tantalizing program, having these two legendary collaborators on the same bill.

Back in New York, both artists performed at the Kool Jazz Festival in the early summer of 1983 at separate events. Jazz critic (and occasional producer) Gary Giddins programmed an Evans tribute, the first half of which formed a retrospective of Gil's work from the late 1940s through the early 1960s. The arrangements (most of which were transcribed from recordings for the event) were performed by a jazz orchestra that included musicians who had worked with Evans over the years: Gerry Mulligan, Lee Konitz, Bill Barber, Johnny Coles, Budd Johnson, and Jimmy Knepper among them. The band performed two visionary arrangements Evans wrote for the Claude Thornhill Orchestra in 1947, Parker's "Yardbird Suite" and Delibes's "Maids of Cadiz," which the Thornhill band never recorded and that Evans reworked for *Miles Ahead*. A reconstituted Nonet (without Miles Davis), featuring Mulligan, Konitz, and Barber, then performed Evans's scores for that group including "Boplicity" and "Moon Dreams." The orchestra reassembled to play a medley of Gil's famous arrangements for Davis, with Jon Faddis putting his own stamp on Davis's parts. Budd Johnson and Johnny Coles, veterans of Gil's ensembles of the late 1950s and early 1960s, were featured on "La Nevada," a signature piece for both. According to Giddins, Evans was nervous about hearing his work in retrospect, and spent the first half of the concert by himself in a dressing room, listening to the concert through huge speakers. Afterward, he was so pleased that he bounded out and made a point of shaking hands with everyone in the band.

The second half of the concert began with the historic clip of Evans, Davis, and the orchestra performing on the *Robert Herridge Television Theater* ("The Sounds of Miles Davis," 1959). Finally, the music moved into the present. Giddins came onstage to introduce Konitz and Gil, who had moments before agreed to perform as a duo. Lee came out, but there was no Gil. A couple of minutes later, Giddins found him standing in the wings with his corncob pipe. Giddins recalled, "When I reached him, I whispered, 'What are you doing?' He genially took the pipe from his mouth and said, 'Sensimilla,' and then went out to play the duet."[8] The Monday Night Orchestra fittingly closed the concert with an electrified Evans bop concoction, the band in rip-roaring form from playing together so frequently all through the spring.

Some jazz writers were onto the magic. Howard Mandel wrote, "Evans has continued to contrive witty, rhythmic, sometimes neo-classical and sometimes pseudo-pop settings for the most incisive soloists of the last forty years...his contexts, whenever they were written, have all the indestructible immediacy of the never-ending present. The reconstructions...could not have sounded more modern."[9]

Others considered Gil a marginal figure who occupied a peculiar spot in the jazz world. He was a bandleader with a barely working band, and an arranger whose output was only scant (a couple of hundred scores compared to Ellington's two thousand plus). Whitney Balliett of *The New Yorker* chose to attend another festival event that night, commenting that the Evans tribute was an "arranger's concert," whereas he was headed to a "performer's concert, which is what jazz is about."

A year later, advertisements for the 1984 Kool Jazz Festival had New York's jazz fans buzzing. Gil and Davis were to perform a double concert at Avery Fisher Hall (a similar event had taken place a month earlier at the Hollywood Bowl). These were the first occasions the two had appeared on a bill together in the United States since their performance at the Berkeley Jazz Festival in 1968. The collective desire that Gil and Davis would actually perform together turned into rampant rumors that they would.

Thanks to Miles Davis, almost all the 2,700 seats in Avery Fisher Hall were filled. In the three years since he had reactivated his career, the legendary trumpet player had garnered a huge audience of old and new admirers. He was also a constant target for the jazz press. On this occasion his playing was strong and his ideas fully developed, but his terse, haunting trumpet felt light-years away from his band, who, with the exception of guitarist John Scofield, functioned as very loud wallpaper; Gary Giddins called this edition of Davis's quintet "the sorriest he's ever had." Nonetheless, the largely young crowd went crazy and clamored for several encores after Davis's hour-long set.

Gil's second set started at 12:30 A.M. The sell-out crowd had dwindled to fewer than two hundred diehards. They all moved down to the first several rows, leaving huge blocks of empty seats behind them. As Gil's eleven-piece orchestra geared up, the night felt like a study in contrasts. Miles had been the superstar improviser among his far less gifted sidemen, while Gil's band was an interactive collective of peers. Gil's program was a Sweet Basil–like mix: a tune by Jimi Hendrix, compositions by Monk and Mingus, a mixture of improvisation and rock and roll, and an original Evans piece. The playing sounded uneven; the soloists failed to sustain any emotional spark or captivate the audience. The music seemed to echo loudly against all those empty seats. This was not one of the band's better nights. As Robert Palmer wrote in the *New York Times*, "The music was interesting, often intriguing, but only rarely exhilarating."

A few months later, in November 1984, Davis and Gil were billed together again, this time in a stadium outside Paris in front of fifteen thousand people, along with the jazz vocalist Bobby McFerrin. Once again, Miles and Gil did not share the stage, but it was by far Gil's largest audience to date. He was finally learning to enjoy the attention.

Gil's and Davis's lack of interaction on stage belied a continuous friendship and collaboration. During Davis's hiatus from his career, while he battled drug abuse, Gil was one of a handful of friends who saw and spoke with him regularly. Gil contributed several arrangements and portions of arrangements to two of Davis's post-"comeback" albums, the Grammy-winning *Star People* released in 1983 and *Decoy*, released in 1984. The two spoke on the phone almost every day when they were both in town, and Davis, a man not generally known for his warmth, frequently said (and wrote in his autobiography): "Gil Evans is my best friend."

Davis was still the superstar, a role to which Gil was as unsuited and uninterested in as ever. But now, Gil's presence in jazz and contemporary music circles gained substance again. In 1984 and 1985 he was honored by BMI and received the "Eubie Award" from NARAS; he was also awarded an "American Jazz Masters" fellowship by the National Endowment for the Arts and an Honorary Doctorate from the New England Conservatory. Tours and projects kept multiplying, and offers streamed in, many of which he declined. He said in July 1986:

> I just got a call from somebody in Japan who wants me to record an album of movie themes. Yesterday I got a package in the mail from London. A record company there wants me to do a jazz version of "Phantom of the Opera," but I don't know.
>
> I never have gotten into the expensive taste department. If I had, I probably would take those jobs. I've never been interested in boats or cars or property or whatever. It's just never been a part of my life. But I have no objection to money as long as I'm doing what I want to do. [10]

Evans started accepting more of the kind of invitations he had thus far resisted, to conduct other ensembles playing his music and to lead band clinics at colleges and universities. In the winter of 1985 he directed a Canadian ensemble in Toronto; in February 1986, he and fellow arranger-composer Mike Gibbs conducted some of their arrangements at the inaugural concert of l'Orchestre National de Jazz in Paris.

During the same period, Gil agreed to work on three film scores. In 1984, he scored six big band pieces and some horn arrangements for *Absolute Beginners*, a song-and-dance film starring David

Bowie that was set in London during the 1950s with *West Side Story* aspirations, but without the artistry. Gil's arrangements for two Charles Mingus pieces used in the film, "Boogie Stop Shuffle" and "Better Get It in Your Soul," bore his signature more than anything else on the soundtrack, but the studio band performing them did not pack the punch of Gil's own orchestra.

The following year, Robbie Robertson (former leader of The Band) invited Gil to help out on a couple of pieces for *The Color of Money*, directed by Martin Scorsese and starring Paul Newman. Unfortunately, common to soundtrack projects, Gil's input is barely detectable in the finished film; a lot of Evans's music ended up not being used. He enjoyed working with Robertson—there was talk of them doing an album together—and he got paid well ("When I got the advance for *The Color of Money*, that $7500.00 was in my pocket like that! I went out and bought an air conditioner, a new tape deck, it was great!").[11]

That same year, the avant-garde director Nicholas Roeg asked Gil to adapt the second movement of Mozart's *Jupiter Symphony* for his film *Insignificance—The Shape of the Universe*. The film was a fantasy about several icons of the 1950s—Marilyn Monroe, Albert Einstein, Joe DiMaggio, and Senator McCarthy—whose lives all intersect one fateful night. Gil's reworking of Mozart's "Adagio" accompanies the climax of the film, when the Marilyn character leaves a platonic, yet provocative rendezvous with Einstein for a highly charged sexual encounter with McCarthy. Gil's arrangement, with Lew Soloff playing the lead on trumpet, was incredibly powerful; unfortunately, it underscores the film's weaknesses—an uneven script paired with unconvincing acting.

The uniqueness of Gil's music was exactly what Robertson, Bowie, and Roeg had been hoping for when they hired him, though Gil's contributions were at times almost too profound for the films themselves. These experiences reconfirmed his reasons for never really seeking this kind of work. Essentially he found it constricting; the music had to be adapted to the images, even in the best circumstances.

Gil did have some assistance on *The Color of Money*. Maria Schneider, now a composer/arranger in her own right, had been his copyist for a few months. Schneider had moved to New York

City after getting her masters degree from the Eastman School of Music the previous year and was working as a music copyist, a good way to see what the other arrangers and composers in town were up to. She became friendly with Tom Pierson, a young arranger/composer who was friends with Gil. Pierson knew that Gil needed a copyist right away. "For a while it was just copying—he was missing some parts for something he needed at Sweet Basil," said Schneider. "At that point, he wrote all the parts on one line, a condensed score on one line. He often wrote sketches on these little score pads—about 5" x 2½". He'd carry those pads around and write on them. I got pretty good at deciphering his sketches."

Gradually Gil started giving her other work when he was pressed for time: transcribing recordings or solos, which were then used as the basis for some arrangements, and re-orchestrating some arrangements or parts of them.

Evans had a couple of commissions from European radio orchestras for his arrangements. He needed to add parts to them; the radio orchestras were generally about twenty-two pieces.

> He started asking me to re-orchestrate some of his music for those groups. That's when I started helping Gil out in a deeper way than copying. It was a little terrifying at first. I felt, who I am to be doing this?
>
> There was one day I'll never forget. There was a passage he asked me to do where one note spans out into a huge sonority. And I did it the way you'd do for college bands, with the instruments in their logical ranges—you know, the trombones at the bottom in a nice fat voicing, and the trumpets on top in a triad, and the reeds filling out in between. I brought it back to him, with my solid Eastman education behind me. Gil just had a fit when he saw it—"No, no, *no*—this is all wrong!"
>
> I said, "What's wrong?" And he said, "I want some of the low instruments to go to the high end of the range, and the high instruments to go to the low end of the range. I want everybody to feel like they're screaming by the end."
>
> That's when I realized that this thing about studying music the right way—the only right way in music is your *own* way that you do with belief and conviction, and when you stick to it,

it becomes your voice. Gil had all sorts of ways to do things that are not in the books, and they all had a very consistent logic. It was a little bit of a parallel universe that went by its own mathematical rules.[12]

The way Maria helped work on the cues for *The Color of Money* sounded unusual, but it was exactly the process Gil had been using to develop his arrangements his entire life. Robbie Robertson taped himself playing guitar to the portions of the film they were scoring, then Gil decided on a "take" or portion to orchestrate. Maria transcribed Robbie's guitar playing, then Gil decided how to develop it and orchestrate it. Gil also handed over a couple of cues for Maria to orchestrate. In the end, most of what they recorded was not used in the film.

Meanwhile, the Monday Night Orchestra remained Gil's most steadfast—and heartfelt—commitment. After four years, Monday nights at Sweet Basil remained well worth catching, the music still fresh and unpredictable. The throngs were augmented to bursting by busloads of Japanese or European tourists on jazz tours of Greenwich Village. The favorable exchange rate of the late 1980s made these tours a very successful enterprise. Like their American counterparts, some of the visitors were familiar with Gil's recent work and were stunned by the power of the band's performance. Others, in tourist mode, thronged the tiny bandstand during the break and coaxed Gil into posing for snapshots with them. Still others—expecting the Evans of *Porgy and Bess*—were turned off and walked out.

By this time, Gil wanted to rein in some aspects of the band's performance style but without sacrificing the spontaneity—first of all, the loudness. Gil said:

I'm so particular about dynamics, and there we are on Monday nights and nobody's paying any attention to that. I wouldn't want to stop their irrepressibility but I can't get them to play soft. So I have to rework the charts, I have to do it within the charts. Once at a rehearsal I said, "Play this as though you are practicing in a clothes closet in your apartment so the neighbors won't hear you." And you could hardly hear them—it was

great. But they won't do that on the job. The only band I had
that wasn't like that was Thornhill's. We played soft, so soft—
wow!

Lew Soloff said that Gil was also very particular about articulation and phrasing and the quality of the unison playing. He spent
a lot of time at rehearsals going over unison passages; he desired a
certain rigorousness but still wanted the individual players' sounds
to come through. And though Gil loved the "teetering-on-the edge"
feeling that was the band's modus operandi, he was ready to give the
music more form and have fewer endless solos. "I have to write
some new pieces for the band," he said. "I want the music to be a
little more structured. I have three saxes now, but I would really
like to add another wind player who plays oboe and English horn.
I'm crazy about them. And since I can't really find that much work,
I might as well have a bigger band."

Several albums' worth of material was recorded at the club during August 1984 and again in December 1986 by the Japanese label
King Records. The first two, *Live at Sweet Basil, Volumes 1 and 2*,
though a bit uneven, capture the raise-the-roof wildness and excellent solos that characterize the *Live at the Public Theater* recordings. Two later volumes, *Farewell* and *Bud and Bird* (which were
not widely available in the states until after Gil's death), are far
more inconsistent, musically and technically. Gil was particularly
unhappy with the third volume. When the record was about to be
released in Japan, Gil said:

> Some of the mix is entirely wrong. I just can't let it come out.
> So I called the producer. He said he'd remix it but he had
> already pressed 1500 albums with the old mix, right? I said that
> I didn't want the records to come out with the mix like that. He
> said, "It's just the first 1500, it's only for Japan." And I said,
> "You mean you don't think the Japanese have as much sensi-
> tivity as Americans or other people?" And this was a Japanese
> person talking like that.
>
> So he gave me some answer like, "I'm going to do what you
> want me to do," which didn't mean a thing, because he was still
> going to release the first batch before he put the new mix on. I

was so mad. It was outrageous, really. Because now the number "Cosmos" doesn't mean a thing. It's a number with three
trios. It's got three flutes, French horn and two bones, and
three trumpets. All three of them play the same thing, three-
part harmony all the way through. Well, if you don't have the
synth playing the same thing, but playing it kind of off to give it
a different kind of sound, it's very stiff and cold and meaning-
less to me. So it's got to be remixed. When Horst [Liepolt] gets
those records, I'm going to drive him crazy. I'm going to tell
him to throw them away—he used to try to sell them right in
the club. But I won't let him sell them—the hell with it.

ı¹ lı ı

The pace continued to quicken into spring 1987. On the Monday
preceding Gil's seventy-fifth birthday in May 1987, Anita appeared
at the club with an enormous birthday cake, while the band played
an Evans-esque version of "Happy Birthday." A few days later, Gil
and the orchestra took off for a three-week whirlwind "Seventy-
Fifth Birthday" tour of England and France. The kick-off concert
on May 13, Gil's actual birthday, took place at the Hammersmith
Odeon in London. It was a gala affair with combined orchestras
and a stream of honored guests, including Steve Lacy, Airto Moreira, several noted European jazz artists, and the pop singer Van
Morrison.

Gil did two concerts that spring in Paris with Laurent Cugny
and the Paris Jazz Orchestra and then went to Montserrat to work
on a recording with another pop star, Sting. Sting was scheduled
to appear at a big concert with Evans and his band at the Umbria
Jazz Festival in July and wanted to include one of the tunes they'd
prepared for the concert on his next album. It was a Hendrix tune,
"Little Wing."

Gil returned to the States briefly before heading up to Canada to
play at the Montreal Jazz Festival and then a concert in Toronto.
Gil and the band then had a couple of weeks back in New York.
For Gil, this was not a break. He still had to complete the arrange-
ments for the Umbria Jazz concert with Sting. He called Maria
Schneider for assistance at the eleventh hour. He was exhausted.

I have a feeling Gil was sick then, he didn't really seem like he had it in him to do that project. He called me a few days before the last rehearsal in New York. He said, "I'm doing this thing with Sting. Here's a book of Sting's tunes, and here's a tape and orchestrate them."

I was just terrified. I was scared to do too much or too little.... So I basically orchestrated what Sting did, and left it up to the band to put that Gil Evans spin on it, improvisationally.

By that time I was so tired. I was writing the sketches so fast that I couldn't really give them to another copyist, so I was doing the copying too. I brought what I'd finished to Gil and told him that was all I was going to do, and that he had to do "Strange Fruit." Then he called me the last night before the rehearsal and said, "I really need you to do this one more piece."

Then he sat at the piano, and played me this bass line and said, "I want it to feel like it's floating, and there is no time." And he was describing that Gil Evans thing—time that's floating, the music just feels like it's floating in space. I wrote some introduction that was trying to use what he did and it was a disaster. I wasn't equipped to do it—so I just wrote what *I* write.

I went to the rehearsal the next day and I was completely wasted. They played "Strange Fruit," and Sting had a question about the form, there was some confusion about repeats. Gil didn't know the answer because he didn't write it—I did. So Gil looked at me and I started talking to the band about what they should do.

Then Sting looked at me—like, "Who is she?" And I knew that Gil never told him that I was helping him. It turned out that I was working from an older tape of Sting's and he wasn't performing the song that way any more. All of a sudden I found myself in a "You did it this way!"—"No I didn't!" with Sting. I just thought, "I don't want to be here!" But later, it worked out and Sting really thanked me for the help.

It was scary working for Gil. I was young and I didn't have a lot of confidence. I felt totally happy to be there, but I always wondered why he would trust me. But if he believed in you that was it—sink or swim. It was your problem, kind of—if you didn't make it, it was your problem.[13]

Umbria Jazz, now one of the world's largest jazz festivals, takes place in Perugia, a city of twenty thousand people that is the capital of the Umbria province in central Italy. Its narrow, winding streets feed up a hill into its majestic main *corso*, still the scene of late afternoon promenades in and around the large cafes. Carlo Pagnotta, a successful local businessman, has run the festival for many years. After the 1986 festival, Pagnotta and his codirector brainstormed about a megastar event that could put the festival in the black. Sting with Gil Evans? It wasn't *that* farfetched. Gil's work crossed a lot of genres, and his score for pop star David Bowie's *Absolute Beginners* was the best thing about the film. Sting was a big jazz fan and had just hired jazz saxophonist Branford Marsalis as one of his sidemen.

While scouting artists in New York that October, Pagnotta dropped by Sweet Basil to hear Gil and make him a two-part offer. First, Gil and the band were invited for the entire ten-day festival. The second was to do a concert with Sting and his own orchestra at Perugia's thirty-five-thousand-seat soccer stadium. Was he interested? Gil accepted.

The festival staff joked about the headaches caused by having what seemed to be *two* festivals in the summer of 1987—Umbria Sting and Umbria Jazz. Extra security forces were called in for Sting's stay; throngs of fans awaited his every move. The Sting–Evans concert was scheduled for the second night of the festival. It was a major media event throughout continental Europe. Many Italian jazz purists condemned the festival's "contaminazione," but the event attracted the largest attendance in the fourteen-year history of Umbria Jazz. The band's Hendrix repertoire provided the meeting ground for Gil and Sting, and Sting's voice had a touch of the haunting cry that is so important to Gil's music. The concert was a huge success.

The next day, besieged by the press, Gil was polite but seemed ready to move on. His response to questions about what it was like to work with Sting were met with a simple comment: "Sting is a very good musician. He's very professional, easy to work with and unpretentious." He'd said the same of David Bowie when asked about their collaboration.

Gil and the band then took up residency at San Francisco el Prato, a medieval church in an evocative state of ruin. The church, accommodating about three hundred people, was their site for the rest of the festival. Every night, the moon shone through the opening where the roof had once been, exposing ancient columns. In this setting, Evans seemed like more of a benign wizard than ever, physically and artistically. After touring almost all spring, the band was charged up. Three additional female musicians—Polish vocalist Urszula Dudziak, harpist Emily Mitchell, and Anita Evans on percussion—heightened the band's exotic look and sound. Dudziak's wordless vocalizing added an airborne soprano line to the already unusual timbre of Gil's voicings for the horns, and she and her voice-activated synthesizer were given ample solo space. A superb musician with a five-octave range, Dudziak brought the crowd to silence, even dumbfounding Gil, who would prop his head on the piano and gaze at her steadily during her improvisations.

Tenor player George Adams was another showstopper, particularly on "Subway" (an update of Evans's "London"). In the latter part of the piece, Adams chanted "Step lively, now! Watch the closing doors!" transporting a largely European audience from the medieval ruins to a late-night New York City subway station.

The Italian jazz critics, even the old guard such as Pino Candini of *Musica Jazz* and Vittorio Franchini of the establishment daily *Corriere Della Sera*, flocked to the church every night. Their enthusiasm sharply contrasted with their counterparts in the States who, while still pointing to Gil as one of the most influential jazz arrangers, had more or less ignored his work for years. The Evans Orchestra was the hit of the festival. French horns and flutes, synthesizers and saxes, bop heads over rock rhythms echoed from the city's centuries-old walls and ancient stones.

Evans quickly became a familiar figure on the streets of Perugia. No matter how late the band played, Gil ate breakfast every morning about ten in the patio of La Rosetta, the restaurant catering to festival artists. A little while later, Gil took off down the hill for a daily swim in the town's well-kept public pool. He strolled through the streets clad only in a bathing suit with a towel draped over his shoulders. He smiled en route at all the little old lady shopkeepers and cafe owners setting up for the day. The old women smiled back, captivated by his total lack of self-consciousness, though his state of undress violated a millennium of tradition.

Gil and the band returned to New York after performing at the San Sebastian Festival in Spain. Gil lined up projects for the next few months. Two of them in particular took him full circle: an album with vocalist Helen Merrill and one with Steve Lacy.

Helen Merrill had wanted to do another project with Gil for years and was now able to do so. Kiyoshi Koyama, editor of the Japanese magazine *Swing Journal*, a longtime admirer of Merrill and of Gil, pulled the financing together to make it possible. Initially, Merrill and Koyama wanted to use new material, but knowing that Gil was now in demand all over the globe and that his eyesight made it harder for him to write, they decided to re-create *Dream of You*, the album Evans and Merrill had made together over thirty years before.

This was the first studio album Gil made in over ten years. In agreeing to take on this project Gil made a completely characteristic decision. He was simultaneously offered a far more lucrative gig that he turned down:

A while ago I got a call from Barry Manilow, of all people. He's making a jazz album and he said, "Nothing is working out right—I need somebody who can make it work!" So I recommended some people—but I could not do it. Because I am not a fan of his at all—I don't know what he sounds like, really. You can make a lot of money if you do those things, but like Anita said, "I don't blame you if you want to work on Helen's album for $5,000 instead of Barry Manilow's for $100,000."[14]

Collaboration: Helen Merrill and Gil Evans was recorded in late August 1987. The album had the same arrangements as *Dream of You*, with the addition of "Summertime" (which took the place of "You're Lucky to Me"). The original arrangements and instrumentation were used, but there was a looser quality throughout, and Merrill's strong clear voice and interpretations have only taken on more depth over the years. "Summertime" opens the album with an improvised introduction between Merrill and Steve Lacy, a surprise guest on the date, who happened to be in New York that week. Feeling that "Summertime" needed "something," Gil asked Lacy to come to the session. Merrill said:

Steve said, "Of course." But Koyama said there was no budget for him, he was already over-budget and up to his eyeballs. Steve said he'd come anyway. The next day, Gil arrived at the studio with his Indian moccasins on. I told him that Steve was coming, and he said, "Wonderful, I anticipated that. Look, Helen." Stuffed in his moccasins was $300.

Steve came in, and we re-did "Summertime" live. I can picture Gil lying on the floor listening to the playback—he looked about nine feet long. He was still very opinionated, very strong. He said, "Helen, just do something with Steve out front. I want you to just get up there and freak out, just do whatever you want." So we did, and "Summertime" is my favorite piece on the album. I understand that later on Koyama repaid him. [15]

Merrill said that Gil stayed at the mixing date until they were through, about three in the morning. The next day he was supposed to go to Brazil. Merrill remembered, "Well, here is this man, who holds himself up like a cricket, then stretches out, sleeps a little bit, then gets up. He's in amazing shape. It's a mistake to put emphasis on his age, because it really doesn't apply. It's as silly as talking about Picasso as an old man." [16]

Gil's intense schedule kept up. In September the band played at a jazz festival in São Paulo. They flew down on a night flight, and the next day Gil had to do a big press conference, a sound check, and the concert. While the rest of the crew had a few days off in Brazil, Gil held a band clinic ("where they ask foolish questions and I give foolish answers," Gil laughed). By this time he had led several clinics and enjoyed them.

In late October, Gil returned to Paris by himself to tour with Lumière, the French big band directed by Laurent Cugny. Gil embarked on a twenty-one-concert tour with Cugny, giving performances in France, Switzerland, Germany, the Netherlands, and Italy. Cugny had adapted several of Evans's arrangements for his ensemble, and while they were traveling Gil adapted a few more that he brought with him. A few days into the tour, Cugny reserved a studio in Paris for two days to record the material the band had been performing. To everyone's amazement, Gil pulled out a just-completed treatment of "Goodbye, Pork Pie Hat," tailor-made for Cugny's ensemble. The group recorded two albums' worth of material.

After this whirlwind tour, Gil decided to stay in Paris a few more days. He was invited to a recording session with Antoine Hervé and l'Orchestre National de Jazz, with whom he had appeared the previous spring; they recorded Evans's arrangement of "Orange Was the Color of Her Dress."

Gil's next recording date in Paris was perhaps the most synchronistic. It was his last complete album, a duo album with Steve Lacy. Lacy had been after Gil to do this project for years, affirming his love of Gil's piano playing and the affinity between the two as musicians. *Paris Blues* was recorded November 30 and December 1, 1987. The pair's musical empathy indeed runs deep through all the selections: inspired flights of imagination on Lacy's own "Esteem," Ellington's "Paris Blues," and the Mingus tunes that surface frequently in both musicians' performances—"Reincarnation of a Love Bird," "Goodbye, Pork Pie Hat," and "Orange Was the Color of Her Dress." Evans's pared-down piano style, on acoustic or electric piano, sound angular and spacious. His dissonant voicings and precise articulations imply the sonorous sounds of his orchestra. Evans's accomplished musicianship on piano—contrary to his frequent denials—was irrefutable in this exposed setting.

Evans became ill during his travels that fall, but he never slowed down. When he flew to Paris in November, he had a raging ear infection and had been advised by his doctor not to go. He returned home in early December, and the band resumed playing at Sweet Basil. Gil looked tired, his thin frame was emaciated. A couple of Monday nights in January were cancelled because Gil didn't feel well. He had been tolerating pain and discomfort for a while, as he did other ailments of his advancing age, like his increasing hearing loss. When he finally went to a doctor in January, it turned out he had been running around with undiagnosed prostate cancer. He entered New York University Hospital for what the doctor and the family considered a routine surgery.

The surgery went smoothly, but Gil felt quite weak when he was released from the hospital. The family decided that he should get out of town to recuperate. Maxine and Dexter Gordon had a place near Cuernavaca with an extra bungalow. In late February Gil flew

down there with his son Noah to recuperate. He brought a synthesizer and a pile of arrangements he was working on. Miles Evans
planned to come down shortly and Noah would return to New
York; they worked out three-week shifts to stay with their father.
Another big European tour was scheduled for May, and everyone
expected Gil would recover. But Gil, still somewhat weak yet working every day, contracted peritonitis. Miles flew down to help out,
but the infection got worse. Miles and Noah were both with their
father when he died on March 20, 1988.

ı' ıı ı

During a leisurely walk in Central Park in late August 1987, in the
midst of all his projects and trips, Evans toyed with a new bird
whistle he'd gotten from the Sierra Club. "All of a sudden the birds
start answering me," he said. "You can make up your own whistle,
too," he told his companion. While he demonstrated, they wandered
to the part of the park where there was a small hidden pond,
totally surrounded by deep foliage in the late summertime. "I used
to come here and there was never anybody around. I'd just take
off all my clothes and jump in the water." Gil Evans—spontaneous,
unpredictable, and out there to the end.

12 epilogue (parabola)

Blues in "C"
in memory: Gil Evans (1912–1988)
2.
And I think of your late band, the dense variety
of sounds overlapping, stopping, starting, waiting,
the loose rhythms washing against one another,
moody and tidal,
nothing urgent to be resolved,
notes milling, out on a limb—
wisecracks, potshots, pratfalls—
then the wild facts gathered, shuffled, swung
into jet streams riffs above drum cauldrons
till precipitation! Hot rain of notes, sleet squalls,
then a shiver of alto joy down the spine of sorrow—
always up to the edge, whelming, striving,
then moving on,
a new timbre, shifting ground,
a lush dissonance bending toward a harmony,
as the sun goes, as Blues in "C" quiets finally,
like two friends tired of quarreling,
like the hush after testimony,
after desire...
Parabola life!

. . . .

New song to the end
The older you got
the younger it got.
The window thrust open,
song letting everything in.

—RON OVERTON

(from *Hotel Me, Poems*
for *Gil Evans and Others*)

Gil's plans kept growing in the last few months of his life. He envisioned several albums in addition to the ones he promised Helen Merrill and Steve Lacy. He was considering a request by Lacy and producer Hal Wilner, who wanted Gil to do a version of *Mahagony* by Bertolt Brecht and Kurt Weill. Gil told Merrill that he wanted to work with her on an album of Stevie Wonder tunes, talked of doing another album with Miles, and thought about an album of his own. When Gil left for Mexico, one of the scores he took with him (possibly meant for his own album) was an arrangement of a Robbie Robertson ballad, "Moon Struck One," that he had been working on sporadically for several years. According to Gil Goldstein, a member of the Gil Evans Orchestra who has studied this score, it is a carefully crafted piece whose subtlety and detail rival Gil's scores of decades earlier. It remains a work in progress.

In the summer of 1988 the Evans family took the Gil Evans Orchestra, minus its leader, on an already scheduled tour to Italy and returned to Umbria Jazz in July. Miles Evans led the orchestra, which remained largely intact from the previous year; Anita played percussion and Noah engineered the sound. The following fall, and for a few months thereafter, the Gil Evans Orchestra, under the direction of Miles Evans, played Monday nights at Sweet Basil.

On July 8, 1991, in a much-heralded event at the Montreux Jazz Festival, Miles Davis played the music he and Gil had collaborated on decades earlier. The program included "Boplicity"—the first Evans and Davis collaboration dating from Evans's famed 55th Street basement apartment—as well as selections from *Miles Ahead, Porgy and Bess,* and *Sketches of Spain.* Friends and admirers had long hoped for this musical reunion or some variation of it—including producer/arranger Quincy Jones—but it had never come off. Anita recalled:

> Every year for the past 25 years somebody would call up and ask Gil if they would get together and so it again. Depending on what year, either Gil would refuse or Miles would refuse. So, I had long ago gotten over the thought that I could possibly ever hear that happen. Gil was always thinking about the future or what he was doing next. He didn't want to look back. Miles had the same attitude. And, after all, some of this paper hadn't been unfolded in 34 years.[1]

Quincy Jones initiated the plans for the Montreux event, and after much discussion, Davis agreed to participate. Anita Evans helped produce and coordinate the event. Jones, to ensure the fullest and most sonorous sound possible, decided to use what was, in effect, a double orchestra. Meanwhile, Miles Davis (rumored to be seriously ill earlier that summer) used a backup, Wallace Roney, a much younger trumpet player who ended up performing all the rehearsals.

Re-creating Evans's scores for the event was a complex, painstaking process. The original manuscripts and the instrumental parts for the Evans–Davis arrangements used for the original recordings were not to be found. Supposedly, Miles Davis had them, but Davis claimed ignorance when asked where they were.

In the months before the Montreux event, Anita, Noah, and Miles Evans sifted through Gil's piles of as-yet-uncatalogued manuscripts and compiled all the relevant drafts, piecemeal versions, and numerous sketches they could find. Gil Goldstein became the key musical restorer for all the music for the program except "Miles Ahead," which was reconstructed by Maria Schneider. Goldstein pored over the material, compared what he had to the recordings, and transcribed what he didn't have from the recordings.

Still, until the last minute, nobody knew how the music would come off. People expressed concern about Davis's health and stamina. Goldstein gave Davis the music ahead of time, but Davis didn't attend the early rehearsals in New York; he showed up only for the last rehearsal in Switzerland the night before the concert, and even then he left the playing to Roney. But when Miles took the stage the following night, he played brilliantly—"one soulful motherf**ker," said Lew Soloff.[2] It was one of Davis's last performances; he died less than three months later, on September 29, 1991.

Meanwhile, a new process had begun: the Evans family slowly started going through all of Gil's manuscripts. The newly organized mountain of boxes full of manuscripts, scores, parts, recordings, and tapes of all kinds filled up half a loft. In several instances there were many versions, fragments, and sketches that all pertain to the same arrangement. This "tonnage of music" is what Gil produced sitting at the piano many hours a day, every day.

In the years since Evans's death, there has been an increasing demand from musicians, schools, and festivals for Evans's work from various phases of his career. In 1992 alone, the eminent but short-lived American Jazz Orchestra presented a concert entitled "An Alternative Vision," devoted to the music of Eddie Sauter and Gil Evans. The Evans portion of the program included several of Gil's most innovative arrangements for the Thornhill Orchestra and four arrangements from *Miles Ahead.* That same year, the Manhattan School of Music presented a tribute to Miles Davis; the program—a shorter version of the Montreux concert, featuring Wallace Roney and Lew Soloff in Davis's role—was virtually a tribute to Evans's arrangements. In June 1992 Gerry Mulligan and Lee Konitz reconstructed the Miles Davis Nonet and the *Birth of the Cool* arrangements for a Carnegie Hall concert and rerecorded all the Nonet scores a few months later.

In 1996 a rented storage area in Philadelphia containing Miles Davis's possessions from his Manhattan brownstone was emptied and inventoried. Among the items found were the long-missing scores and parts from the Evans–Davis recorded collaborations. Many musical questions were answered when the music was examined and catalogued, particularly regarding Evans's instrumentation and doublings; for instance, how many instruments a given woodwind player used on particular arrangements (this information was included in the discographical notes for the 1998 Davis–Evans Columbia box set). The parts were loaded with "goof-tapes"—gummed staves pasted over existing parts—revealing, literally, the numerous layers of revisions Evans often made to his music.

Coincidentally, a book of several study scores of Evans's arrangements called *The Gil Evans Collection* (Hal Leonard) was nearing completion; the score for "My Ship" was thus able to be included at the last minute. Prior to the discovery of the Davis–Evans scores and the publication of *The Gil Evans Collection*, recordings of Evans's work had to be transcribed whenever anyone wanted to perform the music; this may still be required for many Evans arrangements. But this is no longer the situation for the Davis–Evans masterpieces; the arrangements have now all been published. Evans's arrangements for Davis, which have been performed at Spoleto, USA; in Carnegie Hall; and in Chicago, London, and Amsterdam, among other cities, have now entered the larger world of contemporary music repertoire.

Other projects involving Evans's legacy have emerged, including "A Magic Science: Celebrating Jimi Hendrix," a Hendrix tribute featuring Evans's arrangements played by the Gil Evans Orchestra, among other artists (performed at the Brooklyn Academy of Music and as part of the Experience Music Project, Seattle). The Gil Evans Orchestra still performs internationally. As audiences hear the music Evans created and re-created over many years, Gil's process continues.

"Students will discover him," Miles said shortly after Gil's death. "They'll have to take his music apart layer by layer. That's how they'll know what kind of genius he was."[3] That prediction has come to pass. Evans's work has influenced and inspired a new wave of jazz composers and arrangers, including Maria Schneider, Bob Belden, Tom Pierson, and Gil Goldstein. As the field of jazz studies has exploded, musicologists such as Robin Dewhurst and Steve LaJoie have rigorously analyzed Evans's music. The authors had to come up with creative ways of analyzing Gil's music, for neither traditional "classical" methodology nor standard jazz analysis was sufficient—they, too, had to go "beyond notation." The music retains its vitality and mystery.

Gil Evans forever transformed the palette of jazz instrumentation and left us with an entirely new sound world. In it, he fine-tuned myriad versions of the resonant cry—at times haunting, at times joyous—he sought to express through his music.

NOTES

CHAPTER 1: STOCKTON

1. Evans's report card, Stockton High School, 1931–32.
2. Wayne Enstice and Paul Rubin, *Jazz Spoken Here,* p. 150.
3. Gil Evans, interview with author.
4. Carmen Spradley, *Stockton: City of the Future,* pp. 140–41.
5. Stockton City Directories, years 1929–33.
6. Ben Wallace, interview with Steve LaVere.
7. Bruse Ross, interview with Steve LaVere.
8. Pat McGuirk, interview with Steve LaVere.
9. Albert McCarthy, *Big Band Jazz,* p. 190.
10. Marshall Stearns, *The Story of Jazz,* p. 205.
11. Gunther Schuller, *The Swing Era,* p. 632.
12. The Casa Loma band remained active until the 1950s under Glen Gray's leadership.
13. Jimmy Maxwell, interview with author.
14. Ibid.
15. Johnny DeSoto, interview with Steve LaVere.
16. Maxwell, Gil Evans's memorial service, April 3, 1988.

CHAPTER 2: PRINCE OF SWING

1. Jimmy Maxwell, interview with author.
2. Ibid.
3. Albert McCarthy, *The Dance Band Era,* p. 34.
4. Hampton started gaining recognition through his recordings (including his first recording on vibraphone, "Memories of You") with Louis Armstrong, when the trumpet star fronted Les Hite's band in 1930 and 1931. The Les Hite Orchestra itself gave Hampton substantial visibility; it was the house band at Frank Sebastian's New Cotton Club in the 1930s, appeared in several films, and found lucrative work recording soundtracks in Hollywood.

5. Lewis A. Erenberg, *Swinging the Dream*, p. 18.

6. Rudy Cangie, interview with Steve LaVere.

7. Anne Grupe, interview with Steve LaVere.

8. Abby Mattas, interview with author.

9. Marshall Stearns, *The Story of Jazz*, p. 200.

10. Lewis Porter has pointed out that the connotations of the term *jazz man* are still widely used among musicians. For instance, in music publishers' brochures describing big band arrangements, the following directions are frequently included: "only the first tenor saxophonist requires jazz," meaning that only the first tenor player would improvise during a performance. Lewis Porter, *Jazz, A Century of Change*, p. 21.

11. Cangie, op. cit.

12. David Stowe, *Swing Changes*, pp. 42–44.

13. Cangie, op. cit.

14. Ibid.

15. Grupe, op. cit.

16. Ibid.

17. Cangie, op. cit.

18. Jimmy Maxwell, Gil Evans's memorial service, April 3, 1988.

19. John De Soto, interview with Steve LaVere.

20. Cangie, op. cit.

21. *Radio and Television Mirror*, September 1939.

22. James Lincoln Collier, *Benny Goodman and the Swing Era*, pp. 180–81.

23. Arthur Rollini, *Thirty Years with the Big Bands*, p. 52.

24. Cangie, op. cit.

25. Mattas, op. cit.

26. Rollini, op. cit., p. 53.

27. Mattas, op. cit.

28. *Tempo*, September 1936.

CHAPTER 3: HOLLYWOOD

1. *Trianon Saturday Night*, for week of January 25, 1937.

2. Maybeth Carpenter, interview with Steve LaVere.

3. Letter from Evans to Pete and Maybeth Carpenter, postmarked January 30, 1937.

4. Ibid.

5. *Trianon Saturday Night*, for week of February 8, 1937.

6. David Stowe, *Swing Changes*, p.108.

7. As was that of other highly successful bandleaders such as Tommy Dorsey. Ibid, p. 101.

8. James Lincoln Collier, *Benny Goodman and the Swing Era*, p. 180.

9. Carpenter, op. cit.

10. Ibid.

11. Jimmy Maxwell, at Gil Evans's memorial service, April 3, 1988.

12. Pasadena Community Dance at Pasadena Civic Auditorium, October 15 and 16, 1937. Airchecks were made.

13. *Pasadena Star News*, October 15, 1937.

14. George Simon, *The Big Bands*, p. 288.

15. Ibid. p. 289.

16. Carpenter, op. cit.

17. Rudy Cangie, interview with Steve LaVere.

18. John De Soto, interview with Steve LaVere.

19. *Tempo*, May 1938. No documents have come to light acknowledging that Gil Evans had a business interest in the Ennis band.

20. Scrapbook clipping re: Third Hollywood Swing Concert (newspaper title cut off).

21. *Tempo*, May 1938.

22. Jimmy Maxwell, interview with author.

23. *Tempo*, 1938.

24. *San Francisco News*, October 7, 1938.

25. Ibid.

26. Cangie, op. cit.

27. Prior to working with Whiteman, Charles LaVere was active in the Midwest and New York and worked with numerous prominent jazz musicians such as Jack Teagarden, Zabbo Smith, and Joe Marsala. He was Bing Crosby's regular accompanist from 1939 to 1947.

28. Skitch Henderson, interview with author.

29. Ibid.

30. *Pasadena Star-News*, June 14, 1939.

31. Carmine Ennis, interview with Steve LaVere.

32. Whitney Balliett, *American Musicans II*, p. 476.

33. Ennis, op. cit.

34. Nat Hentoff, *Down Beat*, May 2, 1957.

35. Henderson, op. cit.

36. *Down Beat*, January 1939.

37. *Swingin Uptown*, BMG Classics/RCA (CD 66746-2).

38. Henderson, op. cit.

39. *Tempo*, April 1939.

40. *Trianon Saturday Night*, July 22, 1939.

CHAPTER 4: THORNHILL—HIS BAND AND HIS SOUND

1. Carmine Ennis, interview with Steve LaVere.

2. George Simon, *The Big Bands*, p. 432.

3. George Paulsen's unpublished memoirs.

4. Ibid.

5. The machinery was the right booking agency, which then served as the prime link to choice hotel jobs, radio networks, and commercial sponsors, which in turn boosted record sales. David Stowe, *Swing Changes*, p. 105.

6. Louis Erenberg, *Swingin' the Dream*, p. 186.

7. *Down Beat*, June 1, 1941.

8. *Metronome*, February 1940.

9. Nat Hentoff, *Down Beat*, May 2, 1957.

10. Paulsen, op. cit.

11. Whitney Balliett, *American Musicians II*, p. 476.

12. Simon, op. cit., p. 434.

13. Review of December 1940 performance at Wilshire Bowl; undated clipping from Jack Crowley's scrapbook.

14. Rusty Dedrick, interview with author.

15. George Simon, *Glenn Miller and His Orchestra*, p. 96.

16. Richard M. Sudhalter, *Lost Chords*, p. 236.

17. Hentoff, op. cit.

18. *Swing*, March 1939.

19. George Simon, *Metronome*, May 1941.

20. Hentoff, op. cit.

21. Paulsen, op. cit.

22. *Music and Rhythm*, October 1941.

23. Edward Jablonski, CD liner notes for *The Historic Gershwin* (BMG Classics 63276-2).

24. Carmine Ennis, op. cit.

25. Charles Garrod, *Claude Thornhill and His Orchestra* (discography).

26. The AF of M recording ban, in effect from August 1, 1942, to September 21, 1943, was the union's attempt to force the record companies to pay musicians royalties for recordings, and to compensate musicians for recordings that were broadcast or played on jukeboxes, among other losses of income.

27. Dedrick, op. cit.

28. Stowe, op. cit., p. 110.

29. Gunther Schuller, *The Swing Era*, pp. 755–756.

30. *Metronome*, October 1942.

31. *The Powers Girl*, United Artists, released in 1943.

32. *Metronome*, October 1942.

CHAPTER 5: WARTIME

1. Roc Hillman, interview with Steve LaVere.

2. Bunny Edwards, interview with Steve LaVere.

3. Al Taylor, interview with Steve LaVere.

4. George Paulsen's unpublished memoirs.

5. Edward Polic, interview with author.
6. Richard Sears, *The Big Bands Go to War*, pp 264–266. The results, of course, were devastating. Shaw suffered two nervous breakdowns while touring in the Pacific. Miller's plane was lost over the English channel in December 1944. His body was never recovered.
7. Edwards, op. cit.
8. Evan Vail, letter to Leonard Feather, August 4, 1988.
9. Ibid.
10. Jimmy Rowles, interview with Steve LaVere.
11. Ralph Harden, interview with Steve LaVere.
12. Evan Vail, interview with Steve LaVere.
13. Rowles, op. cit.
14. Ibid.
15. Jimmy Maxwell, interview with the author.
16. In fact, the Carpenters' second child was a girl, Nancy.
17. Frank Buchmann-Møller, *You Just Fight For Your Life: The Story of Lester Young*, p. 126. Documents the story of Young's incarceration in the Army in great detail.
18. Rowles, op. cit.

CHAPTER 6: 52ND STREET ANNEX
1. Miles Davis, *Miles: The Autobiography*, p. 55.
2. Gil Evans, interview with author.
3. Jimmy Maxwell, Gil Evans's memorial service, April 3, 1988.
4. Evans, op. cit.
5. Hortense Lambert, interview with author.
6. Davis, op. cit, p. 122.
7. Nat Hentoff, "The Birth of the Cool," in D. Cerulli, B. Korall, M. Nasatir, Eds., *The Jazz Word*, p. 171.
8. Johnny Carisi, interview with author.
9. Gerry Mulligan, interview with author.
10. Ibid.
11. George Russell, interview with author.
12. Scott DeVeaux, *The Birth of Bebop*, pp. 424–25.
13. Excerpt from transcribed tape discussion with George Russell, "Where Do We Go from Here?" in *The Jazz Word*, p. 187.
14. Ibid, p. 172.
15. Whitney Balliett, *American Musicians II*, p. 476.
16. Ibid, p. 474.
17. Ira Gitler, *From Swing to Bop*, p. 251.
18. Balliett, op. cit., p. 477.
19. Johnny Carisi, op. cit.
20. Lawrence Koch, *Yardbird Suite*, p. 88.

21. Cerulli et al., *The Jazz Word*, p. 171.
22. Davis, op. cit., p. 116.
23. Hentoff, op. cit., p. 171.
24. Bill Barber, interview with author.
25. Carisi, op. cit.
26. George Simon, *The Big Bands*, p. 438.
27. Balliett, op. cit., p. 474.
28. Balliett, op. cit., p. 476.

CHAPTER 7: MOON DREAMS
 1. Hal Webman, interview with author.
 2. Marc Crawford, *Down Beat*, February 1961, p. 18.
 3. Ibid.
 4. Nat Hentoff, *Down Beat*, May 1957.
 5. Ibid.
 6. Dameron had also come up in the Big Band Era and had written
    arrangements for Earl Hines, Harlan Leonard, Jimmie Lunceford,
    Coleman Hawkins, and Billy Eckstine. A foremost member of his 1948
    band was trumpet player Fats Navarro.
 7. Webman, op. cit.
 8. Gerry Mulligan, interview with author.
 9. Hentoff, op. cit.
10. Johnny Carisi, interview with author.
11. Mulligan, op. cit.
12. Hentoff, op. cit.
13. Miles Davis, *The Complete Birth of the Cool*, Capitol Jazz CDP 7243 94550 2.
14. The recordings of the Miles Davis Nonet's broadcasts from Birdland
    had been "bootlegged" on LPs several times.
15. Pete Rugolo, interview with author.
16. Mulligan, op. cit.
17. Musically, it's fortunate that Clarke went ahead and played the piece.
    Over the years, the blues-based "Israel" remains one of the most criti-
    cally acclaimed of the Nonet's recordings.
18. Miles Davis, *Miles: The Autobiography*, p. 117.
19. Gary Giddins, *Visions of Jazz*, p. 341.
20. Hentoff, op. cit.
21. André Hodeir, *Jazz: Its Evolution and Essence*, p. 116.
22. Ibid.
23. Max Harrison, *A Jazz Retrospect*, p. 171.
24. Stanley Crouch, "Play the Right Thing," *New Republic*, February 1990.
25. Bill Cole, *Miles Davis, A Musical Biography*, pp. 50–51.
26. Krin Gabbard, "Jazz on Video at the Library of Congress," *Performing
    Arts*, 2001.

27. Mulligan with Hentoff, *Down Beat,* July 2, 1964.

28. Webman, op. cit.

29. Carisi, op. cit.

30. George Endrey, "Evans," *Sounds & Fury,* July–August 1965.

31. Laurent Cugny, *Las Vegas Tango,* p. 93.

32. Endrey, op. cit.

33. Cugny, op. cit., p. 93.

34. Ben Sidran, *Talking Jazz,* p. 19.

35. Ibid., p. 20.

36. Jimmy Maxwell, interview with author.

37. Hentoff, op. cit.

38. Gertrude Maxwell, interview with author.

39. Jimmy Maxwell, op. cit.

40. Hentoff, *Down Beat,* January 28, 1953.

41. *Bird: The Complete Charlie Parker on Verve,* liner notes, p. 30.

CHAPTER 8: JAMBANGLE

1. Nat Hentoff, *Down Beat,* May 1957.

2. Gil Evans, interview with author.

3. "In 1954, a Federal Court injunction ordered Reich's hardcover books banned from circulation and his softcover books, including all his English-language science periodicals, burned." W. Edward Mann and Edward Hoffman, *The Man Who Dreamed of Tomorrow,* p. 37.

4. Evans, op. cit.

5. Gil would re-use the opening bars of this arrangement as a motif in his new arrangement of "King Porter Stomp," featuring Cannonball Adderley (1958).

6. Hal McKusick, interview with author.

7. Evans, op. cit.

8. A *Down Beat* review in May 1957 awarded the McKusick record five stars. "This is the most important of Victor's Jazz Workshop series thus far and the one that most fits the 'workshop connotation.' Writers Johnny Mandel, Russell, Giuffre, and Evans have particularly been among the key workers in providing jazzmen more challenging written material contexts within which to grow and blow."

9. Russell had been writing his *Lydian Theory of Tonal Orgnization* around this time.

10. In late 1956 and early 1957, Evans also did some arrangements for the albums of two other vocalists, Marcy Lutes and Lucy Reed.

11. Evans said that "Where Flamingos Fly" was collected by musicologist Harold Coulander with John Brooks's help. Ben Sidran, *Talking Jazz,* p. 23.

12. Evans, op. cit.

13. Jack Chambers, *Milestones: The Music and Times of Miles Davis*, p. 161.

14. Gary Giddins, *Visions of Jazz*, p. 341.

15. Chambers, op. cit., p. 240.

16. George Avakian, interview with author. Apparently, some of the music was written for flugelhorn. Davis had gone to Clark Terry for advice on the instrument.

17. Miles Davis, *Miles: The Autobiography*, p. 184.

18. There was a cover mishap with the album *Miles Ahead*. Davis did not see the cover—picturing a white female model on a sailboat— until the cover was already printed, and thousands of albums were in circulation. Avakian complied with his complaint—"that a black girl" should have been used. Subsequent runs of the album pictured Miles Davis on the cover. *Miles Davis–Gil Evans, The Complete Columbia Studio Recordings*, booklet, p.140.

19. Gil was impressed with a different approach to Delibes's "Maids of Cadiz" by Jimmy Rowles, who had recorded it with Benny Goodman, arranged for small band.

20. Evans, op. cit.

21. Avakian, op. cit.

22. Joe Bennett, interview with author.

23. Columbia Records also issued the soundtrack album of *Porgy and Bess* in 1959.

24. Davis, op. cit., p. 229.

25. John S. Wilson, *High Fidelity*, June 1959.

26. Martin Williams, *The Jazz Tradition*, p. 160.

27. Evans, op. cit.

28. Bennett, op. cit. Columbia started recording stereo tapes around 1956; stereo albums entered the market around two years later, as affordable home stereo equipment became more available.

29. Ibid.

30. Richard Williams, *Melody Maker*, March 1978.

31. Bennett, op. cit.

32. Amiri Baraka, *The Music: Reflections on Jazz and Blues*, pp. 297–306.

33. Dan Morgenstern, interview with author.

34. Steve Lacy, interview with author.

35. Evans, op. cit.

36. The Santa Anita band also performed Evans's "Arab Dance," which he'd written before the war for Claude Thornhill. Most of the Army band's repertoire was not so exotic.

37. *Miles Davis–Gil Evans*, op. cit., booklet, p. 18.

38. Davis, op. cit., pp. 242, 244.

39. Nat Hentoff, liner notes to *Sketches of Spain*.

40. Ibid.

41. A *zortziko* is a very fast Basque dance rhythm in 5/4. Evans first recorded "Zee Zee," a blues in 5/4, in 1971; he said he got the rhythm from the *zortziko* (though "Zee Zee" is performed at a slow tempo).

42. Steve LaJoie methodically determines the "original" amount of material in some of Evans's arrangements, supporting a contention that Evans should have received more royalties as a composer. Steven Lajoie, *An Analysis of Selected 1957 to 1962 Gil Evans Works Recorded by Miles Davis*, Ph.D. Thesis, New York University, 1999.

43. Ralph Gleason, *Down Beat*, December 12, 1957.

44. Bill Mathieu, *Down Beat*, September 29, 1960.

45. Williams, op. cit., p. 160.

46. Lajoie, op. cit.; Robin Dewhurst, *A Study of the Jazz Composition and Orchestration Techniques Adopted by Gil Evans*, Master's Thesis, University of Montfort, Great Britain, 1994.

47. Baraka, op. cit., pp. 292–293.

48. Ibid., p. 304.

CHAPTER 9: OUT OF THE COOL

1. Steve Lacy, interview with author.

2. Ibid.

3. Gil Evans, interview with author.

4. Lacy, op. cit.

5. Kenneth Noland, interview with author.

6. *Down Beat* gave *Jamaica Jazz* a rave review, with kudos specifically for Gil: "The real glory belongs to Evans, whose kaleidoscopic arrangements dominate the album." *Down Beat*'s "Jazz Record Reviews," 1956–1960.

7. Gil Evans interview with Helen Johnston, Jazz Oral History Project, IJS, Rutgers.

8. Ashley Kahn, *The Making of* Kind of Blue, p. 112.

9. Teo Macero Collection, New York Public Library for the Performing Arts.

10. Ibid.

11. There were no further memos clarifying why the deal fell through. It seems rather odd, considering that the Evans–Davis collaborations had been commercially successful and the fact that Irving Townsend was as ardent about Gil's work with Miles as George Avakian had been. Townsend, also like Avakian, was as convinced of the appeal of albums like *Porgy* and *Sketches* to the non-jazz follower.

12. Clipping from Institute of Jazz Studies, byline cut off.

13. Creed Taylor, interview with author.

14. John S. Wilson, *Down Beat*, May 25, 1961.

15. Teo Macero Collection, op. cit.

16. Ibid.

17. The concert was picketed by people who protested the African Research Foundation; the protesters believed the group was in league with South African diamond interests. Ian Carr, *Miles Davis: The Definitive Biography*, p. 177.

18. Jack Chambers, *Milestones*, Vol. 2, p. 36.

19. Gil Evans, interview with author.

20. Teo Macero Collection, op. cit., *Melody Maker* clipping.

21. Teo Macero Collection, op. cit.

22. Lacy, op. cit.

23. Anita Evans, interview with author.

24. Ibid.

25. As far as Anita knew, Gil did not use Reich's controversial "orgone boxes," though in 1967 Gil retitled his composition "Gone," from the Davis–Evans *Porgy and Bess,* "Orgone." Much of Reich's work was considered controversial. His books had been banned in the United States in 1954. Reich was imprisoned for mail fraud in 1955 in connection with the orgone boxes and died of heart failure in prison in Maine in 1957. W. Edward Mann and Edward Hoffman, *The Man Who Dreamed of Tomorrow: The Life and Thought of Wilhelm Reich,* pp. 36–38.

26. Gil Evans, interview with Helen Johnston, op. cit.

27. Teo Macero Collection, op. cit. Gil received payment for eight arrangements (three hundred dollars per arrangement), though only four of them appeared on the record. The following memo indicates that Gil either billed in advance or completed the arrangements before the sessions. Davis's request for additional payment for Gil predates the first *Quiet Nights* session by two months.

> May 24, 1962
> From: Teo
> To: Dave Kapralik
>
> Miles Davis has requested that we pay Gil Evans an additional $500 for his services in connection with the forthcoming album. To date Gil has been paid $2400 for his arrangements. With the additional $500 the total arranging costs will be a little more than what we normally pay Gil for an album. However, Miles is willing to assume this advance against his royalties.

28. While the Davis–Evans Columbia box set makes note of Oct. 9 and 10, the AFM contract has Oct 10 and 11, 1963, listed as the session dates with Gil Evans as leader.

29. Gil Evans, op. cit.

30. *San Francisco Chronicle*, probably October 1963 (date cut off on clipping).

31. Gil Evans, interview with author.
32. Ibid.
33. Leonard Feather, *Down Beat*, February 1967.

CHAPTER 10: SVENGALI
1. Gil adapted this tune, which was released on *Miles Smiles*, for Miles Davis.
2. Leonard Feather, *Down Beat*, February 1967.
3. Teo Macero Collection, New York Public Library for the Performing Arts.
4. Ibid.
5. Ibid.
6. Ibid.
7. Martin Williams, *Jazz Masters in Transition*, p. 276.
8. Sammy Mitchell, *Down Beat*, June 13, 1968.
9. John S. Wilson, *New York Times*, May 8, 1968.
10. Teo Macero Collection, op. cit.
11. Ibid.
12. *Melody Maker*, March 4, 1978.
13. Leonard Feather, *Down Beat*, June 13, 1968.
14. The Ampex label's aim was "locating and developing significant contemporary artists for a variety of audiences." *Down Beat*, February 19, 1970. Other artists included the folk duo Ian and Sylvia, a teenage Todd Rundgren, and blues harmonica player Furry Lewis.
15. Anita Evans, interview with author.
16. Gil Evans, interview with Helen Johnston, Oral History, IJS.
17. Anita Evans, op cit.
18. Ibid.
19. Ibid.
20. Martha Sanders Gilmore, *Down Beat*, May 11, 1972.
21. Kenneth Noland, interview with author.
22. Masabumi Kikuchi, interview with author.
23. Noland, op. cit.
24. Anita Evans, op. cit.
25. Noland, op. cit.
26. Maxine Gordon, interview with author.
27. Ibid.
28. Anita Evans, op. cit.
29. Gordon, op. cit.
30. Ibid.
31. Ibid.
32. John S. Wilson, *New York Times*, March 23, 1974.
33. Alan Douglas, interview with author.

34. Peter Occhiogrosso, *Village Voice*, October 24, 1974.

35. Gary Giddins, *Village Voice*, May 23, 1977.

36. Kikuchi, op. cit.

37. Anita Evans, op. cit.

38. Gordon, op. cit.

39. Robert Palmer, *New York Times*, May 13, 1977.

CHAPTER 11: SWEET BASIL

1. John S. Wilson files at IJS, Rutgers, Newark.

2. Wayne Enstice and Paul Rubin, *Jazz Is Spoken Here*, 1992.

3. Ibid.

4. Gil Evans, interview with author.

5. Lew Soloff, interview with author.

6. Tom Malone, interview with author.

7. Evans, op. cit.

8. Gary Giddins, *Village Voice*, April 5, 1988.

9. Howard Mandel, *Village Voice*, 1983.

10. Evans, op. cit.

11. Ibid.

12. Maria Schneider, interview with author.

13. Ibid.

14. Evans, op.cit.

15. Helen Merrill, interview with author.

16. Ibid.

CHAPTER 12: EPILOGUE (PARABOLA)

1. Bill Milkowski, "Miles Plays Gil," *Down Beat*, October 1991.

2. Ibid.

3. Burt A. Folkart, *Los Angeles Times*, March 22, 1988.

BIBLIOGRAPHY

A selected listing of books and articles used or drawn from in this work (refer to notes for numerous short articles and reviews).

Albertson, Chris. "The Unmasking of Miles Davis," *Saturday Review*, November 27, 1971.

Balliett, Whitney. *American Musicians II: 72 Portraits in Jazz.* New York: Oxford University Press, 1996.

———. "Claude Thornhill," *New Yorker*, April 18, 1988.

———. "Love Match," *New Yorker*, August 26, 1996.

Baraka, Amiri [LeRoi Jones]. *Blues People.* New York: Morrow Paperback Editions, 1963.

Baraka, Amiri. *The Music: Reflections on Jazz and Blues.* New York: William Morrow, 1987.

Blumenthal, Bob. "Miles and Quincy Re-Create Gil Evans," *Boston Sunday Globe*, September 5, 1993.

Buchmann-Møller, Frank. *You Just Fight for Your Life—The Story of Lester Young.* New York: Praeger, 1990.

Carner, Gary. *The Miles Davis Companion.* New York: Schirmer Books, 1996.

Carr, Ian. *Miles Davis: The Definitive Biography.* New York: HarperCollins Publishers, 1998; London: Quartet Books Ltd., 1982.

Castle, Patrick Douglas. *Aspects of Style in the Repertory of the Claude Thornhill Orchestra: 1940–1948.* University of Illinois at Urbana-Champaign, D.M.A., 1981, Ann Arbor, MI: UMI Dissertation Services.

Cerulli, Dom, Burt Kurall, and Mort Nasati, eds. *The Jazz Word.* New York: Ballantine Books, 1960.

Chambers, Jack. *Milestones. The Music and Times of Miles Davis.* New York: Da Capo, 1998; Toronto: University of Toronto Press, 1960.

Charters, Samuel B., and Leonard Kunstadt. *Jazz: A History of the New York Scene*. New York: Da Capo, 1962, 1981.

Chilton, John. *Who's Who of Jazz: Storyville to Swing Street*. London: Peridon Ltd., 1970.

Cole, Bill. *Miles Davis: A Musical Biography*. New York: William Morrow, 1974.

Collier, James Lincoln. *Benny Goodman and the Swing Era*. New York: Oxford University Press, 1989.

Connors, D. Russell. *Benny Goodman: Listen to His Legacy*. Metuchen, NJ: Scarecrow Press, 1988.

Crawford, Marc. "Miles and Gil—Portrait of a Friendship," *Down Beat*, February 16, 1961.

Crosbie, Ian. "Claude Thornhill," *Coda*, October 1975.

Crouch, Stanley. "Play the Right Thing," *New Republic*, February 12, 1990.

Cugny, Laurent. *Las Vegas Tango: Une Vie de Gil Evans*. Paris: Collection Birdland, P.O.L., 1989.

Davis, Miles, with Quincy Troupe. *Miles: The Autobiography*. New York: Simon and Schuster, 1989.

Dewhurst, Robin. *A Study of the Jazz Composition and Orchestration Techniques Adopted by Gil Evans*. Masters of Arts in Music [Thesis], University of Montfort, Great Britain, 1994.

DeVeaux, Scott. *The Birth of Bebop: A Social and Musical History*. Berkeley: University of California Press, 1997.

Early, Gerald. *Tuxedo Junction: Essays on American Culture*. New York: Ecco Press, 1989.

Endrey, George. "Evans," *Sounds & Fury*, July–August 1965.

Enstice, Wayne, and Paul Rubin. *Jazz Spoken Here: Conversations with Twenty-Two Musicians*. Baton Rouge: Louisiana State University Press, 1992.

Erenberg, Lewis A. *Swingin' the Dream: Big Band Jazz and the Rebirth of American Culture*. Chicago: University of Chicago Press, 1998.

Feather, Leonard. *The Encyclopedia of Jazz*. New York: Horizon Press, 1955.

———. *The Encyclopedia of Jazz in the Sixties*. New York: Horizon Press, 1966.

———, and Ira Gitler. *The Encyclopedia of Jazz in the Seventies*. New York: Horizon Press, 1976.

———. "A Magnificent Innovator" (obit.), *Los Angeles Times*, March 27, 1988.

———. "The Modulated World of Gil Evans," *Down Beat*, February 23, 1967.

Firestone, Ross. *Swing, Swing, Swing: The Life and Times of Benny Goodman*. New York: Norton, 1993.

Gabbard, Krin, ed. *Jazz Among the Discourses*. Durham: Duke University Press, 1995.

Garrod, Charles. *Claude Thornhill and His Orchestra* (discography). Zephyrhills, FL: Joyce Record Club, 1996.

Giddins, Gary. *Celebrating Bird: The Triumph of Charlie Parker*. New York: William Morrow, 1986.

————. "The Scene Changes" (obit.), *Village Voice*, April 5, 1988.

————. *Visions of Jazz: The First Century*. New York: Oxford University Press, 1998.

Gitler, Ira. *Swing to Bop: An Oral History of the Transition of Jazz in the 1940s*. New York: Oxford University Press, 1987.

Goldberg, Joe. *Jazz Masters of the Fifties*. New York: Macmillan, 1965.

Gonzalez, Fernando. "In the Key of Evans," *Boston Globe*, May 1983.

Gottlieb, Robert, ed. *Reading Jazz*. New York: Pantheon Books, 1996.

Haley, Alex. "Playboy Interview: Miles Davis," *Playboy*, September 1962.

Harrison, Max. "Gil Evans and Miles Davis, Part 1," *Jazz Monthly*, December 1958; "Part 2," *Jazz Monthly*, February 1960 (reprinted in Harrison, *A Jazz Retrospective*, and Kirchner, *Miles Davis Reader*).

————. *A Jazz Retrospective*. London: Quartet Books, 1991.

Hentoff, Nat. "Birth of the Cool," *Down Beat*, May 2, 1957.

————. "I'm No Grandaddy: Gil Evans," *Down Beat*, May 16, 1957.

————. "Miles Davis: Last Trump," *Esquire*, March 1959.

————. *Speaking Freely*. New York: Alfred A. Knopf, 1997.

Hoeffer, George. "The Birth of the Cool," *Down Beat*, October 7, 1965.

Horricks, Raymond. *Svengali, or the Orchestra called Gil Evans*. Spellmont: Tunbridge Wells, Great Britain, 1984; New York: Hippocrene, 1984.

Kernfeld, Barry, ed. *The New Grove Dictionary of Jazz*. London: Macmillan Press Ltd., 1988.

Khan, Ashley. *The Making of Kind of Blue*. New York: Da Capo, 2000.

Kirchner, Bill, ed. *The Miles Davis Reader*. Washington: Smithsonian Institution Press, 1997.

————, ed. *The Oxford Companion to Jazz*. New York: Oxford University Press, 2000.

Lahey, Don. "Gil Evans, Out of the Cool," *Coda*, December 1985–January 1986.

Lajoie, Steven. *An Analysis of Selected 1957 to 1962 Gil Evans Works Recorded by Miles Davis*. Ph.D. thesis, School of Education, New York University, 1999, Ann Arbor, MI: UMI Dissertation Services.

Lees, Gene. *Arranging the Score: Portraits of the Great Arrangers*. London, New York: Cassell, 2000.

————. "He Fell from a Star," *Gene Lee's Jazz Letter*, June, July, August 1995.

Mandel, Howard. "Gil Evans, the Lone Arranger." *Down Beat*, April 1984.

Mann, W. Edward, and Edward Hoffman. *The Man Who Dreamed of Tomorrow: The Life and Thought of Wilhelm Reich.* Los Angeles: J. P. Tarcher, Inc., 1980.

McCarthy, Albert: *Big Band Jazz.* New York: Exeter Books, 1983, 1974.

———. *The Dance Band Era.* Radnor, PA: Chilton Book Co., 1971.

Milkowski, Bill. "Miles Plays Gil," *Down Beat,* October 1991.

Muccioli, Joe, ed. *The Gil Evans Collection: 15 Study and Sketch Scores from Gil's Manuscripts.* Milwaukee, WI: Hal Leonard Corp., 1996.

Nicholson, Stuart. *Jazz-Rock: A History.* New York: Schirmer Books, 1998.

Nisensen, Eric. *'Round About Midnight: A Portrait of Miles Davis.* New York: Dial Press, 1982.

O'Meally, Robert, ed. *The Jazz Cadence of American Culture.* New York: Columbia University Press, 1998.

Ostransky, Leroy. *Jazz City: The Impact of Our Cities on the Development of Jazz.* Englewood Cliffs, NJ: Prentice-Hall, 1978.

Overton, Ron. *Hotel Me: Poems for Gil Evans and Others.* Brooklyn, NY: Hanging Loose Press, 1994.

Palmer, Robert. "Refocus on Gil Evans," *Down Beat,* May 23, 1974.

Porter, Lewis. *Jazz: A Century of Change.* New York: Schirmer Books, 1997.

Priestley, Brian, and Stan Tracey. "Discourse," *Jazz Journal International,* London, July, August 1978.

Reese, Jérôme. "Gil Evans, l'arrangeur qui dérange," *Jazz Hot,* Paris, April 1984.

Reisner, Robert George. *Bird: The Legend of Charlie Parker.* New York: Bonanza Books, 1962.

Rollini, Arthur. *Thirty Years with the Big Bands.* Urbana: University of Illinois Press, 1987.

Rouy, Gérard. "Gil Evans," *Jazz Magazine,* Paris, July–August, 1974.

Ruff, Willie. *A Call to Assembly: The Autobiography of a Musical Storyteller.* New York: Viking, 1991.

Russell, Ross. *Bird! The High Life and Hard Times of Charlie Parker.* New York: Charterhouse, 1979.

———. *Jazz Styles in Kansas City and the Southwest.* Berkeley: University of California Press, 1971.

Sanders Gilmore, Martha. "Brand New World of Gil Evans," *International Musician,* November 1972.

Schuller, Gunther. *Early Jazz: Its Roots and Musical Development.* New York: Oxford University Press, 1968.

———. *The Swing Era: The Development of Jazz, 1930–1945.* New York: Oxford University Press, 1989.

Sears, Richard S. *V-Discs: A History and Discography.* Westport, CT: Greenwood Press, 1980.

Sharaf, Myron. *Fury on Earth: A Biography of Wilhelm Reich*. New York: St. Martin's Press, 1983.

Shapiro, Nat, ed. *Popular Music: An Annotated Index of American Popular Songs*. New York: Adrian Press, 1965.

Shaw, Arnold. *The Jazz Age: Popular Music in the 1920's*. New York: Oxford University Press, 1987.

———. *52nd St.: The Street of Jazz*. New York: Da Capo, 1977, 1971.

Sidran, Ben. *Talking Jazz: An Oral History*. New York: Da Capo, 1995.

Simon, George. *The Big Bands* (4th ed.). New York: Schirmer Books, 1981.

———. *Glenn Miller and His Orchestra*. New York: T.Y. Crowell Co., 1974.

Smith, Arnold Jay. "Gil Evans: 21st Century Man," *Down Beat*, May 20, 1976.

Stearns, Marshall. *The Story of Jazz*. New York: Oxford University Press, 1956.

Stewart, Rex. *Jazz Masters of the Thirties*. New York: Macmillan Co., 1972.

Stewart, Zan. "Gil Evans," *Musician, Player and Listener*, January 1982.

Sudhalter, Richard M. *Lost Chords: White Musicians and Their Contributions to Jazz, 1915–1945*. New York: Oxford University Press, 1999.

Tajiri, Tetsuya. *Gil Evans Discography, 1941–82*. Tokyo, National Press Co., 1983.

Taylor, Arthur. *Notes and Tones: Musician-to-Musician Interviews*. New York: Coward, McCann & Geoghegan, 1982.

Tate, Greg. "The Electric Miles," *Down Beat*, July 1983.

Tomlinson, Gary. "Miles Davis, Music Dialogician," *Black Music Research Journal II, No. 2*, Fall 1991.

Troupe, Quincy. *Miles and Me*. Berkeley: University of California Press, 2000.

Tucker, Sherrie. *Swing Shift: All Girl Bands of the 1940s*. Durham: Duke University Press, 2000.

Tucker, Mark. *Porgy and Miles*. Center for Jazz Studies at Columbia University, New York: Rhythm-a-Ning: A Symposium on Jazz Culture, May 8, 2000.

Walker, Leo. *The Wonderful Era of the Great Dance Bands*. Garden City, NY: Doubleday, 1972.

Way, Chris. *The Big Bands Go to War*. Edinburgh: Mainstream Publishing, 1991.

Williams, Martin. *The Jazz Tradition*. New York: Oxford University Press, 1970.

———. *Jazz Masters in Transition, 1957–69*. New York: Macmillan Co., 1970.

Williams, Richard. *Miles Davis: The Man in the Green Shirt*. New York: H. Holt, 1993.

———. "Sketches of Gil," *Melody Maker*, March 4, 1978.

SELECTED DISCOGRAPHY

This selected discography was adapted and edited from Laurent Cugny's Evans discography, which is currently posted on the Internet (www.gilevans.org), with his permission. I have also referred to the Evans discography compiled by Cugny and Georges Wagner (in Cugny's book *Las Vegas Tango*); *Gil Evans Discography 1941–82*, by Tetsuya Tajiri; and *Claude Thornhill and His Orchestra* by Charles Garrod. With the exception of the Skinnay Ennis recordings and the Claude Thornhill recordings (which, for the most part, were originally issued as 78rpm singles), and those by the Miles Davis Nonet (which were originally issued as singles), this discography is primarily based on original LPs and their reissues as CDs, listed chronologically by recording date. This discography is intended as a user-friendly, comprehensive guide to Gil Evans's recorded work; it is by no means complete, nor does it use the format of standard reference jazz discographies. All arrangements are by Gil Evans unless otherwise noted.

ABBREVIATIONS

afl	alto flute	flh	flugelhorn
arr	arranger	g	guitar
as	alto sax	key	keyboards
av	alto violin	mand	mandolin
b	bass	mar	marimba
bas	bassoon	mello	mellophone
bcl	bass clarinet	or	organ
bfl	bass flute	p	piano
bj	banjo	perc	percussion
bs	baritone sax	pic	piccolo
btb	bass trombone	pictp	piccolo trumpet
cel	celeste	ss	soprano sax
cl	clarinet	tp	trumpet
cond	conductor	tb	trombone
dm	drums	tim	timpani
dir	director	ts	tenor sax
elg	electric guitar	tu	tuba
elb	electric bass	tv	tenor violin
elp	electric piano	vcl	vocal
enh	English horn	vib	vibraphone
fh	French horn	vln	violin
fl	flute	ww	woodwinds

Skinnay Ennis and His Orchestra

Skinnay Ennis (vcl), Ralph Liscom, James Maxwell, Wade Schlegel (tp)
Pete Carpenter, Noris Hurley (tb), Ryland Weston, Jack Crowley, Herb
Stowe (ww), Gil Evans (p, arr), Sonny Dawson (g), Fred Whiting (b), John
DeSoto (dm). Hollywood, September 11, 1938.
1. The Girlfriend of the Whirling Dervish [Vi 26047-B]

Skinnay Ennis (vcl), Wade Schlegel, Harry Johnson, James Maxwell (tp),
Pete Carpenter, Noris Hurley (tb), Ryland Weston, Jack Crowley, Herb
Stowe, Fred Peters, Rudy Cangie (ww), Charles LaVere (p), Sonny Dawson
(g), Fred Whiting (b), John DeSoto (dm), Gil Evans (arr). Hollywood,
March 24, 1939.
2. Strange Enchantment [Vi 26207]

2 on *Swingin' Uptown*, RCA Victor CD 66746-2

Claude Thornhill and His Orchestra

Randy Brooks, Conrad Gozzo, Steve Steck (tp), Tasso Harris, Bud Smith

(tb), John Graas, Vincent Jacobs (fh), Danny Polo (cl), Jack Ferrier, Bob Walters (cl, as), Ted Goddard, George Paulson (cl, ts), Buddy Dean (cl, bs), Barry Galbraith (g), Claude Thornhill (p), Marty Blitz (b), Irv Cottler (dm), Gil Evans (arr). New York, June 19, 1942.
1. Buster's Last Stand

Jake Koven, Conrad Gozzo, Steve Steck (tp), Tasso Harris, Bud Smith (tb), John Graas, Mike Glass (fh), Danny Polo (cl), Jack Ferrier, Conn Humphreys (cl, as), Ted Goddard, George Paulson (cl, ts), Buddy Dean (cl, bs), Barry Galbraith (g), Claude Thornhill (p), Marty Blitz (b), Irv Cottler (dm), The Snowflakes (Lillian Lane, Terry Allen, Martha Wayne, Buddy Stewart) (vcl), Gil Evans (arr). New York, July 24, 1942.
2. There's a Small Hotel 3. I Don't Know Why 4. Moonlight Bay

Rusty Dedrick, Louis Mucci, Jake Koven, Clarence Willard (tp), Tasso Harris, Bob Jenny, Ray Schmidt (tb), Fred Schmidt, Sandy Siegelstein (fh), Bob Walters (cl), Jack Ferrier, Ted Goddard (cl, as), John Nelson, Carl Swift (cl, ts), Chet Pardee (cl, bcl, bs), Barry Galbraith (g), Claude Thornhill (p), Richard "Iggy" Shevack (b), Bill Exiner (dm), Gil Evans (arr). New York, July 17, 1946.
5. Under the Willow Tree 6. Arab Dance

Rusty Dedrick, Louis Mucci, Jake Koven, Clarence Willard (tp), Tasso Harris, Bob Jenny, Tak Tavorkian (tb), Fred Schmidt, Sandy Siegelstein (fh), Bob Walters (cl), Jack Ferrier, Ted Goddard (cl, as), John Nelson, Joe Reisman (cl, ts), Chet Pardee (cl, bcl, bs), Barry Galbraith (g), Claude Thornhill (p), Richard "Iggy" Shevack (b), Irv Cottler (dm), Buddy Hughes (vcl), Gil Evans (arr). Liederkranz Hall (live), New York, late August, 1946.
7. Sorta Kinda 8. Twilight on the Trail 9. La Paloma 10. The Troubador (Pictures at an Exhibition) 11. Arab Dance

Eddie Zandy, Emil Terry, Louis Mucci, Clarence Willard (tp), Tak Tavorkian, Allan Langstaff (tb), Walt Welscher, Sandy Siegelstein (fh), Bill Barber (tu), Danny Polo, Lee Konitz (cl, as), Mario Rollo (cl, ts), Bill Bushey (cl, bcl, bs), Mickey Folus (bcl, bs), Barry Galbraith (g), Claude Thornhill (p), Joe Shulman (b), Bill Exiner (dm), Gene Williams (vcl on 4), Gil Evans (arr). New York, September 4, 1947.
12. Anthropology

Eddie Zandy, Paul Cohen, Louis Mucci (tp), Tak Tavorkian, Allan Langstaff (tb), Walt Welscher, Sandy Siegelstein (fh), Bill Barber (tu), Danny Polo, Lee Konitz (cl, as), Mario Rollo (cl, ts), Bill Bushey (cl, bcl,

bs), Mickey Folus (bcl, bs), Barry Galbraith (g), Claude Thornhill (p), Joe Shulman (b), Bill Exiner (dm), Gene Williams (vcl on 2), Gil Evans (arr). New York, October 16, 1947.
13. Robbin's Nest 14. I Knew You When 15. Lover Man 16. Poor Little Rich Girl

Same personnel
New York, October 17, 1947.
17. Robbin's Nest

Eddie Zandy, Red Rodney, Louis Mucci (tp), Tak Tavorkian, Allan Langstaff (tb), Walt Welscher, Sandy Siegelstein (fh), Bill Barber (tu), Danny Polo, Lee Konitz (cl, as), Mario Rollo (cl, ts), Bill Bushey (cl, bcl, bs), Mickey Folus (bcl, bs), Barry Galbraith (g), Claude Thornhill (p), Joe Shulman (b), Bill Exiner (dm), Gil Evans (arr). New York, November 6, 1947; December 17, 1947, (6) add Ed Stang (pic, fl).
18. Lover Man 19. Polka Dots and Moonbeams 20. The Happy Stranger 21. Donna Lee 22. Yardbird Suite

Louis Mucci, Emil Terry, Ed Zandy (tp), Johnny Torick, Allan Langstaff (tb), Walter Wechsler, Sandy Siegelstein (fh), Bill Barber (tu), Danny Polo (cl, as), Lee Konitz (as), Myron Mickey Folus, Jerry Sanfino (ts), Gerry Mulligan (ts, bs), Barry Galbraith (g), Claude Thornhill (p), Russ (Savakus) Saunders (b), Bill Exiner (dm), Gil Evans (arr). New York (live), April, 1948.
23. Spanish Dance #5 24. Anthropology 25. Arab Dance 26. Robbin's Nest 27. Royal Garden Blues 28. Polka Dots and Moonbeams

1–4, 17, 18, 21, 22 on *The Memorable Claude Thornhill,* Columbia 32906 2LPs
1, 2, 5, 6, 12, 17–22 on *Claude Thornhill—The Best of the Big Bands,* CK 46152-CD
7–12, 17–22 on *The Real Birth of the Cool,* CBS/Sony 25DP5321-CD
13–16 on *The Uncollected Claude Thornhill and His Orchestra,* Hindsight HCD-108-CD
23–28 on *Claude Thornhill—The 1948 Transcription Performances,* Hep CD17
1 on *American Pop: An Audio History—from Minstrel to Mojo,* West Hill Audio Archives WH-1017 (9CDs)

Miles Davis Nonet
Miles Davis (tp), Mike Zwerin (tb), Junior Collins (fh), Bill Barber (tu), Lee Konitz (as), Gerry Mulligan (bs), John Lewis (p), Al MacKibbon (b), Max Roach (dm), Kenny Hagood (vcl on 1), Gil Evans (arr). New York,

Royal Roost (live), September 4 (1), September 18 (2), 1948.
1. Birth of the Cool Theme 2. Moon Dreams

Miles Davis (tp), J. J. Johnson (tb), Sandy Siegelstein (fh), Bill Barber (tu),
Lee Konitz (as), Gerry Mulligan (bs), John Lewis (p), Nelson Boyd (b),
Kenny Clarke (dm), Gil Evans (arr). New York, April 22, 1949.
3. Boplicity

Miles Davis (tp), J. J. Johnson (tb), Gunther Schuller (fh), Bill Barber (tu),
Lee Konitz (as), Gerry Mulligan (bs), John Lewis (p), Al MacKibbon (b),
Max Roach (dm), Gil Evans (arr). New York, March 9, 1950.
4. Moon Dreams

1–4 on *The Complete Birth of the Cool,* Capitol Jazz CDP 7243 4 94550 2 3-CD
3, 4 on *The Birth of the Cool,* Capitol CP32-5181-CD

Billy Butterfield and His Orchestra

Billy Butterfield, Andy Ferretti, Jimmy Maxwell, Yank Lawson (tp), Will
Bradley, Cutty Cutshall (tb), Toots Mondello, Hymie Shertzer (as), Al
Klink, Hank Ross (ts), Ernie Caceres (bs), Mickey Crane (p), Sam Bruno
(b), Buzzy Drootin (dm), Gil Evans (arr). New York, February 1, 1950.
1. Singin' the Blues

1 on *The Billy Butterfield Orchestra,* London 622-LP

Pearl Bailey

Pearl Bailey (vcl), Chris Griffin (tp), Will Bradley (tb), Hymie Shertzer
(as), Ray Tunia (p), Barry Galbraith (g), Frank Carroll (b), Terry Snyder
(dm), Gil Evans (arr, cond). New York, July 20, 1950.
1. Vagabond Shoes 2. He Didn't Have the Know How 3. Down in the Cellar 4. Some Days There Just Ain't No Fish

1, 4 on Columbia 38928
2, 3 on Columbia 38969
2, 4 on *It's a Great Feeling,* Sony Special Products

Charlie Parker and His Orchestra

Charlie Parker (as), Junior Collins (fh), Hal McKusick (cl), Tommy Mace
(oboe), Manny Thaler (bas), The Dave Lambert Singers (vcl), Tony Aless
(p), Charles Mingus (b), Max Roach (dm), Dave Lambert (vcl-arr), Gil
Evans (arr, cond). New York, May 25, 1953.
1. In the Still of the Night 2. Old Folks 3. If I Love Again

1–3 on *The Complete Charlie Parker on Verve,*Verve 837 141-2-CD

Dancing for Two in Love—Billy Butterfield and His Orchestra
Billy Butterfield, Tony Faso, Bernie Glow, Al Mattaliano (tp), Cutty Cut-shall, Lou McGarity (tb), Hank D'Amico (cl, as) Paul Ricci (as), Nick Caiazza (ts), Ernie Caceres (ts), John Barrows (frh), Lou Stine (p), Felix Giobbe (b), Cliff Leeman (d), Gil Evans (arr, prob on 2). New York, 1954.
1. I Got a Right to Sing the Blues 2. Struttin' with Some Barbecue 3. It's Easy to Remember

1–3 on *Dancing for Two in Love,* Westminster WP6006-LP

Teddy Charles Tentet
Teddy Charles (vib), Art Farmer (tp), Don Butterfield (tu), Gigi Gryce (as), J. R. Monterose (ts), Sol Schlinger (bs), Jimmy Raney (g), Mal Waldron (p), Teddy Kotick (b), Joe Harris (dm), Gil Evans (arr). New York, January 11, 1956.
1. You Go to My Head

1 on *The Teddy Charles Tentet,* Atlantic LP 1229; reissued on Atlantic Jazz 790 983-2-CD

Gerry Mulligan Sextet
Gerry Mulligan (bs), Bob Brookmeyer (vtb), Zoot Sims (ts), Jon Eardley (tp), Bill Crow (b), Dave Bailey (dm), Gil Evans (arr). New York, January 25, 1956.
1. La Plus Que Lente

1 on *Mainstream of Jazz, Special Edition,* Phonogram 826 993-2-CD

Johnny Mathis
Johnny Mathis (vcl), Buck Clayton, Jimmy Maxwell (tp), J. J. Johnson (tb), Tommy Mitchell (btb), John LaPorta (as), Hank Jones (p), Bill Pemberton (b), Bill Exiner (dm), Gil Evans (arr). New York, March 21, 1956.
1. Love, Your Magic Spell Is Everywhere 2. It Might as Well Be Spring 3. Easy to Love

1–3 on *Johnny Mathis,* Columbia CL887-LP; reissued as CK 64890

The Jazz Workshop—Hal McKusick
Hal McKusick (as), Art Farmer (tp), Jimmy Cleveland (tb), Gene Allen (bs), Barry Galbraith (g), Jimmy Raney (rhythm-g), Milt Hinton (b), Osie Johnson (dm), George Russell (perc on 2), Gil Evans (arr). New York, April 3, 1956.

1. Jambangle 2. Blues for Pablo

1–2 on *The Jazz Workshop*—Hal McKusick, RCA Victor LPM1366-LP; *The RCA Victor Jazz Workshop: The Arrangers*, RCA Bluebird 6471-2-CD

Dream of You—Helen Merrill
Helen Merrill (vcl), Hank Jones (p, cel on 4), Barry Galbraith (g), Oscar Pettiford (b), Joe Morello (dm), strings, woodwinds unknown, Gil Evans (arr, cond). New York, June 26, 1956.
1. He Was Too Good to Me 2. I'm a Fool to Want You 3. I've Never Seen 4. Troubled Waters

Helen Merrill (vcl), Art Farmer (tp), Joe Bennett (tb), John LaPorta (cl, as), Jerome Richardson (fl, as, ts), Danny Bank (bs), Barry Galbraith (g), Hank Jones (p), Oscar Pettiford (b), Joe Morello (dm), others unknown, Gil Evans (arr, cond). New York, June 27, 1956.
5. Anyplace I Hang My Hat Is Home 6. A New Town Is a Blue Town
7. I'm Just a Lucky So and So 8. Where Flamingos Fly

Helen Merrill (vcl), Art Farmer, Louis Mucci (tp), Jimmy Cleveland (tb), John LaPorta (cl, as), Barry Galbraith (g), Hank Jones (p), Oscar Pettiford (b), Joe Morello (dm), others unknown, Gil Evans (arr, cond). Note: according to Gil Evans, Joe Morello only played on one of the sessions for "Dream of You"; Osie Johnson played on the others. New York, June 29, 1956.
9. By Myself 10. Dream of You 11. People Will Say We're in Love 12. You're Lucky to Me

1–12 originally issued as *Dream of You*, EmArcy MG36078; reissued as EmArcy 314 514 074-2-CD; *The Complete Helen Merrill on Mercury*, Mercury 826 340-2

They're Playing Our Song—Billy Butterfield and His Orchestra
Billy Butterfield, Tony Faso, Bernie Glow, Jimmy Nottingham (tp), Lou MacGarity, Cutty Cutshall (tb), Hank D'Amico (cl, as), Toots Mondello (as), Nick Caiazza, Boomie Richman (ts), Danny Bank (bs), Mickey Crane (p), Jack Lesberg (b), Cliff Leeman (dm), Dottie Smith (vcl), Gil Evans (arr). New York, December 5, 1956.
1. Singin' the Blues 2. Again and Again and Again (composed by Gil Evans, prob. arr. by Bill Stegmeyer)

1–2 on *They're Playing Our Song*, RCA Victor LPM 1441-LP

This Is Lucy Reed—Lucy Reed

Lucy Reed (vcl), Jimmy Cleveland (tb), Tommy Mitchell (btb), Romeo Penque (afl, enh), David Kurtzer (bas), Harry Lookofsky (tv), Bill Pemberton (b), George Russell (dm), Gil Evans (p, arr). New York, January, 1957.
1. Love for Sale 2. A Trout, No Doubt 3. No Moon at All

1–3 originally issued on *This Is Lucy Reed*, Fantasy 3243-LP

Debut—Marcy Lutes

Marcy Lutes (vcl), Shorty Baker (tp), Hal McKusick (as), Al Cohn (ts), Oscar Pettiford (b), Paul Motian (dm), others unknown, Gil Evans (arr). New York, February 1957.
1. Cheek to Cheek 2. Trav'lin Light 3. Aren't You Glad You're You

1–3 issued on *Debut*—Marcy Lutes, Decca DL8552-LP; reissued on *Gil Evans*, GRP 9895-2-CD

Miles Ahead—Miles Davis + 19/Orchestra under the direction of Gil Evans

Miles Davis (flh), Ernie Royal, Bernie Glow, Louis Mucci, Taft Jordan, John Carisi (tp), Frank Rehak, Jimmy Cleveland, Joe Bennett (tb), Tom Mitchell (btb), Willie Ruff, Tony Miranda (fh), Bill Barber (tu), Romeo Penque (fl, cl, bcl, oboe), Sid Cooper (fl, cl), Danny Bank (bcl), Lee Konitz (as), Paul Chambers (b), Art Taylor (dm), Gil Evans (arr, cond). New York, May 6, 1957; May 10, 1957; May 23, 1957, Jimmy Buffington (fh) replaces Tony Miranda; May 27, 1957, Tony Miranda (fh) replaces Jimmy Buffington, Eddie Caine (fl, cl) replaces Sid Cooper, Wynton Kelly (p, 13, 14, 16, 18–20, does not appear on mastered takes).
1. Springsville 2. The Maids of Cadiz 3. The Duke 4. My Ship 5. Miles Ahead 6. Blues for Pablo 7. New Rhumba 8. The Meaning of the Blues 9. Lament 10. I Don't Want to Be Kissed (by Anyone but You)

1–10 originally issued as *Miles Ahead—Miles Davis + 19*, Columbia CL1041; reissued as CK40784; CK53225-CD; plus all alternate and rehearsal takes on *Miles Davis–Gil Evans—The Complete Columbia Studio Recordings*, Columbia CXK 67397; *Miles Davis–Gil Evans—The Complete Columbia Studio Recordings*, Mosaic MQ11-164 LP

Gil Evans & Ten—Gil Evans and His Orchestra

John Carisi (1 only), Lou Mucci, Jake Koven (tp), Jimmy Cleveland (tb), Bart Varsalona (btb), Willie Ruff (fh), Steve Lacy (ss), Lee Konitz (=Zeke Tolin) (as), Dave Kurtzer (bas), Paul Chambers (b), Jo Jones (1 only), Nick

Stabulas (dm), Gil Evans (p, arr, cond). Hackensack (NJ), September 6, 27, 1957; October 10, 1957.
1. Remember 2. Ella Speed 3 Nobody's Heart 4. If You Could See Me Now 5. Big Stuff 6. Just One of Those Things 7. Jambangle

1–7 originally issued as *Gil Evans & Ten, Prestige LP7120;* reissued as Prestige OJCCD-346-2

Jamaica Jazz—Don Elliott
Don Elliott (tp, mello, mar, bongo), Don Aswarth, Phil Bodner, Romeo Penque (fl, oboe, enh), Al Klink (bcl, ts), Barry Galbraith (g), Ernie Furtado (b), Art Taylor (dm), Gil Evans (arr, cond). New York, November 23, 1957.
1. Pretty to Talk With 2. Napolean 3. Push De Button 4. Ain't It the Truth 5. Savanna

Don Elliott (tp, mar, vib), Jimmy Buffington, Willie Ruff (fh), Frank Rehak (tb), Hal McKusick (fl, as, bcl), Dave Kurtzer (bas), Paul Chambers (b), Art Taylor (dm), Candido (conga), Gil Evans (arr, cond). New York, November 26, 1957.
6. Cocoanut Sweet 7. Little Biscuit 8. What Good Does It Do?

1–8 originally issued as *Jamaica Jazz*—Don Elliott Octet, featuring Candido, ABC Paramount AC228-LP
2, 3, 5, 6 on *Gil Evans,* GRP 9895-2-CD

New Bottle, Old Wine—Gil Evans Orchestra featuring Cannonball Adderley
Julian "Cannonball" Adderley (as), John Coles, Louis Mucci, Ernie Royal, Clyde Reasinger (replaces Royal on 6, 7, 8) (tp), Joe Bennett, Frank Rehak (tb), Tom Mitchell (btb), Julius Watkins (fh), Harvey Phillips, Bill Barber (replaces Phillips on 5, 6, 7, 8) (tu), Jerry Sanfino, Phil Bodner (replaces Sanfino on 5, 6, 7, 8) (pic, fl, bcl), Chuck Wayne (g), Paul Chambers (b), Philly Joe Jones, Art Blakey (5 only) (dm), Gil Evans (p, arr, cond). New York, April 9, 1958; May 2, 1958; May 21, 1958; May 26, 1958.
1. Saint Louis Blues 2. King Porter Stomp 3. 'Round Midnight 4. Lester Leaps In
5. Willow Tree 6. Struttin' with Some Barbecue 7. Manteca! 8. Bird Feathers

1–8 originally issued as *New Bottle, Old Wine*, World Pacific WP1246; reissued as *Pacific Jazz Collection*—Gil Evans, EMI CDP 74 6855-2; CDP 74 6822-2-2 CDs; *New Bottle, Old Wine* (Pacific Jazz CP 32-5372)

Porgy and Bess—Miles Davis Orchestra under the direction of Gil Evans
Miles Davis (flh, tp on 4), Ernie Royal, Bernie Glow, John Coles, Louis Mucci (tp); Dick Hixon, Frank Rehak, Jimmy Cleveland, Joe Bennett (tb); Willie Ruff, Julius Watkins, Gunther Schuller (fh); Bill Barber (tu); Phil Bodner, Romeo Penque (fl, afl, cl), Danny Bank (afl, bcl), Julian "Cannonball" Adderley (as); Paul Chambers (b), Philly Joe Jones (3, 4, 9), Jimmy Cobb (dm), Gil Evans (arr, cond). New York, July 22, 1958; July, 29, 1958; August 4, 1958 (Jerome Richardson replaces Romeo Penque); August 18, 1958.
1. Buzzard Song 2. Bess, You Is My Woman Now 3. Gone 4. Gone, Gone, Gone 5. Summertime 6. Oh, Bess, Oh Where's My Bess 7. Prayer (Oh, Doctor Jesus) 8. Fisherman, Strawberry and Devil Crab 9. My Man's Gone Now 10. It Ain't Necessarily So 11. Here Come De Honey Man 12. I Loves You, Porgy 13. There's a Boat That's Leaving Soon for New York

1–13 originally issued as *Porgy and Bess*, Columbia CL1274 (mono), CS 8085 (stereo); reissued as CK 40647-CD; plus all alternate, rehearsal takes, *Miles Davis–Gil Evans—The Complete Columbia Studio Recordings*, Columbia CXK 67397; Mosaic MQ11-164 LP

Great Jazz Standards—Gil Evans and His Orchestra
John Coles, Louis Mucci, Allen Smith (tp), Curtis Fuller, Bill Elton, Dick Lieb (tb), Bob Northern (1, 2, 5), Earl Chapin (fh), Bill Barber (tu), Al Block (ww), Steve Lacy (ss), Chuck Wayne (g), Dick Carter (b), Dennis Charles (dm), Gil Evans (p, arr, cond) New York, probably January 1959.
1. Davenport Blues 2. Straight, No Chaser 3. Django

John Coles, Louis Mucci, Danny Stiles (tp), Jimmy Cleveland, Curtis Fuller, Rod Levitt (tb), Earl Chapin (fh), Bill Barber (tu), Ed Caine (ww), Steve Lacy (ss), Budd Johnson (ts, cl), Ray Crawford (g), Tommy Potter (b), Elvin Jones (dm), Gil Evans (p, arr, cond). New York, February 5, 1959.
4. Ballad of the Sad Young Man 5. Joy Spring
6. Django 7. Chant of the Weed 8. La Nevada (theme)

1–8 originally issued as *Great Jazz Standards*—Gil Evans Orchestra featuring John Coles, World Pacific WP1270-LP; reissued as EMI CDP 74 6855-2; CDP 74 6822-2-2 CDs

Sketches of Spain—Miles Davis, arranged and conducted by Gil Evans
Miles Davis (tp, flh), Ernie Royal, Bernie Glow, Louis Mucci, Taft Jordan (tp), Dick Hixon, Frank Rehak (tb), Jimmy Buffington, John Barrows, Earl Chapin (fh), Jimmy MacAllister (tu), Al Block, Ed Caine (fl), Romeo

Penque (oboe), Harold Feldman (oboe, cl), Danny Bank (bcl), Jack
Knitzer (bas), Janet Putnam (harp), Paul Chambers (b), Jimmy Cobb
(dm), Elvin Jones, probably Jose Mangual (perc), Gil Evans (arr, cond).
New York, November 20, 1959.
1. Concierto de Aranjuez

Miles Davis (tp), Ernie Royal, Bernie Glow, Louis Mucci, John Coles (tp),
Dick Hixon, Frank Rehak (tb), Jimmy Buffington, Joe Singer, Tony
Miranda (fh), Bill Barber (tu), Al Block, Harold Feldman (fl), Romeo
Penque (oboe), Danny Bank (bcl), Jack Knitzer (bas), Janet Putnam
(harp), Paul Chambers (b), Jimmy Cobb (dm), Elvin Jones, probably Jose
Mangual (perc), Gil Evans (arr, cond). New York, March 10– 11, 1960.
2. The Pan Piper 3. Song of Our Country 4. Solea 5. Will O' the Wisp
6. Saeta

1, 2, 4–6 originally issued as *Sketches of Spain* Columbia CS 8271-LP
stereo; Columbia CK 40578-CD
3 on *Directions*—Miles Davis, Columbia KC2 36474-2 LPs
1–7 plus all alternate, rehearsed takes on *Miles Davis–Gil Evans—The
Complete Columbia Studio Recordings,* Columbia CXK 67397; Mosaic
MQ11-164-LP

Out of the Cool—Gil Evans and His Orchestra
John Coles, Phil Sunkel (tp), Jimmy Knepper, Keg Johnson (tb), Tony
Studd (btb), Bill Barber (tu), Ed Caine 1–4, Ray Beckenstein 5, 6 (as, fl,
pic), Bob Tricarico (bas, fl, pic), Budd Johnson (ts, ss), Ray Crawford (g),
Ron Carter (b), Elvin Jones, Charlie Persip (dm, perc), Gil Evans (p, arr,
cond). New York, probably November 18 and 30, December 10 and 15,
1960.
1. La Nevada 2. Where Flamingos Fly 3. Bilbao Song 4. Stratusphunk
5. Sunken Treasure 6. Sister Sadie

1–5 originally issued as *Out of the Cool*—The Gil Evans Orchestra,
Impulse A4-LP; Impulse 254 615-2-CD; 1–6 on GRP0000186

Miles Davis at Carnegie Hall, with Gil Evans and His 21 Piece Orchestra
Miles Davis (tp), Ernie Royal, Bernie Glow, John Coles, Louis Mucci (tp),
Jimmy Knepper, Dick Hixon, Frank Rehak (tb), Julius Watkins, Paul
Ingraham, Bob Swisshelm (fh), Bill Barber (tu), Romeo Penque, Jerome
Richardson, Ed Caine, Bob Tricarico, Danny Bank (ww), Hank Mobley (ts
on 1), Janet Putnam (harp), Wynton Kelly (p on 1-2), Paul Chambers (b),
Jimmy Cobb (dm), Bob Rosengarden (perc), Gil Evans (arr, cond).
Carnegie Hall (live), New York, May 19, 1961.

1. So What 2. Spring Is Here 3. The Meaning of the Blues/Lament 4. New Rhumba 5. Concierto de Aranjuez

1–4 on *Miles Davis at Carnegie Hall*—Miles Davis, Columbia CL 1812-LP
5 on *More from the Legendary Carnegie Hall Concert*—Miles Davis, Columbia CJ 40609-LP
1–5 on *Miles Davis at Carnegie Hall—The Complete Concert,* Columbia/Legacy C2K 65027-2

Quiet Nights—Miles Davis/Arranged and conducted by Gil Evans
Miles Davis (tp), Ernie Royal, Bernie Glow, Louis Mucci, Harold Shorty Baker (tp), J. J. Johnson, Frank Rehak (tb), Ray Alonge, Julius Watkins, probably Don Corrado (fh), Bill Barber (tu), Al Block (fl), Jerome Richardson, probably Ray Beckenstein (fl, reeds), unknown (reeds, ww), Bob Tricarico (bas), Garvin Bushell (bas, cbas), Steve Lacy (ss), probably Janet Putnam (harp), Paul Chambers (b), Jimmy Cobb (dm), William ("Willie Bobo") Correa (perc), Gil Evans (arr, cond). New York, July 27, 1962; August 13, 1962; November 6, 1962.
1. Corcovado 2. Aos Pes Da Cruz 3. Song #1 4. Wait 'Til You See Her 5. Once Upon a Summertime 6. Song #2

1–6 originally issued as *Quiet Nights*—Miles Davis, Columbia CS 8906-LP stereo; Columbia 85556-2-CD; *The Complete Columbia Studio Recordings*—Miles Davis–Gil Evans, Columbia CXK 67397; Mosaic MQ11-164-LP

The Individualism of Gil Evans
Jimmy Cleveland (tb), Gil Cohen, Don Corado, Julius Watkins (fh), Al Block (fl), Eric Dolphy (fl, bcl), Steve Lacy (ss), Bob Tricarico (ts), Margaret Ross (harp), Barry Galbraith (g), Paul Chambers, Richard Davis, Ben Tucker (b), Elvin Jones (dm), Gil Evans (p, arr, cond). New York, September 1963.
1. Flute Song

Ernie Royal, John Coles, Louis Mucci (tp), Jimmy Cleveland, Tony Studd (tb), Jimmy Buffington, Bob Northern (fh), Jerome Richardson (fl), Eric Dolphy (as, fl,bcl), Steve Lacy (ss), Bob Tricarico (ts), Margaret Ross (harp), Barry Galbraith (g), Milt Hinton, Paul Chambers, Richard Davis (b), Osie Johnson (dm), Gil Evans (p, arr, cond). New York, September 1963.
2. El Toreador

John Coles, Bernie Glow (tp), Jimmy Cleveland, Tony Studd (tb), Ray Alonge (fh), Bill Barber (tu), Eric Dolphy (as, fl, bcl), Garvin Bushell, Bob

Tricarico (ww), Steve Lacy (ss), Kenny Burrell (g), Ron Carter, Paul Chambers (b), Elvin Jones (dm), Gil Evans (p, arr, cond). New York, April 6, 1964.
3. Hotel Me 4. Las Vegas Tango

probably Johnny Coles (tp), Frank Rehak (tb), Ray Alonge, Julius Watkins (fh), Bill Barber (tu), Al Block, Andy Fitzgerald, George Marge, Bob Tricarico (ww), Wayne Shorter (ts), Bob Maxwell (harp), Kenny Burrell (g), Gary Peacock (b), Elvin Jones (dm), Gil Evans (p, arr, cond). Englewood Cliffs, New Jersey, October 29, 1964.
5. Proclamation 6. Nothing Like You

1–4, plus The Barbara Song (6 from July 9, 1964, date) originally issued as *The Individualism of Gil Evans*, Verve V6-8555-LP
1–6 on *The Individualism of Gil Evans*, Verve 833 804-2-CD; *Verve Jazz Masters Vol. 23—Gil Evans*, Verve 521 860-2 - CD.

Gil Evans Orchestra, Kenny Burrell & Phil Woods
Tony Studd (tb), Paul Chambers (b), Clifford Jarvis (dm), Gil Evans (p, arr). New York, March 4, 1964.
1. Blues in Orbit 2. Isabel (incorrectly titled; the correct titles are Cheryl and Ah Moore, respectively)

Thad Jones, Louis Mucci, Bernie Glow (tp), Jimmy Cleveland, Jimmy Knepper (tb), Ray Alonge, Julius Watkins (fh), Bill Barber (tu), Andy Fitzgerald, George Marge, Bob Tricarico (ww), Steve Lacy (ss), Phil Woods (as), Harry Lookosky (tv), Kenny Burrell (g), Paul Chambers (b), Elvin Jones (dm), unknown (celeste), Gil Evans (p, arr, cond). New York, May, 25, 1964.
3. Concorde 4. Spoonful

Frank Rehak (tb), Ray Alonge, Julius Watkins (fh), Bill Barber (tu), Al Block, Andy Fitzgerald, George Marge, Bob Tricarico (ww), Wayne Shorter (ts), Bob Maxwell (harp), Kenny Burrell (g), Gary Peacock (b), Elvin Jones (dm), Gil Evans (p, arr, cond). Englewood Cliffs, New Jersey, July 9, 1964.
5. Barracuda (=Time of the Barracudas) 6. The Barbara Song

1–5 originally issued as *Gil Evans Orchestra with Kenny Burrell & Phil Woods*, Verve V6-8838-LP
6 originally issued on *The Individualism of Gil Evans*
1–6 reissued on *The Individualism of Gil Evans* Verve 833 804-2-CD
3–5 on *Gil Evans—Verve Jazz Masters, Vol. 23*, Verve 521 860-2-CD

The Time of the Barracudas (incidental music for the play) **Miles Davis/Arranged and conducted by Gil Evans**
Miles Davis (tp), Dick Leith (btb), Richard Perissi, Bill Hinshaw, Art Maeba (fh), Paul Horn (fl, afl, as), Buddy Collette (fl, afl, ts), Gene Cipriano (oboe, afl, ts), Fred Dutton (bas), Marjorie Call (harp), Herbie Hancock (p), Ron Carter (b), Tony Williams (dm), Gil Evans (arr, cond). Hollywood, October 10 and 11, 1963.
1. The Time of the Barracudas

1 on *Miles Davis–Gil Evans—The Complete Columbia Studio Recordings*, Columbia CXK 67397; Mosaic MQ11-164-LP.

Guitar Forms—**Kenny Burrell with the Gil Evans Orchestra**
Kenny Burrell (g), John Coles or Louis Mucci (tp), Jimmy Cleveland, Jimmy Knepper (tb), Ray Alonge or Julius Watkins (fh), Bill Barber (tu), Andy Fitzgerald, George Marge (fl, enh), Ray Beckenstein (fl, bcl), Bob Tricarico (ts, bas, fl), Richie Kamuca (ts, oboe), Steve Lacy (ss), Lee Konitz (as), Ron Carter (b), Elvin Jones or Charlie Persip (dm), Gil Evans (arr, cond). Englewood Cliffs, New Jersey, December 4, 15, 1964.
1. Moon and Sand 2. Last Night When We Were Young 3. Greensleeves 4. Lotus Land 5. Loie

1–5 originally issued as *Guitar Forms*, Verve V6-8612-LP; Verve 521 403-2 - CD
1–3 on *Gil Evans—Verve Jazz Masters, Vol. 23*, Verve 521 860-2-CD

Look to the Rainbow—**Astrud Gilberto/Orchestra arranged and conducted by Gil Evans**
Astrud Gilberto (vcl), John Coles (tp), Bob Brookmeyer (vtb), Ray Alonge (fh), maybe Al Cohn (ts), Kenny Burrell (g), Grady Tate (dm), Dom Um Romão (berimbau on 1), Gil Evans (p, arr, cond), other musicians unknown. Englewood Cliffs, New Jersey, May 18, June 14, 1965; February 4, 1966 (omit Um Romão); 9, 10 arr. and conducted by Al Cohn.
1. Berimbau 2. Once Upon a Summertime 3. Felicidade 4. I Will Wait for You 5. Frevo 6. Maria Quiet 7. Look to the Rainbow 8. Bim Bom 9. Lugar Bonita (Pretty Place) 10. El Preciso Apprender a Ser So (Learn to Live Alone) 11. She's a Carioca

1–7 originally issued as *Look to the Rainbow*, Verve V6-8643 LP; Verve 821 556-2-CD; Verve 539 675-2-CD
11 on *Gil Evans—Verve Jazz Masters, Vol. 23*, Verve 521 860-2-CD

Miles Davis/Arranged and conducted by Gil Evans

Miles Davis (tp), Julius Watkins, Ray Alonge (fh), Howard Johnson (tu), Hubert Laws (fl), probably Danny Bank (fl, afl), Romeo Penque (enh), probably Karl Porter (bas), Wayne Shorter (ts), Gloria Agostini or Betty Glauman (harp), Herb Bushler (hawaian g), Joe Beck (g), Lawrence Lucie (man), Herbie Hancock (Wurlitzer elp), Ron Carter (b), Tony Williams (dm), Warren Smith (mar, tim), Gil Evans (arr, cond)., New York, February 16, 1968.
1. Falling Water

1 on *Miles Davis–Gil Evans—The Complete Columbia Studio Recordings*, Columbia CXK 67397; Mosaic MQ11-164 LP

Filles de Kilimanjaro—Miles Davis Quintet

Miles Davis (tp), Wayne Shorter (ts), Herbie Hancock (el pno) Ron Carter (b), Tony Williams (dms), Gil Evans (arr 1 and 5, probably other selections). New York, June 19, 20, 21, 1968; September 24, 1968.
1. Frelon brun 2. Tout de Suite 3. Petits machins 4. Filles de Kilimanjaro 5. Mademoiselle Mabry

1–5 originally issued as *Filles de Kilimanjaro*, Columbia, CS9750; reissued as CK 46116

Gil Evans—Gil Evans

Snooky Young, Mike Lawrence (tp), Jimmy Cleveland, Jimmy Knepper (tb), Julius Watkins (fh), Howard Johnson (tu), Hubert Laws (fl), Billy Harper (ts), Joe Beck (g), Gene Bianco (harp), Herb Bushler (elb), Elvin Jones (dm), Sue Evans (perc), Gil Evans (p, elp, arr, cond). New York, 1969.
1. General Assembly 2. Proclamation 3. Love in the Open 4. Variation on the Misery 5. Spaced 6. So Long

Ernie Royal, John Coles (tp), Jimmy Cleveland (8 only), Garnett Brown (tb), Julius Watkins, Ray Alonge (fh), Howard Johnson (tu) (7 only), George Marge (fl, ss), Billy Harper (ts, fl), Trevor Koehler (bs, 8 only), Joe Beck (g), Herb Bushler (elb), Alphonse Mouzon (dm), Donald MacDonald (perc), Gil Evans (p, elp, arr, cond). New York, probably 1969.
7. Thoroughbred 8. Blues in Orbit

1–8 originally issued as *Gil Evans*, Ampex A10102-LP; reissued Enja R2 79611-CD.

Where Flamingos Fly—Gil Evans

John Coles (tp), Howard Johnson (tu, bs), Billy Harper (ts), Harry Lookofsky (tv), Joe Beck (g, mand), Don Preston (key), Herb Bushler (elb),

Lenny White (dm), Sue Evans (perc, mar), Airto Moreira, Flora Purim
(perc, vcl on 1), Gil Evans (elp, honky tonk piano, arr, cond). New York, 1971.
1. El Matador 2. Zee Zee

John Coles, Hannibal Marvin Peterson, Stan Shafran (tp), Jimmy Knepper
(tb), Howard Johnson (bs, flh on 3), Trevor Koehler (ss, bs), Billy Harper (ts,
chimes), Bruce Johnson (g), Phil Davis, Don Preston (key), Bill Quinze (elb),
Richard Davis (b), Bruce Ditmas (dm), Sue Evans, Airto Moreira, Flora
Purim (perc on 4), Gil Evans (p, elp on 2, arr, cond). New York (studio), 1971.
3. Love Your Love 4. Hotel Me 5. Where Flamingos Fly 6. Naña

1–6 issued in 1981 as *Where Flamingos Fly*, Artists House AH14-LP; A&M
390 831-2-CD.

Masabumi Kikuchi + Gil Evans
Masabumi Kikuchi (elp), Hannibal Marvin Peterson (tp, flh), Billy Harper
(ts, fl, perc), Kunitoshi Shnohara, Takehisa Suzuki (tp, flh), Hiroshi
Muneyiko (tb), Tadataka Nakazawa (btb), Tadashi Yamamoto, Chiyosige
Matsubara (fh), Ikuzo Tato (tu), Kohsuke Mine (as, ss), Shigeo Suzuki (as,
fl), Yukio Etoh, Masami Nakagawa, Takashi Asahi (pic, afl, bfl), Masayuki
Takayanagi, Sadayuki Nakamura (g), Isao Etoh (elb), Yoshio Suzuki (b),
Yoshiyuki Nakamura, Masahiko Togashi (dm), Koichi Yamaguchi (tim),
Michiko Takahashi (mar, vib), Hideo Miyata (perc), Gil Evans (p, ring-
modulator, arr, cond). Tokyo, July 5, 1972.
1. Ictus 2. Thoroughbred 3. Priestess 4. Love in the Open 5. Drizzling Rain
6. Eleven 7. Cry of Hunger 8. Love in the Open

1–6 originally issued as *Masabumi Kikuchi + Gil Evans*, Nippon Phonogram FX8525-LP; Philips 6385928 - LP
1–8 on *Masabumi Kikuchi + Gil Evans*, EmArcy EJD 3028-CD

Svengali—Gil Evans and His Orchestra
Hannibal Marvin Peterson (6 only), Tex Allen, Richard Williams (tp),
Joseph Daley (tb, tu), Sharon Freeman, Pete Levin (fh), Howard Johnson
(tu, bs, flh), David Sanborn (as), Billy Harper (ts, fl), Trevor Koehler (bs,
ss, fl), Ted Dunbar (g), David Horowitz (key), Herb Bushler (elb), Bruce
Ditmas (dm), Sue Evans (perc), Gil Evans (p, elp, arr, cond). Trinity
Church (live), New York, May 30, 1973; (6) Philharmonic Hall (live), New
York, June 30, 1973.
1. Thoroughbred 2. Blues in Orbit 3. Eleven 4. Cry of Hunger 5. Summertime 6. Zee Zee

1–6 originally issued as *Svengali*, Atlantic SD 1643 LP; KOC-CD- 8518

The Gil Evans Orchestra Plays the Music of Jimi Hendrix—**Gil Evans**
Hannibal "Marvin" Peterson (tp, vcl), Lew Soloff (tp), Tom Malone (tb, btb, fl, key), Howard Johnson (tu, bcl, elb), Peter Gordon (fh), Pete Levin (fh, key), David Sanborn (as, ss, fl), Billy Harper (ts, fl), Trevor Koehler (ts, as, fl), John Abercrombie, Ryo Kawasaki, Keith Loving (g), David Horowitz (key), Michael Moore (elb, acb), Don Pate (b), Bruce Ditmas (dm), Sue Evans (perc, dm), Warren Smith (perc, vib), Gil Evans (elp, arr, cond). New York, June 11–13, 1974.
1. Angel (arr. Tom Malone) 2. Crosstown Traffic/Little Miss Lover (arr. Tom Malone) 3. Castles Made of Sand (arr. G. Evans)/Foxey Lady (arr. Warren Smith) 4. Up From the Skies 5. 1983—A Merman I Should Turn to Be (arr. Dave Horowitz) 6. Voodoo Chile (arr. Howard Johnson) 7. Gypsy Eyes (arr. Trevor Koehlor) 8. Little Wing 9. Up from the Skies

1–7 originally issued as RCA CPL1 0667-LP; reissued as RCA Bluebird 8409-2-CD; 8 originally issued on *There Comes a Time* APLI1-1057

Montreux Jazz Festival '74—**Gil Evans**
Hannibal Marvin Peterson, Lew Soloff (tp), Tom Malone (tb, tu, fl, pic, elb, key), Peter Gordon (fh), Pete Levin (fh, key), Howard Johnson (tu, bs, bcl, flh), John Stubblefield (ss, ts), Billy Harper (ts, fl), Trevor Koehler (bs, ss, fl, arr on 3), Paul Metzke (g), Don Pate (b), Bruce Ditmas (dm), Sue Evans, Warren Smith (perc), Gil Evans (p, elp, arr except 3, cond). Montreux, Switzerland (live), July 7, 1974.
1. Parabola 2. Lunar Eclipse 3. Amadama 4. Hotel Me 5. Waltz

1–5 issued as *Montreux Jazz Festival '74*, Nippon Phonogram RJ6043-LP

Nasty Gal—**Betty Davis**
Betty Davis (vcl), Carlos Morales (g), Fred Mills (key), Larry Johnson (elb), Nicky Neal (dm), Miles Davis (arr), Gil Evans (brass arr), other personnel unknown. New York, 1975.
1. You and I

1 on *Nasty Gal*—Betty Davis, Island ILPS 9329-LP

Gil Evans
Billy Harper (fl), Joe Beck (g), Warren Smith (key, perc), Herb Bushler (elb), David MacDonald (dm), Gil Evans (p, elp, arr, cond).
1. Bluefish

1 on *New American Music, Vol. 1*, Various Artists Folkways FTS33901-LP

There Comes a Time—Gil Evans

Lew Soloff, Ernie Royal (tp, flh, pictp), Hannibal Marvin Peterson (tp and vcl on 1, koto, perc), Peter Gordon, John Clark (fh), Peter Levin (fh,key), Tom Malone (tb, btb, tu, key), Howard Johnson (tu, bcl, bs, tb), Bob Stewart, Joe Daley (tu), David Sanborn (as, ss, fl), Billy Harper (ts, fl), George Adams (ts,fl), Ryo Kawasaki (g), David Horowitz (key, org), Joe Gallivan (key, g, perc), Paul Metzke (elb), Bruce Ditmas (dm, on 1), Tony Williams (dm), Warren Smith (perc), Sue Evans (perc, celeste), Gil Evans (key, arr, cond). New York, March 6, 12, 1975; April 11, 14, 1975.
1. King Porter Stomp 2. Makes Her Move 3. The Meaning of the Blues 4. Joy Spring 5. So Long 6. Buzzard Variation 7. There Comes a Time 8. Anita's Dance 9. Little Wing 10. Aftermath the Fourth Movement Children of the Fire

1–3, 7–10 originally issued as *There Comes a Time,* RCA APLI-1057-LP; 1–8 issued as *There Comes a Time* RCA Bluebird 5783-2-CD (with newly edited form for 3)
9 on *The Gil Evans Orchestra Plays the Music of Jimi Hendrix,* RCA Bluebird 8409-2-CD

Synthetic Evans—Gil Evans

Lew Soloff, Ernie Royal (tp), Tom Malone (tb), Bob Stewart (tu), Arthur Blythe (as, ss), George Adams (ts), John Clark (g), Pete Levin (key), Mike Richmond (elb), Sue Evans (dm), Gil Evans (p, elp, arr, cond). Warsaw, Poland (live), October 23, 1976.
1. Priestess 2. Gone 3. Summertime 4. Rhythm-A-Ning 5. The Meaning of the Blues

1–4 originally issued as *Synthetic Evans,* Poljazz Z-SX-0636-LP; reissued as *Live '76*—Gil Evans, ZETA 714-CD

Priestess—Gil Evans

Lew Soloff (tp, ptp), Ernie Royal, Hannibal Marvin Peterson (tp), Jimmy Knepper (tb), John Clark (fh), Howard Johnson, Bob Stewart (tu), Arthur Blythe, David Sanborn (as), George Adams (ts), Keith Loving (g), Pete Levin (key), Steve Neil (elb), Susan Evans (dm, perc), Gil Evans (elp, arr, cond). St. George Church (live), New York, May 13, 1977.
1. Priestess 2. Short Visit 3. Lunar Eclipse 4. Orange Was the Color of Her Dress, Then Silk Blue

1–4 Originally issued as *Priestess,* Antilles AN1010-LP; reissued as Antilles 422-826 770-2-CD

Live at the Royal Festival Hall London 1978—Gil Evans

Lew Soloff (tp, ptp), Ernie Royal (tp, fgl), Hannibal Marvin Peterson (tp, perc), John Clark (fh, g), Bob Stewart (tu, flh), Arthur Blythe (as, ss), David Sanborn (as, ss, fl, sopranino sax), George Adams (ts, ss, bcl, afl), Pete Levin (key), Masabumi Kikuchi (org), Herb Bushler (elb), Sue Evans (dm, perc, tim), Tom Malone (arr on 1), Howard Johnson (arr on 11), Gil Evans (p, elp, arr, except 1 and 11, cond). Royal Festival Hall, London (live), February 25, 1978.
1.Angel (arr. Tom Malone) 2. Parabola 3. Orange Was the Color of Her Dress, Then Silk Blue 4. Stone Free 5. Fugue from Concorde 6. Blues Inc. Medley: Cheryl–Birdhead–Relaxin' at Camarillo 7. Epilogue 8. Rhythm-A-Ning 9. Up from the Skies 10. Variation on the Misery 11. Voodoo Chile (arr. Howard Johnson).

1–7 on *Gil Evans Live at the Royal Festival Hall London 1978*, RCA (GB) PL25209-LP
8–11 on *The Rest of Gil Evans Live at the Royal Festival Hall London 1978*, TAA/Mole3-LP

Parabola—Gil Evans

Lew Soloff (tp), Earl MacIntyre (tb), Steve Lacy (ss), Arthur Blythe (as, ss), Pete Levin (key), Don Pate (elb), Noel MacGhee (dm), Gil Evans (elp, arr, cond). Rome, July 29, 1978.
1. Waltz 2. Up from the Skies 3. Parabola 4. Stone Free 5. Variation

1–5 originally issued as *Parabola,* Horo HDP31-32-32 LP

Little Wing—Gil Evans Orchestra

Lew Soloff (tp, ptp), Terumasa Hino (tp), Bob Stewart (tu), Gerry Niewood (as, ss, fl), George Adams (ts, fl, perc), Pete Levin (key), Don Pate (elb), Rob Crowder (dm), Gil Evans (elp, arr, cond). West Germany (live), October, 1978.
1. Dr. Jeckyll 2. The Meaning of the Blues 3. Little Wing

1–3 originally issued as *Little Wing—The Gil Evans Orchestra Live in Germany,* Circle RK101978/13 -LP; reissued as *Little Wing—The Gil Evans Orchestra featuring George Adams,* West Wind 2042-CD

Lee Konitz/Gil Evans

Lee Konitz (as, ss), Gil Evans (p). Greene Street (live), New York, January 11–12, 1980.
1. Prince of Darkness 2. Reincarnation of Lovebird 3. Aprilling 4. What Am I Here For 5. All the Things You Are 6. Prelude #20 in C, Op. 28

7. Blues Improvization/Zee Zee 8. Lover Man (Oh, Where Can You Be?)
9. Orange Was the Color of Her Dress, Then Silk Blue 10. The Moon
Struck One 11. Drizzling Rain 12. Gee Baby, Ain't I Good to You 13. The
Buzzard Song 14. How Insensitive 15. Copenhagen Sight

1–8 issued in 1991 as *Heroes—Lee Konitz & Gil Evans,* Verve 511 621-2-CD
9–15 issued in 1991 as *Anti-Heroes—Lee Konitz & Gil Evans,* Verve 511
622-2-CD

Live at the Public Theater—Gil Evans
Lew Soloff, Hannibal Marvin Peterson, Jon Faddis (tp), George Lewis (tb),
Dave Bargeron (tb, tu), John Clark (fh), Arthur Blythe (as, ss), Hamiet
Bluiett (bs, afl), Masabumi Kikuchi, Pete Levin (key), Tim Landers (elb),
Billy Cobham (dm), Alyrio Lima (perc), Gil Evans (elp, arr, cond). Public
Theater (live), New York, February 8 and 9, 1980.
1. Anita's Dance 2. Jelly Rolls 3. Alyrio 4. Variation on the Misery
5. Orgone 6. Up from the Skies 7. Copenhagen Sight 8. Zee Zee
9. Sirhan's Blues 10. Stone Free 11. Orange Was the Color of Her Dress,
Then Silk Blue

1–6 originally issued as *Live at the Public Theater, Vol. 1*, Trio PAP9233-LP
7–11 on *Live at the Public Theater, Vol. 2*, Trio PAP25016-LP; reissued as
Evidence ECD 22089 and ECD 22090

Star People—Miles Davis
Miles Davis (tp), Mino Cinelu (perc), Bill Evans (ts, ss), Al Foster (dm),
Marcus Miller (elb), John Scofield (g), Mike Stern (g), Gil Evans (arr).
New York, August–November, 1982.
1. It Gets Better 2. Star on Cicely

1–2 on *Star People*, Columbia FC38657; 25395

Gil Evans/Steve Lacy
Steve Lacy (ss), Gil Evans (p, elp). New York, 1984.
1. Bemsha Swing

1 on *That's the Way I Feel Now—A Tribute to Thelonious Monk*—Various
Artists, A&M SP6600-LP; A&M CD6600-CD

Live at Sweet Basil—Gil Evans and The Monday Night Orchestra
Lew Soloff, Hannibal Marvin Peterson, Miles Evans, Shunzo Ohno (tp),
Tom Malone (tb), Howard Johnson (tu, bs, bcl, arr on 7), Chris Hunter
(as), George Adams (ts), Hiram Bullock (g), Pete Levin (key), Mark Egan

(elb), Adam Nussbaum (dm), Mino Cinelu (perc), Gil Evans (p, elp, arr except 7, cond). Sweet Basil (live), New York, August 20, 27, 1984.

1. Parabola 2. Voodoo Chile 3. Orange Was the Color of Her Dress, Then Silk Blue 4. Prince of Darkness 5. Blues in "C" 6. Goodbye, Pork Pie Hat 7. Up From the Skies 8. London 9. Jelly Roll 10. Friday the 13th 11. Gone 12. Prelude to Stone Free 13. Stone Free 14. Snowflake Bop

1–6 originally issued as *Live at Sweet Basil, Vol.1*—Gil Evans & The Monday Night Orchestra, King K19P 9395-6; reissued as Evidence ECD 22026
7–11 on *Live at Sweet Basil, Vol. 2*—Gil Evans & the Monday Night Orchestra, King K19P 9395-6; reissued as Evidence 22027
1–11 on *The Complete Gil Evans & The Monday Night Orchestra at Sweet Basil,* King K25Y9531-38-8 CDs

Absolute Beginners—David Bowie, Various Artists
Sade, Style Council (vcl on 7), probably Chris Hunter (as), probably Don Weller (ts), Gil Evans (p, arr, cond; brass arr 7–10); rest of personnel unknown. London, 1985.
1. Absolute Beginners 2. Killer Blow 3. Have You Ever Had it Blue? 4. Va Va Voom 5. That's Motivation 6. Having It All 7. Riot City 8. Boogie Stop Shuffle 9. Cool Napoli 10. Better Get It in Your Soul 11. So What 12. Absolute Beginners

1–12 on *Absolute Beginners*—Original Motion Picture Soundtrack, Virgin VD 2514-LP

Insignificance—The Shape of the Universe—Various Artists
Lew Soloff (tp), Gil Evans (arr, cond), rest of personnel unknown. Prob. London, 1985.
1. Jupiter Suite

1 on *Insignificance—The Shape of the Universe*—the Original Motion Picture Soundtrack, Zenith ZTT1Q4-LP

Hanalei Bay—Lew Soloff
Lew Soloff (tp, flh), Hiram Bullock (g), Gil Evans (elp only), Pete Levin (key), Mark Egan (elb), Adam Nussbaum (dm except 5), Kenwood Dennard (dm on 5), Manolo Badrena (perc). New York, March 4, 1985.
1. Salazar 2. My Buddy 3. Hanalei Bay 4. A Felicidade 5. La Toalla 6. Emily 7. Well You Needn't

1–7 on *Hanalei Bay,* King K32Y 6032

The Color of Money—Various Artists
Robbie Robertson (tp), Gil Evans (arr), personnel unknown. Prob. New York, 1986.
1. The Main Title 2. Modern Blues

1–2 on *The Color of Money*—Original Motion Picture Soundtrack, MCA 6189-LP

Gil Evans Orchestra
Stanton Davis, Shunzo O'no, Miles Evans (tp), George Lewis (tb), Howard Johnson (tu, bs, bcl), John Clark (fh), Chris Hunter (ss, as, fl), Bill Evans (ts, ss), Hiram Bullock (g), Pete Levin (key), Mark Egan (elb), Danny Gottlieb (dm), Gil Evans (p, elp, arr, cond). Paris, France, July 23, 1981 (6); Lugano, Switzerland, May 3, 1986 (1); Milan, Italy, May 5, 1986 (2–5); all recorded live.
1. Here Come De Honey Man 2.Voodoo Chile 3. Eleven 4. Boogie Stop Shuffle 5. Goodbye, Pork Pie Hat 6. Drizzling Rain

1–6 on *The Gold Collection*—Gil Evans, issued 1999, Fine Tune 2234-2.

Bud and Bird—Gil Evans and the Monday Night Orchestra Live at Sweet Basil
Lew Soloff, Shunzo O'No, Miles Evans (tp), John Coles (flh on 5, 8), Dave Bargeron (tb), Dave Taylor (btb), John Clark (fh, hornette), Chris Hunter (as, ss, fl), Bill Evans (ts, ss, fl), Hamiet Bluiett (bs, cl, bcl), Hiram Bullock (g), Pete Levin (key), Gil Goldstein (key), Mark Egan (elb), Danny Gottlieb (dm), Gil Evans (p, elp, arr cond). Sweet Basil, New York City, December 1, 22, 1986.
1. Bud and Bird 2. Half Man, Half Cookie (arr Bill Evans) 3. Gates-Illumination (arr Mark Evans) 4. Nicaragua Blues (arr Mark Egan) 5. Groove from the Louvre (arr John Clark) 6. Let the Juice Loose (arr Paul Holderbaum) 7. Your Number (arr John Clark) 8. Waltz 9. Little Wing

1–5 on *Bud and Bird*, King K32Y 6171-CD
6–9 on *Farewell*, King K32Y 6250-CD
1–9 on *Complete Gil Evans & The Monday Night Orchestra at Sweet Basil*, King 25Y9531-38-8 CDs

Nothing Like the Sun—Sting
Sting (vcl), Hiram Bullock (g), Mark Egan (elb), Kenwood Dennard (dm), Gil Evans (arr). Montserrat, Switzerland, spring 1987.
1. Little Wing

1 on *Nothing Like the Sun*, A&M 39 3912-2-CD

Gil Evans/Sting

Sting (g, vcl), Lew Soloff (tp, pictp), Shunzo O'no, Miles Evans (tp), George Lewis (tb), Tom Malone (tb, btb), Dave Bargeron (tu, tb), John Clark (fh), Chris Hunter (as), George Adams (ts, fl, vcl on 6), Branford Marsalis (ts, ss), John Surman (bs, key), Emily Mitchell (harp), Pete Levin (key), Delmar Brown (key, vcl), Mark Egan (elb), Danny Gottlieb (dm), Anita Evans (perc), Urszula Dudziak (vcl), Gil Evans (elp, arr, cond). Perugia, Italy (live), July 11, 1987.
1. Bud and Bird 2. Up from the Skies 3. Strange Fruit 4. Shadows in the Rain 5. Little Wing 6. There Comes a Time 7. Introduction of the band 8. Consider Me Gone 9. Synchronicity 10. Roxanne 11. Tea in the Sahara 12. Orange Was the Color of Her Dress, Then Silk Blue 13. Message in a Bottle

1–13 on *Umbria Jazz Festival—Gil Evans Orchestra & Sting*, Live 11-787-CD

Live at Umbria Jazz—Gil Evans Orchestra

Lew Soloff (tp, pictp), Shunzo O'no, Miles Evans (tp), George Lewis (tb), George Lewis, Tom Malone (tb), Dave Bargeron (tu, btb), John Clark (fh), Chris Hunter (as), George Adams (ts, fl, vcl), John Surman (bs, key), Pete Levin (key), Delmar Brown (key, vcl), Mark Egan (elb), Danny Gottlieb (dm), Anita Evans (perc), Urszula Dudziak (vcl, keyb), Emily Mitchell (harp), Gil Evans (elp, arr, cond). Perugia, Italy (live), July 12–19, 1987.
1. Up from the Skies 2. Orange Was the Color of Her Dress, Then Silk Blue 3. Subway 4. Orgone 5. Sometimes 6. Bud and Bird

1–6 on *Gil Evans Orchestra Live at Umbria Jazz* (issued 2000), EGEA-UJ EUJ 1001

Collaboration—Helen Merrill / Gil Evans

Harry Lookofsky (v, tv), Lamar Alsop (v, av), Theodor Israel, Harold Coletta (av), Jesse Lavy (cello), Phil Bodner (ww), Jay Berliner (g), Gil Goldstein (p, key), Buster Williams (b), Mel Lewis (dm), Gil Evans (arr, cond). New York, August 18, 1987.
1. I'm a Fool to Want You 2. Troubled Waters 3. I've Never Seen 4. He Was Too Good to Me

Jimmy Knepper (tb), Steve Lacy (ss on 1 and 4), Danny Bank (fl, bcl), Phil Bodner (fl, afl, bcl), Jerry Dodgion (fl,ss), Chris Hunter (fl, cl, oboe), Wally Kane (bcl,bas), Roger Rosenberg (bcl on 5), Joe Beck (g), Gil Goldstein (p, key), Buster Williams (b), Mel Lewis (dm), Gil Evans (arr, cond). New York, August 25, 1987.

5. Summertime 6. Where Flamingos Fly 7. I'm Just a Lucky So and So 8. Anyplace I Hang My Hat Is Home 9. A New Town Is a Blue Town

Lew Soloff (tp), Shunzo Ono (tp, flh), Jimmy Knepper (tb), Dave Taylor (btb), Chris Hunter (as, ss, pic), Danny Bank (bs), Joe Beck (g), Gil Goldstein (p, key), Buster Williams (b), Mel Lewis (dm), Gil Evans (arr, cond). New York (studio), August 26, 1987.
10. Dream of You 11. People Will Say We're in Love 12. By Myself

1–12 on *Collaboration*, EmArcy 834 205-2

Rhythm-a-Ning/Golden Hair—Gil Evans–Laurent Cugny/Big Band Lumière Christian Martinez, Stéphane Belmondo, François Chassagnite (tp), Gilles Salommez (tb), Bernard François (fh), Philippe Legris (tu), Denis Barbier (fl, afl, pic), Bobby Rangell (ss, as, fl), Pierre-Olivier Govin (as, fl), Andy Sheppard (ts, ss), Lionel Benhamou (g), Benoit De Mesmay (key), Dominique Di Piazza (elb), Stéphane Huchard (dm), Marilyn Mazur (perc), Xavier Desandre (perc on 2), Laurent Cugny (key, co-arr 2, arr 3, cond), Gil Evans (p, elp, arr, cond). Paris, November 3, 1987.
1. London 2. La Nevada 3. Golden Hair 4. Zee Zee 5. Goodbye, Pork Pie Hat

Christian Martinez, Stéphane Belmondo, François Chassagnite (tp), Gilles Salommez (tb), Bernard François (fh), Philippe Legris (tu on 1, 2, 5), Didier Havet (tu on 3, 4), Denis Barbier (fl, afl, pic), Bobby Rangell (ss, as, fl), Philippe Sellam (as), Pierre-Olivier Govin (as), Charles Schneider (ts except 5), Andy Sheppard (ts on 1, 5), Lionel Benhamou (g), Benoit De Mesmay (key), Dominique Di Piazza (elb), Stéphane Huchard (dm), Marilyn Mazur (perc), Xavier Desandre (perc), Laurent Cugny (key, cond), Gil Evans (p, elp, arr, cond). Paris, November 26, 1987.
6. Rhythm-a-Ning 7. Stone Free 8. C Blues 9. Orange Was the Color of Her Dress, Then Silk Blue 10. Parabola

1, 2, 6, 7 on *Rhythm-a-Ning*, EmArcy 836 401-2
3–5, 8–10 on *Golden Hair*, EmArcy 838 773-2-CD
1–10 on *The Complete Recordings*, EmArcy 838 794-2-CD

O.N.J.'87—Orchestre National de Jazz, direction Antoine Hervé
Philippe Slominski, Antoine Illouz, Michel Delakian (tp), Denis Leloup, Glenn Ferris, Jacques Bolognesi (tb), Didier Havet (tu), Alain Hatot, Gilbert Dall'Anese (as), Francis Bourrec (ts), Jean-Pierre Solvès (bs), Nguyen Lê (g), Philippe Guez (key), Jean-Marc Jaffet (elb), André Cecca-

relli (dm), François Verly (perc), Antoine Hervé (key, cond), Gil Evans (p, arr, cond). Paris, November, 1987.
1. Orange Was the Color of Her Dress, Then Silk Blue

1 on *O.N.J. '87*, Label Bleu LBL C6511

Paris Blues—Gil Evans/Steve Lacy
Steve Lacy (ss), Gil Evans (p, elp). Paris, November 30, December 1, 1987.
1. Reincarnation of a Lovebird 2. Paris Blues 3. Esteem 4. Orange Was the Color of Her Dress, Then Silk Blue 5. Goodbye, Pork Pie Hat 6. Jelly Roll 7. Esteem

1–7 on *Paris Blues*, OWL 049CD

Why Not Now—Ray Russell
Ray Russell (g on 1–3, tg on 2, synth on 1), Mark Isham (tp on 1, 2), Gil Evans (elp), Mo Foster (acb on 1), Frank Riccotti (perc on 1). London, Los Angeles, New York, [Gil Evans], early 1988.
1. The Pan Piper 2. Sketches of Gil 3. Goodbye, Pork Pie Hat

1–2 on *Why Not Now*, Theta 834 107-2
3 on *Take Me to the Sun*—Gil Evans with RMS, Last Chance Music LCM 002

Tribute to Gil—The Gil Evans Orchestra
Lew Soloff, Hannibal Marvin Peterson, Miles Evans (tp), Dave Bargeron (tb, tu), Tom Malone (tu, tb, bs), Dave Taylor (btb), John Clark (fh), Chris Hunter (as, fl), Alex Foster (ts, ss), Michael Urbaniak (el vln), Gil Goldstein (concertmaster p, key), Pete Levin (key), Bireli Legrene (g), Mark Egan (elb), Danny Gottlieb (dm), Anita Evans (perc, vcl), Urszula Dudziak (vcl, keyb). Umbria Jazz and Sicilia Jazz, Italy (live), July 8–24, 1988.
1. Prelude to Orgone 2. Orgone 3. Moon Struck One 4. London 5. Duet 6. Eleven

1–6 on *Tribute to Gil*, Soul Note, 121 209-2 CD

Miles & Quincy Live at Montreux
Miles Davis (tp), Quincy Jones (cond), Kenny Garrett (as), Wallace Roney (tp), Gil Evans (arr), The Gil Evans Orchestra: Lew Soloff, Miles Evans (tp), Tom Malone (tb), Alex Foster (as, ss, fl), George Adams (ts, fl), Gil Goldstein, Delmar Brown (key), Kenwood Dennard (dm on 8, perc on others). The George Gruntz Concert Jazz Band: Marvin Stamm, John D'earth, Jack Walrath (tp, flh), Dave Bargeron, Earl MacIntyre (eup, tb),

Dave Taylor (btb), Howard Johnson (tu, bs), Sal Giorgianni (as), Bob Malach (ts, fl, cl), Larry Schneider (ts, oboe, fl, cl), Jerry Bergonzi (ts), George Grunz (p, leader), Mike Richmond (b), John Riley (dm, perc). Additional musicians with the George Gruntz Concert Jazz Band: Manfred Schoof, Ack Van Royen (tp, flh), Roland Dahinden, Conrad Herwig (tb), Alex Brofsky, Claudio Pontiggia (fh), Anne O'Brien (fl), Julian Cawdry, Hanspeter Frehner (fl, pic, afl), Michel Weber (cl), Christian Gavillet, Roger Rosenberg (bcl, bs), Tilman Zahn, Dave Seghezzo, Xavier Duss, Judith Wenzicker (oboe), Christian Rabe, Reiner Erb (bas), Xenia Schindler (harp). Additional participating musicians: Benny Bailey (tp, flh), Carlos Benavent (b, elb on 12, 13), Grady Tate (dm). Montreux (live), July 8, 1991.
1. Boplicity 2. Springsville 3. Maids of Cadiz 4. The Duke 5. My Ship 6. Miles Ahead 7. Blues for Pablo 8. Gone 9. Gone, Gone, Gone 10. Summertime 11. Here Come De Honey Man 12. The Pan Piper 13. Solea

1–13 on *Miles & Quincy Live at Montreux*, Warner Bros 9362-45221

Rebirth of the Cool—Gerry Mulligan
Gerry Mulligan (bs), Wallace Roney (tp), Dave Bargeron (tb), John Clark (fh), Bill Barber (tu), Phil Woods (as), John Lewis (p), Dean Johnson (b), Ron Vincent (dm). New York, January 29, 30, 31, 1992.
1. Moon Dreams 2. Boplicity

1–2 on *Rebirth of the Cool*—Gerry Mulligan, GRP GRD-9679

Gil Evans on Film and Video
Miles Davis Quintet/Gil Evans Orchestra (Robert Herridge Television Theater, 1959), Jazz Masters Vintage Collections, Vol. 2, A Vision 50240-3.

World of Rhythm Live—Gil Evans and His Orchestra (live at Montreux, 1983), View Video 1301.

Jazz à Paris—Gil Evans/Laurent Cugny/Big Band Lumière, 1987, Polygram Music Video 041780-2.

Gil Evans, documentary, Amerimage-TV Ontario, 1998.

INDEX

Abercrombie, John, 282
Absolute Beginners (film), 312–313
Ada Leonard and her orchestra,
    120
"Adagio," from *Concierto de Aranjuez*
    (Rodrigo), 207, 243
"Adagio," from *Jupiter Symphony*
    (Mozart), 313
Adams, George, 280, 291, 305–306,
    307, 320
Adderley, Cannonball, 201, 204,
    227–228, 239, 251, 276
"Aftermath the Fourth Movement
    Children of the Fire," 292
"Again and Again and Again," 226
"Ah Moore," 254
Ahmet, Ertegun, 282–283
"All Alone at a Table for Two," 38
"All the Things You Are," 300
"Alternate Vision, An" concert, 328
"Alyrio," 301
"America, I Love You," 92
American Jazz Orchestra, 328
American Society of Composers,
    Authors and Publishers
    (ASCAP), 94
Ampex, 196, 268
"Anthropology," 143, 145, 152
"Antigua," 264
"Aos Pes da Cruz," 249–250
Apollo Theatre, 205, 229
"Arab Dance," 91, 200

Armstrong, Louis, 3, 5, 26, 107, 122,
    164, 170, 174, 193, 204, 228, 245,
    255–256
Artists House records, 276, 299
Atlantic Records, 282–283
Avakian, George, 182–183, 189–195,
    199, 205, 210, 227, 228, 283
Avery Fisher Hall, 310–311

Bachianas Brasileiras, 213
Bailey, Pearl, 174, 199
Balboa (dance), 32
Band Training Unit (BTU), 103, 104,
    105–106, 107, 111
Baraka, Amiri, 204, 205, 215–216, 243
"Barbara Song, The," 253
Barber, Bill, 143–144, 157, 184, 228,
    253
Bargeron, Dave, 277, 305
Basie, Count, 11, 40, 50, 53, 73, 78, 99,
    125, 135, 136, 138, 157, 158, 222,
    276
Basin St. West, 174
"Be Careful, It's My Heart," 92
bebop (bop), 125–126, 134–138,
    144–145
Bennett, Joe, 196, 202, 203
Bennett, Tony, 174, 268
Berkeley Jazz Festival, 264, 311
Berlin Jazz Festival, 274
Bernie, Ben, 21
"Bess, You Is My Woman Now," 199

"Better Get It in Your Soul," 313

Bewitched, The, 224

Big Band Lumière, 322

"Bird Feathers," 228

"Birth of the Blues, The," 80

Birth of the Cool, The (Davis Nonet), 145, 161, 162, 165–167, 194, 216, 293, 299, 328

Bitches Brew (Miles Davis), 204, 269, 281, 282

Bitter End, 279, 287

"Blues in Orbit," 269, 284

"Blues for Pablo," 184–185, 187, 194, 207, 230

Bluiett, Hamiett, 300

Blythe, Arthur, 280

Bob Hope show. *See Pepsodent Show*

"Boogie Stop Shuffle," 313

Booth, Helen, 8–9

bop, 144–145

"Boplicity," 161, 165, 167, 194, 309, 326

Borden, Bill, 74–75, 80, 84, 85

Bowie, David, 313–314, 319

bossa nova, 166, 249, 253

Brass Society, 190–191

Briggs, Clark, 10

Briggs, Ned, 8–11, 16, 44, 47, 55, 96

Briggs-Evans Band, 9

Broadcast Music Incorporated (BMI), 94, 296

Brown, Clifford, 186–187, 188, 229

Buckmaster, Paul, 298

"Bud and Bird," 307

Bud and Bird (Evans), 316

"Budo," 160, 165

Bullock, Hiram, 280, 305

Burrell, Kenny, 253, 254, 256, 299

"Buster's Last Stand," 91, 92, 132, 226

Butterfield, Billy, 174, 226

"Buzzard Song," 199–200

"Buzzard Variations," 292

Calhoun, Carmine, 64, 66, 72, 87–88, 90, 103

Calloway, Cab, 26, 108, 137

Camel Caravan radio show, 24

Camp Lee, Virginia, 103–112, 121

Cangie, Rudy, 25–28, 33, 34–35, 38, 39, 42, 55, 56, 62, 67, 68

Capitol Records, 159–160, 165, 275–276

Capitola Ballroom, 20–27, 30, 33

Carisi, Johnny, 128–129, 131–132, 141, 144, 157–158, 171, 185–186, 197, 248

Carnegie Hall concerts, 217, 241–243, 287, 328

Carpenter, Maybeth Carr, 2, 30, 47–50, 51, 54, 55, 244

Carpenter, Pete, 38, 44, 47–50, 55, 64, 67, 69

Carpenter, Pete and Maybeth, letters to, 47–49, 88–89, 90, 93, 95, 104–106, 110–113, 114–120, 171, 220, 230–232

Carter, Ron, 237, 251, 259

Casa Loma band, 10–12, 15, 18, 24, 27, 38, 57, 58, 120

"Casa Loma Stomp," 11

"Castles Made of Sand," 290

Cavanaugh, Page, 103–104

Chambers, Paul, 196, 201–202, 217, 218, 228–229, 245, 253

Charles, Teddy, 183

"Cheryl," 254

"Chicken Reel," 79

"Christopher Columbus," 38

City University of New York, master classes at, 302–303

Clark, Dick, 51, 67

Clarke, Kenny, 135, 125, 126, 134, 164, 165

Claude Thornhill Orchestra (*see also* Thornhill, Claude), 74, 76, 78, 79, 82–83, 85, 86, 91–97, 101, 138–141, 143–145, 147–148, 152, 155–157, 171, 182, 201, 309

Cleveland, Jimmy, 186, 221, 223, 253

Clique Club, 160

Cobham, Billy, 300

Cole, Bill, 169

Cole, Buddy, 36, 38, 42, 44, 47, 55

Coleman, Ornette, 235, 299

Coles, Johnny, 228, 237, 253, 269, 309

Collaboration: Helen Merrill and Gil Evans (Merrill/Evans), 188, 321

College Swing (film), 54, 59
Colonna, Jerry, 59, 81
Color of Money, The (film), 313, 315
Coltrane, John, 189, 229, 239, 245, 246, 251, 262, 269
Columbia Records, 189–190, 194, 202, 204–205, 227, 231–235, 238–240, 242, 243, 248–250, 261–264, 266–267
Concierto de Aranjuez, 206–207, 211, 212, 215, 242–243
"Concorde," 254, 287
"cool jazz," 165–170, 189
"Copenhagen Sight," 300
"Corcovado" (Quiet Nights), 249
"Corinna Corinna," 79
Cosey, Pete, 293
"Count Me In," 92
Crosby, Bing, 22, 54, 65, 82, 103
Crosby, Bob, 74, 77, 83
"Crosstown Traffic," 290
Crouch, Stanley, 168
Crowley, Jack, 40, 46, 56, 60, 69, 80, 88
"Cry of Hunger," 279, 284
"Cubana-Be," 133
"Cubana-Bop," 133
Cugny, Laurent, 322–323
Cyclops (Gil's Great Dane), 84, 90, 93, 96

"Dallas Blues," 42
Dameron, Tadd, 154, 158, 160, 188, 222
"Darn That Dream," 165
Davis, Betty Mabry, 281
Davis, Clive, 261–263
Davis, Miles, 151–152, 154–173, 180, 188–192
  and Carnegie Hall concert, 240–243
  and Columbia Records, 238–240, 261–264
  and Evans/Hendrix collaboration, 288–289
  and Gil Evans
    collaborations with, 156–157, 159–165, 198–218, 210, 248–250, 250–252, 259, 292–294, 298, 309–312, 326–328

  first contact with, 146–147
  first impressions of, 130–31
  on Gil's mentoring, 192
Davis, Phil, 275
"Day I Let You Get Away, The," 38
Dearie, Blossom, 129
Debussy, Claude, 17, 180
"Deception," 161
Dedrick, Rusty, 82–83, 84, 92–93
"Deep in a Dream," 67
DeJohnette, Jack, 293
"Desafinado," 166
De Soto, Johnny, 14, 23, 33–34, 38, 55, 56, 60, 67
DeVeaux, Scott, 136–137
Directions (Miles Davis), 213
"Dizzy Atmosphere," 136
"Do That to Me," 174
"Doll Dance, The," 79
Dolphy, Eric, 253
"Donna Lee," 152, 153
Dorham, Kenny, 151
Dorsey, Jimmy, 41, 44, 47, 47, 77, 85, 86, 98, 99, 125, 174
Dorsey, Tommy, 50, 51, 73, 57, 85, 86, 175
Douglas, Alan, 289
Douglas, Jack, 77
Doyle, Norman, 31, 45, 52–53
Dr. Doolittle (film), 263
Dream of You (Merrill/Evans), 186–188, 321
Dreamland Ballroom, 13, 19, 35
"Drizzling Rain," 279
Dudziak, Urszula, 121, 320

"Early Autumn," 147
"Easy to Love," 183
Eckstine, Billy, 137
Eden, Roger, 66–67
El Amor Brujo (ballet), 207–208
"El Toreador," 253
"Eleven," 267, 279, 284
"Ella Speed," 223
Eldridge, Roy, 77, 125
Ellington, Duke, 15, 26, 28, 40, 49, 73, 74, 75, 86, 90, 91

Elliot, Don, 225–226
Endrey, George, 172–173
Ennis Orchestra, 68–70, 71–72, 80–81, 87–90
Ennis, Skinnay, 53–70, 67–70, 99–100
Erenberg, Louis, 17, 73–74
ESP (Miles Davis), 261
"Esteem," 323
Evans, Anita Cooper, 245–246, 251–252, 254, 270–274, 295–296, 320, 326–327
Evans, Bill (pianist), 239, 242–243, 251
Evans, Bill (saxophonist), 282
Evans, Gilmore Ian Ernest Green (Gil)
  college days of, 8
  divorce from Lillian, 244–245
  family life, 5–6, 254–255, 270–271, 301
  first band, 5–8
  final illness of, 323–324
  foreign tours of, 274–275, 279, 294, 302, 309, 311, 317, 320, 322
  high school days of, 3
  honors awarded to, 255, 270–271, 297, 302, 312
  marriage of
    to Anita Cooper, 254
    to Lillian Grace, 173
  and Miles Davis
    collaborations with, 156–157, 159–165, 198–218, 250–252, 259, 292–294, 298, 309–312, 326–328
    first contact with, 146–147
    as mentor to, 192
  on Thornhill's influence, 166–167
Evans, John, 2, 4
Evans, Lillian Grace, 171–173, 176, 220, 244–245
Evans, Margaret Julia McConnachy (June), 2–3
Evans, Miles, 217, 270–271, 306, 324, 326
Evans, Noah, 270–271, 306, 324
Evans, Sue, 121, 274, 277
"Ev'body Clap Hands," 174
Exiner, Billy, 129, 151

Faddis, Jon, 217, 277, 300
Falla, Manuel de, 17, 185, 207–208, 217
"Falling Water," 264
Farewell (Evans), 316–317
Fatool, Nick, 84
Fazola, Irving, 83–84, 93, 164
Filles de Kilimanjaro (Davis/Evans), 266–268, 293
Field, Herbie, 132
"Flute Song," 253
Fragments (film), 266
Frazier, Brenda, 59
"Freedom Jazz Dance," 260

Gabbard, Krin, 169–170
Galbraith, Barry, 84, 129, 153, 155, 186
"Garden of the Moon," 60
Garden of the Moon (film), 60
"Gardenias," 67
Garland, Judy, 59, 63, 67
Gardner, Sylvia, 129
"General Assembly," 251, 269
Gershwin, George, 89, 198–200, 213, 215, 217
Getz, Stan, 166, 188, 253
Giddins, Gary, 292, 309–310
Gifford, Gene, 11, 120
Gil Evans (Evans), 269, 274, 276
Gil Evans & Ten (Evans), 220–224
Gil Evans Collection, The (book), 329
Gil Evans and His Youngsters, 32
Gil Evans and the Monday Night Orchestra, 310, 315
Gil Evans Orchestra (early bands), 9, 37, 39, 43–44, 49, 51
  late band, 326–329
Gil Evans Orchestra with Kenny Burrell and Phil Woods, The (Evans), 254
Gilberto, Astrud, 253, 256, 259
Gilberto, João, 249, 253
Gillespie, Dizzy, 126, 129, 133, 134–137, 153, 154, 228, 235
Gillian Music, 212, 232, 245
"Girlfriend of the Whirling Dervish, The," 60

Glaser, Joe, 255–256
Glen Island Casino, 82–85, 139, 148, 149
Glenn Miller Orchestra, 73–74, 76, 82
Globin's Cabins and Chalet, 16–18
"Godchild," 160–161, 168, 169
Goldstein, Gil, 326–327, 329
"Gone," 200–201, 213, 305
"Gone, Gone, Gone," 200
Goober Club, 5–6, 13, 20, 24
"Goodbye, Pork Pie Hat," 223, 281, 322, 323
Goodman, Benny, 11, 25, 27, 37–38, 41–46, 50–51, 53, 58, 65, 67, 69, 73, 74, 79, 82, 84, 88, 90, 97, 95, 100, 107, 127, 136, 149, 226
"Goody Goody," 38
Gordon, Maxine Gregg, 284–287, 296, 323
Gozzo, Conrad, 82–83
Granz, Norman, 177–179
Great Jazz Standards (Evans), 228–229
Greene St., 299
Grossman, Albert, 268, 275
Grossman, Steve, 282
Grupe, Anne, 23, 28–30, 36
Grupe, Bernyce, 28–29
Grupe, Greenlaw, 4, 5, 7, 20, 21, 23–24, 33–35, 36
Guggenheim Fellowship, 259, 270
Guitar Forms (Evans/Burrell), 256

Haig, Al, 160
"Half Nelson," 151
Hallenbach, Ralph, 58, 63
Hammersmith Odeon concert, 317
Hammond, John, 43–44, 50, 259
Hampton, Lionel, 21–22, 43, 73
Harden, Ralph, 107–108
Harper, Billy, 260, 269, 274, 277, 279, 284, 286
Harrison, Max, 168
Hawkins, Erskine, 108
Henderson, Fletcher, 3, 10, 22, 26, 34, 38, 90, 136

Henderson, Joe, 277
Henderson, Skitch, 62–64, 66–67, 68, 90
Hendrix, Jimi, 259, 267, 269, 288–291
Hentoff, Nat, 66, 131, 154, 181, 191, 209, 211
Herman, Woody, 100, 153, 188
heroin, 151, 188
Hervè, Antoine, 323
Hillman, Roc, 98–99
Hines, Earl, 135, 137
Hino, Terumasa, 302
Hodeir, Andre, 167
Hogan, Clair "Shanty," 174
Holiday, Billie, 66, 77, 108, 125, 204
"Honeysuckle Rose," 42
Horowitz, Dave, 277
"Hooray for Spinach," 67
Hope, Bob, 58–59, 81–82
Hotel Drake, Miami, 112–114
Hotel Mark Hopkins, 22, 61, 72, 82
Hotel Pennsylvania, 31, 50, 76, 77, 138–139, 149
"Hotel Me," 251, 253, 254, 275
Hurley, Noris, 10, 38, 55, 67

"I Don't Know Why," 91, 92
"I Got Plenty of Nuttin'," 200
"Ictus," 279
"Ida, Sweet as Apple Cider," 6
"If I Love Again," 177
"I'm Forever Blowing Bubbles," 67
Impulse! records, 235, 237, 248
"In the Mood," 73
In a Silent Way (Miles Davis), 269
"In the Still of the Night," 177–178
Individualism of Gil Evans, The (Evans), 253, 255, 268
Insignificance—The Shape of the Universe, (film), 313
Into the Hot (Evans), 248
"Israel," 161, 164, 167, 185
"It Ain't Necessarily So," 200
"It Might as Well Be Spring," 183

Jamaica (Arlen/Harburg), 226
"Jambangle," 185, 222

James, Harry, 73
Jazz Gallery, 231, 235, 236, 276
jazz-fusion, 301–302
jazz-rock fusion, 267
"Jelly Roll," 251
"Jeru," 160–161
Jobim, Antonio Carlos, 249, 253, 283
Johnny Mathis (Johnny Mathis), 183
Johnson, Budd, 228–229, 309–310
Johnson, Howard, 260, 269, 274, 275,
    280, 285, 305, 307
Johnson, J. J., 160, 165
Jones, Elvin, 209, 228–229, 236–237,
    253, 269
Jones, Philly Joe, 196, 201, 228
Jones, Quincy, 186, 227, 327
"Joy Spring," 291–292
Judd, Leroy, 5, 10
Jurgens, Dick, 17–18, 31
"Just Friends," 177, 179
JVC Jazz Festival, 217

Kemp, Hal, 53–54, 56, 60, 61, 63–65,
    70, 89
Kennedy Center concert, 276–277
Kenton, Stan, 36, 40, 42, 58, 153, 159,
    260
Kikuchi, Masabumi, 279–280, 282,
    293, 294, 300–302
"King Porter Stomp," 38, 260, 291
King Records, 316–317
Knepper, Jimmy, 237, 309
"Koko," 136
Konitz, Lee, 129, 153, 155, 157, 159,
    161, 164–166, 169–170, 184, 221,
    328, 299–300, 309–310
Kool Jazz Festival, 302, 309–310
Koseinenkin Hall concert, 279
Koven, Jake, 221
Koyama, Kiyoshi, 321–322
Krupa, Gene, 73, 128, 132
KWG radio station, 13

"La Nevada," 229, 236–237, 310
"La Paloma," 185, 206–207
"La Plight," 80
La Porta, John, 135

Lacy, Steve, 185, 205–206, 219,
    221–222, 224–225, 228, 230, 244,
    253, 275, 317, 321–323, 326
Lake Tahoe, 16–18
Lambert, Dave, 129, 177–179
Lambert, Hortense, 129
"Lament," 197
Lampley, Calvin, 199
Landers, Tim, 300
"Las Vegas Tango," 253
LaVere, Charles, 62, 69
Lee, Peggy, 172, 174
Les Hite Orchestra, 22, 33
"Let's Do It," 80
"Let's Face the Music and Dance," 38
"Let's Swing It," 22
Levin, Pete, 277, 305–306
Lewis, George, 280, 300
Lewis, Jack, 184
Lewis, John, 129, 131, 137, 156–160,
    173, 190–191, 229, 238
Lieberson, Goddard, 204, 211, 234,
    239, 240, 268
Liepolt, Horst, 304, 317
Lima, Alyrio, 300
Liscom, Ralph, 10, 38, 55, 67
"Little Brown Jug," 82
"Little Willie Leaps," 151
"Little Wing," 292, 317
Little Wing (Evans), 294
Live at the Blackhawk (Miles Davis), 241
*Live at the Public Theater, Volumes 1
    and 2* (Evans), 301
Live at Sweet Basil, Volumes 1 and 2
    (Evans), 316
"Loch Lomond," 65, 94
Look to the Rainbow (Gilberto/Evans),
    256
Lombardo, Guy, 22, 73
"Love for Love," 147
"Love Tales," 79
"Love, Your Magic Spell Is Every-
    where," 183
Lunceford, Jimmie, 15, 22, 26, 73, 74,
    78, 91
Lush Life, 295
Lynch, Reuel, 38, 44, 57, 58, 67, 69, 88

Macero, Teo, 183, 197, 210–211, 212, 213, 233–234, 240, 241–243, 249, 262–263, 266, 281, 283
McGuirk, Pat, 10
McKusick, Hal, 184, 222
"Mademoiselle Mabry," 267
"Magic Science, A: Celebrating Jimi Hendrix," 329
"Maids of Cadiz," 193, 197, 309
Malone, Tom, 290, 306, 308
Manilow, Barry, 321
"Manteca," 228
Martin, Freddid, 65, 73, 78
Martin, Kupie, 16
Mathis, Johnny, 182–183
Mattas, Abby, 9–10, 13, 17, 24, 25, 42, 302
Maxwell, Gertrude Bernstein, 127, 176
Maxwell, Jimmy, 7, 10–11, 12, 13–16, 19, 29, 28–29, 33, 38, 44, 52, 57, 66, 67, 88–89, 98, 113–114, 127, 175–176, 180
"Meaning of the Blues, The," 197, 291–292
Merrill, Helen, 186–188, 191, 192, 237, 227–228, 230, 321–322, 326
"Miles Ahead," 193–194, 197, 227
Miles Ahead (Davis/Evans), 180, 186, 190, 192–198, 214–216
Miles Davis–Gil Evans: The Complete Columbia Studio Records (1998 box set), 194, 252, 264
Miles Davis Nonet, 157–165, 167–170, 179, 183–183, 190, 309, 328
Miles in the Sky (Miles Davis), 264
Miles Smiles (Miles Davis), 261
Millar, Bob, 30–31
Miller, Glenn, 50, 73–74, 79, 94, 101
Mingus, Charles, 169, 177, 183, 202, 280–281, 305, 307, 311, 313, 323
Mitchell, Emily, 320
Mitchell, Louis, 88, 100
Modern Jazz Concert, (Brass Society), 191
Modern Jazz Quartet, 129, 144, 165, 184

Monk, Thelonious, 134, 144, 188, 204, 224, 229, 235, 307, 311
Monterey Jazz Festival, 259
Montreal Jazz Festival, 317
Montreux Jazz Festival, 326–327
Moog, Robert, 275
"Moon Dreams," 161, 309
"Moon Struck One," 300, 326
"Moonlight Bay," 92
"Moonlight Serenade," 73
Moreira, Airto, 275, 276, 277, 281–282, 317
Morgenstern, Dan, 205, 245, 256
Moten, Bennie, 10–11, 26
"Move," 160, 165
Moussorgsky, Modest, 141, 147
Mucci, Louis, 221, 228
Mulligan, Gerry, 128, 132–133, 137, 142–145, 151, 156–160, 162, 163, 165–166, 170–174, 184, 188, 227, 306, 309, 328
Music for Brass (Brass Society), 191
Music Corporation of America (MCA), 31
Musso, Vido, 36, 40–46, 50–51, 57–58
"My Man's Gone Now," 200
"My Ship," 197, 329

Nasty Gal (Betty Mabry Davis), 281
Naval Reserve Band 501 (The Rangers), 102
Navarro, Fats, 151
"Near You," 148
Nelson, Dick, 26, 30
New Bottle, Old Wine (Evans), 227–228
"New Rhumba," 194
New York Jazz Repertory Company, 287–288
Newport Festival West, 284
Newport Jazz Festival, 188
Noble, Ray, 22
"Nobody's Heart," 223
Noland, Kenneth, 225, 278, 282–284
Norvo, Red, 82–83
"Nothing Like You," 254
Nut Club, 174

"Oh, Lawd, I'm On My Way," 201
"Old Folks," 177
"Old Wien," 79
Olsen, Kenneth, 88
"One Bass Hit," 137
"Orange Was the Color of Her Dress, Then Silk Blue," 223, 281, 300, 305, 323
Orchestra USA, 190–191
Orchestre National de Jazz, l', 323
"Orgone," 200, 305, 307
Out of the Cool (Evans), 235–238, 248
Overton, Ron, 326

Pacific Jazz Festival, 259
Pagnotta, Carlo, 319
"Pan Piper," 209, 212, 213
Parachute to Paradise (film), 266
"Paraphernalia," 264
"Paris Blues," 323
Paris Blues (Evans/Lacy), 323
Parker, Charlie (Bird), 125, 134–135, 137–138, 141–145, 147, 151, 153–154, 173, 177–179, 181, 188, 228, 306
Partch, Harry, 224, 259
Patti Page Show, 175
Paulsen, George, 72–73, 78, 84, 86–87, 101
Pepsodent Show (Bob Hope show), 59, 65, 71–72, 76–77
Persip, Charlie, 237
Peterson, Hannibal Marvin, 274, 277, 279, 286, 306
"Petits Machins," 267, 279
Pettiford, Oscar, 134–135
Philharmonic Hall concert, 283–284
Piano Concerto (Grieg), 139
"Plenty of Money and You," 41
Poem for Brass (J. J. Johnson), 191
Polo, Danny, 83–84
Porgy and Bess (Davis/Evans), 89–90, 180, 198–204, 214–216, 217–218, 223, 238, 240, 287, 288, 315, 326
Potter, Tommy, 142, 237
Powell, Bud, 125, 126, 135, 150, 164, 222, 245

"Prayer," 200
Prestige records, 188, 190, 220, 223, 239
Preston, Don, 275
Priestess (Evans), 292
"Proclamation," 254, 264, 269
Public Theater concerts, 300–301, 302
"Punjab," 205, 254
puntature, 197–198
Purim, Flora, 121, 276, 277

Quiet Nights, 248–250

RCA Records, 290–291
RCA Victor's Jazz Workshop series, 184
Ravel, Maurice, 17, 131, 180
Redman, Don, 3, 229
Reich, Wilhelm, 182, 225, 246–247, 248, 278
"Reincarnation of a Love Bird," 323
"Remember," 223
Rendezvous Ballroom, 31–32, 35–37, 41, 47, 51, 53, 56, 76, 79, 260
"Requiem," 200
Rey, Alvino, 26, 101
"Rhythm Is Our Business," 22
ring modulators, 275
"Ritual Fire Dance," 207
Roach, Max, 129, 135, 142, 155, 157, 177, 242
"Robbins' Nest," 143, 152
Robert Herridge Television Theatre, 229, 310
Robertson, Robbie, 313, 315
"Robins and Roses," 38
Robinson, Sugar Ray, 192
"Rocker," 161
Rodney, Red, 151, 155
Rodrigo, Joaqin, 206–208
Rollini, Art, 41–42
Roney, Wallace, 327–328
Ross, Bruce, 6
"Rouge," 161
"'Round Midnight," 190, 228
'Round Midnight (Miles Davis), 190
Rowles, Jimmy, 100, 107, 108–109, 111, 122, 148–150, 222

Royal Festival Hall concert, 294
Royal Roost, 158–159
Rugolo, Pete, 159–160, 162
Russell, George, 128, 133, 137, 138, 142, 142, 144, 156, 163, 172–173, 184–185, 186, 270, 280

"Saeta," 209
St. George's Church concert, 292
"San Sue Strut," 11
Sanborn, David, 280, 291, 305–306, 307
Santa Anita Army Band (360th Ordnance Band), 99–103
Sauter, Eddie, 74, 79, 82, 90, 328
Schneider, Maria, 217–218, 222, 313–315, 317–318, 327, 329
Schuller, Gunther, 11, 144, 259, 190–191
Scofield, John, 282
Sea in Your Future, The (film), 266
Shad, Bob, 186–187
Shaw, Artie, 50, 73, 84, 86, 101–102
Shaw, Woody, 277
Shelley's Manne-Hole, 260
"Short Visit," 305, 307
Simon, John, 275, 292
Sims, Zoot, 164
"Singin' the Blues," 174, 226
"Sippin' at Bell's," 151
"Sirhan's Blues," 301
Six Hits and a Miss, 59, 66, 78
Sketches of Spain (Davis/Evans), 180, 198, 206–213, 214–216, 217–218
Slug's, 276, 278
"Smoke Rings," 11
"Snowfall," 86, 139, 288
Snyder, John, 299
"So Long," 269, 292
"So What," 229, 243
"Solea," 209, 211, 212
Soloff, Lew, 275, 300, 305–307, 313, 328
"Somebody Nobody Loves," 92
"Song #1," 250
"Song #2," 249
"Song of Our Country," 213–214

"Sorta Kinda," 152
"soundies," 92
Southern California Sector Headquarters Band, 98–99
"Spaced," 269
"Spanish Dance," 207
"Spoonful," 254
"Spring Is Here," 243
"Springsville," 186, 193, 197, 232
Strayhorn, Billy, 74, 141
Sting, 317–319
"Stompin' at the Savoy," 38
Stone, Sly, 293
Stowe, Herb, 10, 38, 55, 56, 69
"Strange Enchantment," 67–68, 81
"Strange Fruit," 318
"Subway," 320
"Summer Night," 249
"Summertime," 200, 284, 321
"Sunday Kind of Love, A," 139, 147
Svengali, 131
Svengali (Evans), 283–284, 285–286
Sweet Basil jazz club, 303–309, 315–317, 326

Taix, Sheldon, 26, 38
Taylor, Al, 100
Taylor, Cecil, 224, 248, 304, 306
Taylor, Creed, 235–236, 248, 252–254
Taylor, Dave, 305
"Teo's Bag," 264
"That Sentimental Sandwich," 67
There Comes a Time (Evans), 291–292
"There's a Boat That's Leaving Soon for New York," 201
"There's a Small Hotel," 91, 92, 139
"Thinking About You," 34
30th Street Studio, 193
Third Hollywood Swing Concert, 57
"Third stream music," 190–191
Thornhill, Claude, 57, 65–67, 71–76, 84, 86–87, 97, 102, 107, 126, 128, 138–141, 143–149, 154–156, 166–167, 171, 181, 201, 205, 216
"Thoroughbred," 269, 279
Three Deuces, 125, 134, 142
Three Little Feelings (John Lewis), 191

"Three Little Words," 80
Tilton, Elizabeth, 39–40
Tilton, Frances, 39–40
Tilton, Martha, 39, 103
"Time of the Barracudas," 251, 254, 269
Time of the Barracudas (play), 250–252
Torin, Symphony Sid, 158–159
"Tormented," 38
"Traumerei," 139
Trianon Ballroom, 46–47, 49–51, 53, 69
Trinity Church concerts, 283
Trio Records, 300
Triscari, Joe, 108–109
Tristano, Lennie, 151, 155, 160, 163, 169
Tropp, Oscar, 247–248
Trotter, John Scott, 54, 61, 70
"Troubador," 147, 206
Tudor, Pops, 35–37
"21 Club," 124

Umbria Jazz Festival, 319–320, 326
University of California at Berkeley, 15–16
"Up from the Skies," 290

Vail, Evan, 102–103, 108
Valencia Ballroom, 32, 44, 47
Vanguard Orchestra, 303–304
Varsalona, Bart, 221
"Venus de Milo," 161
Verve records, 252–254, 256, 259
Victor Hugo restaurant, 55–56, 62–63, 66, 69, 72, 81
Victor Records, 52, 67
Villa-Lobos, Heitor, 213
Village Vanguard, 279, 280, 286, 303–304
"Voo-doo Chile," 291

"Wait 'Til You See Her," 250
Walkin' (Miles Davis), 188
Wallace, Ben, 4–5
Warren, Fran, 147
Weaver, Hart, 20, 33
Webman, Hal, 147–148, 155, 156
Wein, George, 283, 287, 294
Weinstock, Bob, 223
West, Ray, 35
Westbeth Cabaret, 276
Weston, Ryland, 10, 19, 38, 55, 67
"Where Flamingos Fly," 187, 237, 275
Where Flamingos Fly (Evans), 276
"Where Has My Little Dog Gone," 92
Whitney Museum concerts, 264–266
"Will I Ever Know," 38
"Will o' the Wisp," 207–208
Williams, Martin, 201, 215, 264
Williams, Tony, 251, 258, 259, 267, 281, 291
"Willow Tree," 228
Wilson, John S., 201, 214, 238, 265, 288, 295, 298
Winding, Kai, 160, 165
"Wishing Will Make It So," 67
"Wonderful, Wonderful," 183
Woods, Phil, 253–254
World Pacific (Pacific Jazz) records, 227–228
Wright, Cobina, 59

"Yardbird Suite," 143, 152, 309
"You Go to My Head," 183
"You Make Me Feel Like a Natural Woman," 264
Young, Lester, 107, 121–122, 126–127, 164, 166–169, 193, 228, 256
"You're Not So Easy to Forget," 147

"Zee Zee," 283–284
Zortziko, 212